90 0631557 1

D1759740

SCIENCE IN THE NINETEENTH-CENTURY PERIODICAL

Reading the Magazine of Nature

For the Victorian reading public, periodicals played a far greater role than books in shaping their understanding of new discoveries and theories in science, technology, and medicine. Such understandings were formed not merely by serious scientific articles, but also by glancing asides in political reports, fictional representations, or humorous attacks in comic magazines. Ranging across diverse forms of periodicals, from top-selling religious and juvenile magazines through to popular fiction-based periodicals, and from the campaigning 'new journalism' of the late century to the comic satire of *Punch*, this book explores the ways in which scientific ideas and developments were presented to a variety of Victorian audiences. In addition, it offers three case studies of the representation of particular areas of science: 'baby science', scientific biography, and electricity. This innovative collaborative volume sheds new light on issues relating to history and history of science, literature, book history, and cultural and media studies.

CAMBRIDGE STUDIES IN NINETEENTH-CENTURY
LITERATURE AND CULTURE

General editor
Gillian Beer, *University of Cambridge*

Editorial board
Isobel Armstrong, *Birkbeck College, London*
Leonore Davidoff, *University of Essex*
Terry Eagleton, *University of Manchester*
Catherine Gallagher, *University of California, Berkeley*
D. A. Miller, *Columbia University*
J. Hillis Miller, *University of California, Irvine*
Mary Poovey, *New York University*
Elaine Showalter, *Princeton University*

Nineteenth-century British literature and culture have been rich fields for inter-disciplinary studies. Since the turn of the twentieth century, scholars and critics have tracked the intersections and tensions between Victorian literature and the visual arts, politics, social organization, economic life, technical innovations, scientific thought – in short, culture in its broadest sense. In recent years, theoretical challenges and historiographical shifts have unsettled the assumptions of previous scholarly synthesis and called into question the terms of older debates. Whereas the tendency in much past literary critical interpretation was to use the metaphor of culture as "background," feminist, Foucauldian, and other analyses have employed more dynamic models that raise questions of power and of circulation. Such developments have reanimated the field.

This series aims to accommodate and promote the most interesting work being undertaken on the frontiers of the field of nineteenth-century literary studies: work which intersects fruitfully with other fields of study such as history, or literary theory, or the history of science. Comparative as well as interdisciplinary approaches are welcomed.

A complete list of titles published will be found at the end of the book.

SCIENCE IN THE NINETEENTH-CENTURY PERIODICAL

Reading the Magazine of Nature

GEOFFREY CANTOR, GOWAN DAWSON,
GRAEME GOODAY, RICHARD NOAKES,
SALLY SHUTTLEWORTH, AND
JONATHAN R. TOPHAM

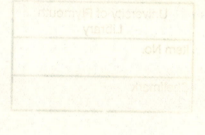

CAMBRIDGE
UNIVERSITY PRESS

PUBLISHED BY THE PRESS SYNDICATE OF THE UNIVERSITY OF CAMBRIDGE
The Pitt Building, Trumpington Street, Cambridge, United Kingdom

CAMBRIDGE UNIVERSITY PRESS
The Edinburgh Building, Cambridge, CB2 2RU, UK
40 West 20th Street, New York, NY 10011-4211, USA
477 Williamstown Road, Port Melbourne, VIC 3207, Australia
Ruiz de Alarcón 13, 28014 Madrid, Spain
Dock House, The Waterfront, Cape Town 8001, South Africa

http://www.cambridge.org

First published 2004

Printed in the United Kingdom at the University Press, Cambridge

Typeface Adobe Garamond 11/12.5 pt.   *System* LATEX 2$_\varepsilon$ [TB]

A catalogue record for this book is available from the British Library

ISBN 0 521 83637 9 hardback

The publisher has used its best endeavours to ensure that URLs for external websites referred to in
this book are correct and active at the time of going to press. However, the publisher has no
responsibility for the websites and can make no guarantee that a site will remain live or that the
content is or will remain appropriate.

Contents

SECTION B: THEMES

Illustrations

FIGURES

TABLE

Preface

The chapters in this volume were written as part of the SciPer (Science in the Nineteenth-Century Periodical) project pursued at the Universities of Leeds and Sheffield, under the direction of Geoffrey Cantor and Sally Shuttleworth. The project was funded by the Arts and Humanities Research Board, the Leverhulme Trust, and the Modern Humanities Research Association. We would like to record our gratitude to all these bodies for making the project possible.

For their generous support of the project we would like to thank Christopher Sheppard and his colleagues in the Brotherton Collection, University of Leeds, the Humanities Research Institute, University of Sheffield, and the staff of the Leeds Library, Sheffield Central Library, and Leeds Public Library. Our warmest thanks are also due to Samuel Alberti, Katherine Fenton, Louise Henson, and our Advisory Panel, Micheline Beaulieu, Dame Gillian Beer, Laurel Brake, William H. Brock, Bernard Lightman, James G. Paradis, Harriet Ritvo, James A. Secord, and Joanne Shattock.

For details of the overall Project and Electronic Index see <http://www.sciper.leeds.ac.uk>.

CHAPTER I

Introduction

Gowan Dawson, Richard Noakes, and Jonathan R. Topham

In an early essay, the physicist James Clerk Maxwell pondered the intelligibility of the universe, contrasting the reassuring image of the book of nature with an intriguing, if somewhat disturbing alternative, the magazine of nature:

Perhaps the 'book', as it has been called, of nature is regularly paged; if so, no doubt the introductory parts will explain those that follow, and the methods taught in the first chapters will be taken for granted and used as illustrations in the more advanced parts of the course; but if it is not a 'book' at all, but a *magazine*, nothing is more foolish to suppose than that one part can throw light on another.[1]

This epistemological reflection is both suggestive and rather surprising. If nature is like a book, Maxwell suggests, or better, a well-constructed textbook, then the explanation of its several parts will form a unified and coherent whole. However, this assumption is far from self-evident, and may well be false. Nature may instead be like a magazine. Just as a magazine contains a miscellany of unrelated articles, argues Maxwell, so the various parts of nature may be unrelated to each other. What is surprising about Maxwell's claim that on this basis it would be 'foolish to suppose . . . that one part can throw light on another' is that he was later outstandingly successful in exploiting such relationships in his research. Using mechanical models of the ether he spectacularly illuminated the analogies between electricity, magnetism, and light. In much the same way, as this book will show, important relationships can be found between the disparate articles which make up a magazine.

Science, technology, and medicine permeated the content of general periodicals in nineteenth-century Britain, appearing not only in avowedly scientific articles, but also in other forms of narrative including fictional representations, glancing asides in political reports, and caricatures and allusions in comic magazines. From the perspective of readers, science was omnipresent, and general periodicals probably played a far greater role than books in shaping the public understanding of new scientific discoveries, theories, and practices. The object of this collection of essays is to analyse the representation of science, technology, and medicine, as well as the inter-penetration of science and literature, in the general periodical press in nineteenth-century Britain. Employing a highly interdisciplinary approach, the following chapters address not only the reception of scientific ideas in the general press, but also examine the creation of non-specialist forms of scientific discourse within periodical formats, and the ways in which they interacted with the assortment of other kinds of articles found in nineteenth-century periodicals.

The prevalence of science in such periodicals as the *Cornhill Magazine*, the *Illustrated London News*, or *Punch* has far-reaching implications for lit-erary scholars and historians of science alike. In an age in which the natural sciences became increasingly demarcated from other fields of learning, and from a self-consciously 'literary' sphere, periodicals frequently served to reincorporate them in a wider culture. Whether in homiletic form in the sermons of the *Wesleyan-Methodist Magazine* or in political form in lead-ing articles of the *The Times*, the cultural significance of the sciences was widely debated in the periodical press. Moreover, the variety or even *brico-lage* of their formats made periodicals unusually open to different subjects and genres being juxtaposed, and most readers were not as fastidious as Maxwell about the analogies thus suggested. Indeed, editors and writers were often fully aware of the opportunities for conceptual and linguistic interchange. Novelists, essayists, politicians, and scientists alike found peri-odicals a common ground for such borrowings. Moreover, with the bounds of the sciences constantly under re-negotiation, non-specialist periodicals presented an invaluable medium for the exploration of new, heterodox, or disputed sciences.

While books are generally intended to be of lasting, if not timeless, value, periodicals are designedly ephemeral: in Margaret Beetham's phrase, literally 'date-stamped'.[2] For the historical scholar, it is, paradoxically, the very time-sensitive nature of periodicals that gives them their permanent value. Of course nineteenth-century books were often written in response to other books, but the fine texture of debate was embodied far more com-pletely in the periodicals. Day by day, week by week, month by month, periodicals addressing widely diverging reading audiences contained im-plicit and explicit dialogues concerning the sciences. Such interchanges, occurring both within and between periodicals, represent a remarkable, almost overwhelming, body of evidence for the cultural history of science in nineteenth-century Britain. Books were also secondary to periodicals in other significant ways. It was in periodicals, for instance, that many of the best-known works of the nineteenth century first appeared, ranging from a considerable proportion of the novels to such scientific classics as John Tyndall's *Fragments of Science* (1871). In addition, those works first published as books were often primarily known through their representations in periodicals, whether in reviews, extracts, abstracts, advertisements, correspondence, or passing comments. As James Secord observes, the achievement of stability in the process of 'literary replication' was far from straightforward: the meanings of paragraphs and epigrams extracted in periodicals often differed widely from those intended by the producers of the original books.[3]

The pervasiveness of science in nineteenth-century periodicals has long been recognized. In 1958, Alvar Ellegård's ground-breaking *Darwin and the General Reader* demonstrated that evolutionary ideas were widely canvassed in the non-scientific press. However, while Ellegård's use of a broad range of periodical sources (he examined 115 titles) remains an achievement not subsequently matched, his approach rested on the assumption that 'periodicals can be taken, by and large, as representative of the ideas and beliefs of their readers, and thus, with some qualifications, of the population at large'.[4] This approach ignores the variety of ways in which periodicals were produced and read. As Secord has recently shown, for instance, newspapers and magazines sometimes functioned as foils for readers' own developing views: they might read them 'not to agree with them, but to think with them'.[5] More fundamentally, periodicals themselves embodied forms of debate. Whether in the interplay of different contributions or in letters pages, they presented a space which, however tightly bounded, allowed for a variety of opinions to be expressed. Ellegård's attempt to codify public opinion by a statistical analysis of press reaction, classified according to five possible positions on each of three 'parts' of Darwinism, obscures such debate.[6] Indeed, by focusing on those articles overtly concerned with evolution, Ellegård inevitably overlooked many apparently non-scientific articles which also engaged with Darwin's theory. Examining the entire contents of a periodical allows the historian to gain a more subtle, nuanced, and often very different picture of how Darwinism emerged, or indeed was submerged, in cultural discourse of the time.

This notion of the interplay of scientific and other subjects in periodical literature is central to Robert Young's well-known thesis, adumbrated in the late 1960s, that for the first eight decades of the nineteenth century British periodical literature reflected a 'common intellectual context' in which the sciences were fully integrated.[7] A major problem with Young's thesis, however, is that it implies a progressive transition from a unified intellectual culture to something resembling C. P. Snow's 'two cultures'. It has little to say concerning the complex changes in notions of the 'literary' and the 'scientific' which occurred over the course of the period, or to the manner in which those changes related to the transformations that took place in the forms of, and audiences for, periodical literature. Indeed, Young focused exclusively on a small number of the highbrow magazines and quarterlies indexed by the *Wellesley Index to Victorian Periodicals*, and, while he attributed the putative break-up of the 'common context' partly to 'the growth of general periodicals of a markedly lower intellectual standard', he otherwise disregarded the continual development over the century of new periodical forms addressed to an increasing range of reading audiences.

While the quarterlies undoubtedly represented the leading medium of discussion and debate among the wealthy middle classes and those in positions of cultural power in the early nineteenth century, there were already signs of strain in this 'common context'. As Richard Yeo has shown, Jürgen Habermas's notion of the bourgeois public sphere is helpful here. Such a sphere developed in eighteenth-century Britain, France, and Germany, as the cultural forum of a newly self-conscious 'public'. While effectively open only to the bourgeoisie and the landed aristocracy, it relied on a notion that men of differing ranks could discourse within it on all subjects on equal terms, through the authenticating token of Enlightenment rationality. The bourgeois public sphere existed, characteristically, in the physical space of the coffee house and in the virtual space of the periodical, where the writer and reader were notionally interchangeable. By the early nineteenth century, however, this notion of a unified public was becoming increasingly tenuous. In particular, the emergence from the 1790s of a self-consciously counter-cultural radical press and the strain placed on synthetic writing by the specialization of knowledge, made it increasingly difficult to maintain the notion of a unitary public sphere. Moreover, as Yeo has shown, science exacerbated these tensions. Divergent and threatening notions of science were prevalent in the radical press and elsewhere, and there was increasing conflict between 'the needs and interests of the lay public and the specialists' in terms of periodical writing on science.[8]

The breakdown of the bourgeois public sphere in early nineteenth-century Britain exposes the inadequacy of Young's exclusive focus on highbrow periodicals. In order to negotiate the increasing diversity of reading audiences for science we need to study the full range of periodical types. As Jon Klancher suggests in his ground-breaking study of early nineteenth-century periodicals, reading audiences are not 'simply distinct sectors of the cultural sphere' that can be considered in isolation; rather, they develop and are maintained in relation to each other.[9] Ultimately, a more extensive familiarity with the periodical press is needed even in order to grasp how the 'intellectual' audience envisaged by Young was redefined during the course of the century. To date, most attention in this regard has been devoted to the rise of the radical press – work which has done much to show that the production of science for fashionable or specialist readers was profoundly informed by the presence of other audiences.[10] However, other important reading audiences remain neglected. Take, for instance, Charles Timperley's calculation that of some 318 periodical titles (other than newspapers) issued in London on 16 December 1837, some fifty-two (16 per cent) were religious, and many of the seventy-one left unclassified (22 per cent) were 'very cheap periodicals, addressed chiefly to children'.[11] The large circulation of religious and children's magazines suggest areas particularly worthy of consideration, but many other reading audiences also demand attention.

A renewed interest in the full range of nineteenth-century writing on science has been a hallmark of the recent historiography of science popularization and science in popular culture. In their 1994 re-appraisal of the field, Roger Cooter and Stephen Pumfrey urged that future work should be 'responsive to a greater plurality of the sites for the making and reproduction of scientific knowledge', asserting the need to scrutinize 'popular prose and non-scientific texts for (or as) signs of orthodox and unorthodox scientific authority' and to explore the histories of scientific metaphors in popular writing.[12] In particular, Bernard Lightman and others have pointed up the importance of widely circulated scientific writings produced by professional popularizers who 'offered different ways of speaking about nature' to the emergent scientific professionals of the late century.[13] Similar perspectives have also emerged from recent work in literary studies. As scholars such as Gillian Beer, George Levine, and Sally Shuttleworth have shown, many literary writers of the nineteenth century actively engaged with scientific themes in essays, fiction, and poetry.[14] Much of this writing first appeared in the non-specialist periodicals which are the focus of the present book.

Periodical studies have also developed apace. Thanks to John North's monumental *Waterloo Directory*, the vast output of the periodical press – North records some 125,000 newspaper and periodical titles in nineteenth-century England alone – has come under increasing bibliographical control.[15] Other resources, notably Alvin Sullivan's *British Literary Magazines* (1983–4) and J. Don Vann and Rosemary VanArsdel's *Victorian*

Periodicals and Victorian Society (1994), give helpful overviews of the development of the press. Theoretical approaches have also become more sophisticated, as scholars have reflected on the distinctive qualities of the periodical genre.[16] To date, however, little has been done to combine these new perspectives on periodicals with recent historiography of popular science or with scholarship on literature and science.

Scholars wishing to draw on periodical literature in their historical work on science have been daunted by the size and complexity of the task. This literature can be difficult to penetrate: few periodicals have adequate indexes, and modern indexes, such as the *Wellesley Index* and *Poole's Index to Periodical Literature, 1802–1906*, are keyed to titles which frequently offer little guidance as to the content of articles. The invaluable *Wellesley Index*, moreover, has exerted a distorting effect upon the field: scholars have tended to follow its example, focusing primarily on 'highbrow' titles, to the exclusion of periodicals aimed, for example, at women, children, artisans, or religious denominations. The 'Science in the Nineteenth-Century Periodical' (SciPer) project addressed these concerns by creating an interpretative electronic index to the scientific content of a range of genres of general periodical, based on inclusive reading of the entire periodical texts.[17] This book is based on this in-depth research.

In this book, we seek to reinterpret the place of science in nineteenth-century British culture by combining insights from the history of popular science, cultural and literary studies, and periodical studies, together with the experience of reading tens of thousands of pages of general periodicals in preparing the SciPer index. The book approaches its subject from two main directions. The chapters in the first section focus on the function of science within the literary economy of various periodical genres. All too frequently, historians have raided periodicals for interesting references to science, paying little attention to the wider frame in which those references existed. Yet periodical articles appeared as elements of larger texts, and they were commonly read (and indeed often written) in relation to the texts that surrounded them. In this book, we consider the place of science in six important periodical genres, reinstating the original contexts in which the constituent articles were initially read, and considering how the formal features of the periodicals shaped the content and meaning.

The chapters in the second section of the book address particular themes across a range of periodicals, recapturing the sense that contemporaries had both of the diversity of approaches to the sciences embodied in different kinds of publication and of the frequent interplay between the several journals. In chapter 8, Sally Shuttleworth shows that many of the key early interventions in the creation of the science of infant development were made in mid-century literary magazines and highbrow reviews. Even after the psychological journal *Mind* had broached the subject, the debate continued to range across a number of non-specialist periodicals. Shuttleworth also shows the difficulties encountered by George Henry Lewes, James Sully, and others in attempting to negotiate the different demands of non-specialist and specialist periodicals, and considers the implications of such writing for scientific reputation. Geoffrey Cantor, in chapter 9, explores how periodicals transmitted the narratives of free-standing scientific biographies to far wider audiences, transforming their meaning by immersing them in radically different contexts. One of the peculiarities of periodicals is that they contain within a single work a whole range of generic forms, and Cantor also investigates the manner in which the different genres of biographical writing were handled. In chapter 10, Graeme Gooday explores the changing literary forms in which the new technologies of industrial and domestic electricity were handled in the periodicals of the late nineteenth century. He argues that the development of new journalistic media – notably W. T. Stead's campaigning *Review of Reviews* (1890) – contributed to the emergence of a 'futurist romance' of electricity, which was to displace the 'technical-didactic exegesis' of the older reviews.

In this introduction we set these detailed case studies within two larger perspectives. First, we survey the increasing range of periodicals in the period and consider the significance of their changing forms and audiences for a wider understanding of the place of science in nineteenth-century culture. Secondly, we consider some of the key historiographical questions entailed in using periodicals in this way.

'CHARTING THE GOLDEN STREAM': SCIENCE IN THE NINETEENTH-CENTURY PERIODICAL[18]

In his *History of Nineteenth Century Literature* (1896), George Saintsbury reflected that no literary phenomenon was 'so distinctive and characteristic' of the era as 'the development . . . of periodical literature'.[19] Since the late seventeenth century, periodicals had been regarded as a potent device for developing the literary marketplace, providing metropolitan publishers with a conduit through which to advertise other literary wares to provincial booksellers and far-flung readers.[20] However, with the increasing commercialization of the book trade in the eighteenth century, and with the emergence of new reading audiences and the mechanization of book manufacture in the early nineteenth century, periodicals took on a new significance. In an unpredictable market, periodicals allowed publishers to develop relationships with particular groups of readers while at the same time avoiding the financial risks of capital-intensive book production. Their periodicity allowed producers to respond readily both to readers' comments and to sales figures in order to match commodity and consumer more effectively. The periodical was thus the perfect vehicle for sounding out and consolidating the diverse reading audiences of the growing and increasingly entrepreneurial literary marketplace. As a result, the number of titles trebled in the first three decades of the new century, and the types of periodical also rapidly increased.

To some contemporaries, periodicals seemed almost to be replacing books. In 1823, Hazlitt famously addressed the complaint that his was 'a Critical age; and that no great works of Genius appear[ed], because so much [was] said and written about them'.[21] The dominance of periodical literature has also been widely recognized by historians. Lee Erickson, for instance, considers that 'the periodical became the dominant publishing format' during the first half of the nineteenth century, and Mark Parker argues that literary magazines were the 'preeminent literary form of the 1820s and 1830s in Britain'.[22] Yet the basic parameters of this new market for periodicals remain largely unexplored. Figures from the *Waterloo Directory* suggest there was a sustained if uneven increase in the number of periodical titles over the course of the century, with the exception of a final decline, which may be a result of the method of sampling (fig. 1.1). The number of periodicals apparently increased at an ever-faster rate as the century progressed, although the greatest proportionate increases occurred in the early part of the century (particularly in the late 1810s/early 1820s and in the early 1830s). Comparing this pattern to figures derived from the *Nineteenth-Century Short-Title Catalogue* seems to confirm that from the 1820s, and more especially from the 1850s, the number of periodical titles grew at a faster rate than the number of book titles (fig. 1.2).

When complete, the *Waterloo Directory* may enable us to generate data about the shifting genres and periodicities of periodical publication, and the changing patterns of periodical prices. To date, however, there is no modern study which, like Walter Graham's *English Literary Periodicals* (1930), seeks to provide a comprehensive assessment of the main phases of periodical publication. Yet the rise and fall of periodical forms clearly impinged heavily on the ways in which the sciences were encountered and discussed in nineteenth-century Britain. In this section we sketch some of the key

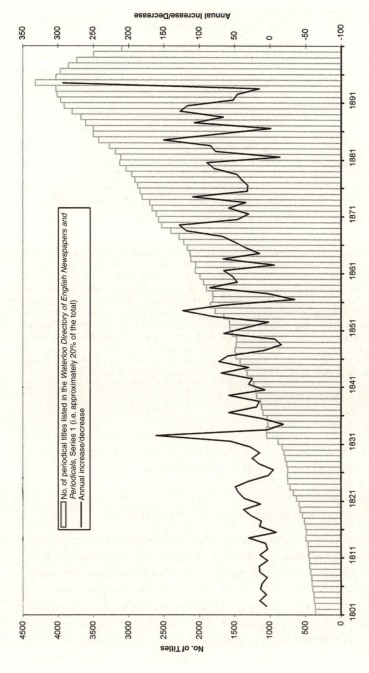

Figure 1.1. Patterns of periodical publication in nineteenth-century Britain.[a]

[a] The data are derived from *Waterloo Directory of English Newspapers and Periodicals, 1800–1900*, ed. by John North (Waterloo: Ontario North Waterloo Academic Press, 2001) accessed 7 March 2001 <http://www.victorianperiodicals.com>. The figures given here are taken from the first of the five planned series of the directory, which, it should be noted, has something of a subject bias. In each series of the directory, all subject areas are covered, but each of the series 'attempts to provide a comprehensive listing of from seven to ten additional subjects, while including many thousands of titles not on those specialty lists'.

9

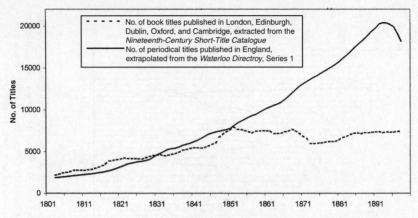

Figure 1.2. Comparative trends of book and periodical publication in nineteenth-century Britain.*a*

a The data (displayed as five-year moving averages) are derived from the *Waterloo Directory* and the *Nineteenth-Century Short-Title Catalogue, Series I & II, 1801–1870 (NSTC)*, CD-ROM (Newcastle-upon-Tyne: Avero Publications, 1996). The *NSTC* is a union-catalogue of the 'British books' in a number of leading research libraries, including all books, periodicals, and pamphlets 'published in Britain, its colonies and the United States of America; all books in English wherever published; and all translations from English'. As a union-catalogue, it does not pretend to be a complete record of publication; while at the same time it contains many foreign publications not germane for our comparison. Thus, we have not only excluded serials from our calculations, but have also followed Simon Eliot in excluding all books not published in London, Oxford, Cambridge, Edinburgh, or Dublin, trusting that these leading publishing centres will give a reasonable reflection of the pattern of British book publishing. See Simon Eliot, *Some Patterns and Trends in British Publishing, 1800–1919* (London: Bibliographical Society, 1994); and Eliot, 'Patterns and Trends and the NSTC: Some Initial Observations', *Publishing History* 42 (1997): 79–104, and 43 (1998): 71–112.

phases of this history, considering how the shifting material and cultural forms of periodicals modified not only how the sciences were represented, but also the audiences to which they were addressed.

Science in early nineteenth-century periodicals

The nineteenth century began with the inception of one of the most commanding new periodical genres, namely, the quarterly review journal, initiated by the *Edinburgh Review* (f. 1802). Far more selective in its reviewing, and also far more opinionated and partisan than the monthly reviews of the previous century, the *Edinburgh* 'plainly set out to break the mould of existing journal culture'.[23] In contrast to the encyclopaedic ambitions and open ethos of the *Monthly Review* (f. 1749) or the *Analytical Review* (f. 1788), the new review prided itself on its discrimination, both in its subject matter and in its contributors. The point was well encapsulated by the *Gentleman's Magazine*, reflecting on the role of literature in the wake of the political unrest of 1819:

since the establishment of the great Quarterly Journals, every subject of any moment to the Publick is sure to be most elaborately discussed, in a proper scientific technical form, by men of rank in life, and high acquisitions, who are above dependence on their professional situations . . . Things of this very high character can only be executed by persons resident in large cities, and who can have access, upon particular subjects, to documents, not of a general kind.[24]

The *Edinburgh* was founded by an ambitious group of young men influenced by the academic specialisms of the Scottish universities, which featured prominently in the review. Several of the editorial coterie had been former members of the Academy of Physics – a student scientific society – and they gave particular emphasis to the natural sciences, as well as to moral philosophy and political economy.[25] By contrast, traditional theological and classical lore, together with the mechanical arts and antiquities beloved of the new middle classes, were notably absent. In addition, the *Edinburgh* viewed medical subjects as generally suitable only for the specialist writers and readers of the medical journals.[26]

By the 1820s, the natural sciences were becoming increasingly problematical for the quarterlies. Marilyn Butler observes that the *Edinburgh*, like its competitor the *Quarterly* (f. 1809), began to reflect an 'ordered *separation* between literature, especially poetry, and independent or reformist or scientific thinking' that was in train by this period. Likewise, Richard Yeo argues that by the 1830s 'it was clear that there was no longer a single educated readership', and writers in the quarterlies had to contend with the 'problem of speaking to both experts and general readers' on scientific subjects. It was also difficult to identify suitable books for review on scientific subjects or to find reviewers who could write in a suitable manner for a non-scientific audience. Nevertheless, around one tenth of articles in the *Edinburgh* and *Quarterly* in the 1830s were devoted to scientific subjects, and other articles often broached scientific themes.[27] Moreover, gentlemen of science like David Brewster and William Whewell who wrote at length in the reviews clearly saw them as important platforms for addressing a non-specialist but culturally powerful public. Such literary performances were of a piece with the conversational interventions gentlemen of science were expected to make in London's fashionable salons, and fulfilled important functions in making the claims of science heard amongst the ruling élite.[28] At the same time, the quarterlies began to provide a platform for emergent men of letters, such as Thomas Carlyle, to explore new developments in specialist knowledge using 'the touchstone of a general humanism'.[29]

The breakdown of the ideal of a bourgeois public sphere and the developing sense of distinct literary and scientific spheres was, if anything, more evident in the monthly magazines. Conceived as storehouses ('magazines') of learning and information, the eighteenth-century miscellanies of the sort typified by the *Gentleman's Magazine* had welcomed contributions from readers on subjects ranging from natural history to the practical arts, and from meteorology to agriculture. The Enlightenment project of amassing observations and experiments flourished in such magazines, as Roy Porter has illustrated in relation to medical subjects.[30] Advertising a reprint of its half-century run in 1782, the magazine claimed: 'There has scarce a new Subject been started, a new Invention introduced, or a Discovery of any Kind, either by Land or Sea, of which a satisfactory Account is not to be found in the GENTLEMAN'S MAGAZINE.'[31]

In the years following the Napoleonic wars, however, this situation rapidly changed, as the older style of miscellany was replaced by self-consciously literary magazines and a growing body of commercial science periodicals appeared. The first of the new magazines, *Blackwood's Edinburgh Magazine* (f. 1817), began in a strictly traditional form, including separate sections devoted to 'Original Communications', 'Select Extracts', 'Literary and Scientific Intelligence', and a 'Monthly Register' of news, commercial and agricultural reports, and births, deaths, and marriages. At the start of the second volume, however, its publisher radically revised the format, removing the traditional sections (with the exception of the 'Monthly Register', which continued – increasingly intermittently – until 1831) and paying handsomely for contributions that were self-consciously original literary creations. This approach to the monthly magazine was soon adopted by other publishers. In January 1820 the *London Magazine* was started in deliberate imitation of *Blackwood's*, and the following year the *New Monthly Magazine* (f. 1814) took on a markedly more literary form. Other existing titles, including the *Monthly Magazine* (which had been one of the most scientific of the monthlies) and the *European Magazine*, soon followed suit.

The *Gentleman's Magazine* maintained its traditional format as a 'living encyclopædia',[32] yet it also contained fewer original scientific observations. Roy Porter has noted that from the 1810s in particular 'there was a dramatic decline in the exchange of medical advice, inquiries, remedies', and that it 'ceased to play any important role in instructing the laity in medical self-help or as a medical talking-shop'; instead, the magazine carried 'reports on what the medical profession was doing, viewed as an organized profession'.[33] In 1817, reports of scientific discoveries and technical innovations began to appear as brief paragraphs in a separate section, often in extracts from other publications. The implication was that readers were consumers of scientific news more than active participants in scientific discovery. An 1820 preface was more explicit, arguing that, especially in such turbulent times, journals like the *Gentleman's Magazine* should suppress erroneous ideas brought forward by partly educated men who believed that 'one man ha[d] an equal right with another to attention'. The magazines were to act 'as Clerks of the Market, to prevent the Literary Public Stomach from being seriously injured by eating unwholesome food'.[34]

The transformation of the monthly magazine into a primarily literary genre did not occur in isolation. While a number of commercial scientific, medical, and technical magazines had been in existence since the later part of the eighteenth century, the period following the Napoleonic wars witnessed a rapid increase in their number and range. Whereas in 1815 there had been approximately ten such magazines, by 1830 the number had trebled; in the same time period the number of society publications had remained around ten.[35] The existing commercial journals, like the *Botanical Magazine* (f. 1787), the *Repertory of Arts* (f. 1794), the *Philosophical Magazine* (f. 1798), and the *Medical and Physical Journal* (f. 1799) were supplemented by a number of competitors, like the *Botanical Cabinet* (f. 1817), the *London Journal of Arts* (f. 1820), the *Edinburgh Philosophical Journal* (f. 1819), and the *Medico-Chirurgical Review* (f. 1820). In addition, however, a wider range of specialized subject journals appeared, ranging from the *Phrenological Journal* (f. 1820) to the *Gardener's Magazine* (f. 1826), and the *Veterinarian* (f. 1828) to the *Magazine of Natural History* (f. 1829). Such magazines opened their pages to original observations from readers in much the way that the Enlightenment miscellanies had; however, their audiences were now clearly fractured along disciplinary lines. Furthermore, a number of the new genres of scientific, technical, and medical periodical which originated at this period emphasized socio-cultural divisions – perhaps most strikingly those which, like the *Lancet* and the *Mechanics' Magazine*, emulated the new cheap weekly miscellanies of the 1820s.

The demise of the traditional Enlightenment miscellany and the development of the new specialized genres of the scientific and literary magazine require much more detailed analysis than can be given here. However, it is not our intention to replace Young's 'fragmentation of the common context' in the 1870s with an alternative fragmentation in the 1820s. Historians have long recognized that this period witnessed the development of specialized scientific disciplines with increasingly technical vocabularies and a developing emphasis on trained experts, and the generic innovations of British periodicals in the years following the Napoleonic wars certainly contributed to the disintegration of an Enlightenment ideal of the bourgeois public sphere. Yet not only the quarterlies, but also the new literary monthlies and other forms of periodical intended for those who were not scientific specialists, manifestly continued to engage with the sciences in a range of important ways, as this book illustrates. Moreover, as the cultural status of the sciences rose in the course of the century, literary magazines carried increasing numbers of articles on scientific subjects, often written by leading practitioners. In assessing the ebb and flow in the representation of the sciences in the periodicals of nineteenth-century Britain, close attention must be paid to the constantly shifting genres of periodical publication.

A striking instance of this is the development in the post-war period of the weekly literary journal of *belles-lettres*, typified by Henry Colborn's *Literary Gazette* (f. 1817). A sixteen-page shilling weekly, the *Gazette* had the advantage of being able to provide readers with literary and other news on a more immediate basis than the monthlies. The new possibilities it raised for the reporting and discussion of science were increasingly exploited in succeeding decades. On William Edward Parry's return from his first Arctic voyage in 1820, for instance, the *Gazette*'s editor, William Jerdan, boarded the ships as they came up the Thames, penning an account which boosted the sale of the journal by five hundred copies.[36] Later, following the founding of the British Association for the Advancement of Science in 1831, Jerdan travelled in person to the peripatetic annual meetings to report on the sessions.[37]

The *Literary Gazette* was the first periodical after *The Times* to be printed using steam presses. The effects of industrialization were felt increasingly in the years after 1815, as stereotype, machine-made paper, and case binding all began to be used in periodical manufacture. Such transformations were fundamental to the production of the penny periodicals in the 1830s. However, the advent of the first cheap periodicals in the 1820s owed more to the growing market for cheap print, signalled by the runaway success from 1816 of the separate two-penny edition of William Cobbett's *Political Register* (f. 1802). Early radical journals, like Thomas Wooler's *Black Dwarf* (f. 1817), tended to eschew scientific matters as not being germane to the immediate political exigencies, although they were often permeated by a discourse of natural law, and frequently used scientific imagery. However, some more extreme publications, like Richard Carlile's atheist *Republican* (f. 1819), explicitly used materialist sciences to iconoclastic effect.[38]

The repressive legislation introduced in 1819 did much to silence the cheap radical press during the 1820s, but the format of the cheap two-penny weekly of sixteen octavo pages was soon pressed into service by small-time entrepreneurs – including Cobbett's erstwhile collaborators – to reach a wider market. At a time when all but a small minority were priced out of the market for most new books and periodicals, the cheap weekly miscellanies like the *Mirror of Literature* (f. 1822) came as a great boon, and were bought in unprecedented numbers. Combining readers' contributions of the type found in the *Gentleman's Magazine* with topical articles, extracts from fashionable books and the new monthly magazines, and innovative wood-engravings, the new genre incorporated science in a range of different ways, as shown in chapter 2. By the 1830s, however, a self-consciously 'popular' science came to predominate, intended for rational recreation, rather than for practical use or debate. Such an approach was adopted by the penny weeklies, such as the *Penny Magazine* (f. 1832) and *Saturday Magazine* (f. 1832), which were produced in response to the resurgence of the radical press during the Reform Crisis.

The specialization of periodical literature in which the scientific and literary monthlies partook was part of a larger development: the emergence of what the Victorians called 'class journalism', directed to the ever-increasing range of specialized reading audiences. Particularly prominent were the many religious magazines which were founded in the early decades of the nineteenth century, the cheapest of which – the *Evangelical Magazine* (f. 1793) and the *Wesleyan-Methodist Magazine* (f. 1778) – were (as chapter 3 shows) by far the most widely circulated periodicals of the period. Some religious magazines – notably the early *Christian Observer* (f. 1802) – emulated the traditional magazines in providing regular reports of the meetings of Europe's scientific societies. More commonly, the science content of religious magazines was overtly directed towards practical devotion, but science nevertheless featured in dedicated articles, missionary reports, obituaries, sermons, and book reviews.[39]

In the growing middle-class leisure market of the eighteenth century, a number of monthly magazines had been directed to ladies, but the new century saw the market expand further. To varying degrees, these ladies' magazines incorporated entertaining and instructive articles on scientific subjects, most particularly natural history. Yet, as Cynthia White has argued, and others have confirmed, there was 'a sudden reversal of the trend which promised [women] wider participation in social affairs' in the 1820s, with women's magazines subsequently being dominated by an ideology of domesticity.[40] Ann Shteir has shown that this transition was marked in the way that both the *Lady's Magazine* (f. 1770) and the *Lady's Monthly Museum* (f. 1798) handled science, and points suggestively to the fact that this transition was coincident with the movement of 'scientific teaching and learning... away from general interest magazines into specialist publications'.[41] The early nineteenth century also saw the first sustained monthly magazines for children and youths. Such periodicals reached amongst the largest reading audiences of the period, their success rooted in their explicitly religious objectives, and in their use of religious distribution networks. They commonly included scientific articles as part of their fare of rational entertainment, and also sought to inculcate a pious approach to scientific reading in their moral tales, homilies, and other articles.[42]

Science in mid-nineteenth-century periodicals

The middle of the nineteenth century saw enormous growth and development in the British periodical press.[43] This expansion had many causes. First, demand rose from increasingly literate and leisured reading audiences for what Patricia Anderson calls 'new and varied sources of knowledge and amusement'.[44] Secondly, technological developments offered ways of catering for this growing and diversifying taste, both with the development of increasingly efficient printing machines, and with the rapid expansion of Britain's railway network which greatly aided distribution of printed matter.[45] Thirdly, changes in taxation massively reduced costs. Following the significant reduction of duties on newspapers in 1836, their subsequent repeal in 1853 and 1855 fostered a sharp growth in the number of new titles and made newspapers more accessible to working- and middle-class readerships.[46] Moreover, the abolition of taxes on paper and rags in 1860 and 1861 lowered the cost of all types of periodical.

Studies by Bill Brock, Susan Sheets-Pyenson, and Ruth Barton emphasise that *Nature* (f. 1869) was only the latest in a large crop of new commercial popular and semi-popular science journals appearing in the period from 1840 to 1870. Some of these built on the examples of cheap weekly mechanics' magazines (e.g. the *English Mechanic* (f. 1865)), some emerged from trade weeklies (e.g. the *Chemical News* (f. 1859)), some developed from the more expensive genre of the monthly natural history magazine (e.g. the *Zoologist* (f. 1843)), and others experimented with the periodical genres traditionally associated with general topics (e.g. the *Popular Science Review* (f. 1862) and the *Reader* (f. 1863)).[47] These journals catered to, and helped define, specialist scientific readerships. They gave scientific practitioners many more alternatives to the existing general media where scientific debate had traditionally taken place and thus widened the gulf between general readers and scientific experts. Nonetheless, as Barton shows, popular science journals occupied a crucial nexus between trained scientists and the increasing number of readers with scientific interests because they functioned as sources of education and recreation and, increasingly during the 1860s, as platforms from which the new breed of scientific professionals could promote arguments for the cultural importance of science.[48]

The new scientific professionals did not, however, use only popular science journals in attempting to address their claims to a wider public. The problem of divergent interpretations of the meaning and uses of science had been spectacularly brought home to many experts during the controversy over *Vestiges of the Natural History of Creation* (1844).[49] What this controversy showed, above all, was that the Victorian reading public now had access to a vast array of printed material in which conflicting views of science were expounded. Readers were not simply picking up claims made in the name of science in specialist journals, but in other established periodical genres, and in the welter of new serial forms that emerged in the period from 1840 to 1870.[50] If the new professionals were to achieve the cultural authority over science that they sought, they would need to make their voices heard in general periodicals, and many did. It was in this mid-century battle for cultural authority that scientific polemicists like Huxley came into prominence in the general periodical press.

One of the most striking developments in early Victorian periodicals was the increase in the quantity and quality of illustration. Exemplified by the *Illustrated London News* (f. 1842), *Reynolds's Miscellany* (f. 1849), and the *Leisure Hour* (f. 1851), illustrated periodicals greatly expanded and unified the Victorian reading public's visual experience and played a central role in creating a mass culture.[51] Moreover, as the chapters in this book show, the increasingly widespread pictorial representations of scientific events, objects, and personalities in the general periodical press significantly shaped public perceptions of science.[52] In the pages of illustrated newspapers, far wider audiences were now introduced to the scientific spectacles of the day, ranging from exhibitions of new technology to shows of exotic specimens. Savants themselves became familiar to a wider public, both collectively as represented at scientific meetings, and increasingly individually, as scientific celebrities. Scientific discoveries, too, began to be represented in pictorial terms, acquiring an appearance of factuality far more immediate than that conferred by textual description.

Illustrations were, of course, a key component in the comic journals that imitated and sought to enjoy the success of *Punch* (f. 1841). *Punch* and such rivals as *Fun* (f. 1861) built on earlier traditions in 'high' and 'low' comic journalism, from the waspish visual caricatures of William Hone and George Cruikshank and the grubby political satire of *Figaro in London* (f. 1831) to the genteel literary humour of *Fraser's Magazine* (f. 1830), Hood's *Comic Annual* (f. 1830), and *Bentley's Miscellany* (f. 1837). What distinguished *Punch* and many other new comic journals from their ancestors – and what constituted major ingredients of their success among their predominantly bourgeois readers – was their development of comic formulæ that combined respectability of tone, topicality, variety, and political conscience. As chapter 4 shows for *Punch*, scientific material played a much bigger part in this formula than hitherto recognized. Major scientific spectacles lent themselves to visual caricature in comic journals as much as sober depiction in the *Illustrated London News*, while the abstruse claims of astronomers, the immoral conduct of doctors, and the ingenious schemes of inventors provided material for comic journalists to continue their humorous, and frequently vitriolic, commentaries on the rights and wrongs of Victorian culture.

Illustrations also contributed to the success of other newcomers to the early and mid-Victorian market for periodicals: fiction-based weeklies and new serials for women and children. One of the outstanding features of mid-Victorian periodical publishing was the enormous circulation achieved by a string of penny fiction-based weeklies catering to a relatively uncultivated audience. By the 1850s, titles such as the *Family Herald* (f. 1842), the *London Journal* (f. 1845), and *Cassell's Family Paper* (f. 1853) were read by several hundred thousand people each week.[53] Building on the earlier tradition of cheap miscellanies, they offered large amounts of fiction, as well as useful information and serious articles, much of which was unoriginal and presented in a patronizing way. Of much higher literary and intellectual quality, though more expensive and lacking illustrations, were the two fiction-based weeklies 'conducted' by Charles Dickens: *Household Words* (f. 1850) and *All-the-Year-Round* (f. 1859). These featured fiction by writers such as Wilkie Collins, Elizabeth Gaskell, and Dickens himself, which frequently engaged with the same scientific, medical, and technological issues raised in the intellectually astute essays appearing elsewhere in the periodicals.[54]

The middle-class readership that Dickens targeted with his journals included the educated though not necessarily affluent women whom other early- and mid-Victorian publishers believed would clamour for cheap periodicals tailored to their needs. The most successful attempt to exploit this market was Samuel Beeton's two-penny *Englishwoman's Domestic Magazine* (f. 1852). In the preceding decades, most women's magazines had been expensive monthlies for upper-class ladies that either focused largely on fashion and beauty or soberly promoted the morality and spirituality of

Christian motherhood.[55] The *Englishwoman's Domestic* offered something very different and was frequently imitated. Its low price guaranteed it enormous sales among middle-class women for whom no comparable publication existed. Like the cheap fiction-based weeklies, it carried a large amount of medium-quality fiction, articles on history and biography, and answers to correspondents, but it trail-blazed with its systematic coverage of aspects of domestic management such as gardening, hygiene, and cookery. These articles best represent Beeton's aim to improve readers' intellectual, moral, and domestic abilities, and they furnished ample opportunities for introducing useful scientific and medical information.[56]

Samuel Beeton also played a pivotal role in the mid-Victorian transformation of children's magazines. Until the mid-1850s, middle- and upper-class children's experiences of periodicals were usually either from family journals or juvenile serials published by religious presses. Juvenile periodicals launched from the 1850s increasingly differentiated between readers of different ages and gender, and offered much more secular material. Beeton's *Boy's Own Magazine* (f. 1855), a two-penny monthly aimed at older middle-class boys, fully exploited falling periodical costs, growing literacy among the more affluent children, and the rising mid-Victorian bourgeois taste for what Kirsten Drotner calls 'moral entertainment where an extrovert, imperial manliness mattered more than introspective piety or dry memorising'.[57] It entertained with exciting adventure stories, puzzles, and a welter of (often coloured) illustrations, and instructed with hagiographies and detailed recipes for nature study, scientific experiments, and workshop projects, many of which were written by recognized experts such as J. G. Wood, who later edited the magazine.[58] The runaway success of the *Boy's Own Magazine* inspired other juvenile magazines. However, many boys wanted more entertainment and less instruction and this was provided by a flurry of immensely successful cheap boys' weeklies published from the late 1860s, such as Edwin J. Brett's *Boys of England* (f. 1866). Although many parents scorned them, Brett emphasized that his serials were designed to give less affluent boys wholesome alternatives to the 'penny dreadfuls' that had flourished in the 1840s. The *Boy's Own Magazine* and *Boys of England* represented different ways of interpreting wholesome entertainment and instruction that shaped the late-Victorian era in juvenile periodicals.

Like Beeton, the publishers of the so-called 'shilling monthlies' – most notably Alexander Macmillan of *Macmillan's Magazine* (f. 1859) and George Smith of the phenomenally successful *Cornhill Magazine* (f. 1860) – were entrepreneurs who sought to exploit a new sector of the mid-Victorian reading public. Shilling monthlies catered for relatively educated but not traditionally affluent readers who were attracted to neither the cheap 'family' journals nor the expensive (2s) monthly literary magazines. They succeeded by offering more fiction, a generous helping of woodcuts and lithographs, and a plethora of serious articles on a wide range of subjects including history, art, and the sciences. Part of the appeal of this material was that it was penned by cultural figures respected by middle-class audiences, ranging from William Makepeace Thackeray, Anthony Trollope, and Sheridan Le Fanu for their high-quality fiction, to Thomas Henry Huxley, William Thomson, and Richard Proctor for their lucid scientific articles. As chapter 5 argues, scientific material in the shilling monthlies fulfilled the same function as scientific discussion in the new comic journals: it was a key element in these periodicals' overall strategy of meeting the middle-class taste for topical, learned, and entertaining discourse. For professionalizing scientists like Huxley, however, these magazines presented an important forum for addressing a wider audience.

The founders of the new monthly reviews of the 1860s devised periodicals which emulated the intellectual debates taking place in societies, clubs, and conversaziones. They identified a gap in the periodical market for a more open intellectual forum, free from the party lines that tainted the quarterlies. The most radical was Chapman and Hall's *Fortnightly Review* (f. 1865) which, paradoxically, was neither fortnightly (at least not after 1866) nor properly a review, primarily featuring free-standing articles that were not directly tied to the current lists of publishing houses. Intended as an English equivalent of the *Revue des Deux Mondes* (f. 1829), the *Fortnightly* was the first major periodical to disavow anonymity and instead enforce authorial responsibility by a strict policy of signature. The initial success of the *Fortnightly* was, according to G. H. Lewes (its first editor), 'mainly owing to the principle adopted of allowing each writer perfect freedom; which could only have been allowed under the condition of personal responsibility'.[59] This policy of openness on questions of religion, politics, philosophy, literature, and the sciences certainly appealed to the scientific practitioners who contributed to its pages, including John Herschel, Huxley, and John Tyndall. The prominence of science was, from the very beginning, one of the defining characteristics of the *Fortnightly*, prompting criticisms that the periodical was politically more liberal than neutral, and theologically more rationalist than unbiased.

Signed journalism was also quickly adopted by a string of other intellectually highbrow serials, most notably the monthly *Contemporary Review* (f. 1866), which like the *Fortnightly* was priced at 2s 6d Founded as a response to the success of the secular *Fortnightly* by Alexander Strahan, the publisher of a string of religious magazines, the *Contemporary* focused more strongly on theological and philosophical issues, especially those that had been raised in the Metaphysical Society – an informal debating club that attracted statesmen, scientists, theologians, and philosophers, most of whom contributed to the *Contemporary*. Despite its Anglican leanings, the *Contemporary* differed strongly from most religious serials of the period in the wide range of theological, philosophical, and scientific positions that it published. Indeed, the *Contemporary*, at least while James Knowles remained as editor, featured some of the most ferocious arguments by Huxley, Tyndall, William Kingdon Clifford, and other scientific professionalizers in favour of the authority of trained scientific experts on social, intellectual, and cultural questions that had traditionally been the province of clergymen.

The insistence on signed articles in the *Fortnightly* and the *Contemporary* had important implications for the treatment of science in both journals, and perhaps induced a greater specialization amongst their contributors which in turn corresponded with the kind of professionalizing programme advanced by Huxley and others. As John Morley, Lewes's successor as editor of the *Fortnightly*, reflected,

One indirect effect that is not unworthy of notice in the new system is its tendency to narrow the openings for the writer by profession. If an article is to be signed, the editor will naturally seek the name of an expert of special weight and competence on the matter in hand.[60]

In the conditions of signed authorship which increasingly prevailed from the 1870s onwards, professional scientific writers were able to establish distinct authorial personas. By expressing consistent individual opinions across a range of different articles they established their expertise and credibility on particular topics, thereby ensuring that those without such intellectual credentials were denied the right to be heard. For Young, the monthly reviews represented almost archetypal exemplars of the 'common intellectual context', ahead of its eventual fragmentation in the 1880s and 1890s. On the contrary, however, they clearly represented a new and distinctive phase in the continuing development and re-negotiation of the relations between science and different periodical forms during the course of the century.

Science in late nineteenth-century periodicals

The last three decades of the nineteenth century witnessed an unprecedented growth in rates of literacy and levels of education, which, along with further technological innovations in printing and paper production

and ever more efficient railway distribution networks, continued to transform the periodical marketplace. These factors sustained the rapid increase
in the number of titles, further reduced their prices, and again increased the
size of the audience. The 1870 Education Act that helped create this newly
literate mass audience (especially when compulsory attendance at Board
Schools began to be enforced in the 1880s) also ensured the centralized
guidance of school curricula which, as José Harris has argued, 'rapidly generated a new national popular culture – a culture that evoked new market
responses in the form of mass-circulation newspapers'.[61] Lower production
costs, larger potential audiences, and the growing homogeneity of popular culture meant that commercial periodical publishing expanded more
rapidly in this period than ever before. Publishers willing to provide magazines and newspapers that were attuned to the demands of this growing mass
audience – with illustrations, short fiction, and answers to correspondents
being particular favourites – could now, in the words of the Liberal politi-
cian Henry Labouchère, 'make the journal a remunerative speculation'.[62]
Indeed, one of the distinguishing characteristics of periodical publishing
in this period was the emergence of corporate owners, including Alfred
Harmsworth (later Lord Northcliffe), who were attracted by the increased
profitability of the press.

The differential between the number of periodical and book titles published each year, which first began to diverge markedly in the 1850s, also
grew exponentially in this period (see fig. 1.2), reflecting the continuing high
price of books – especially the hugely expensive first editions bought prin-
cipally by circulating libraries – at a time when periodicals were becoming
ever cheaper. The 'periodical seems destined to supersede books altogether',
noted Mark Pattison in 1877, the year in which the Royal Commission
on Copyright declined to alter the arrangements between publishers and
libraries that maintained inflated book prices.[63] Pattison's hardly impartial
observation appeared in the *Fortnightly*, which cost 2s 6d for each monthly
issue of around 170 pages; a triple-decker novel at the time would generally
cost at least 10s 6d for each volume. Only after 1894 were book prices revised
downwards and, with the demise of the three-volume novel, brought into
line with the changes in the cost of periodicals over the previous three
decades. One of the consequences of the removal of taxes on newspapers
and paper in the 1850s and 1860s had been the supplanting of quarterly titles
by monthlies and weeklies, and the trend continued at an even greater pace
in the later years of the century, with the emergence of highly influential
dailies like the *Pall Mall Gazette* (f. 1865). The increasing speed of production, as well as the proliferation of journals, had important consequences

for the consumption of periodicals in the final decades of the century (see chapter 7).

At the expensive end of the periodical market, monthly reviews like the *Fortnightly*, *Contemporary*, and the new *Nineteenth Century* (f. 1877) continued to take over the cultural role previously performed by the quarterlies that had established the pattern for intellectual debate at the beginning of the century. While, as Pattison observed wryly, 'venerable old wooden three-deckers' such as the *Edinburgh* and *Quarterly* 'still put out to sea', the 'active warfare of opinion [was] conducted by three new iron monitors, the *Fortnightly*, *Contemporary*, and the *Nineteenth Century*'.[64] The *Nineteenth Century*, founded by James Knowles after a contretemps with the owners of the *Contemporary*, emerged as the principal flagship of the monthly reviews' values of liberal impartiality, signed articles, and reasoned debate. Additionally, the *Nineteenth Century* also pioneered roundtable formats of intellectual discussion (in the celebrated 'Modern "Symposium"' feature), and devolved ever-greater authority from the periodical and its editor to highly paid 'star' contributors like Huxley, Tyndall, and William Gladstone. Meanwhile, in the mid-priced sector of the market, imported American magazines costing a shilling like *Harper's New Monthly Magazine* (f. 1850) were successfully challenging the former hegemony of home-grown shilling monthlies like the *Cornhill* and *Temple Bar* (f. 1859), largely because of the unmatched quality of their illustrations. The success of *Harper's*, which was selling over 25,000 copies in Britain by the mid-1880s, also signalled the growing internationalism of the periodical press during the last decades of the century.

The most significant changes and innovations, however, took place at the cheaper end of the periodical market. The popular marketplace in the 1870s and 1880s was dominated by penny weeklies such as *Tit-Bits* (f. 1881) and sixpenny monthlies like the illustrated *Cassell's Family Magazine* (f. 1874) and the religious *Good Words* (f. 1860). The market leaders in the 1890s were populist and aggressively imperialist monthly miscellanies like the *Strand Magazine* (f. 1891) and *Pearson's Magazine* (f. 1896) which, priced at 6d, sold over 250,000 copies each. These titles were also joined by a number of periodicals, such as the *New Review* (f. 1889) and the *Review of Reviews* (f. 1890), which espoused a new and distinctive style of journalism that was more vivid and self-consciously demotic. Organs of this so-called 'New Journalism', as is discussed at length in chapter 7, engaged in crusades against the vested interests of the political and intellectual establishment as well as pioneering new formats such as 'talking' headlines. These populist crusades and novel forms of presentation were an attempt to make journalism less estranged from the lives of its ordinary readers, and to transform periodicals into fully inclusive public forums.

The rise of the new journalism also coincided with significant changes in the organization of the sciences as well as the ways in which they were presented. It has become a historical commonplace that during the 1870s and 1880s the practice of science became increasingly specialized and detached from the general culture. With the establishment of modern laboratories and salaried positions, as well as the further development of specialist scientific societies and journals, professional men of science became ever more isolated from the wider public. As we have seen, Young sees this as the fragmentation of his 'common context', and attributes it, at least partially, to the 'growth of general periodicals of a markedly lower intellectual standard' in which the reporting of science was left to 'pretentious hacks and . . . more or less competent amateurs'.[65] Similarly, Peter Broks suggests that mass-circulation family journals of the last decades of the century restricted the possibilities for public participation in science, and instead represented science 'as a commodity, a product not a process, to be consumed not participated in'. Even the presentation of science in the popular print media, he argues, 'reinforced the idea of a great gulf between the scientist and the public'.[66] The relationship between science and the popular print media, however, was considerably more complex and less one-sided in this period than Young and Broks have allowed.

This becomes especially evident when stylistic differences between the so-called 'New' and 'Old' journalisms are taken into consideration. Rather than simply maintaining 'lower intellectual standards' than earlier periodicals, organs of the 'New Journalism' presented a wide range of scientific material to new audiences in radically different ways.[67] These new journalistic methods of presenting science, including encouraging plebeian readers to submit details of their own experiments on a variety of subjects, often explicitly challenged the authority relations that men of science had been able to establish in the press earlier in the century. Additionally, innovative formats such as the celebrity interview (which had been imported from North America) could be used to generate an unprecedented sense of intimacy, cleverly mediated by increasingly powerful editors and proprietors, between the mass audience of the journals and producers of expert knowledge. The treatment of science in the popular print media could be considerably more dynamic and less élitist in this period than Young and Broks suggest. Indeed, the boundaries between what might be considered 'élite' and 'popular' understandings of science became

increasingly blurred in the self-consciously democratic pages of the periodicals that came to prominence during the final decades of the nineteenth
century.

The repeated shifts in the forms and audiences of nineteenth-century periodicals rule out any progressive history from a 'common intellectual context' to its fragmentation. The proliferation of socially and ideologically
divided audiences and periodicals in the decades after the French Revolution, and the 'invention' of modern disciplinary science in the same period,
were aspects of the transformation of the eighteenth-century bourgeois
public sphere which radically altered the position of science in the general
periodical literature. Yet the development of new kinds of writing about
science served to reintegrate it in the new kinds of general periodical that
were developed. Indeed, this seems to have occurred to an ever-greater extent as the cultural prominence and prestige of science increased over the
course of the century. Such writings ranged from what Richard Yeo calls
the 'metascientific' essays of gentlemanly scientists like Whewell and the
humanistic assessments of men of letters like Carlyle in the early-century
quarterlies, through the highbrow popularization of aspiring professionals
like Huxley and scientifically inclined writers like Lewes in the mid-century
literary magazines and reviews, to the campaigning journalism of Stead in
the late-century populist weeklies and monthlies. The chapters in the first
part of this book begin to sketch out in more detail some of the phases of
these developments.

COMMUNICATING SCIENCE: RETHINKING THE ROLE OF THE PERIODICAL

The insight that periodicals represent some of the most significant material and cultural forms through which the sciences were communicated
and debated in nineteenth-century Britain has far-ranging consequences
for students of the period, and the accompanying historiographical issues
require further consideration. Notwithstanding recent developments in
periodical studies, historians of science still often use periodicals as relatively
transparent records of the opinions either of the authors of individual articles or of particular publics, rather than considering periodicals as objects
in themselves. On the other hand, periodical historians have tended not to
pay particular attention to science, and when they have, they have usually
focused on the self-consciously scientific articles rather than on the inter-
penetration of scientific and other forms of discourse or on the fluctuating

and disputed boundaries of what is considered to be scientific. This book attempts to combine the best of these two approaches, showing that the characteristics that distinguish periodicals from other nineteenth-century media have a significant bearing on the history of science. In the remainder of this introduction we outline some of the most important characteristics of periodicals in this regard, considering the significance of how they were used and produced, their importance as sites of controversy and interchange, and their signal role in processes of literary replication.

Audiences

One of our central concerns in this book is with the issue of audience. As we have seen above, periodicals fulfilled a pivotal role in the nineteenth-century literary marketplace, allowing publishers, editors, and writers to attempt to shape the interpretative frameworks and self-awareness of readers in order to carve out new audiences, all the while adjusting their approach in response to the rapid and detailed feedback periodicals invited. As a result, they are, in Jon Klancher's phrase, 'probably the clearest framework for distinguishing the emerging publics of the nineteenth century'.[68] Such an insight brings a new perspective to the history of science in popular culture. A recurrent problem in the field has been the dominance of those approaches which prioritize the activities of science popularizers (often implicitly invoking the notion of 'diffusion') or which presuppose the relative autonomy of science in popular culture. Periodicals can be used to develop an alternative to these approaches: a dynamic history which brings into focus the interaction of readers and writers. Not only do periodicals embody debate, but they provide evidence of how individuals encountered and engaged such debate in relation to collective formations like class, gender, or ideology. Using periodicals like the *Wesleyan-Methodist Magazine* (chapter 3) and the *Boy's Own Paper* (chapter 6) to explore the reading audiences in relation to which individuals conceived of themselves, allows the historian to integrate the merely anecdotal records of encounters with science found in autobiographies, diaries, correspondence, and marginalia, into a wider account.

In his *Making of English Reading Audiences*, Jon Klancher draws on the work of Mikhail Bakhtin to argue that the mutual creation of audiences is embodied in the dialogic form of periodical writing: it is in the representation of other social languages, he argues, that readers become aware of themselves as members of particular audiences. Such semiotic analysis must also be supplemented by historical evidence about the strategies employed in periodicals to consolidate groups of consumers as self-conscious audiences and the manner in which periodicals were distributed and used. As chapter 3 shows, with respect to the *Wesleyan-Methodist Magazine*, some periodicals were managed by, and largely encountered through, heavily centralized authority structures – so much so that the book advertisements on the magazine's wrappers had to be scrutinized by a sub-committee. Of course, even here individual readers were by no means ineluctably bound by attempts at audience-creation. Yet, the recognition that, even in less extreme cases, periodicals bear linguistic and historical traces of such attempts allows the historian to begin to grapple with the fluid notions of audience with which historical readers themselves were confronted.

Producers

Given the importance of periodicals as sites for communicating and debating science, it is striking that the interests and activities of the publishers, editors, and journalists responsible for producing them have remained largely unexplored with reference to science. More than a quarter of a century has passed since Steven Shapin and Arnold Thackray argued that, instead of merely relying on the received historical canon, scholars should 'find out who published science, then assess the intellectual and cultural significance of their association with the enterprise of natural knowledge'.[69] It is only recently, however, that historians have begun to address this issue more systematically. One of the gains engendered by a renewed focus on periodicals is that it brings into view a wide range of people involved in producing scientific literature whose sometimes very considerable historical significance has been overlooked.

The vast majority of nineteenth-century periodicals were commodities: their form and content were critically shaped by the demands of the book trade in which they were manufactured, marketed, and distributed. As several of the chapters in this book demonstrate, publishers who developed new genres of periodical were responsible for changing the representation of science. Publishing entrepreneurs like John Limbird of the *Mirror of Literature* frequently used innovative periodicals to establish themselves in previously unexploited niche markets. As chapter 2 shows, the result of Limbird's entrepreneurship was a new genre – the cheap weekly miscellany – which conveyed scientific writing in distinctive ways to a new mass market. Even established publishers, like George Smith of the *Cornhill Magazine*, were prepared to invest huge sums in periodicals, not only because of the regular and reliable income they could generate, but also because of their value both in marketing other publications and in cultivating a coterie of authors. As a result, as chapter 5 reveals, Lewes had to sell scientific articles to Smith as part of a blend which would 'be felt as a reason for buying the Magazine', while Smith was uneasy about the potential commercial consequences of even a cautious endorsement of Darwinism in the magazine.[70]

While publishers exercised significant control over the representation of the sciences in periodicals, the power of the nineteenth-century editor could also be considerable. The transformation of the editor from a mere 'bookseller's drudge' into a 'distinguished functionary' took place early in the century with Francis Jeffrey's trail-blazing editorship of the *Edinburgh Review* (1803–29), and, as we have seen, the journal's distinctive approach to the sciences rested on the predilections of Jeffrey and his editorial coterie.[71] By the 1880s, Stead, the campaigning editor of the *Pall Mall Gazette*, proclaimed the coming of a new era of 'Government by Journalism' in which the 'editor's mandate' would be 'renewed day by day', while 'his electors register[ed] their vote by voluntary payment of the daily pence'.[72] In the burgeoning 'New Journalism' of the 1890s, editors like Stead (then at the helm of the *Review of Reviews*) emerged as demagogues of the era of mass democracy, appealing directly to readers – who were encouraged to send in details of their experiences with ghostly apparitions and to purchase the wares of homeopathic doctors – above the heads of even scientific contributors, such as Grant Allen, who wrote for the journal. Many journals upheld well-defined editorial positions, often (at least until the 1870s) with unsigned essays presenting the façade of a single authorial 'we'. The management of such a corporate voice was no trivial feat. As chapter 4 makes clear, the fictional 'Mr Punch' who was notionally responsible for the contents of his journal was constantly renegotiated in weekly meetings in the *Punch* offices. Even where periodicals relied on signed contributions, editorial control was often draconian, particularly in cases like the *Wesleyan-Methodist Magazine* (chapter 3), where the journal was taken to speak for a well-defined ideological faction.

Under the system of anonymous publication, of course, it was often impossible for the majority of readers to ascertain what specific form of authority lay behind a scientific article. Written interventions by men of science in the leading reviews and magazines nevertheless helped establish their reputations among the cultural élite and were often financially indispensable in a pre-professional age. Later in the century, signed journalism enabled scientists like Huxley not only to state the claims of the nascent professional community, but also to establish their own reputations as scientific celebrities. Throughout this history, however, the lines of demarcation between men of science, men of letters, and scientific popularizers were far from clear, and were constantly being renegotiated. As discussed in chapter 8, writers like Lewes and James Sully struggled to establish their higher scientific ambitions while financing themselves by popular scientific journalism, and the two objectives often merged. Of course, the growth and diversification of periodical forms involved a similar expansion in journalism, and there is a large body of writers, many of them drawn from the medical professions, whose contributions to making nineteenth-century science remain unconsidered. Ranging from the religiously inspired writers of the *Wesleyan-Methodist Magazine* and the *Boys' Own Paper*, through the hack writers of such pot-boilers as the *Mirror of Literature*, to the Bohemian contributors of *Punch*, such writers, and the forms of journalism they developed, clearly shaped the encounters with science of nineteenth-century periodical readers.

Controversy

Scholars have long recognized the historical value of studying controversies in the sciences. Less familiar, however, is the extent to which scientific controversies of the nineteenth century were conducted in, or extended to, semi-popular scientific journals and generalist periodicals. Indeed, as chapter 8 demonstrates in relation to the creation of 'baby science', such debates contributed significantly to the making of natural knowledge. This view runs counter to the prevalent distinction between what Harry Collins and Trevor Pinch call the 'constitutive' forum for scientific debate (the specialist periodicals, formal conferences, and other settings where actions are believed to be based on 'universalisable non-contingent premises') and the 'contingent' forum (namely the popular journals, after-dinner speeches, private gossip, and other settings where actions are not supposed to affect scientific knowledge). Yet even in the late-twentieth-century debate about parapsychology, Collins and Pinch could find no epistemological distinction between discussions in these two forums, and it is clear that in the nineteenth century such distinctions were even less easily made.[73]

There is now a growing literature demonstrating the insights into scientific controversies that can be gained by exploring the rich and relatively unexploited material in specialist and non-specialist periodicals.[74] In particular, James Secord's analyses of the tumultuous reception accorded Andrew Crosse's electrical production of insects and of the sensation caused by the *Vestiges of the Natural History of Creation* (1844) demonstrate the considerable power of nineteenth-century mass-circulation newspapers and magazines to dictate the terms of scientific controversies.[75] He shows that with the rapid rise of steam technologies and expansion of reading audiences, tensions developed between the local cultures within which experimental claims were produced and the public arena where the meaning of such claims was transformed. What began as a claim in a private laboratory was dramatized and 'replicated', with a range of literary and graphical techniques, into a fact or chimera, a discovery or non-discovery, in periodicals. Journalists, editors, publishers, and others involved in periodical production had the power to control the meaning of an experiment, and to force scientific practitioners to join the fray – whether by redirecting their laboratory projects or by writing to daily newspapers – and to promulgate their own views on what was fact and what was fancy.

Common contexts

The generic *mélange* of the periodical particularly lent itself to the interpenetration of language and ideas that scholars have, in recent decades, found to characterize literary and scientific writing in the nineteenth century. One of the abiding insights of Robert Young's 'common context' thesis is that the verbal and conceptual interconnectedness of the sciences, politics, theology, and literature were both sustained and revealed by their juxtaposition in periodical articles. However, since articles on the sciences are still habitually read in isolation from the larger periodical text which surrounds them, these connections are often missed. For instance, the insight that the language of materialism passed from attacks on scientific naturalists like Huxley and Tyndall to criticism of aesthetic poets such as Algernon Charles Swinburne and Dante Gabriel Rossetti has been obscured by a compartmentalized historiography. This linguistic slippage, though, becomes readily apparent when one examines the periodical press, where the same reviewers 'commonly wrote notices of both scientific and poetic publications, often identifying almost identical transgressions in both'.[76] Observing the conjunction of these subtly different usages reveals a wider play of connotations than would otherwise be apparent.

Reading across an entire periodical text has the effect of highlighting developing patterns of discourse which are not immediately apparent in an isolated text. The *Cornhill Magazine*, for instance, has generally been regarded as making little attempt to engage with Darwin's evolutionary theorizing. Yet, as is discussed in chapter 5, the language and concepts of Darwinism were far more prevalent in the magazine than might appear from reading any single article. In particular, the Darwinian language of struggle and competition soon featured in articles on the nutrition of the poor and on nutritional physiology, and even in the fiction of Anthony Trollope, while the affinity between humans and other primates was explored – often in a racially charged context – in Thackeray's fiction. Such appropriations were, of course, mutual. Lewes, for instance, developed a distinctively familiar language in which to relate the subjects of his scientific articles in the *Cornhill* to quotidian concerns. Thus his 'Studies in Animal Life' passed from the sexual dimorphism in Entomostraca to a discussion of the inferiority of the male sex in some great biological families, 'confess[ing]' to the presumptively male reader 'that our sex cuts but a poor figure' and adding, 'this digression is becoming humiliating'.[77] Elsewhere, it was 'the music of our deeply meditative' Tennyson which, for Lewes, elucidated digestive assimilation and the law of organic development.[78] The stylistic demands of scientific journalism also had consequences for the manner in which scientific fields developed. As chapter 8 demonstrates, Lewes's familiarizing use of the term 'baby' in the title of his pioneering *Cornhill* article on 'The Mental Condition of Babies' (1863) raised questions both about his own ambiguous status as a scientist, and about his claim for scientific status for the study of infant development.

The value for the history of science of taking seriously the original periodical context in which writings first appeared is amply illustrated when the re-examination of familiar works in this way reveals hitherto unsuspected conceptual and linguistic linkages with the sciences. The serial appearance of George Eliot's *Romola* in the *Cornhill* in 1862–3 is a case in point. The collaborative writing practices of Eliot and Lewes are well known, and Lewes's periodical essays have often been juxtaposed with Eliot's fiction. By reading *Romola* in its original context, however, it becomes clear that the highly intelligent heroine of the novel was presented to contemporaries in association with a discussion of recent scientific evidence concerning the relative size of male and female brains in Lewes and John Herschel's 'Notes on Science' column for February 1863. The dialogue between Eliot's novel, with its study of female intellectual aspiration, and Lewes and Herschel's article, with its refusal to accept brain size as unambiguous evidence of female intellectual inferiority, becomes clear once the distinctive qualities of the original publication format are considered.[79]

In many cases, of course, it is not clear to what extent the interplay between the elements of a periodical were intended to be deliberate. From a reader's perspective, however, this was not necessarily particularly relevant. The appearance of *Punch*'s continual attacks on medical quackery (discussed in chapter 4) across the page from the advertisements for patent medicines which appeared weekly on the magazine's cover (see fig. 4.4), was eloquent, whether premeditated or not. In many cases, however, the interplay was quite obviously intentional. As editor of *Household Words*, for instance, Charles Dickens juxtaposed the death and regeneration motif of novels such as *Bleak House* with articles on the chemistry of decay and recomposition and the conservation of energy.[80] Less-well-known editors also had a vested interest in relating different elements of the periodical. As chapter 2 shows, the death of 'Chuny', the famous menagerie elephant, prompted a spate of articles in the cheap weekly miscellany, the *Mirror of Literature*, which sought to capitalize in diverse ways on the topicality of the subject. Similarly, as discussed in chapter 10, Stead intermingled scientific romance and more sober futuristic writing on electricity as part of his socialist utopianism in the pages of the *Review of Reviews*.

Literary replication

The peculiar combination of multiple texts within the covers of the periodical is given an additional twist by the frequent appearance in periodicals of extracts, abstracts, and other representations of texts first published elsewhere. These processes of literary replication constituted significant interventions in the literary marketplace. As chapter 9 urges, for instance, leading scientific biographies of the nineteenth century were primarily known through the extracts and reviews published in the periodical press. Such reviews often read very differently from the biographies on which they were based, as when the *Victoria Magazine* used Henry Bence Jones's *Life and Letters of Faraday* to urge the cause of women's scientific education. As James Secord has recently argued, the processes of extracting, abstracting, and reviewing undergone by such key works of nineteenth-century science as *Vestiges of the Natural History of Creation* contributed significantly to shaping their meaning for readers. Such processes could be extremely complex. Readers of the two-penny *Mirror of Literature*, for example, were in 1830 treated to extracts, not from Charles Lyell's expensive *Principles of Geology* itself, but from George Poulett Scrope's supportive review of the first volume. Moreover, since Scrope's review had been published in the six-shilling *Quarterly Review*, few readers of the *Mirror* are likely to have been able (as advised by the *Mirror*) 'to turn to the Review, read it, and judge' for themselves.[81] To such readers, the *Mirror* stood in place of both Lyell's and Scrope's original texts. In these circumstances, the potential for the transformation of meaning was considerable – an insight not lost on contemporaries. When, for instance, Stead approached Huxley to support his new abstracting journal, the *Review of Reviews*, Huxley was cautious, counselling that 'passages without context often give a very wrong impression of the writer's meaning'.[82] Moreover, Huxley's fears were well placed, and, as chapter 7 demonstrates, he soon found that Stead's practice of abstracting could transform the meaning of his own writings in a number of significant ways, ranging from deliberate partiality to unintended blunders.

A comparative approach to studying the use of extracts, abstracts, and reviews in a range of periodicals reveals how different kinds of writing about science were developed for diverse audiences. Thus, while Scrope's *Quarterly* review of Lyell's *Principles* was an authoritative and sober assessment, the extracts from the review in the *Mirror of Literature* emphasized merely the wonder of natural phenomena, seizing on, as the editor had it, only 'a few points interesting to the general reader'.[83] Elsewhere in the *Mirror*, material that was intended to be narrative colour in articles published in the fashionable monthlies became, in extracted form, the substantive content of shorter articles. More generally, the appearance of particular genres of scientific writing across the full range of periodical types, allows the historian to consider how the use of such genres varied on the grounds of class, age, gender, or religion. Chapter 9 explores some of these issues in relation to the genre of scientific biography, showing how obituaries, reviews, biographical sketches, and passing references were put to work to serve an assortment of moral, ideological, and educational purposes in different periodical contexts. Moreover, the development of new genres of scientific writing sometimes took place as a form of dialogue between different kinds of books and periodicals. Thus chapter 10 shows how the emergence of electrical futurist writing in a British context depended heavily on W. T. Stead's borrowings from American books and journalism, but also on the responses of existing periodicals like the *Nineteenth Century* and *Fortnightly Review* to Stead's innovations in the *Review of Reviews*.

The rich intertextual field afforded by nineteenth-century periodicals offers historians and literary scholars a varied and plentiful harvest. Far more than mere records of opinion, periodicals provide some of the most important sources of evidence about the ways in which the sciences came to be such a potent aspect of modern culture. They constitute one of the best means of exploring the shifting audiences for science, and of examining the agency of assorted writers, illustrators, and publishers in manipulating those audiences. They also reveal how scientific controversy was conducted and controlled across specialist and non-specialist forums, and how the sciences and other forms of discourse were continually interlinked. The incentives for combining the study of nineteenth-century periodicals and the history of science in the period are thus manifold. However, the field is still in its infancy. Large phases of periodical history in relation to science remain uncharted, and many historiographical themes remain to be explored. The chapters in this book begin the process of sketching out the terrain, but it is to be hoped that they might inspire a future generation of scholarship in this area.

Section A: Genres

CHAPTER 2

The Mirror of Literature, Amusement and Instruction *and cheap miscellanies in early nineteenth-century Britain*

Jonathan R. Topham

When, in the autumn of 1820, the *Monthly Repository* listed the twenty leading secular reviews and magazines, their average subscription was 2s per month.[1] Within three years, however, there had appeared dozens of weekly miscellanies selling for a third of that price, the most successful being the *Mirror of Literature, Amusement and Instruction* (1822–49). Since the recently imposed 'taxes on knowledge' had effectively gagged the cheap radical press, the only other cheap periodicals of the 1820s were the populist religious monthlies discussed in chapter 3. Appearing at a time when new publications were more expensive than ever before, the most successful of these 2d weeklies rapidly achieved sales numbering in the tens of thousands. Within a decade similar journals priced 1d or $1\frac{1}{2}$d were selling as many as 200,000 copies.[2] The cheap miscellany became a primary means of structuring a new 'mass' reading audience, as both commercial and ideologically motivated publishers began to appreciate not only the vast increase in readers but also the potential of emerging technologies of book production.[3]

The appearance of these first mass-circulation periodicals marked a key moment in the histories of both science and literature. In both fields, the profound changes in reading audiences between the French Revolution and the first Reform Bill contributed significantly to redefining cultural roles. In particular, the emergence of a radical working-class audience from the 1790s has been emphasized by historians of science, and scholars have detailed the manner in which the dominant sciences of the period took shape in the face of continual anxiety about the readings to which they might be submitted by such an audience. In this context, the production of mass journals like the *Penny Magazine* of the Society for the Diffusion of Useful Knowledge (SDUK) has been seen as part of a campaign to discipline potentially revolutionary working-class readers, using highly objectified scientific material in an attempt to quell their interpretative dissidence.[4]

In literary history, too, the emergence of mass journals has been related to the concern of contemporary writers with proliferating reading audiences. As Jon Klancher argues in his imposing study, *The Making of English Reading Audiences*, English writers of this period were the first to become 'radically uncertain of their readers', facing 'the task Wordsworth called "*creating* the taste" by which the writer is comprehended'. According to Klancher, Wordsworth and Coleridge's 'worst fears' were realized in the new cheap journals of the 1820s. Such journals, he argues, sought to shape a mass audience by representing the previously undifferentiated crowd as comprising a typology of all social classes. This allowed them to 'sidestep both class conflict and cultural alienation' by 'making the crowd a metonymy for personal and national togetherness'. To become an audience, however, the crowd had to be 'quieted, the dialogic murmur of its innumerable voices displaced by [the] proxy of the mass writer himself'. In the 'unique discursive space' of cheap miscellanies 'the mass reader never becomes the interlocutor of political or philosophical argument'.[5] Like historians of science, Klancher associates the cheap miscellany with attempts to create a mass audience which consumes representations generated elsewhere.

In this literature, the focus on the mass writer's *attempts* to render working-class readers submissive consumers of bourgeois culture is combined with a conviction that working-class readers were not so easily converted. Radical artisans seeking to mould a distinctively working-class audience conspicuously resisted the attempts of SDUK activists to – as they put it – 'stop our mouths with *kangaroos*'.[6] Yet, the primary focus on the self-consciously ideological conflict of such parties tends to oversimplify the role of cheap miscellanies in the development of reading audiences for science. As Susan Sheets-Pyenson has argued, several of the cheap miscellanies of this period were explicitly intended to involve artisanal readers in the production of scientific and technical knowledge – to engage, as she puts it, in a form of 'low' scientific culture in which the object was not the popularization of 'high' science.[7] More generally, however, the developing genre of the cheap miscellany cannot be viewed simply as an ideologically motivated product aimed at and read by the working classes. As this chapter demonstrates, the cheap miscellany developed in a highly contingent manner in response to the shifting commercial demands of the post-war book trade, and the early miscellanies were neither primarily intended for, nor mainly read by, working-class readers. Moreover, while some prominent later offerings, such as the *Penny Magazine* and the *Saturday Magazine*, were avowedly more narrowly aimed, they succeeded in reaching a *petit bourgeois* rather than a working-class readership. The *Penny* and *Saturday Magazines* even formed the 'chief reading' in such *haute bourgeois* households as that of the Darwins.[8]

In this chapter, I seek to explore how science, technology, and medicine were represented in one leading cheap miscellany of the 1820s and 1830s. I focus particularly on how these representations reflected the distinctive features of the genre as they developed in response to the commercial pressures and opportunities of the literary marketplace, as well as to shifting political and cultural concerns. In the first section, I briefly explore the emergence of the cheap miscellany in relation to the high-price post-war book market of the 1820s. I then examine the scientific content of the *Mirror* under its first editor, reflecting on how it was structured by the journal's eclectic format. In the final section, I briefly consider changes in the scientific content of the *Mirror* under its second major editor, particularly in the light of the specialization of the periodical marketplace which took place during the 1820s.

CREATING THE CHEAP MISCELLANY

> Evolution has been defined as the 'origination of species by development from earlier forms'; and in nothing is this more apparent than in the periodical press of this country. In various histories of newspapers it is common to read of claims to originality, of new departures, of landmarks, and so forth; but in nearly every one of these it will be found that what is claimed as new is largely a development – not the entirely original idea of one man or a group of men, but the improvement on many experiments.
>
> W. Roberts, *Chambers's Journal* (1936)[9]

As Adrian Johns has argued in the case of the *Philosophical Transactions*, successful periodicals tend to naturalize themselves, effacing by their success the traces of their uncertain origins.[10] In particular, historians of mass-market periodicals have focused on the period from 1832, when the founding of *Chambers's Edinburgh Journal*, the *Penny Magazine*, and the *Saturday Magazine* represented the inception of a recognizably Victorian genre of cheap miscellany: they were written increasingly by paid contributors whose original work was kept to high standards by an editorial staff, and produced using the latest techniques of stereotyping and steam printing. The producers of these new journals emphasized the novelty of their enterprise, which they contrasted with the cheap miscellanies they sought to supplant. Moreover, at 1d and 1½d, they radically undercut the 2d and 3d publications of the preceding decade (though not the cheap political weeklies that had sprung up during the Reform Crisis). As commentators were quick to point out, however, many of the existing cheap weeklies had been offering similar unobjectionable fare for a decade. Indeed, the *Athenaeum* actively campaigned against what it saw as an attempt by the SDUK to destroy valuable existing miscellanies by using charitable subscriptions to establish a 'huge monopoly'.[11] The better-known miscellanies of the 1830s, for all their novelty, thus drew heavily on the experimental cheap periodical publishing of the previous decade.

The *Mirror of Literature*, arguably the most important of the earlier miscellanies, was itself by no means original. Started by the London publisher, bookseller, and stationer John Limbird (1796?–1883) on 2 November 1822, the *Mirror* was an obvious imitation of the *Hive; or, Weekly Entertaining Register* (1822–4), begun the preceding August. Both combined in sixteen closely printed octavo pages a mixture of original articles together with a large mass of extracted material from contemporary books and periodicals. However, Limbird's miscellany, edited by the hack journalist Thomas Byerley (1788–1826), improved on the *Hive* by adding one or two wood engravings per number. These were a significant attraction, which the *Hive* quickly emulated, and regular sales of the *Mirror* soon exceeded 10,000 copies.[12] The unprecedented success of the *Mirror* led Byerley to claim to have 'created a new era in the history of periodical literature', by alerting literary entrepreneurs to the market for such cheap periodicals and providing them with a model for their productions.[13] The spate of such journals contributed significantly to a rapid expansion of periodical titles in the early to mid-1820s, which was similar to that occurring in the early 1830s (Fig. 1.1).[14]

The early cheap miscellanies should be interpreted as commercial ventures in the competitive literary market of the early 1820s, rather than being read as precursors of the later 'useful knowledge' movement. This was a pivotal moment in the history of the British book trade. With the prices of new books at a peak, as a result both of the war with France (which had increased the cost of both paper and labour) and the conservative practices of the trade, middle-class readers struggled to purchase fashionable reading matter. While standard works could be obtained in cheap reprint editions, new works of fiction, poetry, and travel, had never commanded higher prices. Like the circulating libraries, reviews in the periodical press provided important – if limited – access to such literature, but, as we have seen, most periodicals were also prohibitively priced. Moreover, the hallmark of the new and dominant *Edinburgh* and *Quarterly* reviews (and to an increasing extent of the monthly magazines) was their selectivity and discrimination in reviewing new works. The new weekly literary journals, commencing in 1817 with the *Literary Gazette*, largely took over the extensive and synoptic reviewing associated with the standard eighteenth-century monthly reviews; however, these were also far from cheap. In such a market, a cheap miscellany providing extracts from highly priced books and periodicals clearly had commercial potential.

The new cheap miscellanies were not directed only to a middle-class market. William Cobbett's immensely successful experiment in 1816 with a 2d abridgement of his *Weekly Political Register* indicated that a working-class reading audience of great size now existed. With the growth of literacy in the wake of increasing elementary education, Cobbett found that his 'vile two-penny trash' could sell 40,000–50,000 copies, or perhaps as many as 70,000 copies a week.[15] As a result, while repressive taxation soon curtailed the cheap radical weeklies, the existence of a sizeable working-class reading audience was now widely recognized. To some, this seemed to offer a commercial opening; to others a dangerous threat. Thus, both the Chambers brothers and the later editor of the *Penny Magazine*, Charles Knight, commenced cheap periodicals at this period in order to supplant radical publications with more anodyne reading matter, although neither attempt achieved lasting success.[16]

As Knight later recognized, the mechanization of many aspects of book manufacture was critical in the development of cheap periodicals.[17] In this regard the 1820s was a transitional decade. The introduction of machine-manufactured paper, of stereotype, and of steam presses were at this period only beginning to bring the great cost savings to periodical publishing on which later cheap journals depended. Paper accounted for between half and two-thirds of the cost of journal production, but while paper prices decreased with the end of war-time restrictions on rag imports, only gradually did the effects of machine manufacture reduce them further.[18] The impact of stereotypes was certainly beginning to be felt, and their use in printing journals like the *Mirror* reduced costs by allowing small numbers of copies to be reprinted.[19] Steam presses also began to be used: in January 1818, for instance, the *Literary Gazette* claimed to be the first weekly paper to be printed by steam, and by the mid-1820s such 3d weeklies as the *Mechanics' Magazine* and *Lancet* were also apparently machine-printed.[20] Yet the full potential of these technologies only gradually came to be exploited.

Starting out as a small-time publisher in the late Regency period, Limbird drew heavily on the practices and personnel of existing journals produced by his neighbours in the Strand to create his successful weekly miscellany. His experience as publisher of two 6d weekly literary journals – both un-dercutting the 1s *Literary Gazette* – and of a 2d essay periodical modelled on Leigh Hunt's successful weekly, the *Indicator* (1819–21), helped him to chart what Knight later called the 'perilous sea' of cheap publishing.[21] These ventures also enabled Limbird to develop the distinctive production and distribution techniques necessary in cheap journalism and to acquire suitably skilled editorial staff and illustrators. Most strikingly, Limbird, like many of the early mass publishers, came from a background in radical journalism, starting out as a close associate of the noted radical bookseller and publisher of Cobbett's *Register*, Thomas Dolby. With the market for cheap political publications crushed by repressive legislation after 1819, Limbird (like Dolby and numerous others) adopted the double-column, sixteen-page octavo format of the *Register* in producing cheap apolitical papers.

Had the *Mirror* included topical political matters, it would have incurred the same 4½d newspaper stamp tax which after 1819 made Cobbett's *Register* a 6d journal. Instead, Limbird refused to engage directly in political debate, thus avoiding the tax. An editorial note to the second number observed: 'We feel much obliged to C. H. S. for his friendly hints, but to adopt them would subject the MIRROR to a stamp duty of double its present price.'[22] As a later commentator observed, the *Mirror*'s apolitical tone was essential at a time when 'the Castlereagh administration watched with great jealousy every publication of a popular tendency'. Yet, while the *Mirror* gave 'no offence' to the government, it was also avowedly 'Bound to no party'.[23] The *Mirror*'s studiously apolitical tone and 'its strict moral character' (articles were rejected that were 'coarse, vulgar, and indecent') enabled it to reach an inclusive audience.[24] This was all the more necessary since Limbird's involvement in the literary underworld of cheap publishing (he had connections with both radical and immoral literature) marginalized him in the wider London book-trade.

The *Mirror*'s political quiescence was thus partly a matter of commercial expediency. However, to publish cheap literature at all during the 1820s was implicitly to engage the charged public debate concerning the education of the people, the possible extension of political representation, and government repression of working-class radicalism. Certainly, Henry Brougham considered the publication of the *Mirror* a significant intervention. Both in the House of Commons, and in his seminal *Practical Observations on the Education of the People*, Brougham cited it in his campaign for popular education, observing that its 'great circulation must prove highly beneficial to the bulk of the people'.[25] This kind of publicity was welcomed by the *Mirror*,[26] and while it is not clear to what extent Limbird and Byerley shared Brougham's political outlook, their rhetoric bears obvious similarities to his.

From his earliest involvement in cheap journalism – as publisher of the *Literary Journal and General Miscellany* (1818–19) – Limbird had been associated with attempts to address 'the people', conceived broadly to include both middle and working classes, rather than the more pejorative 'populace' or 'masses'.[27] As later with Brougham, the rhetoric was that of bourgeois-led social rapprochement, in which the 'prince' and the 'artisan' could be addressed using the 'same language'.[28] The *Mirror* continued this inclusive idiom. The second preface welcomed the great advance in elementary literacy achieved by 'our public institutions', but argued that this had made it necessary 'to give to the public at large a journal which, while it embraced the most ample range over the vast domain of English literature, should be published at a price that would place it within the reach of ALL'.[29] The journal claimed that it circulated among all classes of society: 'it is to be found in the cottage of the peasant, on the loom of the manufacturer, in the counting-house of the merchant, in the parlour windows of the affluent, and in the carriages of the nobility'.[30]

Of course, the actual readership of the *Mirror* is far less easy to determine. Reviewers certainly considered that it formed an amazing 'annual library' not only for 'the poor man's fireside' but also for 'higher ranks'.[31] Moreover, it was reputedly 'patronised very largely by the middle and upper classes' and 'was a great favourite with the clergy and the respectable classes'.[32] This view is confirmed by the concern expressed by the established trade that the *Mirror* undercut the market for high-priced publications, which resulted both in a refusal to stock Limbird's works and in legal action for copyright infringement. At the same time, Limbird's unorthodox distribution techniques – developing his own agency system and advertising using both posting and hand bills (fig. 2.1) – probably increased the number of working- and lower-middle-class readers.[33]

Conceived in the hack world of metropolitan journalism, and constrained by the political repression of the years after 1819, the *Mirror* was a fundamentally commercial venture, albeit occasionally underpinned by a moderately reformist rhetoric of social rapprochement and educational progress. In its vision of a 'vast commercial audience' it was undoubtedly, as Klancher assumed, 'inspired by Cobbett' and the other late Regency radical journalists.[34] At the same time, however, it sought a far wider audience priced out of the literary marketplace by the unprecedented cost of fashionable literature. Its blend of 'Literature, Amusement, and Instruction' was thus intended to maximize its market, rather than to accomplish an ideological objective. It was – in Klancher's phrase – as shopkeepers 'gazing out [of] a window at the crowd of possible buyers' that Limbird and

Figure 2.1. A London street scene, 1835. Cheap literature had to compete in the crowded visual field of the London street: here a posting-bill for the *Mirror* jostles with advertisements for exhibitions, theatrical performances, and coach travel. Detail from a watercolour by John Orlando Parry. Reproduced by kind permission of The Dunhill Museum and Archive, St James's, London SW1.

Byerley conceived the *Mirror*.[35] The new 'mass' audience inscribed in the *Mirror* was thus undoubtedly a socially typologized crowd of customers, as Klancher suggests. As we shall see, however, the extent to which it was a 'quieted' crowd was rather more limited than Klancher implies.

'LITERATURE, AMUSEMENT, AND INSTRUCTION': NATURAL KNOWLEDGE IN THE *MIRROR*

The *Mirror* was not simply – as the later rhetoric had it – a 'useful knowledge' miscellany. Its professed objects were to 'afford the greatest quantity of "Amusement and Instruction" at the lowest possible expense, and to enable readers in the humblest circumstances to become acquainted with the current and expensive literature of the day'.[36] According to Limbird's initial advertisement, the *Mirror* was to comprise:

1. The Spirit of the most expensive Works connected with Literature, the Arts and Manufactures, the Drama, Public Exhibitions, Life, Manners, &c. 2. The Spirit of the Public Journals, useful Domestic Hints, Fugitive Poetry, Anecdotes, Bon-mots, the Wit of the Day, &c. &c.[37]

In this miscellaneous format, references to natural knowledge of diverse kinds appeared in many forms, extending from articles that were self-consciously instructive to amusing sketches, anecdotes, poetry, and topical reports of public sensations, exhibitions, and discoveries.

Although its structure became increasingly fluid, the *Mirror* continued to retain certain common structural features established in the early numbers. Each issue generally began with several editorial and contributed articles, the first one usually being illustrated. Two core sections appeared in the central portion of each issue: 'Spirit of the Public Journals', containing extracts from contemporary magazines, and (from the third volume) 'The Selector; or, Choice Extracts from New Works'. Towards the end an assemblage of anecdotes and epigrams usually appeared under the section heading 'The Gatherer' and the journal generally concluded with responses to correspondents. However, with an increasing range of other section headings only intermittently employed and with numbered occasional features continually being added (e.g. 'The Novelist', 'Peter Pindarics', and 'The Sketch Book') the journal had a somewhat irregular and unpredictable appearance. Such generic freedom reflected not only the *Mirror*'s attempt to remain amusingly miscellaneous but also its physical format: since each issue extended only to sixteen pages, readers were not dependent on a rigid structure, nor was it practical to commence each section on a new page. The *Mirror* thus adopted and amplified the looser structure of the weekly literary journal (Byerley had already for several years edited Limbird's *Literary Chronicle*), rather than the regular sections of the traditional magazine. In comparison with other types of periodical, therefore, the weekly miscellany presented many different kinds of scientific allusion in close proximity.

Science and the learned miscellany

In its blend of original contributions and choice extracts, the *Mirror* was clearly reflecting the traditional gentlemanly miscellany typified by the *Gentleman's Magazine*.[38] The octavo format, with text in double columns, was typical of such monthly magazines, as well as of the radical weeklies. Moreover, like traditional miscellanies, the early *Mirror* contained increasing numbers of articles by largely pseudonymous and apparently unpaid contributors, although these were generally shorter and less substantial than those typical of the monthlies. Byerley's literary apprenticeship had been served writing such articles for the *Monthly Magazine*, when, as a Yorkshire carpenter's son whose talent had earned him a grammar-school education, he first came to London.[39] He was keen to encourage similar contributions in the *Mirror*, as the repeated acknowledgements in prefaces indicate.

The identities of the *Mirror's* correspondents remain largely unknown. Although Byerley presented them as a community of all classes, many were evidently of social standing. The one known contributor from Byerley's editorship was Peter Thomas Westcott, who wrote frequently for the journal under the acronym 'PTW'. According to the *Mirror's* later editor, John Timbs, Westcott was 'a gentleman of independent property, who, in his ubiquitous career of utility, did "good by stealth", and carried "the twopenny", as he called the "Mirror", into public institutions and intellectual resorts of a description most calculated to extend its circulation'.[40] Nevertheless, the fiction of a classless community of contributors allowed readers to conceive of themselves as equal interlocutors. Moreover, contributors referred to each other in terms which implied a sense of community, and Byerley would sometimes respond to correspondents with substantial advice on their contributions.[41] However, while contributed articles often referred to each other, Byerley rarely allowed, and certainly did not encourage contributors to engage in controversy.

Many of the *Mirror's* original articles intended for 'amusement and instruction' resembled the content of the traditional monthly miscellanies, ranging widely over the field of learning and including many scientific topics. Such pieces extended from brief paragraphs and sets of instructions to histories, biographies, and essays. Under Byerley, natural philosophy, natural history, and the practical arts were treated as part of a wider learned culture, and the articles written on such subjects – which were largely penned either by Byerley or, increasingly, by his central core of contributors – were written in the manner of learned gentlemen. Moreover, these articles typically drew on similar library-based resources to the antiquarian and historical articles that were commonplace in the *Mirror*, and, indeed, often included observations on the history of science. They gave the impression that scientific knowledge was permanent and cumulative.

This notion of the sciences was well illustrated when, in February 1826, Byerley began an occasional feature under the title 'The Encyclopædist; or, The Circle of the Sciences'. Byerley completed only one subject under this heading, a four-part examination of 'Architecture'. This was later supplemented by a philological article on the 'English Language' and a contributed article on 'Electricity' and, after Byerley's death, by 'Geometry'.[42] The editor considered, however, that in a systematic arrangement 'Agriculture' should probably have begun the series as 'the first of the arts'. Byerley drew on older encyclopaedic approaches in his emphasis on recording the historical accumulation of learning.[43] He reported that he intended to 'give in almost every number an account of some branch of science or art', but not to teach it in detail, as this would be beyond the limits of the publication and the 'great diversity' of its readers. The object was to 'trace the history of a science, and explain or develope the theory of it', rather than to 'teach its practice'. This approach, it was hoped, would excite interest 'not only in the artisan', who might be 'more immediately concerned with [a] particular branch of science or art', but also in the 'general reader'. The order of subjects was not to be systematic, however, since it was hoped that correspondents would contribute extensively.[44]

This was typical of the learned approach taken to the 'arts and sciences' in many of the instructive and amusing articles in the *Mirror*. One frequent contributor, for instance, contributed four linked articles on the history of arithmetic, book-keeping, logarithms, and algebra.[45] Here, mathematical principles were introduced within the historical narrative, but to become active in the field, the articles suggested, one had to master a library of references, many of which were in Latin.[46] Other articles were less systematic and more eclectic. The short piece entitled, 'The Rose of Jericho', written by Peter Westcott ('PTW') in response to another reader's inquiry, encompassed, in a couple of hundred words, an account of the plant's natural range, its introduction by John Tradescant into the Royal Botanic Gardens, Kew, the superstitious origin of one of its common names, the *Rosa*

Mariæ, the peculiarities of its physiology, advice on its propagation using hot-beds, the significance of its Latin name, and suggestions for further reading in two standard sources from the previous century – Abraham Rees's *Cyclopaedia* and Philip Miller's *Gardener's Dictionary*.[47] Other articles drew self-consciously on the flotsam and jetsam of learned reading both in brief anecdotes and in more extended form, such as the 'Multum in Parvo' submitted by several contributors at various times. The latter were remarkable for their cacophony of references:

Æsculapias invented the probe. By means of æther, water can be made to freeze in summer . . . Chemical names of metals were first given to the heavenly bodies. There has been an instance of an elephant that walked upon a rope (see Suetonius). Fuller's earth was used by the ancients for washing.[48]

Some articles were more self-consciously literary than learned. Essays – like that by 'ABC' on marriage – often contained discussions of natural knowledge. Ranging widely over the subject – from the universal adoption of marriage by all nations to the dangers of match-making – the writer devoted a few sentences to criticizing Francis Place's advocacy of contraception. Similarly, literary articles on natural phenomena blended poetic and other imagery with more scientific approaches.[49] Westcott ('PTW') was particularly adept at such articles, and his piece 'On the Resplendent Beauties of the Fire-Fly' combined detail from Maria Merian's *Metamorphosis Insectorum Surinamensium* (1705), Friedrich Lesser's *Theologie des Insectes* (1742), and observations from Nehemiah Grew, with quotations from Thomson's *Seasons*, Anna Barbauld, and Erasmus Darwin.[50] Other contributors sent poetry which represented nature in scientific ways, or which, as in the case of 'Lucubrations in an Apothecary's Shop' by 'DS',[51] took scientific or medical practice as the subject.

From the second volume, the *Mirror*'s title-page detailed its miscellaneous contents in a lengthy subtitle which included 'Discoveries in the Arts and Sciences' alongside 'The Spirit of the Public Journals'. The implication was that the arts and sciences were progressive, open-ended, and as pertinent to the well-read person as was the latest new work of literature. This notion was in keeping with the practice of the established monthly miscellanies, which reported scientific or technical developments in a regular section, often including accounts of the proceedings of learned societies. The *Mirror*, however, had no such section; instead, it carried brief paragraphs, often comprising extracts from new books or recent periodicals and newspapers. Sometimes these were evidently justified by their extraction from sources which readers were unlikely to access directly, as when 'TAC' extracted articles on the invention of 'River Spectacles' from 'an American Paper', and on a possible treatment for 'hydrophobia' from the *Hamburg Correspondent*. At other times, extracts were combined with a commentary. When 'WF' sent extracts from William Bullock's *Six Months' Residence and Travels in Mexico* (1824), he included a covering letter describing the recent sale of Bullock's 'London Museum', a popular attraction at the Egyptian Hall in Piccadilly. However, there was no systematic attempt to record the leading scientific discoveries of the age.

While most scientific articles in the *Mirror* were not of a practical cast, a significant minority were deliberately so. The 'Useful Domestic Hints' which the magazine included from its inception frequently contained advice (often from contributors) on health, domestic economy, and horticulture. This might range in a single issue from 'Medicinal Properties of the Wild Valerian' to the management of cauliflower plants to secure winter produce, and from an old lady's specific for the treatment of impure water to the use of copper sulphate in the treatment of croup.[52] Another regular feature went under the title 'Scientific Amusements', and included simple experiments which required either basic scientific equipment or familiar household materials. In one such article, for instance, 'TL' gave instructions (with no theoretical explanations) for 'obtaining flowers of different colours on the same stem' by planting different seeds in the pith of an elder twig, for making 'Phosphorus Match Bottles', for melting iron using a 'roll of sulphur', for extracting the silver out of a gilted ring using *aqua fortis*, and for writing on paper using gum-arabic and gold leaf.[53]

The *Mirror* was clearly neither a magazine of the practical arts emphasizing artisanal innovation like its imitator, the *Mechanics' Magazine* (1823–72), nor a 'useful knowledge' miscellany offering instruction rather than amusement, in the later sense of the *Penny Magazine*. An unlearned reader would have struggled to derive from it any systematic or useful knowledge of the arts and sciences. However, in its openness to contributed articles, the *Mirror* followed the long-established miscellanies in portraying its readers as potential contributors. In this regard it is important to reflect that the *Mirror* provided the inspiration for the *Mechanics' Magazine* – edited by Byerley's friend and literary collaborator, the patent agent Joseph Clinton Robertson (1788–1852) – with its provision of an open forum for artisanal debate.[54]

Science and fashionable literature

In addition to its original contributions, the *Mirror*'s success was also evidently due to the access it provided to fashionable literature. It sought to

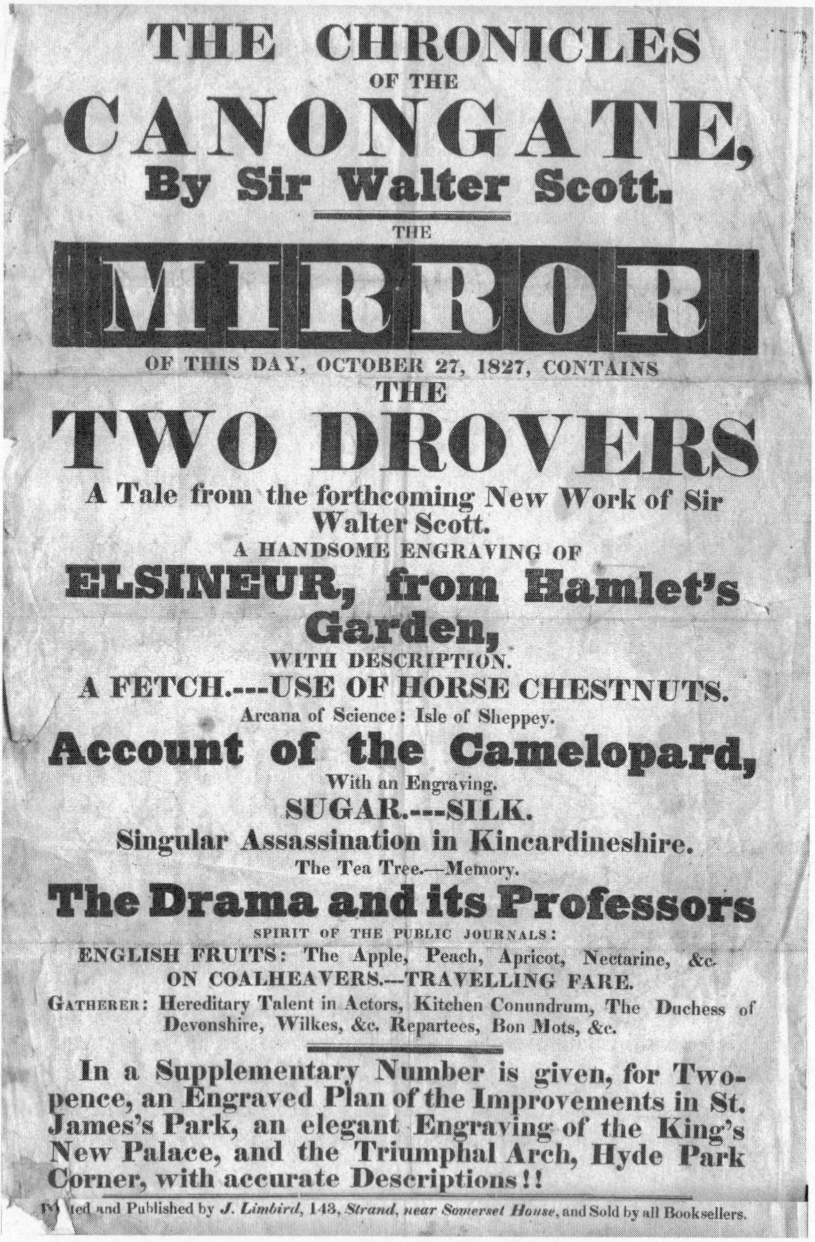

Figure 2.2. Posting-bill for the *Mirror of Literature*, 27 October 1827. Reproduced by kind permission of Mavis Eggle.

secure the 'essence of new works, however expensive' as soon as they were published, notably giving each new novel of Walter Scott extensive coverage.[55] A surviving advertising placard indicates that such material received top billing (fig. 2.2). The *Mirror* offered its extracts 'unmixed with the cant of criticism', and its manner of extracting and abstracting new works clearly drew on the journalistic mores of the weekly literary journal. As editor of the *Literary Chronicle*, Byerley had prided himself on his synoptic reviews that put readers 'in possession of such an abstract as [would], in some measure, enable them to form their own opinion of the merits of the work under consideration'.[56] These representations of fashionable literature were replete with scientific references. Prominent among the fashionable works of the 1820s, for instance, were travel narratives, often written by military men on half pay whose frequently dangerous explorations were the subject of intense public interest. Fashionable memoirs were also popular and often alluded to scientific themes. For example, an extract from *The Private Journal of Madame Campan* (1825) provided detailed observations of Franz Anton Mesmer's practice in Paris.[57] Other works, like Edward Baines's *History, Directory, and Gazetteer, of the County Palatine of Lancaster* (1824–5), detailed the mechanical and commercial triumphs of the age, such as the power loom.[58]

Outnumbering the extracts from new books, however, were the regular excerpts taken from the fashionable magazines of the 1820s. We have already seen that the *Mirror* drew heavily on the format of the traditional miscellany in its reliance on contributed articles. However, following the emergence of the new, more self-consciously literary magazines, which relied on increasingly highly paid 'literary' (rather than hack) writers, the *Gentleman's* and *Monthly* magazines had soon begun to appear rather dated. It was from the new arbiters of middle-class taste – *Blackwood's Edinburgh Magazine* (1817–1980), the *New Monthly Magazine* (1814–84), and the *London Magazine* (1820–9) – that the *Mirror* drew most heavily. Moreover, while some of the extracts were sober factual articles and essays, the great majority were the distinctively literary forms which gave the fashionable magazines their cachet – notably fiction and poetry. These fictional and poetic extracts contain some of the most imaginatively powerful scientific references in the *Mirror*. Moreover, since these references were commonly to contemporary mores, inventions, and discoveries, they conveyed a more progressive, open-ended, and contentious perspective on the arts and sciences.

Humorous verse particularly relied on current events. A couple of stanzas from William Maginn's anonymous *Blackwood's* poem entitled

'A Twist-imony in Favour of Gin-Twist', for instance, alluded to geological controversy in contemporary Edinburgh:

> Geologers all, great, middling, and small,
> Whether fiery Plutonian or wet Neptunist,
> Most gladly, it seems, seek proofs for their schemes,
> In the water, or spirit, of a jug of gin-twist.
>
> These grubbers of ground (whom God may confound!)
> Forgetting transition, trap, hornblende, or schist.
> And all other sorts, think only of quartz,
> I mean of the quarts in a jug of gin-twist.[59]

Maginn's introductory note to the poem cited Bacon as a literary authority, reporting that he had 'been lately be-scoped and tendencied by Macvey Napier, Esq.' – a reference to a paper recently published in the *Transactions of the Royal Society of Edinburgh*. Such topical allusions were also common in humorous verse written by the *Mirror*'s own contributors. For instance, a poem by 'JB' of Orchard-Street, Hackney, on the balloon-ascent of aeronautical pioneer George Graham, appeared in print within a month of the event.[60]

The often-rambling fictional sketches popular in the fashionable magazines also relied heavily on passing events and perceptions. 'The Night Walker in London', again from *Blackwood's*, drew on the introduction of gas lighting for its narrative colour. 'Multitudinous avocations' banished rest from the streets, the narrator reflected, just as 'the broad glare of gas' drove 'darkness even from our alleys'. Medical practitioners formed part of the metropolitan backdrop: between midnight and two o'clock, the coffee-houses in the vicinity of Fleet Street and the Strand were 'beset by habitual idlers, or late-stirring "professional people"', including 'medical students guiltless of physic'. The medical allusion then took a more sinister turn:

> This is the very 'witching time,' par excellence, of night,
> 'When graves yield up their dead!'
> (because resurrection-men will have it so).[61]

Such broadly scientific references were commonplace in the fictional sketches extracted in the *Mirror*, and the sobriety of the factual articles was thus tempered with more topical representations of technological innovation, of medical and scientific practitioners, and of theoretical controversy.

Science and metropolitan spectacle

As Marilyn Butler has shown, the 'sense of place' of the new fashionable monthlies of the late Regency period was one of their most striking

features.[62] *Blackwood's*, the *London*, and the *New Monthly* magazines revelled in the distinctive characteristics of the cities in which they were
produced, providing 'thick', almost ethnographic descriptions of urban
scenes and characters. Significantly, Limbird's earlier short-lived 2d weekly,
The Londoner (1820), had taken this as its guiding principle, framing its essays around the scenes and incidents of life in the city. The *Mirror* adopted
a similar emphasis. Produced in the Strand, at the heart of journalistic
London, the journal reflected a city that was the commercial and cultural
heart of the world's first industrial nation, and the hub of a great and
growing empire.

Topicality was another quality that Byerley explicitly emphasized in the
Mirror, telling impatient correspondents on more than one occasion that
'articles on temporary subjects, or subjects that excite interest at the time'
took 'precedence over those of a general nature'.[63] The inception of the
weekly literary journals – like the *Literary Chronicle* which Byerley also
edited – had certainly changed expectations. As Thomas Dibdin observed
in 1825, the 'reading man' now looked for 'his *weekly* Journal, or Register,
or Chronicle, with the same eagerness and certainty that he used to anticipate monthly supplies of mental food'.[64] Indeed, as several authors have
shown, this also applied to the reporting of scientific news, which in the
weekly literary journals was so much more immediate than it had been
a decade earlier.[65] While the *Mirror* tended not to furnish the earnest reports of scientific news found in the weekly literary journals, its immediacy
in responding to the scientific spectacles of London and elsewhere was
striking.

The *Mirror* made its scientific and technical themes more topical by its
innovative use of illustration. In the early nineteenth century, the reintro-
duction of end-grain wood engraving by Thomas Bewick made possible
the integration of high-quality images and printed text at moderate cost. By
the end of the 1810s some of the traditional monthlies – like the *Gentleman's*
and *Monthly* magazines – were beginning to experiment with wood engravings to illustrate articles.[66] Wood engravings were also occasionally used
by some of the new weekly literary journals, including Limbird's *Literary
Journal*, and from about 1820 the *Observer* and other newspapers occasionally included woodcut illustrations of sensational news events.[67] The
Mirror's use of a regular leading half-page engraving was modelled directly
on a similar experiment made by the *Monthly Magazine* from July 1821,
and the same engraver, Matthew Urlwin Sears (fl. 1826–59), was employed
(figs. 2.3 and 2.4). The *Mirror's* illustrations proved so popular that issues
increasingly included a second, usually smaller, illustration, often at the
mid-point.

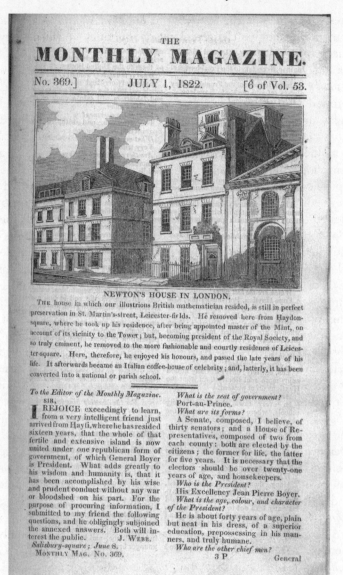

THE
MONTHLY MAGAZINE.

No. 369.]   JULY 1, 1822.   [6 of Vol. 53.

NEWTON'S HOUSE IN LONDON.

THE house in which our illustrious British mathematician resided, is still in perfect preservation in St. Martin's-street, Leicester-firlds. He removed here from Haydon-square, where he took up his residence, after being appointed master of the Mint, on account of its vicinity to the Tower; but, becoming president of the Royal Society, and so truly eminent, he removed to the more fashionable and courtly residence of Leicester-square. Here, therefore, he enjoyed his honours, and passed the late years of his life. It afterwards became an Italian coffee-house of celebrity; and, latterly, it has been converted into a national or parish school.

To the Editor of the Monthly Magazine.

SIR,

I REJOICE exceedingly to learn, from a very intelligent friend just arrived from Hayti, where he has resided sixteen years, that the whole of that fertile and extensive island is now united under one republican form of government, of which General Boyer is President. What adds greatly to his wisdom and humanity is, that it has been accomplished by his wise and prudent conduct without any war or bloodshed on his part. For the purpose of procuring information, I submitted to my friend the following questions, and he obligingly subjoined the annexed answers. Both will interest the public.   J. WEBB.

Salisbury-square; June 8.
MONTHLY MAG. No. 369.

What is the seat of government?
Port-au-Prince.
What are its forms?
A Senate, composed, I believe, of thirty senators; and a House of Representatives, composed of two from each county: both are elected by the citizens; the former for life, the latter for five years. It is necessary that the electors should be over twenty-one years of age, and housekeepers.
Who is the President?
His Excellency Jean Pierre Boyer.
What is the age, colour, and character of the President?
He is about forty years of age, plain but neat in his dress, of a superior education, prepossessing in his manners, and truly humane.
Who are the other chief men?
3 P   General

Figure 2.3. 'Newton's House in London', *Monthly Magazine* 53 (1822), 481. The magazine announced in July 1821 that 'nearly every number' was to begin with a half-page wood engraving of a 'view of some house, building, or site, consecrated by some name dear to Poetry and Philosophy, or by some event deeply interesting to the feelings or curiosity of Englishmen and mankind'. Reproduced by kind permission of the Leeds Library.

The Mirror
OF
LITERATURE, AMUSEMENT, AND INSTRUCTION.

No. CLX.] SATURDAY, SEPTEMBER 17, 1825. [PRICE 2*d.*

Sir Isaac Newton's House.

IF there is anything to be regretted in the modern improvements of the British metropolis, it is in the destruction of those places with which some of our most pleasing recollections are associated. Many a spot in London, once the residence of the good and great of the olden time, is now very differently occupied. A few of these, however, remain, and amongst them, the residence of the greatest of philosophers, and one of the best of men, Sir Isaac Newton, of whose house we present an engraving. This house is situated in St. Martin's Street, the south side of Leicester Square, and was long occupied as an hotel for foreigners, and kept by Mr. Pagliano, though it is now more ap-

propriately used for the purpose of education.

About the year 1814, Mr. Pagliano left this house, when the committee of the Sunday school belonging to the chapel adjoining took it, for the purpose of converting it into school-rooms for boys and girls, for which purpose it is still used.

The observatory, which is at the top, and where Sir Isaac Newton made his astronomical observations, had lain dormant, and been in a dilapidated state for some years, when, in 1824, two gentlemen, belonging to the committee of the school, had it repaired at their own expense, and wrote a brief memoir of the great and immortal Newton, which was

VOL. VI.   O   193

Figure 2.4. 'Sir Isaac Newton's House', *Mirror of Literature* 6 (1825), 193. The *Mirror's* early illustrations not only shared their engraver with those in the *Monthly Magazine*, but they even sometimes depicted the same scenes. Reproduced by kind permission of the Sheffield Central Library.

As a cheap journal which made a prominent weekly feature of its relatively sophisticated wood engravings, the *Mirror* set illustrated journalism on a new track. Compared to the cheap religious literature, chapbooks, and broadsides which had previously provided most people with their visual experiences in print, the *Mirror's* illustrations were striking for their quality.[68] Moreover, they were 'expressly engraved for the work' rather than being the generic images common in cheap literature, and they were executed with considerable accuracy.[69] Many of the illustrations were consciously topical, representing scenes which related to contemporary events, spectacles, or publications – 'nine-day wonders' as John Timbs observed.[70] Like the satirical engravings sold to the wealthy, or viewed in print shop windows, the *Mirror's* illustrations thus brought contemporary characters and sights into the visual field. At the same time, however, the *Mirror's* illustrations were placed in direct juxtaposition to printed text. In this regard, they represented a development on which the illustrated newspapers and comic journals of the 1840s were to build.[71]

The early numbers of the *Mirror* exemplify how its illustrations incorporated scientific, technical, and medical themes. The first issue began with an illustrated article on 'The Tread-Mill at Brixton', which had 'excited so much attention' that 'a correct view and description of it' was considered to be a sure inducement.[72] The second opened with an illustration of an alleged mermaid – 'the great source of attraction in the British metropolis' which 'three to four hundred people' were daily paying a shilling to see.[73] Succeeding numbers illustrated the splendid mansion of the former industrial chemist John Farquhar – the sale of which had captured the public imagination – and the recent eruption of Mount Vesuvius.[74] Illustrations of each of these sights also appeared variously in the monthly magazines, weekly literary journals, and in topical prints, but the *Mirror* made them available to a far wider range of readers.

As a weekly which published original illustrations, the *Mirror* could exploit the huge public interest in the contemporary events of the metropolis. A city of unparalleled size, wealth, and global power, London provided unprecedented opportunity for such reportage. Moreover, in the early decades of the nineteenth century, an increasing proportion of its sensational events related to natural and technical phenomena. New metropolitan extravaganzas ranged from the fashionable scientific demonstrations at the Royal Institution (f. 1799) and the exotic specimens of the Zoological Society's gardens (f. 1828) to the fantastical machines displayed at the National Gallery of Practical Science in Adelaide Street (f. 1832).[75] These supplemented the more familiar round of menageries, exhibitions, and shows

Figure 2.5. Exeter Royal Exchange, 1829. Exeter 'Change was situated 'near the middle part of the ever-crowded, noisy, tumultuous thoroughfare called the Strand', which was 'the very focus – the hot-bed, the forcing house – of the "Newspaper-Press"'. In the early 1820s the shop here marked 'Andrews' was the office of the *Mirror of Literature*, and that with the inverted-T-shaped name-board was the office of the *Literary Gazette*. Thomas H. Shepherd, *London and Its Environs in the Nineteenth Century* (London: Jones & Co., 1829), opposite p. 65. Reproduced by kind permission of Leeds University Library.

to provide a vibrant and constantly changing assortment of natural and technical spectacles. The *Mirror*'s offices in the Strand – initially next to Exeter Royal Exchange, with its noted menagerie, then across the road next to Somerset House (home not only to the Royal Academy but also to many of the learned societies) – placed it at the centre of one of London's busiest and most visually spectacular thoroughfares (fig. 2.5). Thus, like the new weekly literary journals, it was well placed to respond to the city's changing sensations, making the monthlies seem lumbering by comparison.

In its desire for topicality, the *Mirror* sometimes reported on newsworthy events – such as the death and funeral of George IV – at great length. More commonly, however, articles responding to metropolitan sensations had a less transient cast than that common in newspaper reportage, relating the events of the passing moment to larger themes. This reflected the journal's multiple format: it was sold not only in weekly numbers and monthly parts, but also in bound bi-annual volumes. For the last of these formats to appeal to readers, events of a specific moment had to be endowed with a more lasting relevance. Thus, while the *Mirror* was not primarily motivated by an educational agenda, articles on natural or technical spectacles were given enduring appeal by the incorporation of scientific discussion.

A good example of this is provided by the three articles published in December 1822, relating to William Bullock's exhibition at the Egyptian Hall in Piccadilly. For over a decade, Bullock's miscellaneous but substantial exhibits had been one of the most popular resorts of fashionable London. In 1822, Bullock returned from a scientific excursion in Norway with a family of Laplanders and a dozen reindeer whom he employed to perform a tableau in his exhibition. The high-profile North Polar expeditions of Ross and Parry had made the Arctic highly topical and Bullock's shilling exhibition attracted 58,000 visitors in the first season. For those unable to visit, or who wanted a keepsake, the leading print-seller Rudolph Ackermann, whose shop in the Strand was just a few doors from the *Mirror* office, published a print of the tableau by Thomas Rowlandson.[76] Such views were, however, prohibitively expensive, and the *Mirror* was ideally placed to capitalize on the demand. Early in the social season of 1822–3, successive issues carried leading illustrated articles on the 'Wapeti' or 'Gigantic Elks of the Missouri' and 'Laplanders and Rein-Deer', giving representations of the relevant exhibits at the Egyptian Hall. The accompanying text, however, was written in an instructive manner. 'Anxious to keep our promise with the public', the first article began, 'in rendering our little work a "MIRROR of Literature, Amusement, and Instruction", we shall occasionally give engravings of some of the most remarkable subjects of natural history, accompanied by accurate descriptions'. The article's relatively untechnical account of the history and habits of the wapeti was presented as the first in this occasional series. Moreover, while the following week's description of the Laplanders and reindeer related more closely to Bullock's exhibit, general information on the Laplanders 'derived from various authentic sources' was provided in the next number.[77]

A further particularly striking instance of the *Mirror*'s exploitation of the interest in topical events was the death in March 1826 of 'Chuny', the elephant at Edward Cross's famous menagerie at Exeter Royal Exchange. The menagerie, described by the *Mirror* as 'an exhibition with which every Londoner is, and every countryman longs to be, acquainted', was one of the leading shows of London.[78] A prime attraction, Chuny had become a celebrity with whom many Londoners and provincial visitors had a strong sense of affinity. He had been brought to England in 1809 but had become increasingly unmanageable with each successive mating season. Faced by a five-ton elephant – situated in a confined space on an upper floor – which it seemed impossible to restrain, the menagerie's owner was finally forced to call in 'some of the Foot Guards from Somerset-house' to put down the animal – for which he had once been offered £1,000. This event excited 'universal interest'. Within 'a few hours' Limbird had procured a drawing of it and within forty he had published a coloured print. This was, the *Mirror* noted, 'a proof of the celerity with which works of art [were] now executed', and it also indicates the importance of the topical print in recording and enhancing the celebrity of public characters.[79] By contrast, it took ten days for the *Mirror* to publish its account of the event – longer by far than the newspapers. However, by combining the reportage of the newspaper with the visual material of the topical print and the more learned and literary effusions of the monthlies, the *Mirror* provided a distinctive commentary on topical events (fig. 2.6).

The commentary was, moreover, replete with scientific reference. Such events, the *Mirror* believed, would interest lovers of natural history, as well as 'every one acquainted with this menagerie'. Important actors in the initial drama were comparative anatomists Joshua Brookes and William Clift, who, 'perfectly acquainted with the anatomy of the animal', had 'pointed out those parts where he was most vulnerable'. The *Mirror* related in great detail the skilful dissection of the elephant, which was attended by a multitude of prominent surgeons and veterinarians, as well as by 'a great number of medical students and other persons'.[80] Further editorial articles discussed the eating of elephant flesh (in which several of those present at the dissection partook), related anecdotes of Chuny, and gave a brief account of the Indian elephant – largely extracted from Johann Friedrich Blumenbach's recently translated *Manual of the Elements of Natural History* (1825). In addition, Peter Westcott ('PTW') contributed an article relating anecdotes of elephants from a range of sources, including works by Buffon, Thomas Bewick, and John Ray, and the *Philosophical Transactions*.[81] Over succeeding weeks seven more articles relating to elephants appeared, ranging from original and extracted articles about animal behaviour and menageries to sentimental poetry and extracts from travel books.[82]

If the shows and exhibitions of London were increasingly spectacular, they were no more so than the massive architectural and engineering projects which were transforming the city's appearance, the runaway industrial expansion that was underpinning its wealth, and the technological innovation that was transforming transport, communication, and daily living. These developments were frequently used in the *Mirror* as objects

The Mirror
OF
LITERATURE, AMUSEMENT, AND INSTRUCTION.

No. CLXXXVI.]   SATURDAY, MARCH 11, 1826.   [PRICE 2d.

Destruction of the Elephant at Exeter 'Change

LORD BYRON, in his Ode on the death of Sir Peter Parker, says, " There is a tear for all that die." This observation, though intended only in reference to the human species, might, we think, without any extraordinary stretch, be applied to that noble creature the elephant, so long one of the many attractive features of Mr. Cross's Menagerie at Exeter Change, an exhibition with which every Londoner is, and every countryman longs to be, acquainted.

This noble animal, which is always of a stupendous size, had increased to a bulk very unusual in this country, and, as it might have been expected from its confinement, become at certain seasons rather ungovernable. Large doses of opening medicines were given, with the view of cooling the temperament of the animal, even to the extent of 24lbs. of salts, 24lbs. of treacle, 6 oz. calomel, 1½ oz. tartar emetic, 6 drams gamboge, one bottle of Croton oil, in 52 hours, without effect. About five years ago, the animal was so furious, that it was found necessary to administer to him larger quantities of medicine. Six ounces of calomel, and 55 pounds of Epsom salts, (a dose which would purge some thousands of his Majesty's liege subjects) mixed with molasses, were given to him within 52 hours, without effect ; but subsequently about five or six pounds of marrow being given, the action upon the medicine already taken was rapid, and the object desired was accomplished. On another occasion, as much as four small bottles of Croton oil, one drop of which is frequently a dose for a man as an active purgative, were administered without the slightest effect being produced. At ordinary times, sulphur mixed with the food was found sufficient to keep the system under, but since the death of the keeper in November last, no person has had sufficient control over the animal, to prevent the probability of danger. The first symptom of actual rage was shown about a week ago, when a portion of the den was destroyed ; and such was the ferocity of the elephant, that the carpenters were unable to repair it. Until within the last few months, with the exception of certain periods, the animal was so docile, that the keeper could safely sleep in the den within reach of the trunk, and the animal might be approached at all times without using a spear ; but latterly the necessary attend-

VOL. VII.   L   145

Figure 2.6. 'Destruction of the Elephant at Exeter 'Change', *Mirror of Literature* 7 (1826), 145. Reproduced by kind permission of Sheffield Central Library.

of fashionable wonder and interest. Their visually striking qualities made them particularly suitable for illustration, and they cohered with the established traditions of antiquarian, topographical, architectural, and technical illustration which the *Mirror* took from the traditional miscellanies. Many numbers of the *Mirror* thus began with illustrated accounts of new bridges, public buildings, and mechanical inventions, and while their subjects were by no means limited to London, the large-scale remodelling of the capital loomed large.[83] These articles were chiefly descriptive and celebratory, often giving considerable technical detail and emphasizing national progress. Such newsworthy achievements, indeed, often gave rise to more general accounts. Regular correspondent 'F R — y', for instance, took the recent 'aerial excursions' and the death of André Jacques Garnerin as the pretext for a history of aeronautics.[84] More triumphantly, an extract from the *New Times* took the occasion of the departure from London of the steamship *Enterprize*, the first to sail for India, to reflect on the 'wonders of the age' as being hardly more chimerical than the extravagant romances of the Scriblerians.[85]

The positive tone of these articles was, however, juxtaposed with the more ambiguous cast of others. In poetry and fiction – both original and extracted – the technological 'improvements' of the age were often used to comic effect. One source of humour lay in the overblown technological utopianism and commercial ambition which characterized the 1820s. The headlong drive to exploit the power of steam in joint-stock companies became a particular target for humour. Here, as articles ridiculed existing schemes and invented others only slightly more ridiculous, the debt to the Scriblerian tradition was obvious.[86] In a climate where speculators could hardly find sufficient schemes in which to invest their surplus capital, 'John Bubble' submitted to the *Mirror* his prospectus for 'The Intellect Company', the projectors of which had 'discovered an ingredient of inestimable qualities . . . which being enclosed in a fillet, and fastened round the pericranium, imparts to the wearer . . . a qualification to fill every station in life with honour to himself, and benefit to the community'.[87]

At times, however, the humour turned to more serious concerns, highlighting the inconveniences, dangers, or undesirability of technological change. One common subject of humorous complaint was the 'improvement' of London's roads following Parliament's adoption of John McAdam's road-stone scheme in 1823. In a poem extracted from the *New Monthly*, for instance, 'Old Thames' drolly raised his complaint against the dirt and dust caused by the road works in Bridge Street, Blackfriars and the increased likelihood of accidents.[88] Pollution and accidents were also associated with the growing use of steam engines, and these became the objects of more barbed humour. A letter extracted from the *Birmingham Gazette*, for instance, urged the editor to 'thwart the designs' of the '*iron*-hearted' railway speculators 'by advice, by entreaty, by warnings, by ridicule, by *any thing*'.[89] While such articles rarely engaged with the technicalities of the subject, they clearly subverted the more celebratory reportage of technological change with which they were juxtaposed.

The *Mirror*'s generic eclecticism has been well captured by Brian Maidment, who wrote that the journal 'sought to extend the eighteenth century gentlemanly tradition of miscellany journalism to a wider public through the introduction of topical woodcut illustration and the development of more topical, more anecdotal, less antiquarian features'.[90] Thomas Byerley, drawing on his own wide experience as a hack writer, combined elements from numerous existing genres to produce a magazine accessible to a wide range of readers at a time when other journals were becoming more highbrow, expensive, and exclusive. Some of these elements – such as the learned original articles of an instructive and amusing variety – tended to place the arts and sciences within the rather sedate learned culture of the eighteenth-century miscellany. Others – notably the sometimes racy extracts from the new fashionable monthlies and the illustrated articles on topics of the day – emphasized novel, spectacular, or controversial aspects of the arts and sciences and their practitioners.

Under Byerley, the *Mirror* presented readers with the possibility of engaging directly with its contents, scientific or otherwise, as potential contributors. It did not provide the same large discursive domain which the monthly miscellanies had presented to their bourgeois readers in the late eighteenth century.[91] Moreover, the rise of the professionally written fashionable monthlies of the late Regency period increasingly placed it in the position of representing middle-class culture at second hand. Nevertheless Byerley's *Mirror* was strikingly different in its openness to readerly intervention from such cheap miscellanies of the 1830s as the *Penny Magazine*. In part, of course, the shift resulted from the resurgence of the cheap political press with the inception of the 'war of the unstamped' in 1831. Many of the producers of the new cheap miscellanies of the early 1830s were consequently concerned with a perceived problem of controlling unruly working-class readers. However, there had been significant developments in the intervening years, and in the final section I sketch how these were manifested in the *Mirror*'s representation of the sciences.

CHEAP MISCELLANIES AND THE INVENTION
OF POPULAR SCIENCE

Even under Byerley, the *Mirror* was by no means static, but following his untimely death in July 1826 the rate of change accelerated. This was not merely a matter of editorial style. The literary marketplace underwent significant change during the 1820s. In the years after the financial crisis of 1825–6, a number of publishers began to issue new or recent literature at much lower prices, ranging from the 6d and 1s numbers of the SDUK's *Library of Useful Knowledge* (1827–46) and *Constable's Miscellany* (1827–35) to the 5s and 6s volumes of the collected edition of Scott's *Works* (1829–33) and John Murray's fashionable *Family Library* (1829–34). These changes might arguably have blunted the edge of the *Mirror*'s appeal to reasonably wealthy readers. In addition, the *Mirror* clearly reflected transformations in the periodical market during the 1820s, as the process of specialization that had been in train for some time reached a critical point. As the fashionable monthlies progressively turned their backs on the traditional format of the miscellany, with its contributed articles on a wide range of subjects, and its attempt to provide a repository of information, the range and number of scientific monthlies radically increased.[92] At the end of the war there had been around a dozen commercial scientific, medical, technical, and natural historical journals; by the end of the 1820s the number had more than trebled. This process of literary specialization quickly became reflected in the *Mirror*.

One reason for relating the changes in the *Mirror* to the wider context in which the journal appeared is the fact that Byerley's successor as editor (after the brief abortive editorship of an unidentified 'Mr. Ray')[93] was another hack writer, John Timbs, with whom he had much in common. Apprenticed to a printer and druggist, Timbs, like Byerley, cut his literary teeth as a contributor to the *Monthly Magazine*.[94] The magazine's proprietor, Sir Richard Phillips, was a political radical and educational publisher whose 'chief importance' was significantly identified by the *Dictionary of National Biography* (*DNB*) as being as a 'purveyor of cheap miscellaneous literature designed for popular instruction, and as the legitimate predecessor of the brothers Chambers and of Charles Knight'.[95] Timbs became Phillips's amanuensis in 1821, before beginning to edit the *Mirror* in the autumn of 1827.[96] Like Byerley, his own interests were primarily antiquarian (he was elected FSA in 1854), and when he later became sub-editor of the *Illustrated London News* in 1842 he was responsible for the antiquarian and topographical departments.[97]

Despite his similarity in outlook to Byerley, the *Mirror* under Timbs sidelined the contributions of readers. Shortly after Byerley's death, replies to correspondents were repositioned from the end of the weekly numbers to the wrappers of the monthly parts, effectively removing them from the reach of many (especially the poorer) readers.[98] In addition, Timbs allowed little scope for controversy. Following an anonymous article on the 'History of Gas-Lighting' in December 1827, T. Hatchard wrote to the journal claiming priority in the use of coal-gas for illumination. Hatchard's claims were roundly rebutted in a letter from John Davy, almost certainly the brother of Humphry. However, Timbs declined to include another letter on the subject, this time by 'Verax', observing that Davy's article had been included in full 'on account of the record' he had 'copied from the "Philosophical Transactions", which, whether considered in connexion with the origin of gas-lighting, or as an interesting experimental research' would 'be acceptable to the reader'.[99] The implication of this – that science came in extracts from expert sources, not in letters from correspondents – was also exhibited elsewhere in the *Mirror*.

Soon after the commencement of his editorship, on 6 January 1827, Timbs introduced a new section called 'Arts and Sciences', which consisted primarily of extracts from learned transactions and commercial scientific journals. After running for eight months, this was replaced in October 1827 by a section headed 'Arcana of Science; or, Remarkable Facts and Discoveries in Natural History, Meteorology, Chemistry, Mineralogy, Geology, Botany, Zoology, Practical Mechanics, Statistics, and the Useful Arts'. Timbs explained that the object of the section was to 'assemble all new and remarkable facts in the several branches of science' selected 'from the Philosophical Journals of the day, the Transactions of Public Societies, and the various Continental Journals'. He continued:

The advantages of such a division in accordance with the high and enlightened character of the present age, must be obvious to every reader of our miscellany. At the same time it will be our object to concentrate or condense from all other authentic sources such new facts in science as are connected with the arts of social life, and which from being scattered through elaborate and expensive works, might thereby be lost to some portion of our readers. In short, popular discoveries in science, or all such new facts as bear on the happiness of society will be the objects of our choice; neither perplexing our readers with abstract research, nor verging into the puerile amusements of a certain ingenious but almost useless class of reasoners; it not being our object to 'ring the changes' on words.

Under the designation 'popular discoveries in science' Timbs introduced a new form of journalistic practice.[100] Scientific information was to be culled from specialist sources and presented in gobbets to readers, who might use or be amused by it, but were in no position to engage critically with it. As a reviewer of the magazine put it, the *Mirror* did not 'pretend to critical or philosophical accuracy' but was rather 'a record of passing matters, not sitting in judgement'.[101] Within a year, Timbs was using the phrase 'popular science' in his preface, writing:

The arrangement of the present Volume, generally, accords with those of its successful predecessors. Fact and fancy; sentiment, poetry, and popular science; anecdote and art; love of nature and knowledge of the world – alternate in its columns. In these several departments popular reading has been our study.[102]

The development of this notion of 'popular science' clearly reflected the changing journalistic context. Where Byerley had emulated the *Gentleman's* and *Monthly Magazines* in allowing learned contributors to submit articles on the arts and sciences, drawing on their own scholarly resources, Timbs now found himself in a situation in which even the *Monthly Magazine* had become a perceptibly more literary magazine under its new publisher and editor, and the *Gentleman's Magazine* increasingly presented science in extracts from specialist sources rather than in readers' contributions. The role of reporting original scientific findings in letters from correspondents had now become increasingly the province of the commercial scientific journals. This was something which Timbs clearly recognized. In March 1828, evidently buoyed by the success of the 'Arcana' in the *Mirror*, Timbs and Limbird published a separate duodecimo volume priced 4s 6d and entitled *Arcana of Science and Art*. Timbs's preface is worth quoting at length:

The object of the following pages is to supply the public with an Abstract of Popular Science, or such a volume as may not inaptly be termed an Annual Register of the Useful Arts. At the present moment, there are published in London, six Periodical Works devoted to Science and Art generally; besides double that number appropriated to their exclusive branches; in addition to which are the Transactions of Public Societies. It should, however, be recollected that many of these works contain but a small portion of what is called Popular Science, their pages being frequently occupied with Correspondence on Discoveries in the higher walks of science – valuable and important, it is true, but not immediately interesting, in detail, to the general reader. In these considerations originated the preparation of the present work.

Timbs reported that he had consulted 'upwards of five-and-thirty' periodicals in compiling the *Arcana*.

A key question, of course, was for whom such 'popular science' was intended. Rather like Byerley some years before, Timbs anticipated a mixed mass readership, writing:

it is not ... unreasonable to anticipate the popularity of the 'Arcana of Science', in the engine-room of the mechanic; the laboratory of the chemical student; the museum of the naturalist; the library of the gardener; the workshop of the manufacturer; the *studio* of the artist; and at the firesides of all classes. Hence, in the selection of his materials, the Editor has kept in view only such new facts as relate to the Arts of Life and Society; whilst household convenience has been remembered in every department of Domestic economy.

Wide as this potential audience was, it appears that Timbs increasingly saw the interest in 'popular science' as distinct from the general literary culture of the *Mirror*. Starting with the following volume of the *Mirror* (volume 12, July–December 1828), the 'Arcana of Science' section was replaced by a new section entitled the 'Spirit of Discovery'. Moreover, over succeeding years this section, and the companion 'Naturalist' section, declined in importance within the *Mirror*. It is perhaps a sign of the increasingly literary emphasis of the *Mirror* that, when Timbs's first spell as editor ended in 1838, Limbird approached Dickens as his successor, and ultimately appointed John Heraud.[103] This, indeed, was the long-term trajectory of the cheap miscellany, as, by the 1840s, the 'useful knowledge' miscellanies of the previous decade were supplanted by fiction-based weeklies of a more self-consciously literary cast. Such periodicals continued, of course, to feature science, technology, and medicine in highly significant ways, but in ways quite distinct from the Enlightenment miscellanies whose ethos the early *Mirror* emulated.

The changes in the *Mirror* during the 1820s are clearly of wider significance. The startling specialization of periodical literature in the decade following the end of the war, with its co-production of increasingly authoritative literary and scientific magazines, remains to be studied. For the purposes of this chapter, however, it is clear that the process by which scientific and technical (and also literary) material became withdrawn from a wider learned culture in the monthly magazines led to an increasing perception that a separate journalistic form was necessary to convey such expert analysis to a wider audience. It is in this that Timbs's notion of 'popular science' has its origin. It has long been recognized that the explicitly ideological programme of the SDUK was an important part of the creation of such a self-consciously 'diffusionist' form of knowledge. What this chapter has shown, however, is that 'popular science' was also the product of commercial imperatives within the book trade.

CHAPTER 3

The Wesleyan-Methodist Magazine *and religious monthlies in early nineteenth-century Britain*

Jonathan R. Topham

Reviewing J. B. Mozley's Bampton Lectures on miracles in the *Fortnightly Review* for June 1867, the physicist John Tyndall found the High Churchman's illustrations of special providence curiously reminiscent of his childhood reading in Ireland in the 1820s:

> The eminent lecturer's remarks on this head bring to my recollection certain narratives published in Methodist magazines, under the title, if I remember aright, 'The Providence of God asserted,' and which I used to read with avidity when a boy. In these chapters the most extraordinary and exciting escapes from peril were recounted and ascribed to prayer, while equally wonderful instances of calamity were adduced as illustrations of Divine retribution.[1]

Tyndall's sketch contrasts sharply with the later recollections of his contemporary, the Yorkshire minister's son Benjamin Gregory:

> An event looked forward to with delight was the arrival of the monthly book-parcel from City-road, bringing the *Youth's Instructor*, and the [Wesleyan-Methodist] Magazine, with a portrait of a minister... [T]here was a store of anecdotes and 'Accounts of Physical Phenomena,' travellers' wonders, and scientific experiments, thrilling Missionary intelligence, 'Facts of Natural History,' and 'Progress of Mechanical Invention.' It was in the Magazine, March 1824, that I heard the first puff of 'the steam-engine'.[2]

These two contrasting accounts of reading nicely encapsulate the ambiguous status of early nineteenth-century religious monthlies for the history of science. From the perspective of the scientific naturalist, Tyndall, the magazines' emphasis on the divine superintendence of mundane events was part of a religious culture whose epoch had been brought to a close by the advent of a new scientific ethos. Its implied datedness could be used to taint more modern theological writings by association. By contrast, the Methodist minister, Gregory – himself for many years editor of the *Wesleyan-Methodist Magazine* – emphasized the magazine's enormous

Table 3.1 *A 'long list' of periodicals, 1809, showing the preponderance and relative cheapness of religious titles*

Magazines	£	s	d
The Athenaeum		2	o
Agricultural Magazine		1	6
Britannic Magazine		1	o
Botanical Magazine		3	o
Christian Observer		1	o
Evangelical Magazine		o	6
European Magazine		1	6
Gentleman's Magazine		1	6
Gospel Magazine		o	9
Literary Recreations		1	6
Literary Panorama		2	6
Ladies Magazine		1	o
Ladies Museum		1	o
La Belle Assemblée		2	6
Le Beau Monde		2	6
Medical and Physical Journal		2	6
Monthly Repository of Theology & Literature		1	o
Methodist Magazine		o	6
Monthly Magazine		1	6
Monthly Mirror		1	6
Naval Chronicle		2	6
Naturalist's Miscellany		2	6
Orthodox Churchman		1	6
Philosophical Journal		2	6
Philosophical Magazine		2	6
Repertory of Arts and Manufactures		2	6
Records of Literature		1	o
Sporting Magazine		1	6
Theological and Biblical Magazine		o	6
Universal Magazine		1	6

Reviews			
Annual Review (a large volume)	1	1	o
Anti-jacobin Review		2	6
British Critic		2	6
Critical Review		2	6
Eclectic Review		2	o
Edinburgh Review (quarterly)		5	o
Monthly Review		2	6
Medical and Surgical Review		1	6
Oxford Review		2	6

Redrawn from *Literary Panorama* 2 (1807), col. 65.

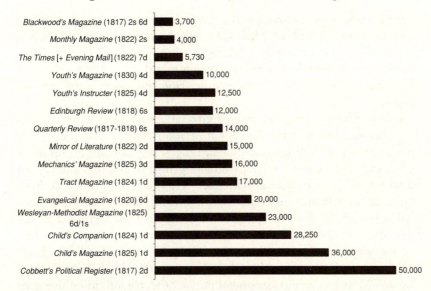

Figure 3.1. Circulations of some leading periodicals, 1817–25.[a]

[a] Figures for the *Child's Magazine, Youth's Instructer,* and *Wesleyan-Methodist Magazine* are taken from Minutes of the Book Room Committee, 1722–1827, Methodist Archives, John Rylands University Library of Manchester (hereinafter 'Methodist Archives') MAW MS641; figures for the *Evangelical Magazine* are taken from *Contemporary Journals,* 541; figures for the *Youth's Magazine* are taken from Jonathan R. Topham, 'Periodicals and the Making of Reading Audiences for Science in Early Nineteenth-Century Britain: The Youth's Magazine, 1828–37', in *Culture and Science in the Nineteenth-Century Media,* ed. by Louise Henson et al. (Aldershot: Ashgate, 2004), pp. 57–69; figures for the *Mirror of Literature* are taken from Chapter 1; figures for the Tract Magazine and Child's Companion are taken from Aileen Fyfe, *Industrialized Conversion: The Religious Tract Society and Popular Science Publishing in Victorian Britain,* PhD thesis, University of Cambridge (2000), p. 33; figures for all other titles are taken from Altick, pp. 392–93.

power in providing poorly provisioned readers with access to a wide range of cultural resources, including scientific ones. For both readers, however, the religious monthlies clearly shaped their developing views of nature and natural knowledge, and they read them with passion.

It is difficult to overestimate the importance of religious monthlies in the first quarter of the nineteenth century.[3] When, in April 1807, the *Literary Panorama* produced a '*long* list' of some thirty-nine leading magazines and reviews then publishing in London, one quarter of the titles were religious (table 3.1).[4] Moreover, these religious magazines, which included the four cheapest magazines on the list, averaged 10d – less than half of the average (1s 11d) for the remaining magazines.[5] The lower prices were reflected in sales figures (fig. 3.1). By the 1820s, the 6d *Evangelical Magazine* and *Wesleyan-Methodist Magazine* sold over 20,000 copies per month, the 4d Wesleyan *Youth's Instructer* and Sunday School Union's *Youth's*

Magazine sold approximately 10,000 copies, and the recently founded 1d children's magazines of the Methodists and the Religious Tract Society – the *Child's Companion* and the *Child's Magazine* – sold about 30,000 copies. Such figures dwarfed those of the fashionable monthlies and quarterlies, but also surpassed sales of the new cheap miscellanies discussed in the previous chapter.

Sydney Smith, citing the reputed circulations of the *Evangelical* and *Methodist* magazines in the *Edinburgh Review* for 1808, observed: 'Their circulation is so enormous, and so increasing, – they contain the opinions and display the habits of so many human beings, – that they cannot but be objects of curiosity and importance'.[6] However, the numerical dominance of the religious monthlies is only one aspect of their significance at this period. In the first quarter of the century the unprecedentedly high prices of books and periodicals made extensive reading a rare luxury. As one minister observed in 1810, the 'poor' in the Methodist body read 'little else' than the *Methodist Magazine*, the Bible, and 'Wesley's Books'.[7] Moreover, as this assessment implies, the religious monthlies generally typified the partisanship which became a growing feature of early nineteenth-century periodical literature, addressing self-consciously distinct audiences. '[E]very little sect among us,' Thomas Carlyle protested in 1829, 'Unitarians, Utilitarians, Anabaptists, Phrenologists, must have its Periodical, its monthly or quarterly Magazine; – hanging out, like its windmill, into the *popularis aura*, to grind meal for the society'.[8] Founded in 1778 as the *Arminian Magazine* – in an attempt to counteract the Calvinist *Spiritual* (1761–84?) and *Gospel* (1766–84) magazines – the *Wesleyan-Methodist Magazine* was one of the earliest to exemplify this trend, but between 1790 and 1825 the religious press increased fourfold, as one after another religious denomination sought its own monthly mouthpiece.[9]

This partisanship has led some historians to treat religious magazines as transparent registers of the scientific opinions of their readerships. However, while denominational magazines like the *Wesleyan-Methodist Magazine* were particularly apt to enforce orthodoxy in core matters of belief, editors usually permitted debate on less fundamental matters. Moreover, given the divergence commonly found between the prominent upholders of religious orthodoxy and ordinary adherents, the views expressed in the official or semi-official publications of a religious denomination or party should not be taken to reflect the opinions of the entire membership. For example, Mark Clement has shown that the cautious 'official' attitude to scientific developments evinced by nineteenth-century Methodist periodicals was at odds with the appropriation of new scientific ideas by practising Methodists – notably the physiologically informed approaches characterized as 'physical puritanism'.[10] More fundamentally, as the quotations at the beginning of this chapter suggest, it was not merely in discussions of new scientific theories that natural knowledge featured in the religious magazines, but also in a range of highly practical contexts.[11] This chapter examines the shifting place of science in the *Wesleyan-Methodist Magazine* (entitled the *Arminian Magazine* until 1797 and the *Methodist Magazine* until 1821), focusing on the first eight volumes of the third series (1822–9). It examines the diverse ways in which scientific subjects were handled in relation to the magazine's rationale and format, and analyzes some of the ways in which science contributed to the practical piety espoused by Methodists.

READING SCIENCE IN THE DENOMINATIONAL MONTHLY

In 1786, Methodist preachers began regularly to visit the village of Sancton in the Yorkshire Wolds, bringing a supply of 'cheap books' with them to week-day services, together with the 6d *Arminian Magazine*, which families combined together to purchase. One farm labourer, Thomas Jackson, resolved that each of his children should have a volume of the magazine, bound in calf. As his son, who subsequently became the editor of the magazine, later recalled:

In this manner a taste for reading was created in families, and profitable books supplanted profane conversation and sports on the Lord's Day. Useful knowledge was diffused, and especially on the all-important subject of true religion.[12]

The evangelical movement which John Wesley was primarily responsible for founding in eighteenth-century Britain, and which became such a prominent part of nineteenth-century culture, was associated from an early stage with the practice of reading. Wesley considered that a close relationship existed between reading and piety, telling one correspondent that 'The work of grace would die out in one generation if the Methodists were not a reading people.'[13] He consequently encouraged the practice at every opportunity, urging his preachers to read continually and publishing extensively in plain language and at cheap prices. Moreover, he soon set up his own press, based at his London chapel, and used his growing network of 'assistants' and 'preachers' – ministers as they later became – to distribute the publications via chapels throughout the country.[14] The *Arminian Magazine* represented a natural development of Wesley's wider publishing programme, and served from the start to unify and regulate, as well as to defend, the Methodist people. Originally planned as a 1s monthly of eighty pages, it was published as a 6d magazine of forty-eight octavo pages, which was consequently available to a far wider readership among what Sydney Smith called the 'common and middling classes of people'. Moreover, although an eighty-page 1s edition was introduced in 1811, an abridged 6d edition continued to be produced alongside it.[15]

Wesley did not confine his writings to strictly religious subjects. As recent studies have emphasized, his outlook drew heavily on the empiricist philosophy of the English Enlightenment, and from an early age he maintained an active interest in natural philosophy, natural history, and medicine. These interests were reflected in his publications, although in a distinctively pragmatic and anti-systematic manner.[16] The electrical therapies of his *Desideratum; or, Electricity Made Plain and Useful* (1760) and the herbal remedies of his *Primitive Physic* (1747) have attracted most historical attention. In addition, however, his compilation *A Survey of the Wisdom of God in Creation* (1763) was a 'compendium of natural philosophy', intended not merely to 'entertain an idle barren curiosity', but to serve a religious purpose in displaying the divine attributes.[17] Scientific references likewise permeated his other publications, including his sermons. Thus, while the *Arminian Magazine*'s predominant fare consisted of theological essays, sermons, biographical sketches, letters, accounts of Christian experiences, and poetry, Wesley maintained a regular supply of articles on natural history and natural philosophy, including extracts from the *Survey*.

After Wesley's death in 1791 the magazine passed with the rest of the 'Book Room' into the hands of the Methodist Conference, which established a management committee consisting of the London-based ministers and other corresponding members. The day-to-day operation was entrusted to a Conference-appointed Editor and Book Steward, but the committee had considerable executive responsibility. In addition, the annual Conference often involved itself in the details of Book Room affairs, sometimes discussing matters of minute detail. The magazine was carefully guarded as the 'official organ of a large body of religious people, whose every movement' was 'watched by hostile parties'.[18] On occasion, it was used to provide *ex cathedra* answers to attacks on Methodism. Moreover, while the offer of remuneration encouraged ministers to write, successive editors were ready to reject, amend, or annotate contributions, in order to maintain denominational orthodoxy. Nevertheless, Methodism maintained a profound ambiguity towards religious authority, and the conduct of the magazine was not infrequently challenged.[19]

The success of the magazine owed much to the alternative distribution network it employed. It was one of the explicit duties of ministers to sell

Book Room publications, on which they received a discount, and it was customary for any new books to be announced from the pulpit at week-night services. However, they were forbidden to sell or advertise other books at the chapels, including their own. Ministers distributed around 90 per cent of copies of the magazine, which was produced a month in advance in order that the parcels could be distributed in time.[20] These measures institutionalized the magazine within the authority structures of the church. Moreover, under the control of the Book Room, the magazine played an important role in creating a distinctive Methodist reading culture by moulding readers' perceptions of the wider literary world. The number of books reviewed or noticed by the magazine was severely limited, and suspect books were not even allowed advertising space on wrappers, which, commonly running to between twelve and twenty-two pages per number, offered an advantageous forum for promoting goods and services, and were consequently carefully scrutinized by a separate Book Room sub-committee (fig. 3.2).[21]

Many contemporaries considered that the unusual literary subculture of the Methodists was narrow-minded and uncultured. The range and quality of material in the magazine, including the number of articles on natural philosophy and natural history, admittedly declined under Wesley's immediate successors.[22] However, when Joseph Benson (1749–1821) became editor in 1804, he commenced a new series, instigating a significant revision of the magazine's format, which persisted until his death. Benson shared Wesley's belief in the religious importance of education. In addition, he was motivated by the consideration that churchmen could not dismiss cultured Methodists as ill-educated enthusiasts.[23] In a printed announcement of October 1803, he declared that the forthcoming changes in the *Methodist Magazine* reflected the wishes of many of the 'more intelligent and judicious members of our Societies', who had 'signified it to be their earnest wish... that more attention should be paid, than heretofore, to render it as far as is possible, a vehicle of useful knowledge and improvement'.[24] The emphasis on education was apparent in the increased formalization of the magazine's structure, with nine (later eleven) sections. In keeping with Wesley's own emphasis, one of these was 'Physico- or Natural Theology' (later 'The Works of God Displayed'), designed to provide readers with 'first, a general, and then, a more particular account of the gracious provisions of Providence, of the wisdom and design of the Creator, and to lead from the admirable works to the more admirable and adorable Work-Master'.[25] Like large portions of Wesley's *Survey*, articles under this heading nevertheless often took the

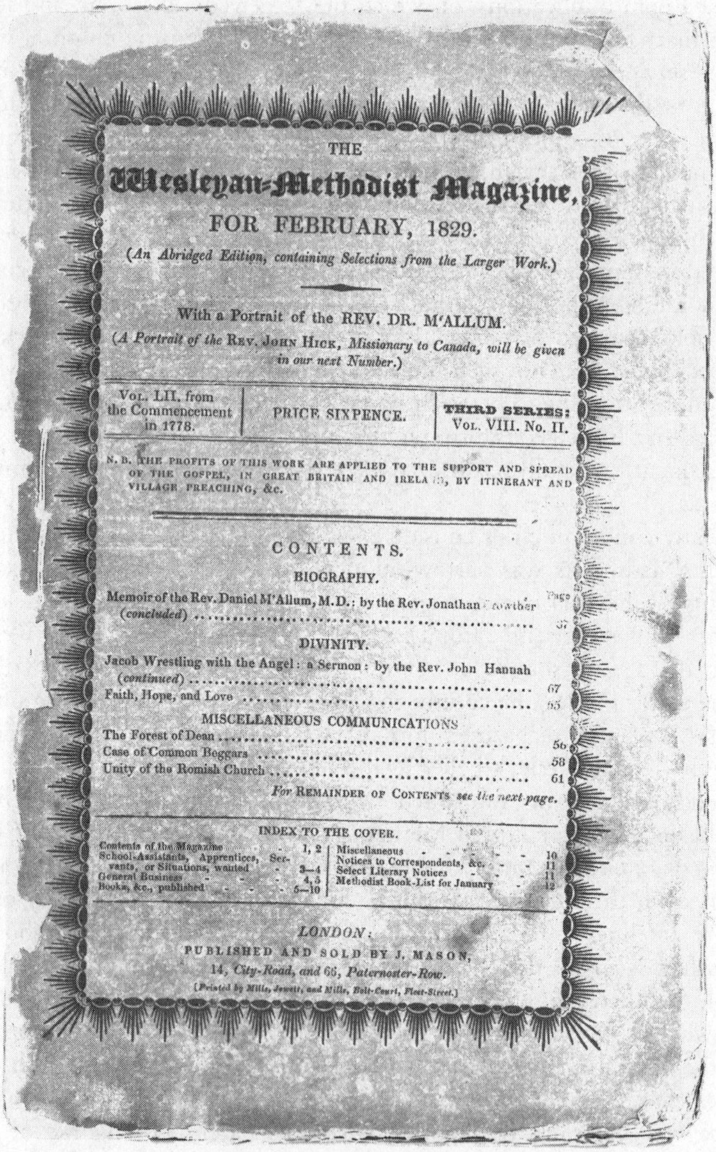

THE

Wesleyan-Methodist Magazine,

FOR FEBRUARY, 1829.

(*An Abridged Edition, containing Selections from the Larger Work.*)

With a Portrait of the REV. DR. M'ALLUM.

(*A Portrait of the* Rev. John Hick, *Missionary to Canada, will be given in our next Number.*)

Vol. LII. from the Commencement in 1778.	PRICE SIXPENCE.	THIRD SERIES: Vol. VIII. No. II.

N. B. THE PROFITS OF THIS WORK ARE APPLIED TO THE SUPPORT AND SPREAD OF THE GOSPEL, IN GREAT BRITAIN AND IRELAND, BY ITINERANT AND VILLAGE PREACHING, &c.

CONTENTS.

For Remainder of Contents *see the next page.*

INDEX TO THE COVER.

LONDON:

PUBLISHED AND SOLD BY J. MASON,

14, *City-Road, and* 66, *Paternoster-Row.*

[*Printed by Mills, Jowett, and Mills, Bolt-Court, Fleet-Street.*]

Figure 3.2a. Front and back wrappers of the abridged edition of the *Wesleyan-Methodist Magazine*, February 1829. The full wrapper ran to twelve pages, including extensive advertisements for other Methodist publications. Reproduced by kind permission of the Rare Book, Manuscript, and Special Collections Library, Duke University, Durham, N.C.

THE NEW PORTRAIT OF MR. WESLEY,

Painted by J. JACKSON, Esq., engraved by THOMSON, and published under the direction of the Methodist Book-Committee in London, is now finished. Fine PROOFS on *India Paper*, price 7s. each, and Fine PRINTS, on *Colombier Paper*, at 3s. 6d., and on *Demy Paper*, at 2s. 6d. each, may be had of Mr. Mason.

N.B. For the Accommodation of Purchasers, the Portraits will be sent framed, when so ordered, at the following prices:—INDIA PROOFS, in plain Gilt Frames, One Guinea; in Maple Frames, French Polish, One Guinea; and in elegant Broad Gilt Frames, Two Guineas each.

METHODIST BOOK-LIST, FOR MARCH, 1829.

THE following PUBLICATIONS have been printed for the Methodist Book-Room, during the last month; and are now on sale, for the benefit of the Connexion, by Mr. MASON, No. 14, City-Road; and 66, Paternoster-Row, London:—

1. THE YOUTH'S INSTRUCTER AND GUARDIAN, FOR MARCH, 1829:

Including an Engraving, representing Stonehenge, with the following Articles:—Stonehenge: Paternus and his Son: the Italian Reformer: Letters from a Father to his Son (Letter III.): An Important Thought: Epitaph on a Pious Youth: Astronomical Sketches (No. III.): Perseverance: The Praying Sailor: The Scolopendra Electrica: Brief Astronomical Notices: Juvenile Obituary: Poetry;—The Sun-Bright Chime: by Mrs. Hemans; Jacob at the Ford of Jabbok; The Decline of Winter; Solitary Musings; Psalm II.

This Juvenile Magazine is published monthly, price 4d. neatly printed in 12mo.

N.B. Sets of the *Youth's Instructer*, from its commencement in January, 1817, may be had in Twelve Volumes, neatly half-bound, including all the Plates, at 5s. per Volume. To the Juvenile Members of Religious Families a Set of this Work would be acceptable as a standing article of the Domestic Library; and it would form a valuable *Prize-Book* at the annual examinations of respectable Schools.

2. THE CHILD'S MAGAZINE, AND SUNDAY SCHOLAR'S COMPANION, FOR MARCH, 1829:

Price One Penny:

Ornamented with Two Wood-Cuts, and containing the following Articles:—Everybody may be of some use: Reflection on Prov. viii. 17: The Word of God: Illustrations of Scripture: Jabez Wilson: Harriet Crump: Choctaw Youth: Poetry;—Verses "To my Brother."

3. THE LARGER EDITION OF THE WESLEYAN-METHODIST MAGAZINE, for March, 1829: Containing many Articles not included in this Abridgment. Price One Shilling. See Notice at the Bottom of the Second Page of this Cover.

4. The Second Volume of a complete and standard Edition of the PROSE WORKS of the Rev. JOHN WESLEY, A.M. Price 8s. boards; or, covered with coloured cambric, and gilt lettered, 8s. 6d.

New Tracts lately published,

No. 259. The SCEPTICAL YOUNG OFFICER. By the Rev. JOHN M. MASON, D.D., of New-York. 12 pages, price 4s. per 100.

260. The INFIDEL CONVERTED; an Account of Mr. Cameron. 8 pages, price 2s. 8d. per 100.

261. "I HOPE WELL;" a Dialogue. By the Rev. R. BAXTER. 12 pages, price 4s. per 100.

REV. J. BENSON'S COMMENTARY ON THE HOLY SCRIPTURES.

The Public are respectfully informed, that the Quarto Edition of the REV. J. BENSON'S COMMENTARY ON THE HOLY SCRIPTURES, which has been long out of Print, has been lately reprinted, and may now be had on application to Mr. MASON; or to any of the Preachers in their respective Circuits: In Five Volumes, boards, price 7l. Any of the Numbers, or Parts, may be had separately.

** A few Sets of the Quarto Edition, on medium paper, are now on Sale, in Five Volumes, price 8l. 8s.

Printed by Mills, Jowett, and Mills, Bolt-Court, Fleet-Street.

Figure 3.2b *(cont.)*.

form of straightforward scientific exposition, sometimes with no explicit religious references.

In his emphasis on the value of secular learning, Benson was also emulating a new competitor in the periodical marketplace. The monthly *Christian Observer* was founded in 1802 by members of the 'Clapham Sect' of Anglican evangelicals as a magazine for the Christian gentleman. The prospectus promised

so to combine information upon general subjects, with religious instruction, as to furnish such an interesting view of Religion, Literature, and Politics, free from the contamination of false principles, as a Clergyman may without scruple recommend to his Parishioners, and a Christian safely introduce into his Family.[26]

In particular, it asserted that the periodical was the tried and tested vehicle for 'rendering the various departments of useful knowledge easy and accessible'. The *Observer* thus promised such secular fare as '*Particulars concerning the Works of God in* CREATION *and* PROVIDENCE' and '*the History and State of* MAN *throughout the World*'.[27] Early volumes contained a regular section of 'Literary and Philosophical Intelligence', similar to that found in secular monthlies, as well as scientific contributions from correspondents. Benson, who claimed to have been a 'constant reader' of the *Christian Observer* since its commencement and to have recommended it 'as a Work well calculated to serve the interests of genuine religion and virtue', intended to achieve parity with this new Anglican rival by reemphasizing the place of secular learning in the *Wesleyan-Methodist Magazine*.[28]

Following Benson's death in February 1821 the editorial chair was temporarily filled by the President of the 1820 Conference, Jabez Bunting (1779–1858), whose role in making early nineteenth-century Wesleyan Methodism a distinct denomination is well documented.[29] From the start Bunting was assisted by Thomas Jackson (1783–1873), a largely self-educated minister who was achieving prominence as a Methodist scholar. When Jackson in turn was appointed editor in 1824, Conference requested Bunting and Richard Watson, a leading Methodist theologian, to assist him.[30] In 1822 when Bunting and Jackson began a new series of the magazine they re-organized its structure in order to address the 'changing circumstances and habits of society'.[31] The new series extended the changes implemented by Benson, the magazine's formal sections increasingly resembling those of secular monthly miscellanies like the *Gentleman's Magazine*. The magazine now commenced with 'Religious Biography' (lives of deceased ministers and other 'eminently pious persons'), followed by 'Divinity' (including theological essays and sermons), 'Miscellaneous Essays, Correspondence, and Extracts', 'Review of Select Theological Publications' and 'Select List of New Books, (chiefly religious)', 'Religious, Philanthropic, and Miscellaneous Intelligence', 'Missionary Intelligence', 'Obituary', and, lastly, 'Poetry'.

In its increasingly sober form, the third series of the *Wesleyan-Methodist* provided many contexts for the discussion of natural knowledge. The most prominent was the 'Miscellaneous Communications' section which, while it included occasional reports of remarkable providential events (as announced in the prospectus), was dominated by earnest and learned articles on theological and practical subjects. Wesley's tradition of publishing scientific articles – perpetuated in Benson's 'Works of God Displayed' – continued to be evident, and in his prospectus Bunting promised 'Selections or original Communications in Natural History and Philosophy' and 'Recent Voyages and Travels'.[32] The magazine set out to give precedence to original, over extracted, articles. An early number apologized for extracting an article entitled 'Providential Arrangements Discovered by Chemistry' from the *Christian Observer*, and requested 'scientific readers' to send 'communications of the same class, adapted for popular use'.[33] Bunting was not, however, prepared to accept what was 'called "free discussion"'. To allow 'the communications of persons who attack the Truth', Bunting averred, even for the purpose of proving them false, would be to put the 'young and uninstructed' in danger. The magazine would therefore only countenance those 'doctrinal sentiments' promulgated by Wesley.[34]

As in other religious magazines of the period, natural theology, strictly defined, was far from prominent in the *Wesleyan-Methodist Magazine*'s scientific articles.[35] Wesley's own natural theology had been distinctively ambivalent. In his *Survey*, he published a fairly standard Enlightenment account of the cosmological argument, but complicated the matter by insisting that '"the light of nature", so called', was a consequence of prevenient grace (i.e. the divine influence which turns the unrepentant heart to God).[36] Some prominent Methodists, including Thomas Jackson, were apparently prepared to endorse traditional natural theology, but in the more theological parts of the magazine writers were often critical of both its epistemological validity and its apologetic utility.[37] Indeed, such sentiments sometimes appeared *ex cathedra*, as when the magazine reprinted by command a sermon on the subject preached at the Wesleyan-Methodist Conference of 1820 by the American representative, John Emory.[38] Contributors nevertheless deployed design in nature to evoke a sense of religious awe and to expand readers' conceptions of divine action. A good example is provided by the two-part article by physician and Methodist minister, Daniel M'Allum, entitled 'Structure of the Human Eye and Ear'. M'Allum explicitly refused to endorse the argument from design as explicated by Paley. Instead, his account *assumed* the 'unquestionable certainty of revealed truth', including the 'existence, supremacy, and other perfections of the Godhead'. Secure in these beliefs, M'Allum used the structure of the ear and the eye as 'illustrations of what the great Creator is, in so far as his character may be inferred from his works, mutilated and reft of original excellence, as by the fall they acknowledgedly are'.[39] Other articles were less explicitly theological, introducing accounts of awe-inspiring natural phenomena – like the longevity of trees – without further comment.[40] Yet articles generally emphasized that scientific knowledge must be made subservient to Christian piety.[41]

Many of the 'Miscellaneous Communications' touching on scientific subjects did so with a particular view to illustrating biblical themes. Fashionable travel literature, in particular, was plundered for descriptions of the ethnography, natural history, meteorology, or other relevant features of the Middle East. Less obvious themes were also canvassed; for instance, a pseudonymous letter from the Methodist school (Woodhouse-Grove) at Apperley Bridge near Bradford debated the identity of the metal alluded to in Rev. 1:15.[42] Other articles tackled points of apparent discord between biblical and philosophical accounts, such as the pseudonymous article on Josh. 10:12, which argued that the injunction of Joshua that the sun should stand still was not intended to be 'philosophical', but that it 'referred merely to the appearance of the scene'. The author nevertheless claimed that a miracle had certainly occurred, and that it was probably 'effected by means of a cessation of the earth's motion on its axis'.[43]

Correspondents occasionally reported their own scientific discoveries, often made with a practical end in view. Wesley's own concern with practical science and medicine was well known and was further publicised when the magazine reprinted one of his letters in 1822.[44] Wesley's letter had been sent in by Thomas Marriott of Bristol, who later submitted an account of the restoration of sight in one of his eyes (which had been afflicted with 'Gutta Serena') following the repeated application of large blisters to his spine. The author claimed that 'the brethren' assembled at the annual Conference had persuaded him to publicize his cure.[45] Nor were contemporary leaders of the church, such as Adam Clarke, averse to making their scientific interests public. Clarke sent a detailed account of an agricultural experiment in which he had cultivated hundreds of plants from three grains of wheat, by means of off-sets. Had some of his crop not been destroyed, the result of the experiment would, he claimed, 'have astonished the most scientific agriculturists in Europe'.[46] Other correspondents, who were engaged in scientific pursuits for amusement, sought to communicate the pleasure to others. For instance, William Rogerson Jr. of Pocklington, near York, submitted his observations on glow worms, which he had kept 'for years in glasses', together with instructions as to how to keep them.[47]

Scientific subjects were also canvassed in the context of public policy. Like other evangelicals, Methodists were involved in various philanthropic and reforming campaigns, which were reflected in articles on such topical issues as the size of the British population and the progress of vaccination. A particularly striking example relates to the campaign against animal cruelty, which received significant support from Methodist activists.[48] Thomas Chalmers's *On Cruelty to Animals* (1826) – the first of a series of annual sermons on the subject – was extracted in the *Wesleyan-Methodist* soon after publication. Arguing that the mistreatment of animals extended to 'cultivated society', Chalmers's sermon opposed scientific cruelty, advocating a 'gradual, and, at length, a complete abandonment of the experiments of illustration, which are at present a thousand fold more numerous than the experiments of humane discovery', and criticizing the 'atrocities' of vivisection conducted by the French physiologist François Magendie. An editorial note expressed the hope that 'other ministers in different parts of the country' would 'take pains to "remind the human savage, whether vulgar or polite, scientific or ignorant", that the creation belongs to its divine author'.[49]

Scientific news items were often carried, especially in the occasional 'Varieties and Gleanings' section, where new discoveries and inventions were reported in brief paragraphs, frequently extracted or abstracted from scientific periodicals. These ranged widely from Charles Babbage's plans for a calculating engine to William Buckland's observations in Kirkdale Cave, and from William Edward Parry's search for a North-West passage to Giovanni Aldini's invention of fire-proof clothing.[50] Reports often stressed the wonders of science and technology: indeed, it was while reading in the 'Varieties' that Benjamin Gregory found himself inspired by the account of steam engines which appeared in an abstract of Benjamin Heywood's 1824 address to the Liverpool Royal Institution.[51] Occasionally, however, such reports were subjected to comment or correction. Thus, in May 1822, following the decision of the Lord Chancellor to refuse copyright protection to William Lawrence's *Lectures on Physiology, Zoology, and the Natural History of Man* because they attacked the Bible, Bunting used his occasional 'Christian Retrospect of General Occurrences Interesting to those who Fear God, on Account of Their Influence on Religion, or on Public Morals and

Happiness' to attack the 'great culprit' who made science the medium of poisonous materialism.[52]

Attempts to vanquish scientific infidelity or to question 'philosophical' findings were much more commonly found in the 'Divinity' and 'Review' sections. Thus (as noted above) contributions to the 'Divinity' section often challenged the epistemological claims of natural theology, suggesting that human reason was both insufficient 'for the purpose of saving knowledge' and could easily alienate the unbeliever from revelation.[53] The disturbing rationalist practice of bringing revelation to the bar of reason was sometimes directly associated with scientific men like Joseph Priestley, or with modern sciences like astronomy and geology.[54] However, other contributions incorporated scientific views within a theology of nature, used scientific language and analogies, and advocated the application to religion of the empirical epistemology of Locke, Newton, Thomas Reid, and Dugald Stewart.[55]

The 'Review' section was one of Bunting's innovations. Although Wesley had refused to publish reviews, Benson had included them in his more general section 'The Truth of God Defended'. However, under Bunting and Jackson, a wide range of largely religious books was reviewed, often with passing remarks on the sciences. Occasionally the magazine reviewed works that directly engaged the sciences, such as books on exploration (usually relating to the Middle East or missionary activities) and religious works like Thomas Chalmers's *Christian and Civic Economy of Large Towns* (1821–6), Thomas Dick's *Christian Philosopher* (1823), and Richard Watson's *Theological Institutes* (1823–9). As the first Methodist systematic theology, Watson's work addressed all major doctrinal matters and inevitably confronted the theological implications of the sciences. In reviews published in the magazine Watson was praised for answering objections 'deduced from the infant science of Geology' while setting out the authority of the Bible, and for criticizing the physiological materialism associated with the writings of the surgeon William Lawrence, while defending the immateriality of the soul.[56]

By the end of the 1820s, the growth of secular education, with the emergence of mechanics' institutes and the expansion of cheap secular publishing, was prompting growing concern in the *Wesleyan-Methodist*.[57] Thus, while the reviewer of the inaugural lectures delivered by the professors at London University agreed with the new institution's repudiation of religious admission tests, he argued that the founders should have maintained the principles of Protestant orthodoxy. The university's leading principle, 'that scientific and literary pursuits have no connexion whatever with the religious persuasion of any individual', cut at the root of Methodist educational practice, which emphasized the religious context of all learning. The reviewer thought it better to say nothing on religion in the lectures, like the closet evolutionist Robert Edmond Grant, than merely to indulge in '"incidental" conveyance of moral and religious instruction', like the medical professor John Connolly.[58] What was really required, however, was for secular subjects to be taught unashamedly within the context of Protestant orthodoxy, an approach exemplified by many of the secular books recommended in Bunting's regular section of brief literary notices and listings.

While science was sometimes discussed in the *Wesleyan-Methodist* in the context of doctrinal beliefs, it occurred more often in practical contexts, ranging from the promotion of an enlightened devotion to the mundane practicalities of medical cures, and from religious activism to pious education. As recent studies have emphasized, beliefs and practices about nature have often been at least as pertinent to religious *practice* as they have been to religious *beliefs*.[59] One of the primary objects of the *Wesleyan-Methodist* was to direct the lives of its readers into particular forms of Christian practice. Indeed, Sydney Smith considered that a far better understanding of Methodism could be obtained by seeing its practical outworkings in the magazine, than merely by 'detailing the settled articles of [Methodist] belief'.[60] In the remainder of this chapter, we will examine two elements of the magazine that particularly emphasized the Methodist life of faith, namely the reports of missionary endeavours and the memoirs and obituaries. In particular, we will examine how discourse about nature, technology, and the sciences featured in these texts, as they encouraged readers to explore the sometimes imaginatively rich possibilities of a fully Christian life.

SCIENCE AND MISSIONARY ENDEAVOURS

[T]he *Missionary Notices* accompanied the *Magazine*, bearing fruit every month – like the trees of Paradise; with their thrilling news from Labrador and the South Sea Islands, from the East and West Indies, from South Africa and North America, from Sweden and from Palestine; seeming to show all seasons at one time, and all climates in one place. Thus my first notions of geography were vividly and charmingly connected with the struggles and successes of the Kingdom of Christ; the martyr and the missionary thus became the heroes of my imagination and my heart.

Benjamin Gregory, *Autobiographical Recollections*[61]

The activism of evangelicals was one of their defining characteristics, particularly in addressing the presumed spiritual, moral, or physical needs of others in domestic and overseas missions, the anti-slavery campaign, and welfare campaigns. As David Bebbington has identified, this emphasis on service could sometimes encourage anti-intellectualism and make learning seem 'a dispensable luxury'.[62] In some contexts, however, the practical concerns of evangelicals entailed a degree of learning. One primary focus of Methodist activism is manifested in the *Wesleyan-Methodist Magazine* by the dominance of the 'Missionary Notices' (which commonly ran to a dozen closely printed double-column pages), by the reprinting of missionary sermons, and by the many reviews of and extracts from missionary narratives. However, as the above quotation shows, rather than militating against knowledge of nature, these accounts of missionary activities contained a huge body of information about the geography, the peoples, and the natural history of the wider world

In August 1826 one avid reader ('WG' of Leeds) penned reflections 'On Reading the Missionary Notices', observing:

We learn from them the true condition of heathen nations, concerning which we had long been misled by the falsehoods of travellers, and the misrepresentations of men who call each other philosophers. They frequently contain interesting information respecting the natural productions, soil, and climate of different countries, as well as correct descriptions of the manners, customs, and superstitions of the people. Above all, they confirm our faith in the great doctrines of the Fall of Man, and the universal efficacy of the Atonement made by Christ.[63]

For 'WG' the magazine made a distinctive contribution to geography and natural history, moulded by the practical concerns and evangelical beliefs of Methodist missionaries. At a purely practical level, many missionaries explored locations which were otherwise largely unknown to Europeans. While 'WG' urged the use of maps to interpret the missionary notices, he observed that many of the places mentioned were not 'in any Atlas extant', and agreed with William Wilberforce that missionaries would be the prime explorers of Africa. Missionaries also paid particular attention to matters of religion and culture. A review of the Baptist missionary William Ward's *Farewell Letters to a Few Friends in Britain and America* (1821), claimed that the moral and general wretchedness of the idolatrous nations had been discovered by missionaries, rather than by 'philosophers, who, though they [had] enriched science by their researches . . . [had] left matters of religion either untouched, or very superficially noticed'. While missionaries had contributed greatly to 'useful and curious knowledge', they had contributed more to the knowledge of religion 'which to Christian philanthropy is in the highest degree interesting'.[64]

As 'WG' observed, the accounts given of other peoples in the *Wesleyan Methodist* confirmed evangelical beliefs about the universal applicability of the doctrines of the Fall and the Atonement. This distinctive outlook resulted in confrontations with secular 'philosophy'. Richard Watson, whose *Religious Instruction of the Slaves in the West India Colonies Advocated and Defended* (1824) was reviewed at length in the magazine, argued against the theory that 'the gradations of animated nature are gentle, and almost imperceptible', and that 'the coloured skin and the peculiar visage of the Negro and the Hottentot' militate 'against their title to humanity'. This theory, he claimed, had been refuted by the 'facts' of religious conversion gathered by missionary societies, which demonstrated the humanity of all races. He concluded: 'Thus have Missionary operations not only enlarged the sphere of benevolence, but extended the vision of a hoodwinked philosophy.'[65]

The contributions of Methodist missionaries to geographical and natural knowledge also contrasted with those of 'philosophers' by being subservient to a higher calling, rather than being an end in themselves. This contrast was often explicitly made. Thus a sermon preached by John Mason to the New York Missionary Society in 1797, and reprinted in the *Wesleyan-Methodist* thirty years later, polemically contrasted the timidity of Christians reluctant to engage in overseas missions with the resoluteness of 'carnal men':

They [carnal men] can visit the savage tribes, can cross rivers, climb their mountains, traverse their forests; can learn their language, conform to their manners, acquire their confidence; can patiently submit to hunger and cold, fatigue and peril: – For what? To decorate earthly science, or to collect the dust of lucre, or the vapours of fame.

Yet, he argued, the missionary's incentive for such physical and mental endeavours was much stronger: 'Duty urges; misery implores; thousands of precious souls are the depending stake; and not a moment is to be lost.'[66] While an interest in 'earthly science' might be acceptable in a missionary, there was a real danger that it would take precedence over such divine concerns. In 1822, for instance, a report in the magazine detailed the founding of an institution 'for the education of pious young men to the work of evangelizing the heathen' by the Basel Evangelical Missionary Society. The directors had learned by experience, it was reported, 'that the minds of pious youths, who devote themselves to the study of the sciences, frequently lose the fervour of devotion in proportion as the understanding becomes enlightened', and they had consequently adopted 'a method of theological instruction, by which the mind [was] not only informed, but the heart and the affections [were] also engaged'.[67]

A similar approach was required in reading the missionary narratives. When the magazine reviewed the *Polynesian Researches* (1826) of William Ellis, a missionary who had been sent to the Society and Sandwich Islands by the London Missionary Society, it averred:

To the naturalist, to those who have a taste for the picturesque of scenery, to the philosopher, and the general observer of human nature, these volumes will afford subjects of entertainment and reflection; but by the Christian, and by those especially whose sympathies, zeal, and hopes, have been most engaged by Missionary exertions, they will be read with the deepest attention; and will at once confirm them in those principles on which they have defended their zeal, and awaken the highest hopes as to the ultimate success of their efforts to bring the whole world to the knowledge of Christ.[68]

Likewise, in his letter 'On Reading the Missionary Notices', 'WG' argued that they served the purposes of maintaining readers' 'sympathies . . . for the miserable and helpless condition of [their] fellow-creatures', of giving 'a fresh stimulus' to their 'desires, exertions, and prayers for the success of the means employed for their salvation', of teaching them 'more perfectly to embrace, in [their] affectionate remembrance, the whole human family', and of causing them properly to appreciate the endeavours of missionaries.[69]

Reports of far-flung places and peoples in the magazine were thus intended to be read as exercises in piety. This did not, however, preclude the reports themselves being secular in origin, and many of the fashionable travel narratives of the period were raided for suitable extracts. The compelling *Narrative of Travels and Discoveries in Northern and Central Africa* (1826) of the ex-military explorers Dixon Denham and Hugh Clapperton was not only mentioned in the magazine's literary listing, but abridgements and extracts from it appeared over numerous succeeding issues.[70] Similarly, naturalist George Finlayson's *Mission to Siam* (1826), edited by Sir Thomas Stamford Raffles, was excerpted in the magazine, chiefly to illustrate the customs and religion of the Siamese.[71] Other extracts reporting new geographical discoveries came from avowedly scientific sources, like the *Edinburgh Journal of Science* and the *Edinburgh Journal of Natural and Geographical Science*.[72] Whatever their original meaning, these texts were transformed within the magazine into contributions to a discourse of missionary endeavour, which the evangelical Christian should study for the practical purposes of prayer, fund-raising, and strategic planning.

Scientific knowledge also possessed a further practical relevance within missionary narratives. In order to undermine the received notions of other cultures, missionaries sometimes gave quite elaborate scientific explanations of phenomena to those they wished to convert. Thus in 1825 Benjamin Clough, a missionary at the Ceylon Mission in Colombo, reported his discussions with a Buddhist priest concerning the geography and cosmology of the Buddhist scriptures: 'I produced some maps, a globe, a quadrant, and a compass, and proceeded to give him as correct an outline of our geography, navigation, &c., as I could, and showed him by a variety of experiments, which he readily understood, how we must in the nature of things understand this matter.' At the end of their interview, Clough claimed, the priest thanked him and begged him to become his spiritual instructor.[73] There is evidence, indeed, that attempts were made to render such practices systematic. Thus, a few years later, in his address to the Auxilliary Wesleyan Missionary Society for the Jaffna District of Ceylon, Sir Richard Ottley reported on the society's efforts to provide Ceylonese children with a general education, including mathematical and scientific as well as religious subjects. Scientific education, he claimed, was useful in correcting the 'errors and superstitions of the idolaters'.[74] Likewise in Sumatra, the Baptist Missionary Society published not only a pamphlet containing the first three chapters of Genesis, but also a small work on astronomy. The rationale for the latter publication was: 'Science will not make them Christians, but it will assist in dispelling the mists of Mahomedanism, and teach them to use their mental powers.'[75]

SCIENCE AND EXEMPLARY LIVES

According to T. W. Herbert, the biographical sections which Wesley made such a prominent feature of the *Arminian Magazine* were a new departure in magazine writing.[76] By the 1820s, Jabez Bunting considered that, 'As a treasury of modern Christian Biography, and of other articles illustrative of the nature and excellence of Experimental Religion' the back issues of the magazine stood 'unrivalled among their numerous periodical competitors'.[77] Likewise, each issue of the *Wesleyan-Methodist Magazine* began with a biographical memoir of a recently deceased Methodist worthy, together with an intaglio portrait of a prominent living Methodist, usually a minister. The physical prominence of these memoirs, and the expense of the intaglio plate (amounting to about one-fifth of the total production cost), emphasizes the importance that was attached to them by the Book Room.[78] In addition, each number also contained shorter obituaries, printed in small type, in double columns. Biographical narratives consequently formed a significant proportion of the magazine. Like their Puritan predecessors, Methodists placed considerable emphasis on the spiritual pilgrimages of ordinary individuals.[79] Wesley himself had meticulously maintained his journal over many years, and he encouraged both children and adults to keep diaries – fragments from such diaries being sometimes quoted in the magazine's obituary notices and memoirs.[80] Biographical narratives formed part of a wider confessional culture. At the weekly class-meetings which formed the basic unit of Methodist organization, members were expected to give verbal accounts of their spiritual experiences.[81] These various biographical and autobiographical performances were intended for mutual edification. However, as life histories were expected to conform to a standard pattern, the biographical material published in the magazine is strikingly formulaic.[82]

As Geoffrey Cantor stresses in his chapter, below, biographical narratives could be used for many different purposes. In the Methodist context, they generally portrayed the spiritual progress of their subjects, indicating the path to salvation and any obstacles overcome. Such narratives usually opened with reflections on the place of education in a pious upbringing, emphasizing the importance of self-improvement and of earnest endeavour in exercising and cultivating the youthful spirit. This provided one of the contexts in which science or medicine might be introduced, usually with an emphasis on their practical value. Thus we are told that, as a young grocer's apprentice in Darlington, George Newton, used his 5s annual pocket-money to buy books on mechanics, geography and astronomy, and the parts to construct a terrestrial globe and a sundial. Such behaviour contrasted with the 'depraved connexions' and 'expensive habits' often acquired by those children 'indulged with a liberal allowance of money'.[83] However, even the desire for self-improvement was fraught with danger. As a girl, Mary Buckley 'cultivated a taste for reading and an ardent desire for mental improvement'; she read widely and acquired 'a correct knowledge of useful science'. Her habit of 'night-reading', however, resulted in repeated colds. A particularly dangerous illness precipitated her religious conversion, after which, 'though she had still an ardent thirst for reading, the Bible became, as she expressed it, her "favourite book"'.[84]

Some Methodists considered scientific reading was an acceptable form of rational recreation. The Revd Joshua Fearnside, for instance, related that his wife 'had within her reach books of amusement, and books of science, as well as books of piety and devotion: and she both regarded reading as a duty, and enjoyed it as a very high gratification'.[85] Such reading was not only divorced from the dangers of romantic fiction, but it could easily be turned to pious ends, and Methodists frequently stressed that scientific reading must be subservient to Bible study.[86] Writing about his father, a Manchester tradesman, the prominent minister James Townley stated: 'Ardent in his attachment to scientific pursuits, it was his delight to trace the wisdom, power, and goodness of GOD in every thing around him; and especially to illustrate Revelation by the discoveries of science.'[87] Scientific reading could also serve an important purpose in enabling Methodists to fulfil their pious educational duties. Women, like Margaret Malley, were particularly represented as being engaged in the education of children: 'Their health, their morals, their proficiency in useful knowledge, but, above all, their salvation, were the subjects of her inquiry, of her exhortations, and of her prayers.'[88] Men, too, had responsibilities, particularly if wealthy like the Local Preacher and Class-Leader, John Lomas. Having 'much leisure', Lomas 'had acquired a variety of useful knowledge; and this he employed for the benefit of the public; which in that retired part of the country rendered him of great value'.[89]

Accounts of education naturally graduated into accounts of vocation. Many of those memorialized in the magazine were ministers, who in some cases had relinquished a secular profession in favour of a ministerial call- ing. Daniel M'Allum, for example, began to practice as a physician after graduating from the University of Glasgow (fig. 3.3). However, 'he found it impossible to divest himself of the conviction, that God was now calling him to a different employment' as a minister. His biographer considered that it was 'useless to conjecture' how successful he might have been in the medical profession, 'had it been the will of God that he should persevere in it' – though his prospects had been 'fair and promising'. M'Allum had wrestled with the thought of 'temporal comfort' and with 'a remembrance of the great expense which had been bestowed on his professional educa- tion', but had followed his calling undeterred.[90] Such narratives did not assert that one particular calling was necessarily preferable, but emphasized that believers should be prepared to sacrifice all to follow the divine will.

Accordingly a wide range of other occupations was represented in the magazine's obituaries and memoirs, including medical and industrial ones. As the biographer of physician James Hamilton made clear, the key point in discussing these occupations was that the subject 'maintained religion in the whole of his conduct'.[91] Starting out as a naval surgeon during the Seven Years War, Hamilton's health had suffered, but

His bodily weakness was sanctified to the good of his immortal spirit; and as he considered, that he who aims to be good himself should strive to do good to others, he became a reprover, adviser, and helper of those who were engaged with him in that perilous service.[92]

Figure 3.3. 'The Late Revd Daniel McAllum', *Wesleyan-Methodist Magazine* 8 (1829), facing 73. Intaglio portraits of prominent ministers were the only illustrations in the magazine. From Jonathan R. Topham's own collection.

Thus, after becoming 'decidedly religious' he pressed 'the great truths of religion on his dying Commander' during a battle.[93] Later, as a surgeon and apothecary in his native Dunbar, Hamilton continued to use his privileged position as a medical man to urge his own form of piety on others. His biographer doubted whether 'he ever had a patient upon whom he did not enforce the necessity and blessedness of religion; and he often prayed with the afflicted'.[94] As a religious duty he willingly treated the poor, later becoming physician to the London Dispensary. In addition, he was portrayed as making his more abstract scientific learning subservient to religious ends, using it as a preacher, and opening his library ('said to be worth five hundred pounds') to ministers.[95]

The practice of medicine gave ample scope for the expression of piety, but other callings were also regarded as giving opportunities for good works. Sometimes the connections were general. For instance, an obituary notice concerning the late Mr Thomas Pengilly, 'Superintendent of the Neath-Abbey Iron-Works, and for many years a member of the Methodist Society there', quoted from the *Cambrian* the claim that 'he was distinguished by his "scientific and practical acquaintance with the mechanical powers . . . " and, above all, "his sincere and influential religion"'.[96] Other examples showed how occupational pursuits could be influenced by piety. Thus William Stephens, a Methodist gardener from St Blazey in Cornwall, had been converted after hearing a sermon on sabbath-breaking, having hitherto sold fruit and vegetables on Sundays.[97]

Biographers could also address medical and scientific themes in recounting the illness and death of exemplary Christians. Often, illness was thought to have been caused by improper action, as in the case of Mary Buckley's night reading mentioned above. Moreover, as Mark Clement has shown, illness was frequently represented in these accounts as bringing on a spiritual crisis or transition, or even a religious conversion.[98] Likewise, the spiritual transition provoked by an illness was often presented as resulting in its cure. This spiritual perspective did not preclude the belief that divine action in illness usually occurred through secondary causation, and accounts of symptoms, medical treatment, and medical practitioners abounded. However, these were always seen as secondary both to the divine will and to the spiritual welfare of the individual. As the obituarist of Elizabeth Berriman observed, 'in most cases, where the Physician is admitted to administer relief to the afflicted body, the faithful Pastor should not be refused the pleasure of administering divine consolation to the immortal mind. He, at least, should not be put off with, "The medical attendant has said, that the patient must not be disturbed".'[99] Thus, for instance, the account of the treatment of glazier Joseph Mitchell's fatal injuries by leading surgeon Benjamin Brodie was incidental to the account of Mitchell's own 'spiritual tranquillity' in the face of death.[100]

For Benjamin Gregory, and doubtless many other Methodists, these evocations of the place of science in the life of faith were extraordinarily powerful. As a young man with limited cultural resources, situated in a tight-knit religious community in which the *Wesleyan-Methodist Magazine* was a central feature of social interaction, Gregory's early encounters with science were intimately connected with the Methodist scheme of practical piety. However, the dominance enjoyed by these denominational magazines in the first quarter of the nineteenth century gradually diminished as the falling price of printed matter and the development of library provision allowed increasing numbers of readers access to a range of reading matter, often including more than one periodical. The religious press itself became gradually more diversified, notably with the inception of religious newspapers like the *Record* in the late 1820s, the experiments in penny weeklies like the *Saturday Magazine* in the 1830s, and the introduction from the 1850s of mass-market family weeklies with a 'Christian tone', like the *Leisure Hour*.[101] By mid-century, denominational periodicals (most selling 2,000 copies or less) were dwarfed in popularity by these newer forms, with mass-market weeklies like *Good Words* selling in tens of thousands.[102] In this new literary market, denominational monthlies like the *Wesleyan-Methodist Magazine* contained more extensive discussions of scientific matter, offering readers accounts of current affairs distinctive of the denominations they represented.[103] However, they no longer possessed as much power to mould the reading culture of a denomination as they had enjoyed in the early decades of the century.

CHAPTER 4

Punch *and comic journalism in mid-Victorian Britain*

Richard Noakes

In 1842 the *Westminster Review* examined a new comic periodical that had apparently been established to meet the demands of a recent 'Committee of Council for Education' launched by the government for improving methods of popular instruction. According to the reviewer, the editor of this new periodical had successfully embraced 'all the moral, scientific, philosophical, political, poetical, and intellectual subjects, requiring to be newly adapted to the wants of the age'. Adopting a more austere tone, the reviewer questioned whether

criticisms on the part of a quarterly review should be confined to high-priced publications circulating exclusively among the wealthy, but having little or no influence among the masses. Let it not be said, can any good come out of Nazareth? All the good that the people at large can desire from the labours of the philosopher or man of science must reach them, if it reaches them at all, through the medium of the cheap literature of the country.

The cheap literary newcomer certainly deserved to be noticed by the *Westminster*. It displayed 'moral superiority' over comparable publications, such as the *Satirist*, the *Age*, and *John Bull*, its elevated 'wit and humour' testified to a growing 'desire for somewhat more healthful and intellectual means of pleasurable excitement than police reports', and its woodcuts demonstrated the 'improvement in the art of wood-engraving for practical purposes'.[1]

The subject of the review was *Punch: Or, the London Charivari*, a weekly that first appeared on 17 July 1841 (fig. 4.1). The *Westminster* clearly anticipated that *Punch* would play an important part in the dissemination of philosophical and scientific labours to the 'masses', because it struck a balance between 'pleasurable excitement' and intellectual stimulation. The formula worked, because *Punch* outlived most of its rivals in the competitive field of Victorian comic journalism. Although *Punch* struggled during its early years, within two decades of its launch this 3d illustrated comic

Figure 4.1. Title page of *Punch* 9 (1845). This illustrates the ways in which *Punch* was a complex space in which its fictional editor, Mr Punch, combined political, social, and scientific material for entertaining and instructing his readership. Here, Mr Punch is portrayed as a wizard in the occult 'science' of comic journalism, surrounded by some of the artefacts of his trade: a potion bottle full of 'jokes', a book of strange recipes, and eminent British politicians (including Robert Peel and Henry Brougham) crammed into specimen jars and hung from the wall. Reproduced by kind permission of Leeds University Library.

journal became one of the most talked about and respectable institutions of British literature.[2]

More has been written about *Punch* than almost any other periodical, but little attention has been paid to its scientific content.[3] Only recently have scholars begun to appreciate the complex representations of science in *Punch*. In particular, Richard Altick's magisterial account of *Punch*'s first decade illustrates how faithfully it tracked major scientific, engineering, and medical developments, and how scientific topics were used to comment on non-scientific issues. In his general study of Victorian satire and science James Paradis has surveyed *Punch*'s ironic portrayal of the increasingly abstract fruits of scientific research. James Secord's exploration of *Punch*'s response to the *Vestiges of the Natural History of Creation* (1844) helps us to understand the periodical in the overlapping metropolitan landscapes of graphic journalism and scientific spectacle. Roy Porter's study of medical illustrations shows that *Punch*'s representations of medical practitioners reflected not only an individual artist's style but also a Victorian tradition of depicting doctors 'phenotypically and physiognomically rather as the profession might have wished itself to have been seen'. Finally, my recent study of *Punch*'s portrayal of technological subjects and its deployment of technological metaphors helps us to understand the embeddedness of engineering and invention in Victorian political, social, and cultural discourses.[4]

For most historians of science *Punch* has been a handy source for documenting 'popular' reactions to scientific topics of the day, ranging from public health to new inventions.[5] They treat *Punch* as a passive *mediator*, rather than an active *medium*, of science. However, recent work on the history of nineteenth-century print culture suggests the importance of understanding *Punch* as an active producer of knowledge. Thus in his analysis of *Punch*'s great contemporary, the *Illustrated London News*, Peter Sinnema rightly urges us to treat any periodical as a 'singular discursive practice, active in the production of truth(s), and engaged with a complex array of other discourses'.[6] Studies by Roy Porter and Brian Maidment reinforce this argument by insisting that graphic prints always 'represent' or mediate historical events 'through aesthetic and gestural convention', and James Secord's *Victorian Sensation* (2002) demonstrates how much popular perceptions of controversial scientific claims owed to the way such claims were represented in illustrated periodicals.[7] Of particular importance to this chapter is Janet Browne's recent discussion of caricatures of Darwin in Victorian comic periodicals. Browne concludes with the compelling suggestion that these humorous portrayals 'are not just a transparent medium of communication, not just illustrations, but could be the actual shapers – maybe even realizers – of nineteenth-century popular thought'.[8]

This chapter attempts to understand how *Punch* functioned as a medium for producing scientific knowledge for what the *Westminster* called the 'people at large'. Concentrating on the first three decades of the periodical – a period corresponding approximately to the tenure of the first editor, Mark Lemon – it argues that *Punch's* production of science was intimately connected with a function that it shared with most weeklies – the representation of news and topical issues. What was specific to *Punch* was its use of the techniques of comic journalism to engage with and reproduce scientific material. Altick has rightly argued that *Punch* 'served as a weekly illustrated comic supplement to the London *Times*, reflecting as in a distorting mirror a selection of the week's news and jauntily editorialising on its significance'.[9] Its dependence on the ebb and flow of news stories was neatly captured by Shirley Brooks, a later editor, who boasted that *Punch* 'set its watch by the clock of *The Times*'.[10] This chapter shows how the scientific material depended on *Punch's* journalistic pulse. The contributors to *Punch* engaged with topical and sensational scientific subjects which their readers would have encountered in reading newspapers, visiting exhibitions, and listening to gossip.

Building on the work of Celina Fox, and continuing themes explored in the introduction to this book and in chapter 2, I shall initially situate *Punch* in the metropolitan world of graphic and comic journalism, and outline how its early contributors developed the periodical in order to appeal to the increasingly affluent Victorian bourgeoisie.[11] I then examine the contributors themselves and show how science figured in their backgrounds, interests, and in their weekly negotiations to produce the periodical's centrepiece – the 'large cut'. Drawing on a systematic study of the entire contents of the periodical between 1841 and 1871, I then survey the kinds of scientific material contained in *Punch*, and the literary and graphical genres deployed.[12] The journalistic preoccupations of *Punch* contributors are spectacularly reflected in its content and form. The scientific topics that *Punch* satirized would have been familiar, entertaining, or of relevance to middle-class readers, and consisted primarily of commentaries on scientific news items.

The final section details *how* different literary and graphic genres deployed by *Punch* engaged with scientific issues. I use this approach to support my central contention that *Punch's* satires on science were not intended merely to entertain readers. Instead, *Punch's* involvement with science was frequently serious, informed, and provocative. Although this material might have prompted a smile or even a laugh, it was ultimately a sober engagement with the world of science. In this sense Leslie Stephen's 1876 description of the 'greatest of modern humourists' applies to *Punch* contributors, for they often seemed to be thoroughly Puritan in their comedy, having the 'strongest perception of the serious issues which underlie our frivolous lives, the profoundest sense of the infinities which surround our petty world'.[13] The moral conscience of *Punch*, so powerfully revealed in its rants over political, religious, and social issues, also shone forth in its discussions of science.

Throughout this chapter, I shall be using 'science' as a convenient shorthand for science, technology, and medicine, and employing an inclusive definition of these related aspects of culture. The former move is not only desirable but justifiable on the grounds that in its first three decades *Punch* often referred to the enterprises and practitioners of medicine and technology as 'scientific'.[14]

THE WORLD CITY, COMIC JOURNALISM, AND *PUNCH*

In chapter 2 Jonathan Topham emphasized that London-based illustrated journals of the late Regency period drew extensively on the spectacles of the metropolitan landscape. *Punch* was no different. From 1843 to 1900 the *Punch* office was in a single-storey building at 85 Fleet Street, in the heart of London's blossoming journalistic empire. Here its writers and artists often composed their material, surrounded by the workplaces of the very professionals whose writings and deeds fuelled *Punch*'s columns – the myriad newspaper offices on Fleet Street, the Middle and Inner Temples, the Apothecaries' Hall, and the Royal College of Surgeons. From the windows of their office, *Punch*'s early contributors watched the Lord Mayor's Show and other spectacles that took place on one of London's busiest thoroughfares, and then turned these displays into cartoons and commentaries.[15] Many of these journalists learnt their trade in, or followed the examples of, the new cheap illustrated periodicals of the 1820s and 1830s which owed their success to their ability to re-present in comic form the funerals of monarchs, the processions of priests, stage dramas, displays of exotic species, exhibitions of new machines, illustrated scientific discourses, and a plethora of other sensations which drew the same London crowds who bought cheap periodicals.

London was the source of events that provided journalists with their copy, but as stressed in the introduction to this book, it also possessed the wealth, the print technologies, artisans, and readers necessary to the success of any new periodical. For the journalists, engravers, artists, and dramatists who launched *Punch* with 'no higher ambition than to put some bread on their tables', the 'World City' was the place to make a living from re-presenting the week's news and events.[16] The introduction to this book also shares with most historians of *Punch* the view that the mass-circulation illustrated periodical was a product of early nineteenth-century industrialized print cultures.[17] During the 1820s and 1830s the success of such cheap illustrated weeklies as the *Mirror of Literature* demonstrated to entrepreneurs that the new steam presses and wood-engraving techniques offered a cheap way of mass-producing weekly journals that blended pictures and text.[18] The new journals also showed the important role that scientific reporting could play in keeping a journal afloat and its team of 'common writers' in work.[19] By the time *Punch* was launched in 1841, journals such as the *Athenaeum* and the *Mirror* had helped create a growing reading audience for digests and other re-presentations of the week's often spectacular stories of scientific endeavour. For the founders of *Punch*, a journal that built its comedy on the week's news, scientific events were an increasingly important source of copy.

Punch drew on the early nineteenth-century traditions in comic journalism that are explored in the introduction. These included the weekly satirical print issued by engravers such as John Doyle (father of early *Punch* cartoonist Richard Doyle); cheap radical satirical journals of the 1810s and 1820s, such as the *Age* and *Satirist*; literary magazines with humorous content, such as *Fraser's Magazine* and *Blackwood's Edinburgh Magazine*; miscellanies that included comic material, such as the *Mirror* and *Bentley's Miscellany*; expensive journals of genteel humour including Thomas Hood's *Comic Annual* and George Cruikshank's *Comic Almanack*; and above all, the cheap satirical weeklies of the 1830s – such as *Figaro in London* (which was edited by *Punch* founders Gilbert Abbott à Beckett and Henry Mayhew), *Punch in London* (edited by leading *Punch* contributor Douglas Jerrold), and the Paris-based *Le Charivari*. Some of the commonest literary and graphic genres found in *Punch* were stock aspects of these earlier genres of periodical publishing: droll commentary on the week's political and social events, literary and theatrical gossip, parodies of literary serials, cartoons, humorous poems and songs, puns, jokes and 'ephemera', and vignette illustrations. Other aspects of the periodical had important precedents: for example, the fictional editor, Mr Punch, was yet another borrowing from the famous, genial, and occasionally irascible fairground character, and the notion of a fictional editor itself had been used successfully in the early years of *Blackwood's*. Likewise, the double-column format and division of the periodical into various 'departments' had been used in *Figaro in London* while *Punch*'s subtitle cleverly exploited the success of *Le Charivari*. *Punch*'s strategies for satirizing science were also not without precedent. For example, its carica- tures of statesmen as physicians and grotesque animals, its spoof reports of scientists pursuing useless trivia about the natural world, and its humorous advertisements for absurdly chimerical engineering schemes were familiar to readers of *Bentley's Miscellany*, William Hone's *Political Showman at Home* (1821), and Cruikshank's *Comic Almanack*, which themselves drew upon standard techniques of scientific satire developed in such celebrated works as Thomas Shadwell's *Virtuoso* (1676), and the *Memoirs of the Extraordinary Life, Works, and Discoveries of Martinus Scriblerus* (1714).[20]

Despite its obvious reliance on earlier forms of comic journalism, *Punch* contained greater variety than most humorous journals of the 1830s: for ex- ample, greater flexibility of page layout was used, as well as a larger range of fonts, and more illustrations.[21] As we shall see, representations of scientific events, and in particular spectacular scientific events, helped achieve this va- riety. However, by the 1850s the layout had become more standardized, but by then *Punch* was established as a British institution and it was no longer necessary to attract readers by experimenting with the format. What chiefly distinguished *Punch* from its predecessors, and what secured its long-term success, was the elevated tone of its humour. As the previously quoted re- viewer in the *Westminster* recognized, *Punch*'s 'moral superiority' set it apart from earlier satirical papers. By the time *Punch* was founded the older and vulgar traditions of comic journalism were dying out, not least because, as Altick suggests, 'a certain climate of propriety, reasonably pervasive though hardly universal, had settled over the court, aristocracy, and the political establishment'.[22] The chief upholders of this new climate of respectability – the middle class – were growing in size and wealth, and they were thus increasingly important consumers of literature. It was to this class that Cruikshank and other early nineteenth-century purveyors of radical print satire increasingly directed their energies, moving away from what Marcus Wood calls the 'confrontational or violently subversive' nature of the print satire towards the 'whimsical and charming social satire' that would become the staple diet of 'respectable Victorian journals'.[23] When *Punch*'s first ed- itor Mark Lemon reminisced that his journal survived by 'keeping to the gentlemanly view of things', he was underlining that its success depended on supplying its bourgeois, largely metropolitan, and predominantly male readers with the kind of humour they increasingly wanted – less vulgar, less personal, more genteel, and more focused on general character types.[24] *Punch*'s shift from the older and more vulgar traditions of comic journalism was not immediate: indeed, during its first decade, the politically turbulent 1840s, it often looked back to those earlier traditions and articulated its political and reformist missions most emphatically. By the mid-1850s, however, this harsher material had largely disappeared and *Punch* had fully accepted its role as a respectable family comic paper, which it retained throughout its mid- and late-Victorian zenith.

This change in tone is reflected in the scientific material that *Punch* carried. Compare, for example, how *Punch* dealt with scientific societies in its early years and in the early 1870s. In the early 1840s, it published a stream of potent satires on the British Association for the Advancement of Science and the British and Foreign Institute. Indeed, *Punch*'s ridicule of the lamentable activities of what it called the 'British and Foreign Destitute' and its *ad hominem* swipes at the Institute's founder, James Silk Buckingham, embroiled it in fierce journalistic controversy.[25] Some twenty-seven years later, *Punch* writers and artists had developed much more respect and even admiration for scientific societies. Thus the 1871 British Association meeting prompted a lengthy poem in which comic descriptions of William Thomson's presidential address were balanced by a serious-toned challenge to Thomson's notion that terrestrial life originated in meteors.[26] The tone of the *visual* representations of scientific subjects also underwent a gradual refinement. This transformation is powerfully shown when we contrast the way medical practitioners were portrayed by leading *Punch* artists of the early 1840s and 1860s. Representative examples are John Leech's 1842 caricature of a drunken medical student (fig. 4.2) and George Du Maurier's 1865 more boldly drawn and 'realistic' cut of a woman physician (fig. 4.3) which highlight the broader trend towards a more genteel visual humour.

Unlike many of its rivals and imitators in the competitive field of comic journalism, *Punch* was, from late 1842, backed by the highly successful printers William Bradbury and Frederick Evans. Not only were Bradbury and Evans innovators in woodcut techniques and steam printing, thus enabling the rapid mass production of illustrated journals, but their substantial capital also enabled contributors to experiment with the periodical's content and format.[27] This flexibility enabled *Punch* to adapt itself to the preoccupations of a predominantly male, middle-class, and metropolitan readership. Indeed, *Punch*'s success owed much to the ability of its contributors to make readers laugh at themselves, an achievement that depended on the culture shared between producers and readers. Thus they drew on a common experience of, say, botanical specimen collecting on holiday, and on a shared knowledge, via reports in the *Times*, of quackery

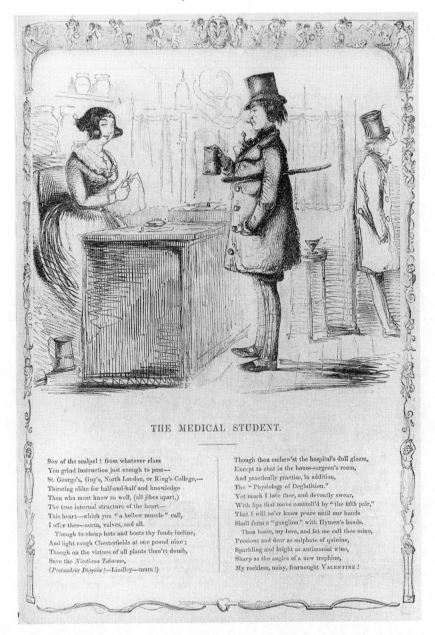

THE MEDICAL STUDENT.

Son of the scalpel! from whatever class
You grind instruction just enough to pass—
St. George's, Guy's, North London, or King's College,—
Thirsting alike for half-and-half and knowledge
Thou who must know so well, (all jibes apart,)
The true internal structure of the heart—
This heart—which you "a hollow muscle" call,
I offer thee—aorta, valves, and all.

Though to cheap hats and boots thy funds incline,
And light rough Chesterfields at one pound nine ;
Though on the virtues of all plants thou'rt dumb,
Save the *Nicotiana Tabacum,*
(*Pentandria Digynia !*—Lindley—mum !)

Though thou eschew'st the hospital's dull gloom,
Except to chat in the house-surgeon's room,
And practically practise, in addition,
The "Physiology of Deglutition."
Yet much I love thee, and devoutly swear,
With lips that move controll'd by "the fifth pair,"
That I will ne'er know peace until our hands
Shall form a "ganglion" with Hymen's bands.
Then haste, my love, and let me call thee mine,
Precious and dear as sulphate of quinine,
Sparkling and bright as antimonial wine,
Sharp as the angles of a new trephine,
My reckless, noisy, fearnought VALENTINE !

Figure 4.2. [John Leech], 'The Medical Student', *Punch* 2 (1842), 71. Reproduced with the kind permission of the Syndics of Cambridge University Library.

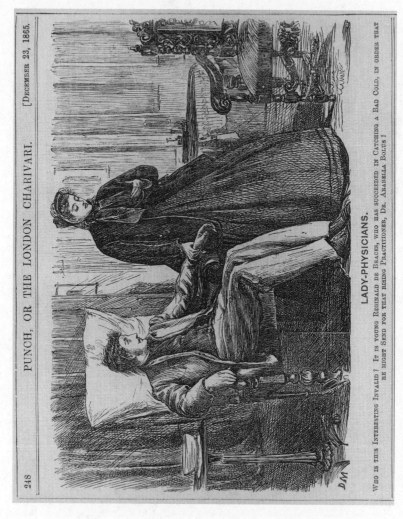

PUNCH, OR THE LONDON CHARIVARI. [DECEMBER 23, 1865.

LADY-PHYSICIANS.

WHO IS THIS INTERESTING INVALID? IT IS YOUNG REGINALD DE BRACES, WHO HAS SUCCEEDED IN CATCHING A BAD COLD, IN ORDER THAT HE MIGHT SEND FOR THAT RISING PRACTITIONER, DR. ARABELLA BOLUS!

Figure 4.3. 'D. M.' [George Du Maurier], 'Lady-Physicians', *Punch* 49 (1865), 248. Reproduced with the kind permission of the Syndics of Cambridge University Library.

and second-class railway travel, and of lectures at the Royal Polytechnic Institution. This is not to suggest that all middle-class readers enjoyed laughing at themselves in the periodical. Humour shaded into brutality in *Punch*'s use of crude stereotypes in portraying Irishmen, Jews, Roman Catholics, and Americans.[28] Neither did it please certain individuals – notably, the Irish statesmen Daniel O'Connell, the journalist Samuel Carter Hall, and the impresario Alfred Bunn – who were subjected to highly personal and defamatory criticism.[29] Even regular subscribers occasionally found some of its material in poor taste and even objectionable. For example, in 1861 Charles Darwin told Thomas Henry Huxley that he 'did not think' the *Punch* poem 'Monkeyana', describing the controversy between Huxley and Richard Owen over man's simian ancestry, 'very good'.[30] There were undoubtedly many literate Victorians who eschewed *Punch* entirely, its rougher edges limiting its appeal to what Susan and Asa Briggs call 'a series of segments' within the Victorian reading public.[31]

SCIENCE AROUND THE *PUNCH* TABLE

Punch may not have appealed to certain segments of Victorian society, but its mid-Victorian circulation was nevertheless impressive for a comic journal. In the early 1860s, for example, *Punch* was selling approximately 60,000 copies each week, compared with the 20,000 copies of *Fun* and the 10,000 of *Tomahawk*, two relatively new comic weeklies.[32] Commentators on *Punch* from the Victorian period to the present agree that the success of the periodical depended greatly on the political and moral character of its satire, but also on the friendships and cordial professional relationships between the periodical's writers, artists, and publishers.[33] Despite differences in social background, personality, and attitude, the periodical's producers became an important British literary community and their informal weekly meetings to discuss the week's 'large cut' functioned as an exclusive club to which many aspiring litterateurs sought invitations. Contributors brought to *Punch* their skills in journalistic reporting, editing daily and weekly papers, writing stage farces, poetry, and novels, and illustrating books and periodicals. They moved in the overlapping worlds of literature, fine arts, the theatre, exhibitions, and pageants. They poked fun at social convention and class, and inveighed against such vices as fraudulence, hypocrisy, and obscurantism. Their periodical was strong on politics and dominated by discussion of the celebrated, notorious, and newsworthy *men* of the day – thus making *Punch* a periodical written largely by men for a predominantly male audience.

The 'Punch Brotherhood' was weakened by bitter rivalries – notably between Thackeray and Jerrold – and occasional disruptions (for example, the Catholic Richard Doyle resigned in 1850 owing to *Punch*'s waspish satires on papal aggression), but Mark Lemon was generally successful in engendering harmony among *Punch* staff. Changes in the group, however, affected the tone of the periodical. The changes between the 1840s and early 1860s noted above were in part due to the loss, by either death or resignation, of many of the initial contributors including Jerrold, Thackeray, Richard Doyle, Gilbert Abbott à Beckett, and Albert Smith. The evolution of the magazine's content led Edmund Yates, the editor of *Temple Bar*, to assert in 1863 that *Punch* had lost the 'wit, humour, and pointed sarcasm of former years' and had degenerated into 'sheer, wilful nonsense'.[34] But its sustained circulation figures suggest that by the mid-1860s a new type of reader enjoyed the subtle social wit of Shirley Brooks, the grotesque cartoons of Du Maurier, the supreme draughtsmanship of Tenniel's political cuts, and the work of the other rising stars of mid-Victorian *Punch*.

Despite the recognition that *Punch*'s brotherhood was crucial to the success of the periodical, little attention has been paid to the question of how this social group negotiated the contents of each week's issue. Although most *Punch* articles were either anonymous or written from the perspective of 'Mr. Punch', ledger books held in the *Punch* library in London enable us to identify writers and artists and thus deepen our analysis of this literary group.[35] A preliminary survey of these ledgers supports the argument that contributors with medical and scientific backgrounds were the foremost producers of the periodical's commentaries on science.[36] For example, John Leech, Albert Smith, and Percival Leigh had been fellow students at St Bartholomew's Hospital, and they contributed most of the cartoons (in the case of Leech) and texts (in the cases of Smith and Leigh) on medical students, medical legislation, and quackery.[37] Contributors who lacked a scientific background constituted a smaller but not insignificant portion of the creators of *Punch*'s scientific content. For these writers and artists, information about science was just as accessible as gossip about politics and fashion, and could likewise be satirized. A good example is *Punch*'s second editor, Shirley Brooks, who abandoned a legal career for journalism in the early 1840s, and subsequently earned an income as a parliamentary and travel reporter on the *Morning Chronicle* and as a writer of comic journalism and stage farces. In 1851 he began writing for *Punch* where he published satirical poems and news commentaries pertaining to science, gleaning information from reading newspapers, hobnobbing with scientific personalities, and visiting metropolitan sites of scientific activity.

His biographer records that, in the 1870s, Brooks developed an acquaintance with the zoologist Thomas Henry Huxley and the science writer John
George Wood. He also attended the Royal Geographical Society's debate
on the expedition to observe the transit of Venus in 1882, and dined with
the explorer Henry Morton Stanley and the biologist St George Jackson
Mivart. Having read Richard Owen's January 1874 letter to the *Times* dis-
missing news of the discovery of a dodo, he scribbled the comic poem,
'The Dodo Demolished', which subsequently appeared in *Punch*.[38] Brooks
was one of many *Punch* contributors who accumulated a stock of material
for scientific journalism through such contacts, and whose careers illustrate
the overlap between Grub Street and scientific London.

Another insight into the weekly business of producing a comic journal
is afforded by the diary of Henry Silver, who recorded his experiences at
the weekly *Punch* dinners between 1858 and 1870.[39] The discussions, dis-
agreements, and anecdotes he documented illustrate that *Punch* men were
surprisingly knowledgeable about scientific developments and frequently
engaged with them intelligently and penetratingly. Around the large deal
table, where food, wine, cigars, jottings, and newspapers circulated, Mark
Lemon recounted his meetings with George Stephenson, 'Professor' Percival
Leigh 'lectured' on phrenology, and others pondered such dramatic news
as Robert Fitzroy's suicide.[40] These interests and passions were reflected
in the serious and informed way in which *Punch* contributors frequently
engaged with scientific news.

How *Punch* contributors worked together to turn scientific news into
an article is illustrated by the following extract from Silver's account of the
'large cut' meeting of 9 April 1862:

S[hirley] B[rooks] proposes Gladstone making a house of cards. But all agree that
the Iron Ships question is the one. So take his Vulcan and Neptune notion of last
week, which J[ohn] L[eech] modifies into sea-nymphs arming Neptune as John
Bull. P[ercival] L[eigh] proposes shoeing the Sea horses, but negatived. M[ark]
L[emon] suggests Britannia in Crinoline – but this repeats this week's 'Jack in
Iron'.[41]

For most of those present at this dinner, Gladstone's budget speech was
far less important than the government's recent decision to save the Royal
Navy by replacing its vulnerable wooden ships with state-of-the-art ironclads. Brooks's, Leech's, and Leigh's proposals were soon rejected, but *Punch*
contributors' support for iron ships was so strong that they adopted an alternative representation of the anticipated 'metallic' state of the Royal Navy –
a cartoon of several sailors dancing below deck in suits of armour.[42]

The deliberations over iron ships highlight the journalistic preoccupations and skills of *Punch*'s writers and artists – their insatiable drive to represent topical and spectacular issues, and their selection of topics that were appropriate for 'the stage of *Punch*'s theatre' (to cite Mark Lemon's phrase).[43] Silver's observations document the immersion of *Punch* contributors in worlds of mid-Victorian comedy and metropolitan science. In bridging these worlds they drew on their mastery of the comic literary and graphical techniques well understood and enjoyed by Victorian readers, and on their acquaintance with contemporary science and scientists. In discussing iron ships they exploited stock aspects of Victorian comedy by articulating many false congruities and unlikely associations. The comic effect of juxtaposing symbols of, on the one hand, the mythological, angelic, and conservative, and on the other, the novel, material, and progressive, underpinned the idea of Britannia in a crinoline. As Leslie Stephen commented in his 1876 analysis of humour, the world was regarded as a 'farce – a melancholy farce, indeed, for otherwise there would be no contradiction – but a farce where the sublime must never be separated from its shadow, the ridiculous'.[44] Later in this chapter, we will see that Stephen's analysis of farce applies to most articles in *Punch*.

PUNCH'S KIND OF SCIENCE

The foregoing analysis of events at the *Punch* table shows how the comic journalistic goals and interests of the periodical's contributors shaped the content of one article. This section takes a much broader approach to the question. It examines broad patterns in the scientific content of the first thirty years of *Punch* and looks at the way in which these trends reflect *Punch* contributors' preoccupations with comedy, topicality, spectacle, the vicissitudes of social, political, and cultural life, and the heroic, ingenious, hypocritical, and corrupt aspects of the Victorian landscape. This section also identifies and analyzes the locations of scientific material within the periodical format of the leading Victorian comic journal. Unlike many other topics covered in *Punch*, such as the long-running 'Punch's Essence of Parliament' or the regular 'Fine Arts' articles that appeared in the early 1840s, there were no dedicated scientific columns. Instead, scientific material was spread over a wide variety of literary and graphic genres, including commentaries on scientific news reported elsewhere, spoof reports on science, mock proceedings of learned societies, pseudonymous letters, poems, songs, large and small 'cuts', burlesques of serialized fiction and stage dramas, illustrated vignettes and illuminated letters, jokes, puns, and other column-filling 'ephemera', and spoof advertisements (many of which poked fun at the very kinds of new medical treatments and contraptions that *Punch* advertised on its wrappers) (fig. 4.4).

In *Punch* the news commentary was the most prevalent genre for discussing science; of 6,200 'scientific' articles published during the first three decades, there were 2,200 news commentaries, compared with 720 cartoons, 520 comic poems, 400 mock letters, 260 spoof advertisements, and 180 droll songs (all figures being approximate). Scientific topics rarely featured in the weekly centrepiece – the 'large cut' – and they were even less likely to appear in such other coveted places as on the title pages of bound volumes. Nonetheless, the foregoing figures give powerful support to the argument that *Punch*'s scientific material – like so much of its other content – was strongly dependent on what was being reported, displayed, or gossiped about elsewhere. A 'scientific' article also often combined literary genres – for instance, a vignette illustration that prefaced a poetic parody, a spoof news report that was followed by a pseudonymous letter, or a poem that was in fact a commentary on an actual item in a newspaper. Few 'scientific' articles in *Punch* existed in isolation and were usually in dialogue with articles appearing in the same or earlier issues, or with entirely separate publications. For example, an 1855 poem describing Faraday's analysis of the Thames water was positioned next to John Leech's large cut of Faraday confronting a gruesome 'Father Thames' emerging from his equally filthy river.[45] Less straightforward was the 1853 spoof prospectus for 'The Locomotive Table Company'. This explained that following proof of 'the facility with which Tables can be moved by means of a Company, through mere volition, after the hands of the Company have been placed for a short time on the Table', the 'Company' believed it could 'supersede Steam Engines on Railways' by placing a table 'where the engine is at present, in front of the train' and having 'a certain number of the Directors of the Company . . . seated at a board in connexion with it; which will insure that additional guarantee of safety so much wanted on railroads'.[46] The comedy depended on an explicit reference to the motive force supposedly exerted by individuals participating in 'table-turning' – a practice much derided in *Punch* – but an implicit allusion to a John Leech cartoon published a few weeks earlier, showing a proposed method of reducing railway accidents: tying two railway company directors to the front of a steam locomotive operated by their firm.[47]

In general, *Punch* focused on those scientific topics that its contributors thought would entertain and provoke a respectable male and metropolitan readership. This audience was particularly aware of those areas of science

Figure 4.4. The wrappers of *Punch* for 14 April 1849 contain puffs for various medical products including the 'Balsam Copaiba' patent organic capsules for remedying nausea (in the left column), a textbook on hydropathy and an 'Invisible Spine Supporter' (in the middle column), and the 'Pomade Depurative' for curing baldness and the 'Amandine' hand-softening treatment (in the right column). Reproduced by permission of Richard Noakes.

that were prominently discussed or displayed elsewhere, or that possessed
general intellectual interest or had direct implications for health, security,
and daily life. *Punch* often selected for comment scientific issues that were
newsworthy; thus a cluster of articles might closely track the development
of a scientific event familiar to most readers. For example, the 1855 cluster
of articles on military technology followed rumours concerning a secret
weapon devised by Lord Dundonald to defeat the Russian Fleet in the
Crimea; and the 1861 cluster on animal behaviour followed the French-
American explorer Paul Du Chaillu's claims regarding the aggressive behaviour of African gorillas. Scientific articles rarely contained just scientific
material. Indeed, the comedy of *Punch* often depended on mixing incongruous subjects, such as statesmen and medical quackery, steam locomotives
and spiritualism, or civil servants and the behaviour of entozoa.

Particularly prominent among the 'pure' scientific topics discussed
in *Punch*'s first three decades were animal behaviour and development,
zoology, astronomy, analytical and industrial chemistry, human development, natural history, and electricity. These topics impinged most extensively on the lives of readers, either because they were intellectually accessible
or stimulating, or because they possessed implications for the readers' daily
routines. Natural history, for example, was often discussed in relation to
amateur collecting activities; analytical chemistry frequently occurred in the
context of polluted water; and electricity typically appeared in discussions
of telegraphy and new electrical machines. The coverage of the physical sciences, and the more technical aspects of all the sciences, was unsurprisingly
small for a journal that sought to hold the attention of non-specialist intelligent readers. Indeed, the most common cause for discussing such abstract
scientific issues was to poke fun at scientific practitioners' obscurantism.

Medical and technological topics were far more prevalent in *Punch* than
the 'pure' sciences, let alone the technically more demanding scientific subjects. This concentration lends further support to the claim that *Punch*
was mainly interested in those scientific topics that were most familiar
or relevant to readers. Among the most common subjects of discussion
were the fair and foul deeds of medical practitioners (physicians, surgeons,
nurses, and quacks), new medical legislation, novel remedies and other
treatments, questions of public health, sanitation, and disease, railways
and steam locomotives (especially as the cause of commercial manias, accidents, and environmental damage), ironclads and other new weapons of
war, the electric telegraph, steamships, balloons, spectacular new engineering structures, and the ingenious and disingenuous accomplishments of
inventors.

As we shall see throughout the remainder of this chapter, the notorious interests of *Punch* contributors in anything that exposed oddities of social convention and class or which smacked of fraudulence, obscurantism, and hypocrisy also informed their choice of scientific topics for discussion. Thus, there are plenty of humorous articles reflecting on the possible advantages of steam locomotives and the electric telegraph to the routines of political and domestic life, the inability of rustics, old sea-salts, and cockneys to come to terms with new inventions, and the curious behaviour and language of delegates at meetings of scientific societies. Similarly, the apparently shady individuals whom *Punch* contributors denounced so passionately at their weekly dinners were targeted for much sober-toned criticism in print. Quacks, dissolute medical students, mercenary railway company directors, inventors of dubious machines, astrologers, and spirit-rappers were caricatured and demonized for much the same reason that *Punch* contributors inveighed against greedy aldermen, misguided statesmen, hypocritical journalists, avaricious merchants, and corrupt priests.[48]

These explanations of *Punch*'s choice of scientific topics also account for the scientific practitioners, places, and publications featured in articles and illustrations. Although patriotism may explain the repeated references to such British scientific worthies as Isaac Newton, Edward Jenner, and George Stephenson, at least as much material was devoted to scientific personalities who would have been familiar to metropolitan readers, such as Richard Owen, Michael Faraday, Charles Darwin, Charles Babbage, and George Airy. *Punch* also covered lesser-known scientific personalities who burst into the news for a variety of savoury or unsavoury reasons. Thus, there are a plethora of articles on, or allusions to, James Glaisher and Henry Coxwell and their heroic balloon ascents, David Boswell Reid and his much-ridiculed apparatus for ventilating the Palace of Westminster, and Cowper Coles and his armoured turret for iron ships that was, according to *Punch*, shamefully neglected by the Admiralty. *Punch*'s engagements with stories of these lesser-known personalities did not simply reflect the news, but actively contributed to the fame or notoriety of these individuals. *Punch*'s frequent allusions to the Zoological Gardens at Regent's Park, to the Crystal Palace, London's hospitals, the Royal Colleges of Surgeons and Physicians, the Royal Polytechnic Institution, the Royal Greenwich Observatory, 'Wyld's Great Globe', and the Social Science Congress, again reflect the interests of the periodical's largely metropolitan audience. References to now-forgotten sites of spectacular new engineering developments, filthy workhouses or polluting factories, or bird-slaughtering gun clubs, also underline *Punch*'s close concern with institutions that might improve or harm the minds and bodies of readers.

References to published works included many to new scientific books (notably the *Vestiges of the Natural History of Creation* (1844), Darwin's *Origin of Species* (1859), and Du Chaillu's *Explorations and Adventures in Equatorial Africa* (1861)). Yet in comparison with the 300-odd references to scientific monographs, pamphlets, and other published works in the period from 1841 to 1871, there were nearly 700 references to scientific periodicals (notably the *Lancet*) or scientific discussions that appeared in general periodicals. Thus, as far as science is concerned, *Punch* drew more heavily on periodicals than on books. This analysis also supports Brooks's contention that *Punch* 'set its watch by the clock of *The Times*' since approximately one third of the references to scientific materials in periodicals were to articles in the leading London daily. The dialogue between *Punch* and other newspapers was, of course, two way, as illustrated by the occasionally stinging exchanges between *Punch* and such dailies as the *Morning Post*, and more flatteringly, the *Times*'s regular inclusion of small extracts from *Punch*.[49] Although *Punch* often made explicit the sources on which it drew, references were sometimes merely implicit. This is powerfully illustrated by the 'Monkeyana' poem which was published in *Punch* on 18 May 1861. The poem ended with the non-referenced phrase, '"To twice slay the slain"', which many readers will have recognized as the last line in a letter that Huxley had written to the *Athenaeum* five days earlier.[50] Thus, the comprehensibility of *Punch*'s scientific articles, like the rest of its material, often depended on readers' familiarity with a broad range of periodicals.

TWISTING SCIENTIFIC NEWS

Although a survey of the contents and literary and graphic forms of science in *Punch* is valuable, we also need to appreciate the complex ways in which individual scientific articles functioned. This section takes a closer look at several 'scientific' texts and illustrations from *Punch*'s first three decades. I shall explore how news was re-presented and adapted for entertainment and instruction, and how science was appropriated in order to enable *Punch* to survive in the cut-throat world of mid-Victorian Grub Street. Throughout the following discussion, we will see that *Punch*'s engagement with scientific topics was not superficial. It depended on and reinforced sober and often profound perceptions concerning the places and uses of science in Victorian culture.

Remaking scientific news

Punch's commentaries on scientific news varied considerably in tone, length, and content. After presenting readers with the outlines of a scientific news item (usually from a named source) or quotations from another publication, contributors to *Punch* typically added expressions of anger, adulation, bewilderment, or amusement, often with allusions to themes already articulated by the periodical. The following example from an 1858 instalment of the 'Essence of Parliament' illustrates how political debates bearing on scientific topics provided ample material for *Punch* to vent its spleen about the more reprehensible aspects of science. Here *Punch* reminded readers that William Cowper's Medical Reform Bill was being read for the second time in the House of Commons, but then pointed out that '*Mr. Punch* intends to move a clause empowering a Magistrate to order any Advertising Quack to be flogged, and branded with a Q', explaining that: 'Nothing short of this will stop the murderous system of heartless traders in misfortune.'[51] The efforts of other scientific practitioners to treat the body politic were represented with much more warmth. In 1855, for example, *Punch* praised Michael Faraday's use of analytical chemistry to address one of the most intractable public health problems – the foul state of the River Thames. After the savant published a letter in the *Times* announcing his discovery of myriad unwholesome constituents in the capital's river, *Punch* hailed the letter as a 'CHEMICAL work of small size and great importance' that would eventually 'effect a saving of life still greater than that which has resulted from his predecessor's [Humphry Davy's] safety-lamp'.[52]

Punch was far less impressed with individuals who, from reports in other periodicals, appeared to be hoodwinking the British public with their apparently dubious inventions supported by unsound arguments. On these occasions *Punch* adopted its idiosyncratic mode of arbitration. In October 1857, for example, it was so puzzled by a description in the *Times* of John de la Haye's method for submerging submarine cables that it compared the invention to 'the devices of the Laputan sages'. The project involved coating telegraph lines with a mysterious compound which delayed the descent of the cables to the sea floor, but *Punch* pointed out that whatever the nature of the compound, it would be washed off by the Atlantic's large waves. *Punch* sought to expose technological fraud with comedy, and suggested that de la Haye's proposal was possible, but only if impracticable conditions were met – the cables should be coated with vast quantities of 'Iced cream' and the Atlantic should be dead calm.[53] The theme of obscurantism appeared again in 1865 when *Punch* noted that a recent issue of the *Mechanics' Magazine* contained a puzzling extract from the French scientific periodical *Cosmos* describing how a savant had calculated that 'the mechanical equivalent of the total light of the sun' was '1,239 septillion of "bougies"'. This news item was neither 'lucid' nor useful because when 'arithmetical athletes . . . distort themselves by piling up these absurd heaps of millions and billions . . . no one cares about giving himself the trouble, either to verify, or disprove them'.[54] *Punch* contributors were, of course, not themselves exempt from abusing language since they exploited new scientific terms as rich sources of puns and word play. For example, a 'Science Gossip' column of 1868 announced that 'A Scientific Ghost-story will shortly appear in fortnightly numbers, founded on Spectrum Analysis'.[55]

It is hardly surprising that a periodical so preoccupied with news and comedy should contain many spoof news reports. These satirical reports presented a newsworthy or familiar topic from a new and comic perspective, typically by associating the topic with other, and often incongruous, themes. As the following examples illustrate, science was often the primary topic of discussion or was woven into a report of what was an ostensibly non-scientific issue. An astonishing range of topics was featured in the 'The Irish Yahoos' appearing in mid-December 1861. This far-fetched report described a rowdy meeting at the 'Pope's Head' where the 'Irish Yahoos' had convened to express 'joy and exultation' at England's imminent involvement in the American Civil War and the anticipated large number of casualties. The mob was 'chaired' by the appropriately named 'O'DONOGHYAHOO' whose cries of abuse against the English were 'hailed with frantic howling and peals of convulsive laughter, like that of a multitude of idiots'. After gloating on the 'calamities they expect[ed] for England' the meeting ended with 'several rounds of hurroos for the POPE' and then 'yelping, whining, and howling, after the manner of the canine species, to which the Yahoo is nearly allied, being a creature between the mongrel and the baboon'.[56] This 'report' featured the common stereotype of the Irish as wild animals but here *Punch*'s racism was linked, implicitly and explicitly, with myriad other themes including Jonathan Swift's bestial 'Yahoos', Britain's growing hostility to America, the evils of Roman Catholicism, and, most significantly, to Paul du Chaillu's recent account of the aggressive nature of African gorillas and Darwinian theories of man's simian ancestry.[57] Despite its obvious comic format, this spoof news report powerfully illustrates *Punch*'s active participation in debates over the possible meanings of science.

News of non-scientific events provided further opportunities for *Punch* contributors to analyze the cultural uses of science. This was particularly common during discussion of alleged miraculous and supernatural phenomena. For example, *Punch* contributors seized on occasional reports of the apparent liquefaction of the blood of Saint Januarius in Naples. In October 1859, for instance, it insisted that this 'so-called "miracle"' could be achieved with greater rapidity and 'dead certainty' by 'science', using steam, bellows, or a hot poker. Moreover, the alleged simultaneous 'appearance' of the Januarius miracle and the appearance of the saint's blood in Puzzoli (where the saint was beheaded) could be 'guaranteed' by connecting Naples and Puzzoli by electricity. Belief in such miracles was 'clearly incompatible with scientific knowledge' because 'In places where the steam-engine has never been inspected, and where electric telegraphs are utterly undreamt of, their agencies might readily affect a so-thought "miracle", and deceive the eyesights blinded by the darkened superstitions which are the stock-in-trade and groundwork of the Romish Church.'[58] On such occasions, when the social order was threatened by tricks perpetrated by cunning priests or other charlatans, *Punch* writers penned forceful endorsements of the superiority of science. Science and engineering could be recruited to reinforce cultural contrasts made more explicitly elsewhere in the periodical. Drawing on such grand spectacles as the Great Exhibition of 1851, contributors to *Punch* revelled in the marvels of science and engineering which, they considered, not only enhanced national pride and confirmed their faith in progress, but also demonstrated Britain's superiority over other nations and the supremacy of Protestants over Catholics.

Illustrating science/politics

Illustrations were crucial to the overall appeal of *Punch* and to the variety it offered its readers (fig. 4.5). Ranging from tiny illustrated vignettes to the week's large cut, *Punch*'s illustrations represent some of the most complex engagements with science in the periodical. Articles were often illustrated by visual vignettes or 'illuminated' letters that evoked comic scenes. Thus a sober 1861 discussion of the sensational trial of a pharmacist was headed by a cartoon showing a quack about to introduce a dubious-looking tablet into the mouth of a frightened patient.[59] Representations of science were often made in the small engravings, which occupied between a quarter and half a page. Like other *Punch* material, these illustrations often explored the comic impact of the eccentric world of science and scientists on social convention. This is succinctly illustrated in Leech's 'Quite a Novelty' of 1854, which shows an 'Amiable Experimentalist' sitting down to dinner with friends in a room whose walls are adorned with pictures of fungi. Much to the distaste of his guests the eccentric savant enthusiastically provides them with technical and stomach-churning descriptions of the mushrooms they are all about to eat.[60]

THE EFFECTS OF A HEARTY DINNER AFTER VISITING THE ANTEDILUVIAN DEPARTMENT AT THE CRYSTAL PALACE.

Figure 4.5. Scientific spectacle adds variety to *Punch*. The striking feature of this page of *Punch* is an illustration by Henry R. Howard of 'The Effects of a Hearty Dinner after Visiting the Antediluvian Department at the Crystal Palace': *Punch* 28 (1855), 50. Reproduced by kind permission of Leeds University Library.

Other *Punch* artists were more renowned for using caricature to reinforce the dangers, ingenuity, and sheer drama of the personalities, practices, and products of science. This is evident in an 1845 illustration of what *Punch* thought Great Britain would look like in 1847: developing its cynical view of the 'benefits' conferred by expanding the railway network, it showed the country entirely covered with railroads.[61] Other examples are Du Maurier's satire on Darwinian evolution portraying a zookeeper's nightmare in which the different species of animals have exchanged heads, and Charles Bennett's busy cartoons of the mid 1860s that caricatured delegates at British Association meetings as the subjects of their papers.[62] In all these cases, the standard techniques of graphic satire – exaggeration, reversal, and incongruous juxtaposition – were used to spectacular effect. Thus in one of his cartoons Bennett drew scientists with large heads atop emaciated bodies, whilst riding, clutching, and embodying the instruments of their trade: the optical expert David Brewster rode a pair of spectacles, the chemist William Crookes upheld, and balanced on, flasks containing his new carbolic spray, and the astrophysicist William Huggins was shown clutching a chemical balance and jar, and sporting an enormous spectroscope prism for a head, the symbols of the optical-chemical approach to celestial objects (fig. 4.6). In a later cartoon Bennett further exploited reports of the British Association drama by showing Thomas Henry Huxley and Richard Owen locked in an affectionate embrace – thus satirizing their widely known antipathy.

Bennett's caricatures are significant in the early history of *Punch* because they were among the few illustrations that depicted identifiable scientific personalities. Rarely were individual scientists portrayed in the week's large cut. Savants who did enjoy such prominent representation – including Richard Owen and Michael Faraday – would previously have been encountered by readers in illustrated periodicals, scientific memoirs, exhibitions of portraits, photographic shops, and public lectures.[63] In contrast to the 1840s, scientific personalities had by the 1860s become far more familiar to the public through illustrated media and public spectacle. Bennett, in particular, exploited this increased visibility of scientists in his cartoons.

Scientific subjects did not often feature in the large weekly cut, the exceptions being mesmerism, railway mania, the Dover–Calais and Atlantic submarine telegraphs, the disease-ridden Thames, solar eclipses, Armstrong heavy artillery, the controversy over gorillas and man's simian ancestry, the hatching of python eggs at the Zoological Gardens, and the Cattle Plague.[64] These topics were chosen for their current newsworthiness – thus displacing less exciting political and social subjects – and because some of

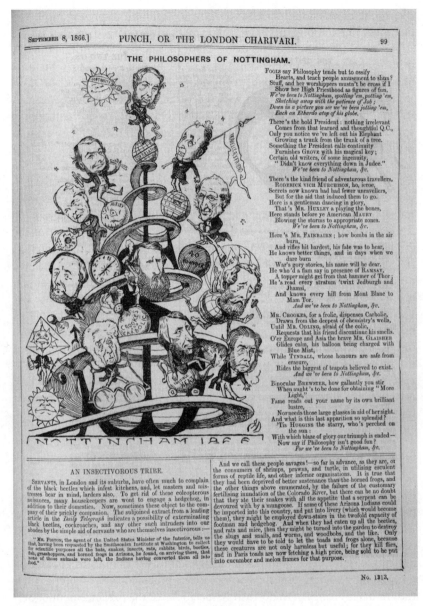

Figure 4.6. 'C. H. B.' [Charles H. Bennett], 'The Philosophers of Nottingham', *Punch* 51 (1866), 99. Reproduced by permission of the Syndics of Cambridge University Library.

them were visual enough to make for powerful graphic re-presentation. Yet, like most illustrations in *Punch*, there are plenty of large cuts that defy a straightforward distinction between 'scientific' and 'non-scientific'. Indeed, it is the cuts that blend scientific and non-scientific material that illustrate most powerfully how *Punch* contributors developed commentaries on non-scientific topics by association with scientific subjects, and vice versa. A striking example is John Tenniel's 'Another Eclipse for India', a large cut appearing in *Punch* for 5 September 1868 (fig. 4.7).[65] The main caption would have reminded readers of the astronomical event of the year – the solar eclipse of 18 August that was best observed from India. The cartoon, the rest of the caption, and, above all, a poem appearing a few pages after the cut, would have helped readers to understand the allusions in the illustration and reflect on the similarity between recent astronomical and political events.[66] The cartoon shows the allegorical figure of India crouching in fear of the shadow of a man wearing an enormous cocked hat, and John Lawrence, the Viceroy and Governor-General of India, who reassures 'India' that she need not fear her 'light' being extinguished by the other 'eclipse' because it is only being caused by Lord Mayo, who had recently been announced as Lawrence's successor and who promised to continue Lawrence's record of raising the socio-economic status of India by developing its resources and improving its administration. Tenniel's cartoon created analogies between the sun and India, and between the moon and Mayo, and however much readers may have dismissed such analogies as the product of a comic artistic imagination, the cartoon was one of many ways in which *Punch* participated in creating and propagating knowledge of a scientific event.

Re-presenting ingenuity and questioning progress

When *Punch* writers parodied the literary genres of science they were simultaneously mocking scientific practitioners themselves. Drawing heavily on the conventions of scientific satire established in such works as *Martinus Scriblerus* and Charles Dickens's 'Mudfog Papers', these writers poked fun at scientific stereotypes for their unconventional behaviour, pomposity, obsessive interest in trivial details, and their pursuit of apparently implausible research projects. Few occasions provided richer material than the annual meetings of the British Association for the Advancement of Science. Unlike most other events in the scientific calendar, British Association meetings were widely reported in the press and would have been familiar to most *Punch* readers. Moreover, its meetings were replete with the pomp, personalities, and pageantry that *Punch* writers were expert at turning into

Figure 4.7. 'J. T.' [John Tenniel], 'Another Eclipse for India', *Punch* 55 (1868), 101. Reproduced with the kind permission of the Syndics of Cambridge University Library.

humorous material. In the 1840s *Punch* published several spoof proceedings of the British Association which were timed to coincide with the annual meeting in late summer. The 1843 series on the 'Brightish Association for the Advancement of Everything' contained the key elements of scientific satire that *Punch* would develop further over the next thirty years. The 'proceedings' of the meeting developed several comic contrasts, notably between the notoriously lofty tone and absurd content of papers delivered, and between the sublime aspirations of scientific men and the utterly trivial, chimerical, or abstruse products of their labours. Thus in *Punch*'s 'Mathematical and Physical Sciences' section a 'DR. SPECTRUM' presented a paper on the apparently important topic of the 'Presence of Prismatic Colours in Potatoes', which described the 'prismatic colours' presented to the eye and the purple colour imparted to the eyelid when the author was struck in the eye by a flying potato.[67] Like other humorous articles, *Punch*'s satires of the British Association evoked contemporary themes familiar to the reader. For example, in 1843 *Punch* informed its readers that Alfred Bunn, the impresario whose plays were a recurrent source of ridicule, had undertaken another futile task: at the forthcoming British Association meeting he would read 'the report of the Committee for the Reduction of Stars on a Method of Hypothetical Representation, as applied to Impossible Results, by PROFESSOR MUDDLEWITZ'.[68] Parodies of scientific reports also gave *Punch* contributors rich literary resources for questioning the benefits and expertise of social types *other* than scientific savants. A hilarious example is 'Political Zoology: The Red-Tapeworm' of February 1855 in which *Punch* combined a powerful reminder of the dry and esoteric style of natural historical description with another swipe at the bureaucrats whom it clearly believed were chiefly responsible for the woeful state of the British soldiers during the Crimean War. Introduced as 'TÆNIA OFFICIALIS' the 'Red-Tapeworm' was characterized as 'one of the *entozoa* which infest the body-politic' characterized by 'a strong attachment to place, and where it once lodges, there it sticks, with prodigious adhesiveness'. 'Like most creatures of low organisation', it noted,

the Red-Tapeworm admits of being cut up almost indefinitely without being apparently the worse for the operation; its separate portions wriggling themselves together again, and uniting, in a short time, as if nothing had happened. The process has over and over again been performed by various journalists; but the Red-Tapeworm has hitherto survived the severest slashing.

The symptoms produced by the Red-Tapeworm are an alarming weakness and wasting away, attended with confusion, and impairment of faculties and functions which it occupies, and which becomes, in the end, hopelessly prostrated by paralysis, and sinks into collapse. The emaciation and atrophy of the troops before Sebastopol have been clearly traced to the agency of the *Tænia Officialis.*[69]

Punch's spoofs of scientific reports and proceedings typically presented readers with ambivalent images of science. On the one hand, they illustrated *Punch* contributors' admiration for scientific ingenuity, which they explicitly and soberly praised for its power to vanquish such afflictions as mortal disease, superstition, and international conflict. On the other hand, *Punch's* parodies of science show how much contributors shared the Scriblerian anxiety that the reach of scientific practitioners, engineers, and doctors often appeared dangerously to exceed their grasp.[70] This tension between admiration and anxiety is succinctly displayed in an 1842 parody of a scientific report on the inane topic of buns, which included such pompous statements as: 'Naturalists having occasionally (very rarely) observed a sort of ossification resembling a currant upon the surface of the bun, were led to undertake a mining speculation, for the discovery of any of these curiosities which might by chance be concealed in the bowels.'[71] Similarly, in the same year *Punch* contributed to the relentless torrent of advertisements for railway schemes with a puff for a railway from England to China. The tunnel would reach from London to Canton 'passing through the centre of the globe', and the whole enterprise was in the hands of the chief engineer 'Sinko Shaft', whose trustworthiness could be judged from his belief that the centre of the globe is inhabited by people who had fallen there during earthquakes.[72]

Punch's ambivalence towards recent scientific developments was developed in a welter of spoof letters, poems, and songs. Spoof letters and comic poems allowed *Punch* contributors to deliver their sharpest criticism and satire on science because they could assume the pseudonymous persona of Mr Punch, or some other individual, animal, place, or inanimate object that praised, condemned, or reflected on recent changes in science. By adopting the style of an obnoxious, arrogant, illiterate, or hopelessly misguided character, *Punch* could represent, ridicule, and promote a range of (often extreme) positions on scientific developments familiar to readers. Few issues prompted this kind of response more forcefully than news of technological development. Take, for example, the different assessments of technology developed in spoof letters from 1846 and 1866, the former from a yokel, and the latter from a 'disinterested' promoter of gas lighting. The earlier letter was from 'Simon Hodgskins', a

farmer of limited literary ability, who explained that while reading a report
of a recent meeting of the Royal Agricultural Society, he was 'took aback
to read about all the noo implements for farmun as was show'd there; –
Nar-weegun Harrers, Hay-band-meakers, Pattent Haxuls'. He could not
help 'laafun' at new clod-crusher and corn-crusher machines and, upholding tradition over innovation, invited Mr. Punch down to his 'farm in
Hampshur' and then 'Take aer a one of my carters, and if you dwoant say
that the best clod-crushers or corn-crushers either be their *boots* never you
trust SIMON HODGSKINS.'[73] *Punch*'s bourgeois readers were implicitly
invited to dismiss the views of this muddled and ignorant sceptic of technological development and instead to sympathize with the producers of
fashionable new inventions.

   Likewise, readers were invited to oppose 'Audi Alteram Patrem', writing
to *Punch* in 1866, who reflected on the news that the Houses of Parliament
had refused the Imperial Gas Company permission to build gasworks in the
lush surroundings of Victoria Park, Hackney Wick. Given *Punch*'s earlier
praise for Parliament's decision, readers might have assumed that this was
another straightforward attack on polluting factories.[74] Closer reading of
the spoof letter, however, shows *Punch*'s more subtle way of questioning
technological development. Presenting himself as an impartial onlooker,
the author explained that the defeat of the Imperial Gas Company had inspired Hackney Wick residents to oppose a parliamentary bill allowing the
Gas Light and Coke Company to establish what they consider an 'odorifer-
ous plant' near Victoria Park. The author's true loyalties were soon revealed
when he praised London gas companies for their 'illuminating power',
low-cost gas, moderate profits, 'readiness to accommodate the public' and
declared his support for 'the interests of a great Company' (the Gas Light
and Coke Company). Readers' sympathies with the author would have
crumbled when he stated that he had advised gas companies to try to
keep their 'Bill to erect Gasworks for that purpose out of the lists of
[Parliamentary] Orders of the Day that appear in the newspapers'. He
also reminded Mr Punch that since 'choicest scents' arise from the 'residual
products' of the Gas Light and Coke Company's works, such a gas plant
would have enhanced the smell of flowers in the park. In conclusion, the
author suspiciously insisted that he had not been bribed by the Gas Light
and Coke Company and was of course 'an entirely disinterested party'.[75]
By satirizing and demonizing a promoter of gas-lighting, an individual so
'interested' that he believed gas companies were actually doing local com-
munities a favour by polluting the air, *Punch* raised dilemmas faced by
many readers who enjoyed gas-lighting and other technological luxuries,

and presented readers with one of its most subtle and powerful strategies for debating technological progress *per se.*

CONCLUSION: 'THE FIRST SCIENTIFIC JOURNAL OF THE DAY'?

In her pioneering study of Victorian reading habits, Amy Cruse recalled an anecdote of a young girl who approached Benjamin Disraeli and, despite having never seen the Conservative statesman before, said: 'I know you, I've seen you in *Punch*.'[76] She was not the only person to believe in a correlation between *Punch* articles and the real world. In 1883 a very different reader, Henry James, opined: 'The accumulated volumes of this periodical contain evidence on a multitude of points of which there is no mention in the serious works – not even the novels of the day. The smallest details of social habits are depicted there.' He also believed that *Punch*'s 'ironical view of these things . . . does not injure the force of the testimony, for the irony of *Punch*, strangely enough, has always been discreet and delicate'.[77] Other Victorian readers would have known the personalities and 'smallest details' of science from reading *Punch*. Recent work by Janet Browne has emphasized the extent to which late-Victorian perceptions of Charles Darwin as a genial sage depended on caricatures published in *Punch* and other mass-circulation comic periodicals.[78] *Punch* writers and artists certainly took the 'ironical view' of scientific 'things', and used the techniques of textual and graphic satire to achieve their journalistic goals. The result was distorted 'testimony' about science, but it was testimony nonetheless, and every week it impacted on several hundred thousand Victorians.[79]

This chapter has suggested several ways of understanding how these Victorians understood science from reading comic periodicals. It has examined the complexities of satirizing science in the most celebrated of all Victorian comic journals, from the kinds of scientific material enriching the variety of *Punch* to the complex ways in which the periodical contributors imposed their 'ironic' views on this material. I have suggested that the content and form of science in *Punch* were determined by the journalistic preoccupations of the contributors who sought to entertain the public each week. Their socializing with scientific personalities, their trawls through daily papers, their discussions around the *Punch* table, and their private jottings and sketches usually resulted in far more than a superficial treatment of scientific material for pure comic effect. Just as *Punch* contributors used satire to make serious moral and intellectual points about thorny political and religious issues, so they exploited comedy to develop serious arguments about the uses and abuses of science. I am not suggesting, as did Mr Punch in 1860, that *Punch* should be recognized as 'the first scientific journal of the day'; rather, I have argued that its role in shaping and determining popular knowledge and opinions about science should not be underrated.[80]

Historians and sociologists of science have long recognized the powerful role of rhetoric and other linguistic and visual techniques of persuasion in the construction of natural knowledge.[81] These studies show that many of the common tropes of Victorian comic journalism – for example, caricature and exaggeration – have been used by scientists themselves to convince each other and their publics of the credibility of their scientific claims. Indeed, scientists themselves were not above exploiting scientific satires in comic journals in their own rhetorical strategies. In 1919, for instance, the ageing physicist Lord Rayleigh addressed the Society for Psychical Research with a speech that used a *Punch* cartoon of mesmerism to illustrate the sceptical attitude of the mid-Victorian 'public' towards an obscure psychical phenomenon that, Rayleigh sanguinely noted, had since become more acceptable to medical practitioners.[82] Rayleigh's strategy reveals how important *Punch* and, for that matter, other comic periodicals, could be in shaping the scientific discourses of élite savants as well as the knowledge of the mass-reading public. His use of *Punch* is a further reminder that far more needs to be known about the places and uses of science in nineteenth-century comic periodicals. Systematic studies of the scientific material in late-Victorian *Punch* and the welter of other Victorian comic journals promises to show in even greater detail the dependence of satires on scientific events taking place, and reported, elsewhere in nineteenth-century cultures; the entanglement of comic journalists and the increasingly professionalized cadre of scientific experts; and the relationship between the public's changing perceptions of science and what made them laugh.

CHAPTER 5

The Cornhill Magazine *and shilling monthlies in mid-Victorian Britain*

Gowan Dawson

When the first number of the *Cornhill Magazine* appeared on bookstalls on 23 December 1859 it was greeted as yet another of the astonishing innovations of the industrial age. It was, according to the *Morning Post*, 'one of the marvels of the time that so much material, and of so excellent a quality, can be provided at so moderate a price', and the *Illustrated Times* and *Notes and Queries* both agreed that a magazine of well over a hundred pages costing just a single shilling was indeed an unprecedented 'marvel of cheapness'.[1] Part of the reason for this amazing cheapness, the magazine's readers were later informed, was that the basic 'material for the *Cornhill Magazine* [i.e. paper]' was almost entirely 'machine-made'.[2] The *Cornhill*, along with other journals of the shilling monthly genre such as *Macmillan's Magazine* and *Temple Bar* (founded in 1859 and 1861 respectively), successfully utilized the new modes of literary production available in mid-Victorian Britain to provide a form of relatively inexpensive periodical that was eagerly purchased by an unprecedentedly large – and as yet largely untapped – middle-class readership. Within two weeks of its initial appearance the magazine's opening number had sold out four different print-runs comprising around 80,000 copies, and, as one observer later recalled, 'the printers were kept working till all hours of the night'.[3]

Paradoxically, the *Cornhill's* founding editor and leading contributor, William Makepeace Thackeray, retained a fogeyish nostalgia for the pre-industrial – 'prærailroad' as he termed it – era, and he frequently betrayed an unease with the emergent values of mechanization and mass-production seemingly embodied by the new magazine so closely identified with himself. The continually whirring 'gigantic . . . Hoe's engines' and the 'reams, and piles, and pyramids of paper' involved in the production of each monthly number of the *Cornhill* were a source of ambivalent and uneasy humour in his novels of this period (which were themselves serialized in the *Cornhill*).[4] Thackeray, as he declared elsewhere in the magazine's pages, was one of those 'of a certain age' who had 'stepped out of the old world on to Brunel's vast deck' and thereby 'belong[ed] to the new time and the old one'.[5] This self-consciously Janus-faced nature of the *Cornhill* was expressed most eloquently in the magazine's orange cover which featured four pastoral figures engaged in timeless agrarian pursuits arranged around the journal's title – which itself alluded equally to rural plenitude and a famously mercantile district of the metropolis – and the most recent date of publication, both of which were rendered in modern typefaces (fig. 5.1). Additionally, the cover's studiedly pastoral illustrations were actually produced using a newly established method of wood engraving and were printed from modern electrotypes to ensure maximum clarity.[6]

Both in terms of price and frequency of publication, the shilling monthly genre of periodicals, of which the *Cornhill* was the most prominent example, was balanced precariously between expensive quarterlies like the *Edinburgh Review* and grubby penny weeklies such as the *London Journal*. Although monthly literary miscellanies like *Blackwood's Edinburgh Magazine* had been in existence since the 1810s, the new shilling monthlies were considerably cheaper (*Blackwood's* sold for 2s 6d), less politically sectarian, and placed a much greater emphasis on the kinds of fictional writing – serialized novels in particular – that had become fashionable since the 1840s. They appealed primarily to new sectors of the mid-Victorian reading public who were previously served neither by the expensive monthly and quarterly titles of the metropolitan intellectual élite nor by the much cheaper weekly journals aimed at a more popular, and sometimes semi-literate, audience. The *Cornhill* in particular, as the *Bookseller* observed, 'opened our eyes to the great fact of there being a very large, and hitherto overlooked mass of readers' for middlebrow periodicals.[7] This new class of relatively educated but not traditionally well-heeled or genteel readers largely consisted of members of the new middle-class occupations, such as manufacturing, finance, engineering, and trade, but also included the bluff working men whom Thackeray's daughter remembered discussing copies of the *Cornhill* that they had lent out amongst themselves.[8]

At the same time, however, shilling monthlies also sought to attract an even greater diversity of readers, from both sexes as well as across generations, by combining non-fictional essays, that often constructed their audience as male, with high-profile novels, stories, and poems, which were largely aimed at female readers. A magazine like the *Cornhill*, Thackeray proposed, would both 'amuse and interest' its different constituencies of readers, but it would never be forgotten that 'ladies and children [were] always present' at its diverse 'social table'.[9] Similarly, the same editor's self-imposed moratorium on 'aggressive politics' and controversial religious

Figure 5.1. Cover of the *Cornhill Magazine*, January 1874. By permission of the British Library, RB.23a. 15320.

subjects – under Thackeray the *Cornhill* was to advance the views of in-offensive 'liberals' and 'look respectfully & kindly on all religious denomi-nations' – ensured that the shilling monthly audience was never confined to readers of particular parties or sectarian groups.[10] In this respect, shilling monthlies like the *Cornhill* resembled other forms of middle-class public culture such as Literary and Philosophical Societies, which, as R. J. Morris has shown, regularly enforced a rule of 'no religion, no politics' at their gatherings.[11] This hybridity and deliberate inclusiveness also gained the initial numbers of the *Cornhill* an exceptionally large circulation, and the magazine's print-run settled at 87,500 during the summer of 1860, while *Macmillan's* and *Temple Bar* sold 20,000 and 30,000 copies respectively.[12]

The *Cornhill* and its nearest rival *Macmillan's* were both founded by leading publishers eager to increase the market for their books, and George Smith and Alexander Macmillan frequently used their respective magazines not only to 'trail' forthcoming titles from their publishing companies, but also to advertise their numerous other wares. The abundant financial back-ing that these arrangements afforded each title was particularly necessary in a literary marketplace that, especially after the repeal of duty on paper in 1861, was becoming increasingly crowded and competitive. At this time, as the publisher William Tinsley (soon to launch his own eponymous shilling monthly) observed, there were 'more magazines in the wretched field than there were blades of grass to support them'.[13] Before the *Cornhill* was launched, Smith had exhausted a huge advertising budget of £5,000 ensuring that even the most isolated members of the mid-Victorian reading public could not remain unaware of his imminent foray into magazine pub-lishing. Additionally, Thackeray, one of the most eminent English writers of the previous two decades, had been hired as editor, on extremely gen-erous terms, partly in order to add an instant distinctiveness and celebrity renown. For Thomas Carlyle, as for many other readers, the *Cornhill* was immediately identifiable as 'the Thackeray magazine', and Smith later re-called how 'His very name as editor gave the new magazine distinction.'[14] Thackeray's expensively acquired editorial imprimatur undoubtedly made the *Cornhill* more attractive as a commodity in a heavily saturated literary marketplace.

The stunning success of the *Cornhill*'s initial numbers, however, only helped to make the market for periodicals still more competitive. A range of imitative shilling monthlies, many also taking their titles from fashionable districts of London like *Temple Bar*, *St James's Magazine* and *Belgravia* (the latter two founded in 1861 and 1866) quickly sprang up, often with former *Cornhill* employees at the helm. Each of these new journals fought extremely hard to secure what the *Economist* termed 'that limited share of public attention which is requisite to keep a monthly shilling magazine afloat', and, as George Henry Lewes, a stalwart of the *Cornhill*, later conceded, although 'they all resembled the "Cornhill" in general . . . each added some special attraction of its own'.[15] With the middle-class audience for such magazines enjoying a greater choice than ever before, established shilling monthlies like the *Cornhill* had to be extremely responsive to changes in the literary marketplace as well as to the shifting tastes of their readers.

One of the most conspicuous ways in which the *Cornhill* and other shilling monthlies responded to changing market conditions and readerly tastes was in the position that scientific material occupied in their pages. From the very outset, almost all shilling monthlies included prominent articles on scientific subjects alongside their usual diet of serialized fiction and poetry, often tackling topical issues, such as engineering, manufacturing, or surgery, that addressed the professional concerns of their largely middle-class readers. In the open letter to contributors and readers printed in the first number of the *Cornhill*, Thackeray insisted that fiction must form 'only a part, of our entertainment', urging that the new magazine should also have 'as much reality as possible', including 'familiar reports of scientific discovery'.[16] While the *Cornhill* never attracted the same calibre of scientific contributors as *Macmillan's*, several prominent men of science were nevertheless enlisted to help behind the scenes. Within the first few weeks of the magazine's existence, for instance, Thackeray had 'asked Sir R[oderick] Murchison . . . who could help us', to which the Geological Survey's Director-General responded by forwarding 'the names of [certain] able and popular scientific writers'.[17] The *Cornhill*'s lead item was always the next instalment of one of the current serial novels, but moving 'back into the world' and away from mere 'novel spinning' was a central plank of Thackeray's editorial agenda, and the balanced discussion of contemporary scientific issues was an essential constituent of the hybrid mix of subjects that made up the shilling-monthly formula.[18]

This chapter, which is based on a close reading of ten volumes of the *Cornhill* from 1860 to 1865, will examine how the presentation of scientific material in shilling monthlies was informed both by commercial considerations and by the need to accommodate science with the kinds of informative and, above all, entertaining reading matter that would appeal across a broad middle-class audience. Taking as its focus two important and ostensibly contrasting forms of scientific inquiry in the 1860s, Darwinism and spiritualism, the chapter will examine how such novel and speculative scientific topics were presented as subjects for stimulating discussion and conversation, perhaps even piquant gossip, often without any judgements being passed on their respective claims to truth. Indeed, there was nothing in the pages of the *Cornhill* during Thackeray's editorship that would necessarily have given readers the impression that Darwinian theories on evolution were any more plausible than speculations about the reality of certain supernatural phenomena. Rather, as the chapter will show, Darwinism and spiritualism were both treated as interesting and stimulating – sometimes even sensational – subjects for conversation, which could be utilized equally as a means of generating readerly excitement in a highly competitive magazine marketplace.

Thackeray had, after all, employed the 'hospitable simile' of a round-table 'conversation' to describe the type of character that he desired for the *Cornhill*, proposing that the magazine would encourage a variety of enticing conversationalists to take 'the turn to speak' and 'tell what they know . . . good-humouredly, and not in a manner obtrusively didactic'.[19] This concern with stimulating conversation, which would follow the pattern of the free-flowing discussion at the magazine's monthly dinners for contributors at the Museum Club, was the dominant trope in the treatment of scientific material in the *Cornhill*. Lastly, the chapter will also examine the shift in the *Cornhill's* tone after Thackeray's resignation as editor in 1862, when a new editorial committee comprising Smith, Lewes, and Frederick Greenwood abandoned Thackeray's breezy *laissez-faire* attitude towards scientific verifiability, and replaced the previous emphasis on science as a form of intriguing conversation with a much greater concern with empirical standards of proof. Such an approach, however, did not appeal in the same way to a diverse middle-class readership, and was one of the factors contributing to the *Cornhill's* steady decline in circulation throughout the late 1860s.

'STRUGGLE-FOR-LIFE, SIR, AT YOUR SERVICE'

It is a remarkable, and rarely remarked upon, coincidence that the very first shilling monthly, *Macmillan's*, was launched just three weeks before the publication of what has come to be regarded as the most significant scientific work of the entire nineteenth century: Charles Darwin's *On the Origin of Species*, which first went on sale on 22 November 1859. A browser at one of London's well-stocked bookshops at the time would probably have had their attention drawn both to Darwin's fat tome, liveried in green cloth and costing 15s, and the attractive pink cover of the new, and innovatively priced, *Macmillan's Magazine*. In little more than a month, the *Cornhill's* own

orange wrapper would join this colourful throng just as the *Origin* was going into a second edition. But Darwin's monograph did not come into connection with shilling monthlies solely on the crowded shelves of bookshops.
The second monthly number of *Macmillan's* – published at the beginning
of December – carried a commendatory review of the *Origin* penned by
Darwin's most vociferous and bellicose advocate, Thomas Henry Huxley.
While Huxley reserved his more combative rhetoric for another notice of
the *Origin* in the radical *Westminster Review* (where he described it as 'a veritable Whitworth gun in the armoury of liberalism'), he nevertheless used
the more middlebrow pages of *Macmillan's* to praise Darwin's 'singularly
original and well-stored mind', and to defend his 'friend's book' against the
'prejudices of the ignorant, or the uncharitableness of the bigoted'.[20] From
its very inception in the autumn of 1859, the shilling monthly genre of
periodicals, itself engaged in a brutal struggle for survival in a fiercely competitive literary marketplace, was inextricably connected with the nascent
doctrines of Darwinism (a term coined by Huxley in his review in the
Westminster).

Shilling monthlies, including the *Cornhill*, engaged with Darwin's theories far more extensively than has generally been recognized by historians.
Alvar Ellegård, for instance, expresses surprise that 'even the enormously
successful *Cornhill* contributed to the discussion' of the *Origin*, and observes
that in general 'notices were sparse in the big-circulation newspapers and
periodicals'.[21] The conclusions regarding the *Cornhill* in Ellegård's account
of the reception of Darwinism in the mid-Victorian press, however, are
based on only two articles from the magazine, the April and May 1860 instalments of Lewes's well-known series 'Studies in Animal Life'.[22] Similarly,
Jennifer Glynn remarks that it is a 'curious gap' that 'in the magazine
produced by the publisher of *The Zoology of the Beagle* [i.e. Smith] the
only mention of Darwin' is contained in the same two articles by Lewes,
and she adds, 'Perhaps Thackeray was simply trying to avoid religious
controversy.'[23] By focusing only on the articles most likely to contain references to Darwin such as those by Lewes, both Ellegård and Glynn, as
well as other historians, have failed to notice that, throughout the 1860s,
topics relating to Darwinian evolution – including its application to humans – were in fact extensively discussed and debated in the *Cornhill*
across a variety of different genres, both fictional and non-fictional. Under
Thackeray's editorship alone, the magazine published at least twelve different articles that discussed some aspect of Darwin's novel and contentious
theories. Despite the misleading but hitherto unchallenged conclusions
of historians such as Ellegård and Glynn, contributors to the *Cornhill*

persistently engaged with even the most controversial aspects of evolutionary theory.

One of the principal objectives of the *Cornhill* and other shilling monthlies was to provide their middle-class audience with the so-called 'useful knowledge' that was previously the preserve of the self-consciously 'wholesome' and inexpensive journals, such as the Society for the Diffusion of Useful Knowledge's *Penny Magazine*, that first emerged during the cheap-literature craze of the early 1830s. Indeed, the *Cornhill*, as the *Economist* immediately recognized, was 'a kind of "Chambers' Journal" of the higher classes of society'.[24] Like the *Penny Magazine*, *Chambers' Edinburgh Journal*, co-edited until 1858 by Robert Chambers, the still anonymous author of the 1844 evolutionary blockbuster *Vestiges of the Natural History of Creation*, offered its putatively plebeian readers information and instruction on a variety of practical topics such as astronomy, mineralogy, and natural history. Despite their democratic designs, however, neither *Chambers'* nor the *Penny Magazine* were much read by the 'portion of the working classes earning less than 16s a week', and, as an 1851 Parliamentary hearing was told, their audience was in fact 'almost exclusively confined to the middle classes'.[25] As the demise of the *Penny Magazine* in 1844 made clear, 'useful knowledge' and rational instruction were only likely to prove remunerative for the publishers of avowedly middle-class periodicals. The *Cornhill*'s own 'mixture of serious matter with the charming & amusing', Lewes assured Smith, would 'be felt as a reason for buying the Magazine' amongst a certain class of readers.[26] To provide these readers with the kind of informative and serious knowledge that they desired (and were apparently ready to pay for), Smith commissioned Lewes himself to contribute a suitable series of articles on natural history at the extremely generous rate of 25s a page.[27]

Over the previous decade Lewes had developed a style of science journalism that skilfully combined serious and more entertaining elements, and the series of six articles that he now penned for the opening numbers of the *Cornhill* presented the leading arguments of mid-Victorian natural history in a style suitable for the readership of a shilling monthly. The instalments of 'Studies in Animal Life' were written in a familiar, but nonetheless authoritative tone, with frequent references to leading Continental scientific authorities as well as to Lewes's own experimental work. Lewes combined traditional forms of 'useful knowledge' like practical advice on the purchase of simple microscopes ('get a good stand and good glasses'), with striking innovations such as employing the term 'Biology' to signify the 'science of life', a contentious neologism which, so Lewes claimed, was both 'needful' and now being 'generally adopted' by the leading young naturalists.[28]

Inevitably, when, in the fourth instalment, Lewes came to consider the underlying anatomical resemblance of widely varying animal forms it was impossible for him to avoid at least touching upon Darwin's recently published speculations on the '"propinquity of descent"'. After quoting a passage from the *Origin*, Lewes alluded to the 'philosophical discussion which inevitably arises on the mention of Mr. Darwin's book', reflecting, with undisguisable enthusiasm, that such discussions are 'at present exciting very great attention' and 'opening to many minds new tracts of thought'.[29] Similarly, in the following month's instalment, he reported excitedly that 'Mr. Darwin's book is in everybody's hands'. Although Lewes insisted that his philosophical and scientific 'object' was simply 'to facilitate, if possible, the comprehension of [Darwin's] book', he also ensured that even those readers not concerned with the finer details of evolutionary theory were nevertheless alerted to the exciting and sensational nature of this new development in biological science.[30] This populist emphasis on the more appealing aspects of Darwin's work was particularly necessary, for, as George Eliot recorded, when she and Lewes first 'read . . . Mr. Darwin's Book on the "Origin of Species"' they considered that a variety of factors – including its 'ill-written' prose – would 'prevent the work from becoming popular'.[31] At the same time, however, Lewes cautioned the *Cornhill*'s more excitable readers that these novel 'opinions', no matter how piquant or interesting, were 'necessarily hypothetical', and 'there can be nothing like positive proof adduced' for them. While evolution '*may* be true', he insisted, 'we cannot say that it *is* true'.[32] Readers were permitted to partake of the vicarious thrill generated by Darwinism's intriguing novelty, but they were then almost at once instructed not to accept it as anything like a verifiable truth.

Alongside the circumspection that was necessary in writing for such a broad audience, Lewes also employed an analogy that only the more erudite of his readers would comprehend to endorse guardedly Darwin's hypothetical reasoning. The evolutionary descent of animal forms, he claimed, was 'not a whit more improbable than the development of numerous languages out of a common parent language, which modern philologists have proved to be indubitably the case'. Without directly stating it, Lewes implied that the 'very remarkable analogy between philology and zoology in this respect' absolved Darwin and his followers from the 'absurdities' ascribed to them by their numerous detractors, and he allowed discerning and well-informed readers to 'see what solid argument they have for the basis of their hypothesis'.[33] Lewes's astute and multivocal discussion of the *Origin* subtly addressed the widely differing concerns – and different tolerances of controversial new ideas – of the divergent groups who made up what he termed the 'immense public of the C.M.'[34]

The instalments of 'Studies in Animal Life' were certainly read in markedly different ways by individual readers. For some, the discussion of recent developments in the field of natural history demanded rigorous attention and intensive study, and Lewes reported that his friend Arthur Helps had 'read parts of Animal Studies three times'.[35] Edward Fitzgerald, on the other hand, evidently considered that Lewes's series was barely worth perusing once let alone reading three times. Linking the discussion of natural historical subjects with the kind of 'useful knowledge' previously peddled in downmarket rags like *Chambers'*, Fitzgerald complained contemptuously that 'Studies in Animal Life' 'lets the Cockney in' to the ostensibly genteel space of the *Cornhill*, and proclaimed that 'Lewes is vulgar.'[36] Although neither Helps nor Fitzgerald were referring to the parts of 'Studies in Animal Life' dealing with evolutionary theory, it is clear that these sections of Lewes's series could likewise have been read in radically divergent ways, both as a populist exposé of Darwinism's most exciting elements and as a cautious but resolute affirmation of some of its more recondite philosophical details (although Lewes still remained dubious about natural selection).

Despite the evident discretion with which he dealt with the highly controversial subject, Lewes's equivocal and carefully qualified espousal of Darwinism nevertheless caused considerable anxiety to the *Cornhill*'s proprietor, who was perhaps concerned with the commercial implications of such support. The sixth instalment of 'Studies in Animal Life' ended somewhat abruptly, and Lewes's close association with Smith and the *Cornhill* was temporarily suspended while he contributed articles to the rival *Blackwood's Edinburgh Magazine*. Lewes had told readers of the series that he 'hope[d]' that it might at some point be 'resumed ... with as much willingness' on their part 'as desire to interest you on mine', but when, in January 1862, Smith requested that his erstwhile contributor recommence 'Studies in Animal Life', Lewes declined, claiming in his journal that he had been 'disgusted with his [i.e. Smith's] behaviour'.[37] Rosemary Ashton has interpreted this as 'in all probability' a reference to Smith's earlier 'complain[ts] about Lewes's heterodoxy and support for Darwin'.[38] It seems clear that it was Lewes's circumspect advocacy of Darwinism's claims to truth rather than his simultaneous focus on its potential for prompting exciting speculation that most perturbed Smith. For, while the discussion of Darwinism in the *Cornhill*'s pages did not continue in the same form, neither did it cease altogether.

In fact, the very same number of the *Cornhill* that carried the final instalment of 'Studies in Animal Life' (June 1860) also contained an article on the nutrition of the poor which employed an explicitly Darwinian language in its analysis of dietary conditions among the destitute. Its author, the *Times* journalist Eneas Sweetland Dallas, remarked archly,

It is a very humiliating reflection that eating and drinking occupy more of our thoughts than anything else in heaven above or in the earth beneath ... Man is like the lower animals in this respect that with the vast majority of our race, the struggle for existence is a struggle for dinner.

This animalistic struggle for food, Dallas contended, is responsible for almost 'all the wars, murders and quarrels' that have afflicted human societies throughout history.[39] Despite the extreme seriousness of the issue he addressed, especially at a time when the devastating effects of the 1846 potato famine were still being felt in Ireland, Dallas's highly topical reference to the conflict for scarce resources between members of the same species nevertheless exudes a sardonic humour. The bitter 'struggle for existence', a locution coined by Darwin in his early notebooks and used recently as the title of the *Origin*'s third chapter, becomes merely the bathetic 'struggle for dinner', while the entire development of the human race is traced to 'this one question of dinner'. Dallas's insistent repetition of the incongruously domestic term 'dinner' makes Darwin's brutally Malthusian terminology appear absurd rather than troubling, translating the incessant death and devastation implicit in the Darwinian 'war of nature' into the familiar idiom of middle-class domestic hospitality ('Nobody shall dine with our good will, if we are starving', he declares). These bathetic observations appear as an aside at the very end of Dallas's article, and he exhibits no concern whatsoever with the verifiability of the Darwinian hypothesis. Rather, he employs these intriguing yet somewhat absurd speculations as the subject of a playful and jocular digression once more important issues, like the 'most wholesome, nourishing, and palatable form[s]' of food available to the working poor, have been adequately discussed.[40] Instead of inciting the kind of existential angst usually attributed to them, in this case Darwin's theories, just six months after the *Origin*'s publication, provided merely a means of endowing dreary subject matter with an outlandish excitement.

In the following months and years, moreover, the 'struggle for existence' was to become a persistent refrain for contributors to the *Cornhill* who wished to add a topical piquancy to their articles. Less than a year after Dallas's mordant observations, the physician James Hinton made a very similar allusion to the role of the 'digestive "struggle for existence"' in a discussion of the physiology of human nutrition, stating that 'Whatever part Mr. Darwin's *Struggle for Existence* may have played in the development of the animal creation, it has certainly had no mean place in the development of man', whose 'energetic efforts' to 'advance from ignorance to knowledge' have been largely prompted by the 'unfailing stimulus which the stomach supplies'.[41] Similarly, the psychiatrist Andrew Wynter added urgency to his warnings about the growing prevalence of diseases of the brain by observing that with the 'struggle for life ... ever straining men's minds to the breaking point' it was imperative that even the slightest manifestation of mental abnormality received immediate medical attention.[42] Even Lewes, once he had returned to the *Cornhill* fold in 1862, augmented a discussion of the dangers of artificial cosmetics by considering how physical beauty always gives 'its possessors a thousand advantages in the "struggle for existence"'.[43] For such contributors, the central position of struggle and competition in Darwin's theory offered a readily available means of adding emphasis to a wide variety of unrelated arguments, though they did not necessarily accept the scientific truth of Darwinism. Additionally, even in the period immediately after the *Origin*'s publication contributors to such a self-consciously family-orientated journal did not shy away from applying Darwin's controversial theorizing directly to humans, as Darwin himself had conspicuously avoided doing. In fact, in the pages of the *Cornhill* Darwinism was applied incessantly to questions of human development and was only rarely mentioned in regard to other species.

The concern with the specifically Darwinian themes of competition and struggle was by no means confined to non-fictional articles in the *Cornhill*. Instead, they were similarly discussed in a range of fictional genres. Anthony Trollope's novel *Framley Parsonage* had been one of the most successful elements of the *Cornhill*'s opening numbers and he was at once commissioned to produce another serialised tale of provincial life. The novella that Trollope hastily produced, *The Struggles of Brown, Jones, and Robinson*, was generally regarded as a failure ('disagreeable & *not* funny,' according to Lewes), and has subsequently been almost entirely ignored by critics.[44] This loose satire detailing the founding of a haberdashery emporium that is to be run according to the latest principles of Political Economy, however, needs to be located in the context of the recurrent discussions of struggle and competition that took place in the *Cornhill* during the early 1860s. Although it was primarily 'intended as a hit at the present system of advertising', *The Struggles of Brown, Jones, and Robinson* nevertheless readily shifted from concerns with commercial competition to more identifiably Darwinian forms of struggle.[45]

When, in 1867, Trollope became editor of *St. Paul's Magazine* (yet another of the imitative shilling monthlies launched in the wake of the *Cornhill's* success) he replied defensively to a prospective contributor that he was 'afraid of the subject of Darwin. I am . . . so ignorant on it.'[46] Despite this vaunted ignorance of the subject, in *The Struggles of Brown, Jones, and Robinson* six years earlier Trollope engaged directly with the highly topical issues raised by Darwin. Most notably, in a chapter of the novella entitled 'The Division of Labour', the droll narrator moves from the theme of mercantile struggle to eulogize wryly 'Competition, that beautiful science of the present day, by which every plodding carthorse is converted into a racer.'[47] Far from being fearful of Darwinism, Trollope makes here an explicit reference to a particular passage in the *Origin's* thirteenth chapter ('Mutual Affinities of Organic Beings') where Darwin reflects on how, although he had always been 'told that the foals of cart and race-horses differed as much as the full-grown animals', he gradually came to 'think it probable that the difference between these two breeds has been wholly caused by selection under domestication'.[48] Evolution by means of either artificial or natural selection – very much a 'science of the present day' in 1861 – insists upon a continuity between ostensibly divergent animal forms which provided a suitably intriguing subject matter for the kind of wry epigrammatic digressions characteristic of the narrator of *The Struggles of Brown, Jones, and Robinson*. The actual plausibility of such organic transmutations was not, as Trollope's later defensive comments make clear, something that necessarily needed to be addressed in a novella.

The fiction published in the *Cornhill's* pages, however, did not always shy away from the more philosophical aspects of evolutionary theory. In 'A Vision of Animal Existences', published immediately after the final instalment of *The Struggles of Brown, Jones, and Robinson* in March 1862, Edmund Saul Dixon offered an ornate fantasy that drew explicitly on concerns prompted by Darwin's writings. Resting in a 'refreshment-room' amidst 'the world of brutes assembled in the Zoological Gardens', the tale's male narrator notices a 'middle-aged lady of thoughtful aspect . . . perusing a thick volume, which [he] recognized'. This familiar 'green-covered book' is, of course, the *Origin*, which, as the narrator observes, 'teaches that the world of plants and animals is a world of incessant change'. The female reader engrossed by Darwin's book is accompanied by 'a curly-pated urchin' who amuses himself with 'a box of toy animals', 'knocking them together, to try which was the strongest, and then throwing the fragments away, only keeping such of the wooden effigies as were able to resist the shock'. The child's ostensibly playful but clearly symbolic activity prompts the narrator to fulminate against the heretical beliefs promulgated by a "'knot of French professors and English imitators'".[49] It is at this point that the tale assumes a distinctly fantastical character.

The middle-aged lady reveals the 'classical Phrygian cap' – a symbol of the French Revolution – previously hidden beneath her bonnet, and hands the narrator a card "'inscribed with [her] name and official title... NATURAL SELECTION! ORIGINATOR OF SPECIES!'". The boy likewise introduces himself as "'STRUGGLE-FOR-LIFE, sir, at your service'".[50] In the form of a dialogue, the two then direct the astonished narrator through the evidence for "'descent'" and "'genealogy'" being "'the clue to the proper classification of all the living things we see around us'", and, with the aid of "'a telescope through which you can look back in time for thousands and thousands of generations'", he views the "'enormous transmutation of habits, aspect, and organization'" that have produced species such as the domestic horse. After reflecting that what he has been told about "'the world of brutes is applicable by implication to the world of men'", and concluding therefore that "'the future... is not cheering'", the narrator suddenly realises that he had fallen asleep and has in fact dreamt the entire exchange. Selection and the struggle for existence, among the most persistent concerns of *Cornhill* contributors over the previous two years, are personified in the narrator's bizarre Darwinian dream as a seditious matron and a mischievous urchin whose vivid account of the earth's history make it clear that "'Strength is to prevail'" in a world where the "'milder qualities of humility, forbearance, modesty, [and] self-denial'" will inevitably be condemned to extinction.[51]

Remarkably, during the first five years of the 1860s 'A Vision of Animal Existences' was one of only two discussions of Darwinism in the *Cornhill* to explore aspects of evolutionary theory that were potentially threatening to middle-class values, not least the prospect of demure middle-aged ladies revealing themselves to be revolutionary incendiaries upholding the necessity of aggression and dominance.[52] By employing the familiar narrative device of the dream, however, the tale is able to quit abruptly the disquieting prospects contemplated in the narrator's dystopian vision and return the reader to the safety of the genteel surroundings of the refreshment-room at the Zoological Gardens, a setting more appropriate for the polite discussion of natural historical topics.[53] Indeed, before departing, the narrator asks the lady – now bonneted once more – her opinion of the *Origin*, and she replies that it "'is conscientiously reasoned and has been patiently written. If it be not the truth, I cannot help respecting it as a sincere effort after truth'".[54] While Dixon's extravagant Darwinian fantasy treats evolutionary theory as a source of profound threat to the kind of values most cherished by the Cornhill and its audience, it also presents Darwinism as a subject eminently suitable for cultivated middle-class conversation. In fact, the reasoned and courteous discussion that constitutes the tale's peroration could even provide a kind of paradigm for how readers of the *Cornhill* might conduct their own conversations about the *Origin* at dinner-parties, civic gatherings, and other forums of middle-class society.

It was during Thackeray's eventful but short-lived reign as editor that Darwin's theories were most commonly employed as intriguing and piquant subjects for topical – and sometimes facetious – discussion in the *Cornhill*. Like Trollope, Thackeray has generally been portrayed as a writer who deliberately eschewed any association with mid-Victorian concerns over evolution, yet in his writing for the *Cornhill* he too can be seen to have contributed to the magazine's distinctive stance on Darwinism. The affinity of humans with gorillas and other simians, as is well known, became a central aspect of evolutionary debate in the early 1860s, especially once the French-American explorer Paul Du Chaillu began displaying pickled gorillas at public lectures in London in 1861. Gorillas were previously almost unknown to the Victorian public, and Du Chaillu's displays of simian specimens and lurid tales of aggressive gorillas soon prompted the celebrated 'Monkeyana' and related cartoons in *Punch*, which showed a variety of apes comically exhibiting their kinship with humans. Du Chaillu was never mentioned directly in the *Cornhill*, but the fascination with all things simian that he helped to instigate, as well as *Punch*'s satirical response to this, soon became a subject for comment in its pages. Even the magazine's editor was compelled to respond to the potent combination of increased interest in the behaviour of higher primates and explicitly Darwinian concerns about human descent.

These contentious subjects, moreover, became especially provocative following the outbreak of the American Civil War, which connected anxieties over apes and evolution with political concerns with race and slavery. The bloody American conflict began in April 1861 and in the very same month the *Cornhill* carried an instalment of Thackeray's serial novel *The Adventures of Philip* in which the narrator, with considerable irony, remarks of a wealthy but odious black character that 'in some of the Southern States of America he would be likely to meet with rudeness in a railway car. But in England we know better. In England Grenville Woolcomb is a man and a brother.'[55] In a *Punch* cartoon published just a few weeks later the same anti-slavery slogan, originally coined by Quaker abolitionists in the eighteenth century, appeared on a placard worn by a gorilla eager to prove his kinship with humans (fig. 5.2). The eponymous hero of Thackeray's novel similarly implies a correspondence between Woolcomb's 'dark complexion' and the faces of '"baboons"' and '"chimpanzee[s]"', and, in a later instalment of the novel, he displays a picture which features an 'undeniable likeness of Mr. Woolcomb' wearing a derogatory placard, closely resembling that worn by a gorilla in the *Punch* cartoon, exclaiming, '"AM I NOT A MAN AND A BRUDDER?"'.[56] The evolutionary speculations about human descent prompted by the *Origin*, despite Darwin's own conspicuous silence on the subject, ensured that the fashionable preoccupation with gorillas and other apes was readily associated in the early 1860s with the burning issues of slavery and racial equality.

In one of the quasi-editorial 'Roundabout Papers' which Thackeray regularly contributed to the *Cornhill* he imagined himself as 'a young surgeon-apprentice' who joins an expedition 'down the Pdodo river' in Central Africa and, after a variety of adventures, encounters a highly developed gorilla civilization.[57] Here he is able, like Du Chaillu, to observe 'the manners and habits of the Gorillas *chez eux*', many of which resemble those of nineteenth-century British society. The level of civilization attained by the gorillas in fact surpasses that of neighbouring human tribes, and the young adventurer, who earlier mistakes a family of gorillas for 'three negroes', is astonished to witness '*several negroes under Gorilla domination*'.[58] The black slaves whose rights were currently being fought over on the bloody battlefields of America, Thackeray's morally ambiguous tale implies, might actually be at a lower stage of evolutionary development than the anthropomorphic gorillas who were the current *cause célèbre* of the mid-Victorian press.

The tone in which such grave and momentous issues were discussed in Thackeray's circuitous tale, however, was anything but serious. Rather, in the self-consciously digressive format of the 'Roundabout Papers', which were modelled on the urbane eighteenth-century journalistic style of Joseph Addison's *Spectator*, the incendiary mixture of evolution, apes, and racial politics was actually employed primarily as a means of discussing a trivial piece of personal gossip that was currently doing the rounds of the metropolitan literati. Thackeray's imaginary narrative of African exploration comes to an abrupt halt when the narrator reveals that it will never be completed because recently, while strolling in town, a friend showed him 'a portrait . . . of your humble servant, as an immense and most unpleasant-featured baboon, with long hairy hands, and called by the waggish artist "A Literary Gorilla"'.[59] This simian caricature, which evokes an anguished cry of 'O horror!' from the narrator, is evidently one of *Punch*'s notorious monkey cartoons, which Thackeray, an erstwhile contributor to the

MONKEYANA.

Figure 5.2. 'Monkeyana', *Punch* 40 (1861), 206. By courtesy of the
University of Leicester Library.

satirical weekly, seems to have felt was directed against himself. In a letter to Smith from the same time he observed, 'About the Gorilla[.] What do you think? That *Punch* picture is certainly against us.'[60] Although it is unclear as to precisely which of the monkey cartoons Thackeray is here referring (and none of the *Punch* gorillas seem to resemble him physically), his comments, both in the format of the 'Roundabout Papers' and in his private letter, show how evolutionary anxieties about human descent could easily become subjects for intriguing gossip and fashionable hearsay.

Evolutionary theories, as James A. Secord has recently shown, had been a 'common currency of conversation' since at least the 1840s.[61] In the *Cornhill* during the early 1860s Darwinism was employed regularly as a source of entertaining conversational gambits, wry epigrammatic digressions and risqué literary table-talk. Indeed, this paradoxical reconstitution of primarily oral forms of communication on the *Cornhill*'s printed page was the dominant trope in the magazine's extensive engagement – hitherto largely unacknowledged by historians – with the evolutionary speculations of the period. With the exception of Lewes's circumspect 'Studies in Animal Life', however, Darwin's intriguing conception of organic transmutation was not assumed to be any more plausible or scientifically verifiable than other similarly contentious speculations about the nature of the universe.

'A GHOSTLY ORGAN'

Alongside the concern with Darwinism, contributors to the *Cornhill* in the early 1860s also engaged extensively with another subject of scientific inquiry that was equally novel and contentious.[62] Spiritualism, which was closely linked to age-old beliefs in spectral apparitions and other supernatural occurrences, had emerged as a distinctly modern concern in North America in 1848, subsequently crossing the Atlantic four years later. During the 1850s visiting American mediums instigated a veritable frenzy of interest in table-rapping, *séances*, clairvoyance, and many other manifestations of a putative spirit world. By the following decade, spiritualism, despite the scepticism expressed by some early participants, had enthralled and convinced men and women of all social classes. While, from a modern perspective, Darwinism represents an eminently orthodox form of science that, self-evidently, has barely any connection with a heterodox pseudo-science like spiritualism, the two subjects would not necessarily have appeared to be so very different to the original readers of mid-Victorian shilling monthlies like the *Cornhill*. Indeed, spiritualism was for many at the time an entirely logical extension of the concern with disclosing otherwise unseen forces and energies which characterized established sciences like physics, and it may well have seemed considerably more plausible than Darwin's apparently outlandish evolutionary speculations about 'race[s] of bears' who, after gradually becoming 'more and more aquatic in their structure and habits', finally come to constitute a completely new 'creature . . . as monstrous as a whale'.[63] Spiritualism, therefore, presented *Cornhill* contributors with another interesting and stimulating – if not always totally credible – subject, which, like Darwinism, was eminently suitable for the kind of free-flowing discussion and enticing conversation advocated by the editor as the magazine's house-style.

In fact, the discussion of spiritualist topics in the *Cornhill* during the opening years of the 1860s was so prevalent that James Fitzjames Stephen, writing in 1863, complained that in 'some quarters' the 'remarkable inference' had arisen that 'the CORNHILL MAGAZINE was a ghostly organ, favouring the pretensions of spirit-rappers and others of the same or analogous persuasions'.[64] The *Cornhill* began to acquire this spectral reputation in August 1860 with the publication of Robert Bell's article 'Stranger than Fiction', a sympathetic eye-witness account of a *séance* conducted by the notorious American medium, Daniel Dunglas Home. Bell, conscious that in writing for a magazine like the *Cornhill* he was 'not addressing the initiated', couched his article in the scientific terminology of law, observation, and evidence, giving 'the driest and most literal account' of his experiences at the *séance* during which various pieces of furniture exhibited spontaneous movement.[65] He rejected the accusation that these phenomena were merely 'illogical absurdities' perpetrated by 'trickery or imposition', and insisted that although 'they may be the unconscious work of the imagination', we should not refuse 'to receive any facts, except such as shall appear to us likely to be true'.[66] Rather, he claimed that it was 'the province of men of science to investigate alleged phenomena irrespective of extrinsic incidents', and insisted on the need for disinterested research conducted without prejudice.[67]

Bell was one of Thackeray's closest friends and he had submitted a longer version of the article as soon as his old ally was appointed editor of the *Cornhill*. Smith, though, seems to have been somewhat 'squeamish' about Bell's piece, and Thackeray agreed to 'put him off a N° or two', telling his impatient contributor that 'the actors are not important enough for N° 1: and that we wont [*sic*] ring up their curtain just at present'.[68] The use here of Thackeray's favourite theatrical metaphor nevertheless intimates that he intended to introduce the still somewhat *outré* subject of spiritualism from the very outset of his editorship of the *Cornhill*.

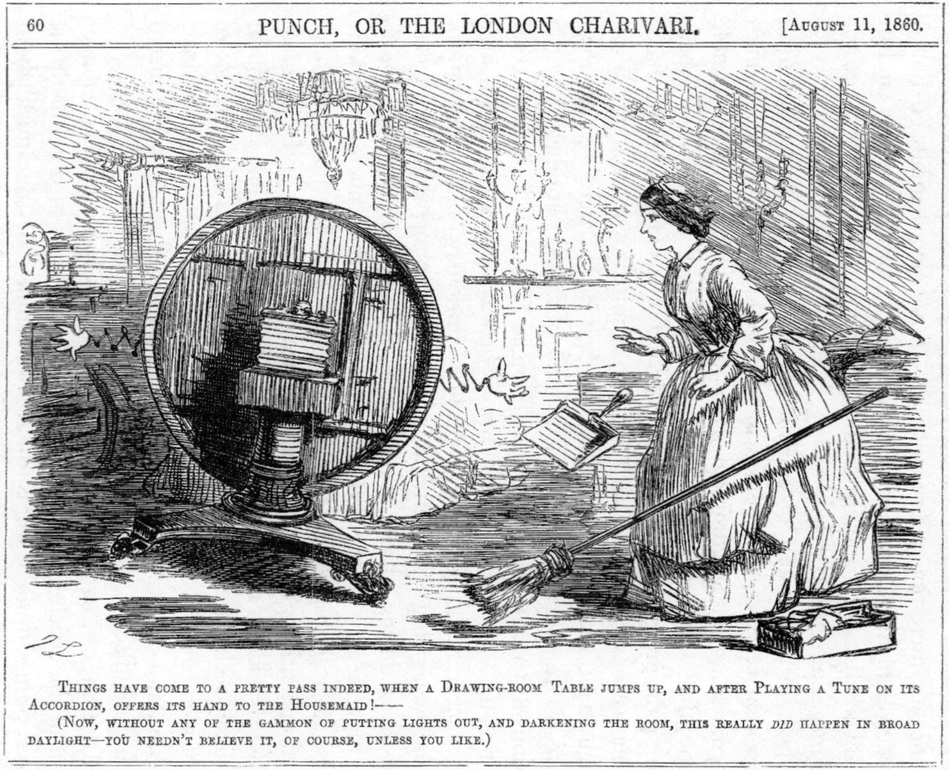

60 PUNCH, OR THE LONDON CHARIVARI. [August 11, 1860.

Things have come to a pretty pass indeed, when a Drawing-room Table jumps up, and after Playing a Tune on its Accordion, offers its hand to the Housemaid!——

(Now, without any of the gammon of putting lights out, and darkening the room, this really *did* happen in broad daylight—you needn't believe it, of course, unless you like.)

Figure 5.3. [John Leech], '[A Drawing-room Table Jumps Up]', *Punch* 39 (1860), 60.
By courtesy of the University of Leicester Library.

Buoyed by the success of the magazine's opening numbers, Thackeray seems to have become confident enough to resist Smith's admonitions and to not only publish his friend's article but also to use his editorial position to instigate a debate concerning the reality of Bell's claims amongst the *Cornhill*'s readers. In a preliminary footnote to 'Stranger than Fiction' he avowed that 'As Editor of this Magazine, I can vouch for the good faith and honourable character of our correspondent, a friend of twenty-five years' standing', but he also encouraged open discussion by allowing that 'readers are . . . free to give or withhold their belief'.[69] Thackeray's blasé editorial attitude towards the trustworthiness of Bell's article was immediately parodied in a droll *Punch* cartoon featuring a levitating table that plays the accordion and offers its hand to a startled housemaid, concerning which readers are told 'this really *did* happen', although 'you needn't believe it, of course, unless you like' (fig. 5.3). Despite *Punch*'s incisive satire, Thackeray's tolerant and self-consciously open-minded editorial stance, seemingly unconcerned with the actual verifiability of his trusted friend's claims, was probably prompted by his recognition that spiritualism, being both eerily intriguing and highly provocative, was the perfect subject to generate stimulating debate amongst readers of, as well as contributors to, the *Cornhill*.

Certainly, Thackeray, perhaps seeking to initiate such discussions, seems to have told different people different things concerning his own opinion of Bell's article. In a letter to Smith he conceded that in his footnote to Bell's essay he had 'expressed only a mild incredulity so as not to spoil the reader's interest in the article',[70] while Lewes, in a letter to John Blackwood, complained that the '"Cornhill Mag." has the immorality (I can call it nothing else) to assist . . . the monstrous folly of Table-turning . . . by a paper in its favour, although Thackeray does not *pretend* to believe it'.[71] A fellow guest at a dinner-party held soon after the number of the *Cornhill* containing Bell's article first appeared, however, reported that Thackeray berated 'several scientific men . . . all of whom availed themselves of the first opportunity to reproach [him] with having permitted the paper in question to appear in a periodical of which he was editor'. He apparently told them with an 'imperturbable calmness' that, following his own experiences at a *séance* in New York a decade earlier, he had already acknowledged 'the truth of spiritualism, and consequently accepted the article on Mr. Home's Séance'.[72] Just as it had at this particular metropolitan dinner-party, Bell's article and Thackeray's seemingly sympathetic editorial response to it soon provoked heated discussions across all sectors of the mid-Victorian print media.

Many rival publications claimed that, in allowing space for such out-landish speculations, the *Cornhill's* prestigious editor had acted irresponsibly and misused the growing renown of his best-selling magazine. The *News of the World*, for instance, maintained, 'It is sad to witness such evidences of credulity as are transpiring; and it is sadder still to find them obtaining publicity through the influence of persons of character and reputation.'[73] The nascent spiritualist press, on the other hand, was delighted by the putative emergence of such a high-profile ally, with the *Spiritual Magazine* declaring, 'All honour to Mr. Thackeray for daring to put forward such a truth. We consider that the insertion of this article in the world-wide *Cornhill Magazine*, is quite an era in the present campaign.'[74] This vigorous interchange of different views concerning the actuality of occult phenomena certainly yielded the *Cornhill* a great deal of media attention in the highly competitive literary marketplace of the early 1860s, even if much of it was savagely critical of the role played by the magazine's editor. Perhaps the most stinging attack came in a rival monthly magazine and from the hands of a former contributor. In an article in *Blackwood's* entitled 'Seeing is Believing' Lewes turned his considerable analytical powers to deriding his erstwhile employers at the *Cornhill*. He noted trenchantly that in 'a paper, which recently appeared in the pages of a contemporary' the author showed himself unable to 'discriminate between fact and inference . . . Stranger than fiction his narrative assuredly is; but the strangeness arises from his method of narration.'[75] Lewes, writing from his old haunt at 'Maga', implied unmistakably that Thackeray had been remiss as an editor in accepting Bell's clearly defective workmanship.

Thackeray seems nevertheless to have revelled in the public discussion and media controversy provoked by 'Stranger than Fiction' and he wanted to print an article '*trumping* Bell's' in the very next issue of the magazine.[76] The article never appeared, but Thackeray himself soon began to use spiritualism as a subject for entertaining conversational gambits and topical narratorial digressions in his own contributions to the *Cornhill*. Just two months after the appearance of Bell's article, Thackeray digressed from his usual nostalgic editorial ruminations, in which he reflects that 'Bodily, I may be in 1860, inert, silent, torpid; but in the spirit I am walking about in 1828', to ask the reader, 'Have you read Mr. Dale Owen's *Footsteps on the Confines of Another World*? – (My dear sir, it will make your hair stand quite refreshingly on end). In that work you will read that when gentlemen's or ladies' spirits travel off a few score or thousand miles to visit a friend, their bodies lie quiet and in a torpid state', and he concludes that 'in this way, I am absent'.[77] The reference to Owen's recently published spiritualistic pot-boiler and the particular practice of 'spirit manifestation', as it was termed by its otherworldly adherents, added a topical – and even invigoratingly hair-raising – piquancy to Thackeray's familiar musings on his long-held desire to inhabit an earlier and more genteel period, even while he whimsically side-stepped any questions regarding the actual possibility of such incorporeal experiences.

The genuineness or otherwise of spiritualism, however, was frequently discussed by the more explicitly scientific writers that Thackeray and Smith had induced to contribute to the *Cornhill*. Hinton, for instance, explained dismissively that certain 'exaggerated' involuntary reflex actions that 'indicate merely the reflecting of a stimulus from the hemispheres of the brain' have recently 'furnished ground for much wonderment and some imposture, and have been set forth, under the name of "electro-biology", and so on, as the basis of new sciences'.[78] Similarly, Stephen drew upon his expert knowledge of jurisprudence in instructing readers that they were to 'disbelieve the assertion . . . that Mr. Home flew around the ceiling of [a] room'.[79] While the attitudes towards spiritualism expressed in the *Cornhill* by men of science and legal experts were, on the whole, as belligerently antagonistic as those promulgated in other less conspicuously open-minded periodicals, they did not preclude the continued discussion of the contentious topic in the magazine's pages.

Instead, many of the fictional works and poems carried in the *Cornhill* at this time articulated a considerably more sympathetic attitude towards spiritualism and its potential for stimulating readerly interest. In an early instalment of Trollope's *Framley Parsonage*, for instance, Miss Dunstable responds to the spiritless rationalism of Lord Boanerges by asking, '"What pleasure can one have in a ghost after one has seen the phosphorus rubbed on?"'. Those who have '"never asked the reason why"', she insists in a spirited defence of frivolous amusements like the belief in disembodied spirits, always '"have the best of it"'.[80] Similarly, Elizabeth Barrett Browning's poem 'Little Mattie' offered a highly particularized vision of a spiritualist eschatology that brooks no equivocation as to its actual reality. The eponymous dead child considers her grieving mother with the

> . . . Grand contempt
> Of the spirits risen awhile,
> Who look back with such a smile![81]

Genres like poetry and fiction afforded a space in which literary figures could engage in the debate over spiritualism and offer a range of alternative perspectives to the authoritative proclamations and superciliously disdainful rhetoric put forward by men of science elsewhere in the pages of the same magazine.

Thackeray's own short fiction 'The Notch on the Axe. – A Story à la Mode' features an 'astounding MEDIUM' called the Count de Pinto, and refers back once more to 'that story stranger than fiction in the *Cornhill Magazine*', which the narrator claims to have read alongside various sensation novels.[82] In one scene the seemingly immortal Pinto, after drinking several bottles of port-wine, tells the narrator of his love for his deceased grandmother. At this point, the dead woman communicates with them by 'three quiet little taps on the table', and when asked if they may have another magnum of port-wine 'the table distinctly rap[s] "No"'.[83] After this spectral encounter, the narrator wakes up, and, as in the ornate Darwinian fantasy discussed earlier, realizes that he has dreamt the whole experience. Thackeray's ghostly tale appeared in the *Cornhill* from April 1862, only a month after the magazine had published Dixon's 'A Vision of Animal Existences', and the almost simultaneous use of fictional dream sequences to explore aspects of Darwinism and spiritualism indicates how, at least to readers of shilling monthlies, both subjects could readily appear equally far-fetched and surreal. Nevertheless, despite the widely – and sometimes violently – opposed opinions of spiritualist phenomena that were expressed in the *Cornhill*, it was, like Darwinism, the source of a great deal of enticing discussion and stimulating conversation within the magazine's pages, and at the conclusion of 'The Notch on the Axe' the narrator expresses himself to be 'rather sorry to lose' the company of the mysterious medium Pinto.[84] The elegiac tone of the story's conclusion was also Thackeray's last editorial comment on the issue which had taken up so much of his attention at the *Cornhill*.

Spiritualism, even more than Darwinism, stimulated discussion and debate in the *Cornhill* as well as across many other areas of the mid-Victorian print media. Once again the use of ostensibly oral modes of communication, echoing the actual conversations that Bell's 'Stranger than Fiction' is known to have generated at metropolitan dinner-parties, was the dominant trope in the magazine's engagement with scientific topics during the early 1860s. Stimulating conversation and free-flowing discussion, however, were not to remain the distinctive characteristics of the *Cornhill*'s science coverage once Thackeray resigned his editorial 'cushion of thorns' in May 1862.

'SAFE & SOUND ENOUGH AS REGARDS SCIENCES'

The discussion of topics such as spiritualism continued in the pages of the *Cornhill* long after Thackeray's involvement with the magazine had ceased. The tone of these discussions, however, veered more and more towards outright hostility. Once Smith, who, as Thackeray implied, was 'squeamish' about spiritualism, had resolved his differences with Lewes, himself an arch-sceptic regarding the supernatural, and appointed him, in May 1862, as 'chief Literary Advisor in the selection of articles, and suggestion of subjects', the *Cornhill* published only articles that maintained a strict boundary between empirical science and spiritualism.[85] Just two months later, for instance, Hinton's 'Seeing with the Eyes Shut' discussed the legitimate scientific method of 'setting free the mind, as it were, by closing the outward sense', but ridiculed the 'much disproved . . . pretences of clairvoyants . . . in the same direction'.[86] The new rigour with which the boundary between so-called legitimate and illegitimate sciences was now maintained also signalled an even greater shift in the *Cornhill*'s treatment of scientific material. The breezy *laissez-faire* attitude towards scientific verifiability encouraged during Thackeray's editorship had been reviled by Lewes in his *Blackwood's* article 'Seeing is Believing', and was now hastily abandoned. Similarly, the previous emphasis on science as a form of intriguing conversation or piquant gossip was soon replaced by a much greater concern with empirical standards of proof (although overall there was no noticeable increase in the magazine's science coverage).

This shift in tone became particularly evident with the introduction in July 1862 of a new regular feature detailing the very latest scientific developments from across the world which closely resembled the separate science sections of highbrow monthly reviews but was unlike anything previously attempted in a shilling monthly. Initially entitled 'Our Survey of Literature, Science, and Art' but soon truncated to just 'Notes on Science', the series, which was begun by Lewes, established new standards of evidence and verification for the *Cornhill*'s non-fiction. Smith even induced the eminent astronomer Sir John Herschel to contribute to it, requesting that he submit an 'occasional scientific article of a popular character'.[87] Although Lewes had at first assured readers that there was 'no intention of competing with the critical journals, either in fullness of information or in elaborateness of criticism', and that the series would merely 'touch lightly, yet firmly, on the . . . glories of scientific progress', it soon became clear that the 'Notes on Science' feature would in fact make hardly any concessions to the interests or competences of the broad middle-class audience which the magazine had earlier cultivated with such assiduousness.[88]

Those sections of the series written by Herschel were particularly uncompromising, assessing, and frequently contesting, specific technical details in the specialist findings of leading experimental researchers on the Continent. Even 'the most brilliant physiologist of the day, Claude Bernard' was criticized for recent remarks he had made concerning the exact status of 'nerves [as] *excitors*', and Herschel, in the pages of a magazine which only a year earlier had been abuzz with speculative gossip about the credibility of spiritualism, insisted that 'the conclusion drawn by M. Bernard is precipitate'.[89] Herschel's highbrow contributions, as Smith soon recognized, were often 'too deep for readers of the "Cornhill Magazine"', and Herschel himself acknowledged that they were 'hardly fitted for the class of readers whom [the magazine's] circulation chiefly embrace[d]'.[90] Inevitably, such technical discussions of recondite experimental details were of more appeal to readers within the scientific community than to the wider middle-class public, and specialist practitioners in a variety of fields certainly paid close attention to them. In November 1862, the naturalist Henry Walter Bates alerted Darwin to 'those capital monthly summaries of science in the "Cornhill"'.[91] Darwin, who had never previously mentioned having read the *Cornhill* in his voluminous correspondence, seems almost at once to have consulted the magazine's most recent number, for, only a fortnight later, he told Huxley that he would 'see in Cornhill mag. a notice of a work by [Ferdinand Julius] Cohn which apparently is important on the contractile tissue of plants'. Indeed, on the basis of the expert views expressed in the *Cornhill*'s pages, Darwin recommended Cohn's book for review in the specialist *Natural History Review*, of which Huxley was editor-in-chief.[92] While the transformation of the *Cornhill*'s science coverage in the months after Thackeray's resignation as editor attracted occasional new readers like Darwin, it unsurprisingly alienated the much larger audience who had grown accustomed to gossipy conversations and lively discussions which attempted, above all, to add an element of excitement to mid-Victorian science.

The issue of the *Cornhill* consulted by Darwin (November 1862) sold just over 72,000 copies; by the following year the magazine's circulation had fallen to around 50,000 and another 10,000 readers were lost over the next twelve months. While this precipitous decline in circulation was not primarily attributable to the *Cornhill*'s new approach to science (the loss of Thackeray's distinctive cachet and the saturation of the literary marketplace were the principal factors), it did not do anything, as the earlier treatment of a topic like spiritualism had, to make the magazine more attractive to potential purchasers who were increasingly spoilt for choice. At the first signs of this contraction in the *Cornhill*'s core audience Lewes warned Smith against responding too hastily by lowering the magazine to the 'trashy' level of salacious penny weeklies like the *London Journal*, the huge circulation of which 'w^d be more profitable – but not so gratifying'.

If the *Cornhill* 'were trashy', he explained, 'I should not suffer in reputation but I should in conscience.'[93] Not long after, however, Lewes relaxed this high-minded resistance to more popular forms of entertainment like sensation novels, and acknowledged that the *Cornhill* had to become once again a 'source of remarkable interest' if it were to 'raise the circulation to a paying point'.[94] The necessity of stimulating greater excitement, as Lewes recognized, extended to the magazine's science coverage too.

In order to effect such a 'change [of] tactics', Lewes advised Smith, it '*would* . . . be prudent to allow me to retire, and concentrate the editing in yourself & Greenwood', neither of whom had been responsible for the magazine's ill-fated shift of direction in its treatment of scientific material (the 'Notes on Science' feature had been scrapped in March 1863).[95] Lewes, however, was to remain on the *Cornhill's* editorial committee for a further year, and his reservations concerning a prospective article on meteorology reveal that he increasingly acknowledged the necessity of making the magazine's coverage of scientific topics more interesting and exciting. The manuscript, he reported, was 'safe & sound enough as regards sciences' and 'scientific readers will find nothing in it to object to'. Nevertheless, if the article were to be published in the magazine a 'little "doctoring" would be necessary' because it 'contains nothing new or suggestive' and was 'not *handled* in a style sufficiently attractive for the C. H. M.'.[96] Lewes, by the end of his period as the *Cornhill's* chief literary adviser, seems to have come to the conclusion that the magazine's coverage of science needed to be not just rigorously empirical – for this was to be merely 'safe & sound' – but, more importantly, to be as 'suggestive' and 'attractive' as it had been during Thackeray's time as editor.

In mid-Victorian Britain the audience for periodicals became increasingly fragmented. Shilling monthlies like the *Cornhill* led the way in providing a new form of magazine that was relatively inexpensive and deliberately inclusive, and which appealed to an unprecedentedly large and diverse middle-class readership. The legendary success of the *Cornhill's* opening numbers, however, ensured that the market for such magazines quickly became saturated with imitative rivals. In response, the *Cornhill* had to become ever more receptive to changes in the periodical marketplace as well as to the shifting tastes of its readers. As has been argued throughout this chapter, one of the most striking ways in which the *Cornhill* responded to changing market conditions and readerly tastes was in its coverage of recent developments and discoveries in mid-Victorian science. In particular, the magazine's discussion of ostensibly divergent forms of contemporary scientific inquiry, such as Darwinism and spiritualism, frequently employed oral forms of communication, including conversation, gossip, and liter-ary table-talk, that were characteristic of forums of middle-class culture like dinner-parties, conversaziones, and metropolitan clubs. In this way, science was accommodated with the kinds of informative and, above all, entertaining reading matter that most appealed to the archetypal middle-class audience of shilling monthlies. The conspicuous failure of the attempt, instigated primarily by Lewes, to alter radically the nature of the *Cornhill's* science coverage after May 1862 only served to demonstrate how much the readers of shilling monthlies had become accustomed to regarding science not as a highly specialized technical vocation but rather as a suggestive and attractive form of middle-class entertainment and leisure.

CHAPTER 6

The Boy's Own Paper *and late-Victorian juvenile magazines*

Richard Noakes

In his 1888 study of children's reading habits, the late-Victorian journalist Edward Salmon presented results of a questionnaire inviting children from selected schools to identify their favourite authors, books, and magazines. Among the most striking revelations were boys' voracious appetite for fiction in books and magazines, and the fact that one of the most common ways in which such readers absorbed 'information' on 'historical, or scientific, or naturalistic subjects' was through the *Boy's Own Paper* (*BOP*) (fig. 6.1).[1] This penny weekly had been launched in January 1879 from the offices of the *Leisure Hour*, itself a hugely successful family weekly issued by one of the leading British publishers of evangelical tracts and periodicals, the Religious Tract Society (RTS). Salmon's evidence was clearly designed to support a pre-existing argument for the desirability of 'healthy' alternatives to the cheap and pernicious 'penny dreadfuls' for which children clamoured each week. Nevertheless, his questionnaire is consistent with the astonishing circulation figures achieved by the *BOP* in its first decades: in early 1880 it was boasting weekly sales of 200,000 copies and was sustaining this figure in the late 1890s.[2] Even if we allow for the *BOP*'s exaggeration of its achievement, it was among the most successful juvenile serials of the late-Victorian period, enjoying a circulation comparable to such prominent general periodicals as the *Daily Telegraph*, being much imitated by later juvenile serials, and offering the strongest competition to such downmarket rivals as *Boys of England*.[3] A substantial portion of the juvenile reading public would have taken the *BOP*, including some of the subsequent movers and shakers in Edwardian Britain.[4]

Scholars have long recognized the importance of mass-circulation juvenile periodicals such as the *BOP* in shaping the young minds of the late-Victorians and early Edwardians. These serials promulgated ideas about empire, race, masculinity, and war, and as John Mackenzie argues, turned the world into a 'vast adventure playground in which Anglo-Saxon superiority could be repeatedly demonstrated *vis-à-vis* all other races, most of whom

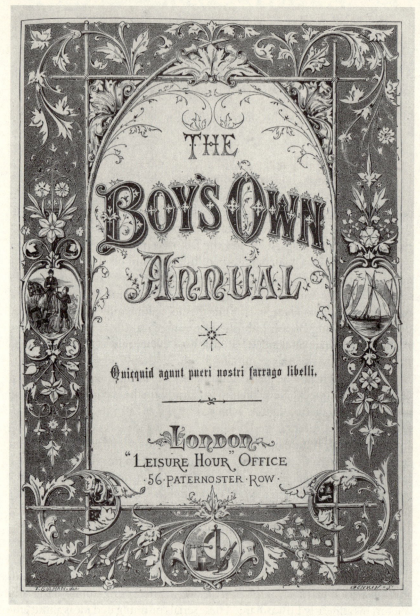

Figure 6.1. Title page of volume 4 (1881–2) of the *Boy's Own Annual*, the annual repackaging of the year's issues of the *Boy's Own Paper*. Reproduced by kind permission of Leeds University Library.

were depicted as treacherous or evil', and made 'violence, boisterousness, and cruelty' acceptable because 'they could be depicted as necessary adjuncts to the spread of civilisation, Christianity, and Just Rule'.[5] Although historians recognize that many of these values were expressed in the context of scientific discussion – for instance, practical advice on killing insects or stories of heroic British explorers – there remain few systematic analyses of scientific material in nineteenth-century juvenile periodicals.[6] Current scholarship on science and juvenile literature *per se*, however, suggests different ways in which we can approach science in journals for boys and girls, from analysis of the literary forms in which science was re-presented to the young, to the role of those dominant producers of nineteenth-century children's literature – the religious presses – in controlling how youths read and used scientific material.[7]

The significant amount of scientific material in the *BOP*, and the high status of its contributors, make it an important case study for understanding mass consumption of the sciences. Recent bibliometric work by David Reed has shown that of fourteen leading popular magazines published in Britain and America in the 1890s, the *BOP* contained one of the highest percentages (approximately 6 per cent) of material on topics relating to science, technology, nature, and health.[8] Moreover, the authors of this material included such important Victorian popularizers of science as the Revd John George Wood and John Scoffern. As Bernard Lightman suggests, these practitioners 'may very well have been more important than the professionals in shaping the public image of science'.[9] The *BOP* was launched in the period when non-specialist reading audiences were increasingly turning to such writers as Wood and Scoffern for the moral and religious teachings of the sciences – elements that once constituted common ground between élite scientists and their audiences but which the former were now expunging from the domain of professional science.

This chapter offers the first systematic analysis of the scientific material in the initial five years of the *BOP*, where 'scientific' is used as convenient shorthand for science, technology, and medicine. In the following section, I examine the foundation and ancestors of the *BOP*. I suggest that the *BOP* was unoriginal in attempting to provide children with healthier alternatives to 'demoralizing serials' and aimed to achieve its goal by combining elements of several successful juvenile periodical genres of the mid-Victorian period, from the expensive monthly magazine for boys to the cheap and racier boys' weekly paper. One of these elements was scientific material which, I argue, constituted an important part of the *BOP*'s strategy of producing a entertaining and wholesome serial that would please middle-class

boys and their high-minded parents and teachers. The remainder of this
chapter demonstrates the insights afforded by an analysis of the scientific,
medical, and technological references in the *totality* of *BOP* material – not
simply articles dedicated to such topics. I begin this task by surveying the
periodical's scientific contents, charting the backgrounds of principal
'scientific' contributors, and examining the types of sciences represented
and in which genres these subjects most frequently appeared. This approach is then complemented in an analysis of the way scientific material
worked in different genres, a task showing that what was being communicated was not just scientific knowledge but Christian and Anglo-Saxon
notions of morality and racial superiority that were more explicitly presented elsewhere in the periodical. The chapter concludes by suggesting
some of the ways in which the lessons of this chapter can help us develop a
fuller picture of the quantity and functions of science in some of the most
widely read publications for juveniles.

'READABLE AND HEALTHFUL, ENTERTAINING AND INSTRUCTIVE'

In January 1879 the *Publisher's Circular* carried an advertisement for a
'journal for boys . . . comprising tales, sports, pastimes, travel, adventure
and a variety of amusement and instruction'. The new journal was the *BOP*
and the authors of the advertisement believed the periodical would satisfac-
torily answer the question of whether anything could be done to 'provide
a Magazine that shall be at once readable and healthful, entertaining and
instructive; or, are the demoralising serials now so widely disseminated to
have it all their own way?'[10] Many readers would have understood that
the *BOP* was addressing an increasing middle-class concern about juvenile
and especially boys' reading habits. The 1870 Education Act and rising
disposable incomes had boosted the already growing market for juvenile
literature.[11] By the time the *BOP* was founded, publishers had long been
exploiting the gradual rise in juvenile literacy and taste for reading with
books, serials, and other publications containing fiction and non-fiction for
children of different gender, age, and class. Many parents, teachers, clergymen, and journalists such as Edward Salmon feared, however, that this
growing market was being dominated by producers of the 'penny dreadful'
rather than the more reputable publishing houses.[12] As John Springhall has
shown, 'penny dreadful' was a pejorative and misleading term coined in the
early 1870s by middle-class journalists to 'amplify social anxiety or "moral
panic"' over the growing number of cheap juvenile periodicals that were

believed to poison young readers' minds.[13] With sensational titles like *Wild Boys of London* (fl. 1864–77) and *Tyburn Dick, the Boy King of the Highwaymen* (fl. 1878), these excitingly written and luridly illustrated stories of adventure and crime commanded enormous readerships which often reached an estimated 1 million.[14] The Religions Tract Society (RTS) knew that representing the *BOP* as the antidote to these publications would win the approval of the affluent and respectable middle classes. But the architects of the *BOP* and its even more successful sister periodical, the *Girl's Own Paper*, recognized that in order to displace the 'penny dreadful' the new periodical would have to ape some aspects of these lower publications.[15] The problem was articulated by RTS member, James Bennett, who in 1882 told an annual meeting of the Society that 'It was absolutely necessary that the publications be of a kind that boys and girls who had been accustomed to buying these abominable publications would be attracted by and induced to purchase.'[16] Parents, teachers, and educationists recognized that children would not be drawn from 'penny dreadfuls' with the heavily religious and dreary didactic material that filled the *Child's Companion*, the *Youth's Magazine* and other early nineteenth-century juvenile periodicals: it had to be achieved with a more appealing diet of exciting but wholesome stories and illustrations about things that interested children. The *BOP*'s first editor, George Hutchison, was acutely aware of this problem and had to persuade the conservative clergymen and evangelical social reformers who formed the RTS General Committee that a periodical 'having articles on common subjects, written with a decidedly Christian tone' rather than 'articles on religious subjects' would be one of the ways of adapting the Society's evangelical mission to juvenile readers of the 1880s.[17]

The *BOP* was, however, an unoriginal solution to an existing concern about mass literacy. As we saw in the introduction, the 1850s was the beginning of a boom in children's literature *per se*, and religious and secular publishers alike exploited both the falling costs of producing and distributing periodicals and growing juvenile literacy to launch a plethora of cheap illustrated weeklies and monthly magazines designed to displace pernicious juvenile reading matter.[18] These included Samuel Beeton's *Boy's Own Magazine* (founded 1855), W. H. G. Kingston's *Magazine for Boys* (founded 1859), and *Aunt Judy's Magazine* (founded 1866) and other journals that catered to juvenile readers increasingly differentiated according to gender, age, and religious denomination.[19] One of the major differences between these serials and most early nineteenth-century children's magazines was the emphasis on fiction, entertainment, and secular instruction and the reduced amount of material on religion. Scientific material constituted a

small but significant part of the new periodicals' blend of wholesome instruction and entertainment, typically appearing in the context of articles
on nature study, pet care, and domestic scientific experiments, and in stories
of fictional adventurers or accounts of virtuous scientists.[20] This material
built on established traditions in religious and secular literature for children
in which scientific subjects were used in a variety of ways, from supporting
a theology of nature and providing the basis for rational amusement, to fur-
nishing material for inculcating mental discipline and satisfying children's
taste for facts.[21]

The shifting focus of children's periodicals to more secular material reflected a more general development in secular *and* religious publishing. For
example, from the mid-1840s, the RTS began issuing cheap books and
periodicals containing secular material written in a Christian tone, publications designed to draw mainly working-class readers away from immoral
literature. As Fyfe has shown, the most successful of these publications, the
Leisure Hour, a family weekly launched in 1852, represented an important
new direction for the Society because unlike most of its juvenile books
and serials of the early nineteenth century, the journal included fiction,
albeit written in a moral tone, and contained far fewer statements of the
atonement and other Christian doctrines.[22] To achieve a similar success in
the mid-Victorian market for male juvenile periodicals, the RTS had to
compete with high-quality serials such as *Boy's Own Magazine*, but more
importantly, the flurry of cheap illustrated boys' periodicals issued from the
mid-1860s by fierce publishing rivals Edwin Brett, William Emmett, and
John Allingham. These astonishingly successful serials, of which Brett's *Boys
of England* (founded 1866) was the most widely read, offered more fiction
and far less pedagogical and factual material than *Boy's Own Magazine* and
similar journals, and although explicitly launched to counter the effects of
'penny dreadfuls', included a large proportion of the sensational material
that parents and teachers abhorred.[23]

One of the editors of the *Leisure Hour* was James Macaulay, a journalist
who rose to the powerful position of the RTS's general editor.[24] In the late
1870s he played a central role in the RTS's agonizing attempt to establish a
new cheap boys' periodical that would counteract the effect of 'demoralising
serials'. In mid-1878 the RTS began its protracted debates on the content of
the journal and commissioned a specimen number from George Hutchison,
the editor of several religious and philanthropic journals and a campaigner
for charitable organizations.[25] The content of the journal proved to be a
major headache for Hutchison before and after its launch because what he
believed boys really wanted to read did not always square with what the RTS

thought they should read. With Macaulay's warm support, the RTS General Committee reluctantly accepted Hutchison's final specimen number for what would be called the *BOP*, on the condition that its evangelical tone be increased once steady sales had been secured. Owing to his greater reputation within the RTS, Macaulay was chosen over Hutchison as the *BOP*'s official editor, but Macaulay, laden with other journalistic work, gave most of the editorial duties to Hutchison, the journal's sub-editor.

The format and content of the *BOP* suggest that Hutchison's solution to the problems of satisfying the conservative RTS and readers of 'penny dreadfuls' was a compromise between many of the juvenile and family journals launched since the 1850s: the expensive, high-quality monthly boys' magazine (for example, the *Boy's Own Magazine*); the cheap, high-quality family weekly containing an even balance between moralizing fiction, essays, and instructional articles (for instance, the *Leisure Hour*); and the cheap weekly containing a greater proportion of fiction and other sensational material (for example, the *Boys of England*). Comparisons between the *BOP* and the RTS's *Leisure Hour* are instructive and reveal many of the ingredients of the *BOP*'s success. For a penny, *Leisure Hour* readers had sixteen double-column pages comprising approximately six long articles, including serialized fiction, biographies of virtuous men and women, essays, poetry, a column of miscellaneous extracts, and between five and six illustrations. Like the *Leisure Hour*, the *BOP* opened with its leading serialized novel, but for the same price and number of pages as the older periodical *BOP* readers got larger pages containing three columns of smaller print. These carried over twice the number of articles, which comprised all the genres appearing in the *Leisure Hour*, and several more including editorial replies to correspondents, competitions, coloured plates, appeals for charitable causes, music scores, and puzzles.[26] It also included a regular column, 'Our Note Book', which more than most genres, set the moral tone of the periodical with its frequent descriptions of individuals whose lives exemplified such moral qualities as courage, honesty, piety, self-sacrifice, and teetotalism. The more eye-catching appearance of the *BOP* was created by its illustrations which were not only more numerous than the *Leisure Hour*'s, but usually more dramatic in order to serve the periodical's racier stories of adventure and articles giving instructions on scientific and other hobbies. The latter set the *BOP* apart from the *Leisure Hour* and put it closer to Beeton's *Boy's Own Magazine* and several other mid-Victorian boys' magazines, although the *BOP* supplied instructions that were less encumbered with the technical details that had deterred many readers of Beeton's publication.[27] The commercial success of the *BOP* depended on its sheer variety, the exciting stories, the high-quality illustrations, but also the stature of its contributors: besides the Revd J. G. Wood, and Dr John Scoffern, it boasted the evangelical fiction writers W. H. G. Kingston and R. M. Ballantyne, and the leading French writer of scientific romances and adventures, Jules Verne.

In several ways, the *BOP* continued the shift to secular publishing begun by the RTS in the 1840s. Compared with RTS publications of the early Victorian period, the *BOP* represented far broader notions of the literary genres and subjects that were considered suitable for establishing the Christian tone of a periodical: it included even fewer references to religious doctrines than the *Leisure Hour*, its RTS provenance was harder to spot, and it boasted even more fiction.[28] Hutchison's plans for the fictional content of the *BOP* did not always meet with the approval of the RTS who believed 'excessive' amounts of the material diverted the journal from its evangelical purpose.[29] But judging by the frequency with which he published praise of the *BOP* from parents, teachers, and clergymen, Hutchison was keen to demonstrate that his formula for fighting 'pernicious trash' was achieving its desired effect.[30]

Like all periodicals, the *BOP* exploited the serial format – in fiction and non-fiction – to entice readers into buying subsequent issues. The format gave writers and illustrators chances to try something different each week, and it was this change that proved a major attraction. Such was certainly the perception of one reader who reminisced that 'The "B.O.P." came quite early into our home, where I was the third of three boys, and it was a scramble to get the first read of the serial story, or the first attempt to solve some new problem, or the excitement to start some new hobby.'[31] As we shall see later, many of these new problems and hobbies were scientific, and it was precisely by instructing readers on these tasks on a week-by-week basis that the *BOP* sought to make science a more appealing aspect of juvenile leisure culture.

Implicit in articles on scientific hobbies was the expectation that any boy could become a participant in science.[32] But the contents of the periodical suggest a more limited readership. True, most boys would have savoured the periodical's engravings and colour plates, but the text assumed a level of literacy that would have put the journal beyond the range of boys below the age of ten. The *BOP* appears to have envisioned readers aged from under sixteen to twenty-three, but from the age of entrants to *BOP* competitions it is clear that the periodical was read mainly by teenagers.[33] Neither would the *BOP* have been appreciated by many plebeian youths. Very little of the *BOP* deals with working-class lives and much of its fiction concerns public schools and middle-class homes. More affluent readers would have been better placed to appreciate the scientific material. Typically, their parents would also have been able to afford the requisite resources for following the *BOP*'s scientific protocols, and they would have attended the better public and grammar schools where, unlike most secondary schools in mid- to late-Victorian Britain, the cultivation of scientific skills was beginning to be part of the curriculum.[34]

PRODUCERS AND TYPES OF *BOP* SCIENCE

Who was responsible for the scientific material in this, one of the most successful of all late-Victorian juvenile magazines? The writers were gener- ally individuals who were already admired by juvenile audiences for other pursuits, whether as writers of textbooks, novelists, popular lecturers, or contributors to other juvenile periodicals. Most were British males, many were retired scientists, technicians, or medical practitioners, some were cler- gymen, several were military officers, explorers, and sporting personalities, and many were journalists and writers of novels and children's books. By far the most prominent were the Revd John George Wood, Gordon Stables, Jules Verne, Theodore Wood, and Dr John Scoffern. As Lightman has shown, Wood's career embraced many clerical and academic appointments but he was best known to Victorian reading audiences for his books and articles on natural historical topics. He was just as energetic for the *BOP*, contributing (often in collaboration with his son Theodore) a plethora of serialized articles on botany, entomology, and other branches of natural history, articles that continued Wood's preoccupation with showing how the wisdom and existence of God was revealed in amateur studies of the natural world.[35]

Stables may have lacked Wood's experience as a popularizer of science, but he was no less successful at presenting *BOP* readers with material for developing their understanding of animal life. In the 1870s, after a career embracing service on a whaling ship, work as a naval surgeon, and ex- ploration, Stables developed a strong interest in domestic pets and animal welfare and his vast number of contributions to the *BOP* reflect his diverse experiences: serialized stories of land and sea adventure (frequently dealing with themes of hunting) and regular columns giving advice on caring for domestic animals.[36] By the time Stables began writing his adventure stories, Jules Verne had already won an international reputation for his contribu- tions to the genre. He had also established himself among male juvenile readers as the author of a string of serialized scientific romances, many of which reached British reading audiences for the first time in the *BOP*.[37] Like Wood, Scoffern had combined careers in teaching and popular science writing, holding a chair of chemistry at the Aldersgate School of Medicine and publishing technical works on industrial chemistry and chemistry texts for the young. He was responsible for much of the physical science content of the *BOP*, producing many series on the application of chemistry and optics to the creation of wholesome indoor entertainments.[38]

Admired as the *BOP* was for including the serialized fiction of W. H. G. Kingston, Robert M. Ballantyne, Talbot Baines Reed, and Ascott R. Hope, these famous authors only occasionally engaged directly with scientific topics in the *BOP*. There were many other authors, however, who made much more substantial contributions in this direction, and who were clearly favoured by Hutchison because of their achievements in other fields. These included Thomas Millington, an Anglican vicar who wrote school and adventure stories, as well as fictional dialogues in which a boy and schoolmaster discuss the mechanical principles illustrated by such juvenile amusements as spinning tops, swings, and balloons; J. Harrington Keene, an angling expert whose serials on fishing and fish-breeding contained detailed discussion of the behaviour and anatomy of fishes; A. A. Wood, a London optician who wrote several articles explaining the scientific principles of magic lanterns and weather forecasting; and W. G. Grace, the famous cricketer whose series on his own sport included extensive discussion of the healthy lifestyle needed to succeed in the game. Whatever their speciality, contributors to the *BOP*'s scientific material seem to have shared a fundamental belief that they were pedagogues, moral guides, and entertainers. They tried to avoid what Gordon Stables called the 'break-jaw Latin' words and other details that would remind readers of the class-book and schoolroom, and developed other textual strategies for showing that learning about and practising science would improve their knowledge, character, and leisure time.[39] As far as scientific illustrations were concerned, many woodcuts were executed by artists such as Alfred Pearse and Warne Browne, although the *BOP* did enjoy the services of more established artists such as George Willis, John Sachs, and William Dickes, and the Kronheim firm of engravers. To save on production costs, the *BOP* reused much of the graphic material that originally appeared in the *Leisure Hour* and secured the rights to the work of L. Poyet and Gaston Tissandier, the leading artists of the French popular science weekly *La Nature*.

Scientific topics were to be found in almost all the periodical genres of the *BOP*, notably serialized pedagogical articles, essays, editorial replies to correspondents, serialized fiction, regular columns of miscellaneous extracts and news items, travelogues, biographies, and the colour plates or woodcuts that often enriched other genres. The scientific topics covered in these genres were extensive and as Dixon suggests this material was 'less academic and more varied than in the boys' magazines of the 1860s'.[40] This does not mean that the *BOP* trivialized scientific material: on the contrary, many *BOP* contributors took very seriously their role as educators and supplied such intellectual matter as the Latin names of insects suitable for private menageries, explanations of physical principles governing toys, and facts relating to geographical features encountered by protagonists of an adventure story. As in many nineteenth-century juvenile periodicals, there is a large proportion of material on natural history, especially in connection with collecting and exhibiting specimens, and an equally significant coverage of geography and topography, much of which is discussed in the context of the wonders of the natural world or the heroic accomplishments of explorers. Even more prominent is the discussion and representation of animal behaviour and animal development – especially in relation to hunting wild species in distant countries, and the health, hygiene, and breeding of domestic animals. While this material was largely non-technical, it clearly played an important part in enhancing readers' understanding of animals in near and distant lands. Of the physical sciences, it is chemistry, optics, and electricity that dominate in the *BOP*, not least as subjects enabling the production of spectacular visual phenomena. Discussion of technology, engineering, and inventions is less prominent but features in a variety of contexts, including biographies of engineers, historical essays on balloon flight and ironclads, and instructions on building yachts and model steam engines. In general, medical topics have a lower profile than scientific subjects and tend to be limited to serialized fiction – notably, the representations of physicians' regular columns on the health of pets, and correspondence columns giving boys suggestions on managing their own health.

The *BOP*'s choice of scientific material reflects the strategy of the editor and contributors to make intellectual topics more interesting by associating them with juvenile hobbies or other leisure activities. This association was implicit in the frequent juxtaposition of scientific topics with those on sport, adventure, and other pastimes. This association is more explicit in the frontispiece of the *Boy's Own Annual* (the annual reissue of the year's *Boy's Own Papers*) which contains several vignettes, some showing such leisure activities as horse riding and yachting, and one depicting a microscope, an electrostatic machine, and a Leyden jar (fig. 6.1). The science–entertainment mixture was articulated most clearly by John Scoffern at the beginning of his series on indoor chemistry amusements. 'It has been suggested to me', he reported,

that boy students of chemistry like nothing so well as coloured fires, bangs, abominable smells, and any chemical teacher who aims at satisfying his young folk must oblige them in this matter. Very good! I bend to the pressure of opinion; but in doing so, I shall not be content except my coloured fires, bangs and evil odours bring forth some product of instruction.[41]

For Scoffern, this way of giving instruction was far preferable to 'chalking [chemical] symbols on a blackboard' because it 'brings into play a number of faculties that would not otherwise be exercised'.[42] Scoffern largely practised what he preached, for in the course of describing how to make such chemical spectacles as a lead fire-shower, he provided instructions on building elementary chemical apparatus and gave basic outlines of inorganic chemical reactions.

Scientific topics also played important roles in creating the sheer variety and aesthetic appeal of the periodical. In early volumes instructions for displaying insects or building steam engines provided a contrast to school stories and historical essays, while woodcuts of optical toys and colour plates of British birds, fishes, anemones, and other species gave lustre to pages of text (figs. 6.2 and 6.3). Equally significant, scientific material played an important role in creating the evangelical and nationalistic tone of the periodical. Indeed, scientific material lent itself to the very genres that the RTS believed fulfilled its purposes – accounts of real exploration, essays, and biographies of the virtuous. Throughout 1880, for instance, a range of different periodical genres featured scientific material conveying Christian messages of various weight. Verne's serialized story 'The Giant Raft' contained long passages describing the beauty and wonder of the Amazon, and its lavish engravings by Leon Benett helped articulate the narrator's belief that the Amazonian forests were 'a magnificent sermon'.[43] A subtly different lesson from the Amazon was drawn months later when an anonymous writer argued that although Amazonian insects caused him to 'shudder' every one had been 'created by the all-wise God for some specific beneficent purpose'.[44] Weightiest of all were a series of hagiographies of scientific practitioners whose lives and works were interpreted to illustrate Christian virtues (fig. 6.4). In keeping with the *BOP*'s nationalistic tone, these were typically *British* practitioners and stories of their heroic rise from humble boys to accomplished adults fulfilled the same ideological function as the myriad pedagogical articles on *British* animals and fictional tales of plucky *British* explorers in foreign climes.

228   The Boy's Own Paper.

OPTICAL TOY SPORTS.

DESCRIBED BY DR. SCOFFERN.

PART II.

THE reader will remember that in my last gossip on this subject certain experiments were described which for their execution needed some device for accomplishing circular motion. I left the choice of the device pretty much to yourselves, not doubting your ability to accomplish it. You will bear in mind that the circular motion already described has been vertical or upright; you viewed your object as you would the face of a clock. I wonder if it occurred to any of you that that very common plaything—a top—would give excellent circular motion? Evidently it would do so; only, using a top, you must be content to operate in a horizontal plane—to look down on your object instead of looking face to face at it. Let me now inform you that tops, like many other playthings, have been laid hold of by grave philosophers to do philosophic work. "Like many other playthings," was my remark. Need you be reminded of Benjamin Franklin and his kite?

The ordinary pegtops used by juveniles can be made to do some honest work in aid of optical illustration. Ordinary pegtops, however, are not very well adapted to this purpose. What the optical experimenter requires is, in the first place, a top of general flat contour, more like the shape of a dinner-plate, so that devices may be dropped down upon it, and there remain. In the second place the experimenter would, for performance of some experiments, at least, have to devise a means of more rapid rotation than ever can be imparted to mere playground tops. However, good optical handiwork has been done by the sort of top represented on this page. It was the device, I believe, of the German Professor Helmholtz, and is, as you see, simplicity itself.

The Helmholtz Top is set rotating by a simple twirling motion. Our picture represents it on the scale of about one-third actual size. Its disc is of metal. Brass is very good, but an alloy of zinc and lead is better. It presents the additional advantage, too, of home manufacture. Any boy can melt zinc and lead together in an iron ladle over an ordinary fire, but he could not in this way melt brass. The mould for shaping the molten alloy may be fashioned in hard-rammed sand, or, what is still easier, a round paper box. A collar-box, or a French

bon-bon box, may be taken, covered with a thin coating of clay, water, and chopped hair on the inside, dried gradually but thoroughly, and then used as the mould. If you only dry the clay partially, an explosion is sure to happen when you pour in the molten metal. As to the spill by which twirling is effected, nothing is better than a proper length of carpet rod. The under, or pointed spill, upon which the top has to rotate, must be of soft, untempered steel. The making of it is beyond a boy's competence. A handy locksmith would be, next to a professed engineer, the best sort of man you could employ.

Take care that he fixes the turning spill at the exact centre of your disc, also that it does not slant. You also must have taken similar care that your turning-spill complies with the same conditions. Hitting the exact centre, and casting in the turning-spill exactly upright, are not matters quite so easy to accomplish as might at first seem. Some boys will succeed, but more will fail, ultimately having recourse to a skilled workman. When this happens, the twirling and the spinning spill may, indeed *ought* to, be in one, and the one should be of untempered steel throughout.

Such a top as that described cannot be made to rotate more quickly than six turns in a

second. That is not considered to be velocity great enough for the performance of some scientific experiments. Three or four minutes is about the maximum duration of spin this sort of top is capable of. I shall presently describe

a top that can be made to rotate no fewer than sixty turns in the second, and to remain spinning for at least three quarters of an hour.

An improvement on the preceding top, or, more correctly speaking, a *development* of it, is here represented. Humming-tops are considered, I believe, not so manly as pegtops—perhaps because girls sometimes use them. Most boys, still, I take for granted, know about humming-tops enough to make description needless. Here is a humming-top which neither hums nor has the shape of a humming-top. However, you must know what I mean.

In one particular, however, this humming-top that does not hum, needs description. Observe the diagram which next follows. The twirling-spill is unscrewed just to show you that when screwed up tight against a cardboard disc with central perforation it necessarily jams the disc against the upper surface of the top, and thus prevents any shifting of the disc during the experiment. This is an important matter to be heeded in some lines of optical investigation. Now for the marvellous top that I just now wrote about—the top that can execute sixty turns in a second of time, and keep spinning for three quarters of an hour. On p. 229 is a picture of that wonderful top, and also what Jonathan would call "its fixings." As for the top, it is a simple thing enough. A boy could make it for himself, but he could not make the fixings. These consist of a strong clamp for attachment to a table, as our artist's picture illustrates, and two steel blades, each notched towards its end, the notches corresponding to the size of the twirling-spill. You will observe that the two notches are on the corresponding sides of the two blades. The lower blade is not close down in contact with the table, as might seem on mere casual inspection of the diagram, but sufficiently removed from it to leave a space of dimensions allowing a dinner plate to be thrust underneath, and upon which plate the top is set upright on its spinning spill. What follows is simple. The top being engaged by its twirling-spill in the two notches, and rotation imparted by a string, as in the humming-top, the plate is removed, and taken to any place the operator chooses. This top should not be less than five pounds in weight, and in diameter should be from three inches and a half to four inches.

Figure 6.2. Page from an instalment of John Scoffern, 'Optical Toy Sports', *Boy's Own Paper* 4 (1881–2), 228–9 (228). Reproduced by permission of the Syndics of Cambridge University Library.

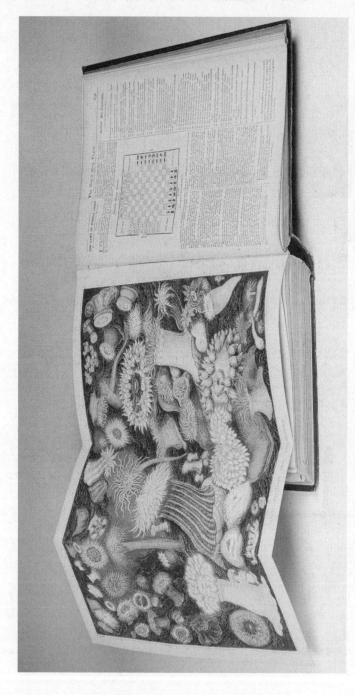

Figure 6.3. The sumptuous foldout coloured plate of 'British Sea-Anemones', *Boy's Own Paper* 4 (1881–2), facing 631. Reproduced by permission of the Syndics of Cambridge University Library.

Figure 6.4. Wonders of engineering and nature. In this issue of the *Boy's Own Paper*, a heroic account of the life and works of Robert Stephenson is directly followed by an instalment of Jules Verne's lavishly illustrated 'Giant Raft', an adventure story set in the Amazon Jungle featuring detailed descriptions and illustrations of the natural wonders of the landscape. *Boy's Own Paper* 3 (1880–1), 596–7. Reproduced by permission of the Syndics of Cambridge University Library.

PEDAGOGY, MORALITY, AND RACIAL SUPERIORITY

Theologies of nature and nationalism were two of many 'non-scientific' themes that the *BOP* aimed to promulgate in its scientific material. In this concluding section I shall look in more detail at the ways in which other non-scientific lessons were conveyed in the different literary genres of the juvenile periodical. We shall see that scientific material helped the *BOP* fulfil its evangelical mission by spreading factual information about the natural world and that such information was underpinned by Christian and Anglo-Saxon notions of masculinity, morality, and racial superiority which featured more explicitly in articles on those common *BOP* subjects of sport, history, warfare, and adventure.

A significant proportion of the *BOP*'s scientific content appears in essays and pedagogical articles. Of the essays featuring scientific content, many were straightforward surveys of a narrow scientific topic (for example, precious stones and electrical machines), and several were written with a strong historical and autobiographical perspective, including histories of arctic exploration and military weapons, and first-hand accounts of trips to such sites of scientific and technological interest as the Amazon and a London sewage works. These articles tended to be more descriptive and narrative-driven, and in general had less technical detail than the more common location for science: the serialized pedagogical article. Most of these articles comprised protocols for conducting experiments or collecting specimens, detailed descriptions of different types of natural object, and in many cases, explanations of scientific principles underlying the topic. By catering to boys' interests in practical hobbies, adventure, and knowledge, *BOP* authors felt they were in a good position to introduce more abstract matters of theory. They believed that it was while pursuing hobbies, walking in the countryside, and playing games, that boys were in a prime position to consider scientific principles and participate in scientific investigation.

Pedagogical articles frequently reminded readers that practical science was not only a source of entertainment and instruction, but also a manly and moral activity. Take, for example, J. G. Wood's introduction to his series on 'Shore Hunting'. He began by describing the type of boy who, wanting to fill his own aquarium with marine animals, visits a shoreline and after merely observing that there are no animals suitable for his collection gives up his search. Believing *BOP* readers to exclude such 'lazy' people who 'expect to gather a harvest without taking any trouble about it', Wood advised that the good shore-hunter manfully roughed it for the cause of science, wearing old clothes and realising that he '*must* get wet'. Wood had little time for the weaklings who protested that '"this shore-hunting interferes with meal-times"', replying that:

Of course it does, but what of that? People ought not to go to the seaside to carry on the regularity of their town hours . . . the genuine shore-hunter troubles himself very little about regular meals, and if he should find himself very hungry while hard at work in the low water, he can make a very good luncheon on the limpets and mussels which cling to almost every rock.[45]

Wood was one of many *BOP* authors who used the conduct of 'genuine' young scientific practitioners to promulgate Christian morality. Few issues revealed this strategy more prominently than cruelty to animals. Like all Victorian juvenile literature, the *BOP*'s attitude towards the treatment of animals was ambiguous, displaying what Mackenzie has called 'a striking sentimentality towards domestic animals while describing in lurid detail the agonies and death throes of wild ones'.[46] This tension is especially noticeable in the periodical format of the *BOP* where, for example, Stables's 1881 series on building a pigeon loft presents a much more humane approach to animals than the same author's 'The Cruise of the Snowbird', a serialized story of adventure and hunting that ran parallel to the pigeon-loft articles. By the time the *BOP* was launched, however, the campaigns of anti-vivisectionists such as Frances Power Cobbe had made the treatment of animals a much more prominent topic of public debate.[47]

The *BOP* generally tried to avoid 'party politics in any shape or form' but it did not evade discussion of vivisection.[48] On the contrary, this topic represents one of the most striking ways in which the early *BOP* used a controversial topic to define Christian morality in the context of scientific pursuits. One of the first *BOP* contributors to raise the issue was J. G. Wood in his 1879 pedagogical series 'On Killing, Setting, and Preserving Insects', which included detailed descriptions of the anatomy of various insects and protocols for dissecting them. He began, however, by rebutting objections that entomologists have 'no right to destroy life needlessly' and that killing insects 'involves cruelty'. To the first objection he insisted that entomology fulfilled important theological needs, emphasizing that: 'We cannot employ our minds on a higher subject than that which is afforded by the works of the Creator, and it is impossible to do so thoroughly without destroying life.' Having 'no sympathy with "sport" as exhibited by shooting creatures merely for the sake of killing them or displaying skill', Wood defended 'killing animals for the sake of natural knowledge' or for the purposes of clothing and eating, and added that Christian objections to slaughtering animals for food were vanquished by the 'recorded fact' that Jesus Christ ate cooked fish after the Resurrection. To the claim that entomology was cruel, Wood responded by insisting that 'An entomologist is never cruel' and never inflicts pain needlessly. He explained that even if the practitioner does inflict pain, 'insects do not suffer pain as mankind does' owing to their different 'nervous organisation'.[49]

The *BOP*'s editor, however, evidently felt that Wood had not sufficiently distinguished entomology from cruel animal sports and added a note explaining that Wood's 'facts do not diminish the guilt of wanton cruelty or the needless destruction of life'.[50] The *BOP* often defined morality through appropriate attitudes to animals in parables, reminiscences, pedagogical articles on pet breeding, and in stories of adventure, but was not always successful in making hunting a topic that could simultaneously carry a moral message and make for exciting reading matter. In 1884, for example, the *BOP* published a story involving a reprehensible character who baits badgers for fun, but this so offended the RTS General Committee that they condemned the periodical's implicit 'approval of the practice of persons for their amusement baiting animals' and felt they needed to have greater control over editorial decisions by urging 'more direct communication' between the Committee and the *BOP*'s editor.[51]

The RTS General Committee had no problems with the *BOP*'s representations of British scientific practitioners and inventors. Telling scientific lives could inculcate national pride and, as in many evangelical periodicals (see chapters 3 and 9), Christian virtues. Typically, the *BOP* imparted basic technical information but implicitly suggested that industry, benevolence, perseverance, courage, and piety, led to greatness in science, engineering, and other fields of endeavour. Thus, the industrialist Josiah Wedgwood was praised for his 'incessant' industry and love of truth 'in everything, great or small', while the baker-geologist Robert Dick was valorized for pursuing scientific interests despite adverse social and financial circumstances, and for learning 'to look from Nature up to Nature's God'.[52] The *BOP* tended to look to long-dead British figures for examples of the 'wise and the good', but the careers of living scientists could be represented to promulgate virtuous behaviour. In one of its rare explicit discussions of Charles Darwin, for example, the *BOP* echoed many evangelical reactions to Darwinian theories of man's origins in opining that: 'Without adopting the Darwinian theory of "evolution" or the development of all creatures from lower forms of life (man included), we cannot but admire [his] shrewd powers of observation and patient industry.'[53]

In many ways, *BOP* hagiographies were in tension with the representations of scientific practitioners elsewhere in the periodical. Much of the fiction promulgates the image of young scientific practitioners whose eccentric habits often land them in trouble. Jules Verne's 'Boy Captain', for instance, features a dishevelled 'observer and collector of insects' whose pursuit of an elusive 'hexapod' in the African jungle is thwarted by the actions of savage natives who have captured him and his friends.[54] A more positive gloss is given to the story of 'Billy Bungler' whose dangerous classroom chemistry experiments prove almost fatal to himself and to his school friends, but who is made to illustrate the virtues of patience and perseverance drawn from the lives of actual scientific practitioners: 'Don't despair if you are a duffer' it advised, 'for you may cure yourself of it, if only you will think and take your time.'[55] These contrasting representations of scientific practice highlight the different forms of didacticism operating within *BOP* fiction. The stories by Ballantyne, Reid, and Hope rarely pause to impart factual information while those by Verne, Stables, and Millington, developing the factual narrative of adventure and travel, sometimes resemble pedagogical articles, complete with footnotes.[56] Verne's 'Boy Captain', for example, includes a history of Western exploration of Africa while Thomas Millington's story of a boys' summer adventure included descriptions of kinematical experiments and refers to the author's *BOP* series on the mechanical principles governing the behaviour of toys.[57]

Verne's 'Boy Captain' may have projected a less than positive image of scientific practitioners but it was still a far cry from the hostile way that this story, like most Victorian juvenile serialized fiction, represented non-English and non-Christian races. As several historians have shown, this literature enforced sharp racial contrasts between Anglo-Saxons and 'others': British explorers, missionaries, and game-hunters were generally heroic and right-thinking individuals on the side of God, progress, and civilization, but natives of Africa, China, and other distant climes were invariably caricatured as barbaric, ignorant, grotesque, and generally inferior individuals who were hostile to the spread of God's word, British values and, as illustrated in Verne's story, scientific progress.[58] The *BOP*'s fictional representations of race were confirmed in the travelogues, essays, and other non-fictional articles contributed to the periodical by RTS missionaries, explorers, and military officers – articles that conspicuously avoided linking racial difference to sophisticated theories of biological development but whose sober and detailed descriptions of the customs, habits, and appearances of 'other' races gave ethnographic plausibility to the periodical's adventure stories.

One of most potent strategies for enticing *BOP* readers to buy subsequent issues of the periodical was its column of editorial replies to correspondents, which often included extracts from letters sent in by (mainly older) boys.[59] In giving greater voice to readers, the *BOP* was typical of late-Victorian juvenile periodicals which, compared with their mid-Victorian ancestors, provided many more opportunities for readers to engage with contributors and to become authors themselves. Scientific material occupied a prominent role in the dialogue between readers and contributors that took place in the *BOP*'s correspondence columns. Common topics included the identity of natural historical specimens that readers had sent in to the journal, methods of caring for domestic animals, advice on scientific textbooks, suggestions on buying and building simple scientific instruments, and technical information about geography, astronomy, and other topics. The tone of replies also varied, from the enthusiastic (as when boys sent in rare fossils) to the downright haughty, as when the *BOP* severely chastised one correspondent for not knowing one of the 'best-known facts' concerning pneumatics.[60] Even in the small space of the editorial reply, the *BOP* sought to impart knowledge as well as inculcate such virtues as perseverance and industry more fully explored in longer articles. Thus, in reply to one correspondent's specific question about chemical filtration and ways of studying chemistry, the *BOP* presented a technical explanation of filtration and then counselled:

persevere with the science, and work hard at it from the very first, no matter what your age may be. You never know what little time you have to spare in the future, and cannot do wrong in making good use of the present. Get some good text-books on Chemistry of recent date – say Roscoe's – first the primer and then the manual, and work out all the experiments therein, noting failures and queer appearances, and clearing up all your difficulties as you go.[61]

Given the immense popularity of the *BOP* it is likely that more readers than the correspondent himself would have read this lesson in chemical practice, perseverance, and humility. Of all genres in the *BOP*, the correspondence column was the place one was most likely to find the more abstruse information on the sciences. But by placing this column at the back of the periodical and by printing it in small type, Hutchison was able to maintain the distance of his periodical from the unpalatable style of the textbook and to propagate the dominant image of his periodical as a welcome blend of entertainment and instruction.

CONCLUSION

This chapter has highlighted some of the ways in which one of the most popular of all late-Victorian boys' weeklies continued the shift begun in the 1850s by many secular and religious publishers towards publishing children's periodicals that responded to changing juvenile tastes by becoming less didactic and more entertaining, less dreary and more colourful, and which accordingly sought to redefine how periodicals could most effectively conduct their pedagogical and moral missions. I have also shown that we can obtain a much better picture of how these missions were conducted by exploring the *totality* of material in the periodical. By this method we not only find that there is far more material on science, technology, and medicine than suggested by merely counting straightforwardly 'scientific' articles, but that this material was frequently entangled with, and helped bolster, such fundamental issues as morality and racial superiority.

Although the *BOP* prided itself on such contributors as Verne whose works were already admired by boys and their parents, it also depended on the writing and artistic skills of myriad other contributors, such as Dr Scoffern, who have now disappeared into obscurity. Many of these writers and artists, however unfamiliar to us now, contributed to the scientific content of one of the most widely read juvenile periodicals of the late-Victorian period. As historians are increasingly recognizing, these scientific popularizers shaped the public's understanding of science more than professional savants, and it is therefore essential that we know more about their backgrounds and roles in the print cultures representing the sciences.

The *BOP* was far from being the only periodical from which late-Victorian juvenile readers would have absorbed scientific knowledge. It had fierce rivals such as *Boys of England* and in the 1890s its market position was challenged by a plethora of imitators and by the flood of cheap halfpenny boys' periodicals issued by Alfred Harmsworth, Cyril Pearson, George Newnes, and similar publishers.[62] We still know very little about how these very different periodicals appropriated and represented science to their readers, and this chapter has suggested some of the key elements of a thorough systematic and comparative study of juvenile periodicals that will force us to revise our notions of how publishing forms that look so very different from the class-book contributed in no small measure to the scientific interests and skills of the late-Victorians.

CHAPTER 7

The Review of Reviews *and the new journalism in late-Victorian Britain*

Gowan Dawson

When he first heard about William Randolph Hearst's notorious campaign to furnish a war between America and Spain in 1896 by filling the *New York Journal* with sensational stories of Spanish despotism in Cuba, William Thomas Stead immediately recognized this 'newest of new journalists' as a kindred spirit. Applauding the *New York Journal* as 'a newspaper which, instead of confining itself to the function of chronicling other men's deeds, boldly asserts its determination to supersede the journalism that chronicles by the journalism that acts', Stead observed that its campaigning style 'reminds me at every turn of what we tried to do in the old *Pall Mall* days'. As editor of the *Pall Mall Gazette* in the 1880s, Stead averred, he had 'succeeded in impressing upon the public mind, a conception of what Matthew Arnold called "The New Journalism" which has never been entirely effaced'.[1] Coined by Arnold in 1887 as a pejorative epithet, the 'New' journalism that Stead claimed to have pioneered was distinguished from the 'Old' by a mixture of journalistic and typographical devices originally used in North America, and appealed primarily to the newly literate mass audience created, in part, by the 1870 Education Act. The new journalism, in fact, had its origins in several newspapers of the 1870s, but came to greater prominence with a number of periodicals that were founded during the 1880s and 1890s.[2] The approach was exemplified in particular by Stead's energetic editorship of the daily *Pall Mall Gazette* (1883–89) and then the monthly *Review of Reviews* (1890–1912), both of which engaged in crusades against various vested interests as well as pioneering new formats such as the interview. Stead boldly rejected the long tradition of 'effete' impersonal journalism and the 'awe of the mystic "We"', and instead enjoined a partisan and distinctly personal style of writing and editing, allowing him to put into practice his conviction that the 'editor is the uncrowned king' of the new era of mass democracy.[3] Like the so-called 'yellow journalism' that Hearst introduced to 1890s America, the new journalism practised by Stead and others significantly altered several aspects of the production and consumption of periodicals and newspapers in late-Victorian Britain.

The emergence of the new journalism, as is discussed in the introduction, coincided with broad changes in the organization of the sciences as well as the ways in which they were presented to the public, with professional men of science becoming ever more isolated from the wider population. This chapter, which is based on a close reading of twenty volumes of the *Review of Reviews* from 1890 to 1899, will examine how the presentation of scientific material in Stead's flagship journal was importantly affected by tactics such as the appropriation and recasting of élite scientific knowledge for a popular audience, the promotion of new ways of reading science that were suited to busy plebeian readers, the use of personality-based formats like the celebrity interview, and the prominent involvement of ordinary readers in the *Review*'s production. In particular, it will suggest that the treatment of science in the popular print media could be considerably more dynamic and less passive in this period than has usually been shown by historians, and will look at the problems which ageing scientific naturalists such as Thomas Henry Huxley, as well as more traditional popularizers of science like Grant Allen, now encountered with the journalistic devices pioneered by Stead. These formal aspects of new journalistic practice, as this chapter will show, were central to the troubled encounters between scientific practitioners and writers and the new type of campaigning editor exemplified by Stead, and signalled wider changes in the relationship between the spokesmen of élite groups, popularizers, and the mass reading public.

Several historians of the press have endeavoured to identify the defining characteristics of the 'New' journalism, with Alan J. Lee suggesting that it 'constituted a new style of journalism, a style which reflected a changing relationship between the newspaper and its reader', and Joseph O. Baylen proposing that 'the New Journalism was . . . a projection of the Nonconformist conscience in Victorian life' in which '"agitations" and "crusades"' were 'an important device . . . to mobilize public opinion'.[4] These were certainly highly conspicuous features of new journalistic practice, but the case of the *Review of Reviews* suggests that Stead's brand of journalism was also importantly characterized by its particular relation to other periodical genres and its position in the marketplace. In 1889 Archibald Grove had founded the *New Review*, which set out to provide the kind of material usually carried in half-crown reviews like the *Nineteenth Century* for the cheaper price of 6d. The *Review of Reviews*, launched less than six months later, was similarly priced as a sixpenny monthly, but it went further by employing the format of so-called 'snippet-papers' like the penny weekly

Tit-Bits (short paragraphs culled from a myriad of other periodicals) in order
to bring the actual contents of the 2s 6d reviews to a far wider readership.[5]
This generic hybridity and peculiar relation to the periodical marketplace
was, as much as any other feature of the new journalism, to have significant
consequences for the treatment of science in organs such as the *Review of
Reviews*.

Stead had resigned his editorship of the *Pall Mall Gazette* in December
1889 after its proprietor Henry Yates Thompson became increasingly ex-
asperated with his controversial editorial style and its deleterious effect on
circulation. He had long harboured plans to edit a monthly journal, and,
even before leaving the *Pall Mall*, had agreed with George Newnes, founder
of the best-selling *Tit-Bits*, to begin a new monthly review, a venture that
would combine Stead's editorial flair with Newnes's business acumen.[6] The
first number of the *Review of Reviews* appeared on 6 January 1890, less than
four weeks after the initial agreement between Stead and Newnes.[7] This
frenetic pace of production was to become one of the hallmarks of the new
journal, which the mercurial Stead moulded in his own image. Stead had
earlier insisted that the 'personality of the editor is the essential centre-point
of my whole idea of the true journalism', and readers of the first number of
the *Review* were assured that while the new journal would 'certainly not be
a party organ', neither would it be merely 'a colourless reflection of the public opinion'.[8] Rather, the *Review* would advance Stead's own idiosyncratic
Dissenting (Congregationalist) and Radical Imperialist outlook, exhibiting
an 'almost awe-struck regard for the destinies of the English-speaking man'
and exhorting 'a revival of civic faith, a quickening of spiritual life'.[9] This
evangelistic and overtly personal style of journalism, as Newnes quickly realized, was not sufficiently popular to 'gather in the shekels' in a mass-market
dominated by fiction-based illustrated magazines, and in April 1890 Stead,
with financial assistance from the Salvation Army, bought out Newnes's
half-share of the fledgling journal.[10]

Stead was now the editor, publisher, and sole proprietor of the *Review
of Reviews*, but he had pledged that the journal would adhere to a certain
standard of disinterestedness and be 'without political prejudice or religious
intolerance'. Above all, its aim would be to 'make the best thoughts of the
best writers . . . universally accessible'.[11] The *Review*, in Stead's grandiose
and somewhat paradoxical vision, would bring 'salvation from untutored
democracy' by popularizing Arnold's elitist conceptions of criticism and
culture, even though Arnold himself had been one of the principal critics
of what he termed the '*feather-brained*' tendency of the so-called 'New
Journalism'.[12] Rather than detracting from the pursuit of these aims, Stead

assured anxious readers that the 'unity of control and concentration of responsibility' brought about by Newnes's departure would in fact enable him to 'carry out more completely the ideal with which the REVIEW was founded', as well as allowing its enlargement from seventy-two to ninety-six pages.[13]

The production of the *Review of Reviews* was initially carried out by Newnes's skilled staff at the *Tit-Bits* office, but after only three monthly numbers it devolved on to the much less experienced personnel at Stead's new Mowbray House office on the Thames Embankment. While the *Review* was predominantly 'mononymous' (the only name mentioned in most issues was that of Stead) and deliberately gave the impression that almost every article emanated from the editor's prolific pen, its rapid production required the collaboration of a number of anonymous contributors, including the young Grant Richards, as well as a host of nameless clerks and typists. In fact, when Stead suffered a mild nervous breakdown in 1895, his younger brother, the Revd Francis Herbert Stead, temporarily took over as editor, although this was never acknowledged in the *Review*'s pages.[14] The staff of the *Review* was particularly distinctive for the large proportion of women that Stead – an advocate of female suffrage – employed at rates of pay equal to their male colleagues, and, under the supervision of the office manager Marie Belloc, female journalists such as Flora Shaw and Virginia Crawford, as well as the 'indexer to the *Review*' Miss E. Hetherington, contributed significantly to the work of the journal.[15] From May 1891, though, the *Review*'s most important employee after Stead was the circumspect business manager Edwin Stout, whose financial prudence helped rein in Stead's editorial recklessness and did much to ensure that the *Review* actually broke even (assisted by dividend payments from Stead's shares in the more successful American *Review of Reviews*).[16] Newnes's hard-nosed concern about the commercial viability of the 'kind of journalism which . . . upsets governments [and] does many other great things' proved to be accurate, and, despite a circulation which began at 80,000 and reached 200,000 after two years, the self-proclaimed flagship of the new journalism struggled to remain financially afloat throughout its existence.[17]

ABSTRACT CONCERNS

To perform the momentous functions that Stead had proposed, the *Review of Reviews* would be 'a combination of two elements, – the eclectic and the personal'.[18] As well as Stead's personal commentary on current events in the opening 'Progress of the World' section, and the regular 'Character Sketch' of a notable personality, the bulk of the remainder of the journal's ninety-six pages comprised the 'Leading Articles in the Reviews' and 'The Reviews Reviewed' sections. These summaries and evaluations of articles from a myriad of domestic and foreign periodicals – which ranged in size from over a page to just a couple of lines – aimed to 'supply a clue' to the 'mighty maze of modern periodical literature' by providing 'a readable compendium of all the best articles in the magazines and reviews', 'winnowing away the chaff and . . . revealing the grain' of the month's journalistic output. This 'humble but useful task', however, was in fact, at least initially, the most controversial aspect of the *Review*'s journalistic practice, and was to have far-reaching consequences for relations between the journal and high-profile scientific experts like Huxley.[19]

One of the reasons that the *Review*'s method of abstracting material from the world's press was contentious was that more expensive rivals feared that it would 'gut' them of their most appealing copy and thereby remove the necessity for readers actually to purchase the periodical in which it had originally appeared. James Knowles, editor of the *Nineteenth Century*, protested that the intellectual property of his expensively acquired 'star' contributors was being unfairly pilfered by Stead, complaining in a letter to Huxley of 'the incredible impudence of this unconscionable cad . . . filching my copyright' and 'living upon other people's brains' with his 'stolen goods truck the "Review of Reviews"'.[20] In actual fact, the *Review*, unlike Newnes's *Tit-Bits*, generally sought the permission of publishers to reproduce their intellectual property; Longman's, for example, gave 'express permission' and 'sent . . . advance proofs for the purpose of quotation'.[21] But even Stead's outraged insistence that the *Review* actually assisted 'the older magazines' by providing them with 'an unexampled publicity . . . given "free gratis and for nothing"' did not allay lingering suspicions about the legitimacy of his journalistic practice, especially among rival editors.[22] Edmund Yates, editor of the illustrated weekly the *World*, dubbed Stead's journal '*Fagin's Miscellany*', and alleged that various publishers were threatening to take legal action against him.[23] Stead strongly repudiated this accusation, but, as with the earlier tradition of cheap 'scissors and paste' journalism, the *Review* did at times flout existing copyright legislation (which remained largely unchanged since 1842) with apparent impunity, vindicating its literary expropriations with an explicitly populist justification.[24] As Stead later claimed, to reproduce in the *Review* maps and diagrams published by the Home Office which only 'a very small proportion of the forty millions of our population will ever have the opportunity of inspecting' was 'a permissible infringement on their copyright'.[25] Similarly, the principal aim of the

'Leading Articles in the Reviews' and 'The Reviews Reviewed' sections was to make the contents of 2s 6d reviews like Knowles's *Nineteenth Century* accessible to a much larger audience.

The problem that editors and contributors from the more expensive end of the periodical market had with this populist piracy, however, was not merely financial. Rather, the practice of abstracting just the main points from long articles in reviews like the *Nineteenth Century* and the *Fortnightly Review* prompted serious epistemological concerns over the control of ideas. Whilst pondering the form that the *Review of Reviews* should take, Stead had canvassed the opinion of many of the most prominent intellectuals and statesmen in late-Victorian Britain, reprinting facsimile reproductions of their hand-written letters of reply in the front pages of the first number. Huxley, in his reply, welcomed 'such a guide to magazinedom as you propose', but counselled Stead that he must 'secure the services of a body of intelligent and painstaking précis writers', warning, 'I am not quite sure that extracts are fair to authors' because 'passages without context often give a very wrong impression of the writer's meaning'.[26] Huxley was less concerned than Knowles with the monetary and commercial implications of abstraction.[27] Instead, his principal anxiety was that the *Review*'s method of journalistic abridgement might erode the author's control over the meaning of an article. By giving an inaccurate summary, or by pulling out only those aspects of an article that were perceived to be of interest to a mass audience or served a journal's ideological agenda, the process of abstracting might actually change the intended meaning of the original article. In the Early Modern period, as Adrian Johns has shown, such literary 'piracy . . . had epistemic as well as economic implications: it affected the structure and content of knowledge', and new journalistic methods of expropriation in the metropolis of the 1890s resembled aspects of the 'rapacious practices of London printers and booksellers' in the unstable print culture of the sixteenth century.[28] What was at stake in the *Review of Review*'s method of abstracting was what has recently been termed 'textual stability': the ability of authors and publishers to control and manage the use of the words that are printed under their names once they are replicated in, amongst many other formats, reviews and excerpts in other publications.[29]

Huxley's pellucid prose was one of the most highly prized commodities in the late-Victorian periodical marketplace. As Joseph Hatton noted in his survey of *Journalistic London* (1882), 'Mr. Huxley often speaks without being reported, yet editors of periodicals . . . will pay him anything to write for them.'[30] Huxley's relationship with these editors, as he told John Morley of the *Fortnightly*, was like being 'as spoiled as a maiden with many wooers', and he promised to 'remain as constant as a persistent bigamist'.[31] Indeed, the lovelorn editors of monthly reviews like the *Fortnightly* and the *Nineteenth Century* were so anxious to retain Huxley's journalistic services that they allowed him a great deal of autonomy in the writing of his articles. Able to dictate details such as length, format, and the kind of printing set-up used for the manuscript, Huxley exerted a high degree of control over how his articles might be interpreted, even to the extent of determining when an article might come out in relation to the timing of other pieces on the same subject.[32] However, when evaluative digests of these same articles appeared in the *Review of Reviews* Huxley lost much of this close control over how they might be understood.

The sexagenarian Huxley, at the height of his celebrity if not his intellectual prowess, was a constant presence in the *Review* during its first year, with five abstracts of his articles in the *Nineteenth Century*, as well as facsimile reproductions of two of his letters to Stead, appearing in its pages. Initially, Stead had asked Huxley to 'cast your eye over a précis, that I have prepared, of your article ['On the Natural Inequality of Men'] for the "Review of Reviews"', claiming that he was 'very anxious to express your view on the one hand without in any way infringing upon the copyright of Knowles on the other'.[33] Such scrupulous concern with accurately representing Huxley's actual views, however, did not last for long. Rather, abstracts of his articles soon began to pick out and dwell on those aspects which apparently demonstrated Huxley's 'sledge-hammer polemic' and 'knock-down method of controversy' and seemed to show that his 'natural vocation was the prize-ring'.[34] Such an incessant focus on Huxley's irascibility could make his arguments seem rash and unreasoned, and might even tarnish his reputation for scientific disinterestedness. Indeed, one abstract of a twenty-page article simply reproduced the four most intemperate paragraphs, which were used to adduce that 'Professor Huxley, as a Biblical controversialist, is rougher than Mr. [Charles] Bradlaugh', thereby associating the ageing scientific naturalist with the notorious atheist and belligerent advocate of free thought.[35] There existed, as Stead acknowledged, 'a gulf difficult to span' between his and Huxley's views on most questions, and, in Stead's adept hands, the process of abstraction could be used to construct particular interpretations of Huxley's writing that were often very different from the intended meanings of the original articles.[36]

When this deliberately partial method of abstraction was combined with the breakneck speed with which the *Review of Reviews* was produced each month, the stability of the author's original meaning became even more contingent. As Stead himself conceded, 'Many of the magazines which are reviewed only come out on the 30th and 31st of each month, and the *Review* goes to press on the 1st of the month of issue; hence many shortcomings of which no one is more conscious than the editor.'[37] Even with Stead's apparent awareness of its inadequacies, however, the *Review* was not closely proof-read, for, as Grant Richards later recalled, Stead '[n]ever spared time to look critically at the actual magazine. By the time it reached his hands it was already a back-number. His mind would be on its successor.'[38] The distorting effect of these shortcomings and the absence of proper proof-reading became particularly evident in July 1890 when a summary of one of Huxley's articles for the *Nineteenth Century* suggested that his judge-ment of 'the accounts given in Genesis of the Creation and of the Deluge as "lies" . . . is significant of the mental temperature in which the article is written'.[39] Adrian Desmond has suggested that this insinuation infuriated Huxley primarily because of his ideological animus against Stead's support for the Salvation Army and belief in spiritualism.[40] In fact, what was prin-cipally at issue was the reliability of Stead's new journalistic method of hurried abstraction, for in the following issue of the *Review* (August 1890) Stead was forced to offer an unconditional apology for printing 'a railing accusation against Professor Huxley last month which he did not deserve', admitting that the 'blunder' had been caused by 'mistak[ing] a verb [i.e. "lies"] for a substantive'.[41] By abstracting it in haste, and with a predisposi-tion to view Huxley as a hot-tempered controversialist, Stead had misread the relevant passage from the article, which stated simply:

Now, not only do I hold it to be proven that the story of the Deluge is a pure fiction; but I have no hesitation in affirming the same thing of the story of the Creation. Between these two *lies* the story of the creation of man and woman and their fall from primitive innocence, which is even more monstrously improbable than either of the other two [my italics].[42]

In the wake of this very public blunder, Stead became, for a short while at least, more circumspect about the way in which he treated Huxley's articles, noting warily that 'even the most daring of reviewers would shrink from attempting to summarize' them.[43] Despite this brief interval of chastened propriety, however, Stead soon reverted to new journalistic type, exasperat-ing Huxley yet again by, once more, playing fast and loose with his public and private statements.

After reading the erroneous abstract in July 1890, Huxley had at once penned a letter of protest to Stead in which he asked archly, 'Will you be so good as to inform me on what pages [of] my article the passage to which you refer occurs; and more particularly where the word "lies" which you specifically quote from it is to be found.' In a subsequent letter he permitted himself the 'small malice of asking whether the mistake . . . is not "significant of the mental temperature" in which your number was written'.[44] Huxley's mordant humour in fact belied a long-running concern with the illicit appropriation and misrepresentation of his words in the popular press, as had happened, most notably, in November 1883 when Charles A. Watts's *Agnostic Annual* reprinted a private letter received from Huxley – who had coined the term 'agnostic' – as if it were an official contribution endorsing the new journal's militant aims.[45] Stead also attempted to arrogate and exploit Huxley's imprimatur to advance his own populist agenda, but, unlike the rationalist Watts, he did this even on issues for which Huxley himself had absolutely no sympathy whatsoever.

When, in January 1891, Huxley had cause to accuse Stead of publishing in the columns of *The Times* 'a partly untrue and wholly misleading account' of their private correspondence regarding a contretemps over the Salvation Army, Stead replied, somewhat disingenuously, that he was 'grieved' that Huxley 'should think [him] capable of intentionally misrepresenting' him.[46] He had in any case, he explained, only referred to their correspondence 'in order to induce the *Times* to publish [his] letter', because, while Huxley was widely regarded as '*persona gratissima*', Stead himself had the 'misfortune to be *persona Ingratissima-issima-issima-issima*' following his imprisonment for abduction during the *Pall Mall Gazette*'s infamous campaign to expose child prostitution in the 1880s.[47] With well-connected editors like Knowles still scorning him as a 'filthy ex-convict', only the apparent endorsement of Huxley could allow Stead's letter to gain access to the venerable pages of *The Times*.[48]

Two years later, Huxley's respectability and intellectual authority were once again co-opted by Stead in support of one of his new journalistic enterprises. In July 1893, Stead sent Huxley a copy of the opening number of *Borderland*, a short-lived attempt to provide a 'quarterly REVIEW OF REVIEWS dealing with subjects which are supposed to lie beyond the pale of human knowledge' that reflected Stead's growing interest in spiritualism and psychic forces.[49] Much to his chagrin, Huxley, who vigorously opposed all forms of supernatural speculation, found that the very first page of Stead's occult organ proclaimed that it would conduct its extrasensory investigations in accordance with 'the principle laid down by Professor Huxley as the fundamental axiom of modern science, "to try all things, and to hold fast by that which is good"'. The same page also carried a lengthy quotation from Huxley's *Nineteenth Century* article 'Agnosticism' (1889), which was presented as if it were an explicit endorsement of open-minded research into all unknown phenomena.[50] Even worse, a few pages later Huxley's apparently sympathetic words were contrasted with the dismissive scepticism of a letter from his close friend Edwin Ray Lankester, with Stead claiming proudly that his own 'invincible reluctance to depart from what Professor Huxley describes as the first principle of modern science gives me much more chance of success than even such an eminent physiologist as Dr. Lankester himself'.[51] Complaining bitterly that Stead had quoted his 'opinion respecting the principles of scientific investigation, as if it were in some way inconsistent with the views expressed by Prof. Lankester', Huxley insisted that this 'conviction' was 'erroneous' and that, notwithstanding the misrepresentation of his views, he in fact fully endorsed 'Lankester's very plain speaking' as to Stead's 'own qualifications for dealing with the question'.[52] Having had his words so distorted and misrepresented that he appeared to be a potential advocate of spiritualism,[53] Huxley wanted nothing more to do with the *Review of Reviews*'s wily editor, and even refused to add his name to a memorial for international arbitration to check the growth of European armaments which Stead sent to several politicians and intellectuals in the following year.[54]

The troubled relations that Huxley experienced with Stead in the early 1890s, so different from his convivial dealings with editors of middle-class reviews like Knowles and Morley, reveal some of the tensions between the producers of expert knowledge and populist campaigning editors that were prompted, at least in part, by the novel publishing formats of the new journalism. Indeed, Huxley's evident irritation and frustration with Stead's incessant appropriation of his imprimatur shows vividly how the traditional relations of authority that men of science had earlier been able to establish with more respectful and deferential journals were now fracturing as the dynamics of the periodical marketplace were transformed by the massive increase in titles aimed specifically at a mass audience.

Stead's self-conscious aim was to bring expert knowledge, whether this be political, artistic, or scientific, to the common reader in a suitably cheap and digested form. As is obvious with the case of Huxley though, the process of abstraction that he employed to do this was never merely a passive mode of diffusion of a simplified form of knowledge. Rather, élite knowledge was transformed by the acts of 'exchange, interaction, translation, and resistance' involved in its condensation, with certain features being emphasized – like Huxley's acerbity – and others – such as Huxley's detailed use of evidence – being more or less overlooked.[55] The process of abstraction, then, was never neutral, and could even become an important resource in Stead's campaigning style of journalism.

Stead believed that science, more than any other area of élite culture, stood in need of being made more accessible to the wider reading public. The *Review of Reviews* regularly abstracted material on a diverse range of subjects from specialist scientific journals like the *Proceedings of the Royal Geographical Society* and the *Journal of Mental Science*, as well as foreign technical periodicals like the *Neue Militärische Blätter*. Such 'periodicals written by savants and specialists', Stead noted in one abstract, had 'the disadvantage of the scientific division of labour' and 'emphasise[d] division and isolation in science'. As such, 'what [was] written in them' needed to be made 'interesting and accessible to the whole reading world' and the 'general public' rather than just 'meet[ing] the eye of the specialist for whom it [was] originally intended'.[56] The rather donnish reports of psychological experiments in the *Proceedings of the Society for Psychical Research*, for instance, could nevertheless be plundered for intriguing and eerie copy such as 'well-authenticated ghost-stories' which expound the 'theory that apparitions . . . can be explained scientifically by the analogy of telepathy'.[57] Indeed, as he became increasingly fascinated by the supernatural, Stead pledged that his new journal *Borderland* would 'attempt to do in a popular and catholic form that which is done in a more or less doctrinaire and exclusive way by the Brahmins of Psychical Research'.[58] Such a campaign to 'democratise . . . the study of the spook', though, was not merely an attempt at a passive diffusionist popularization, for Stead insisted that to improve psychical research the 'collection of the evidence about the phenomena must necessarily be entrusted to a multitude of witnesses'.[59] Reliable substantiation of psychical phenomena, Stead urged, could only be achieved by breaking down the exclusivity of the Cambridge-based Society for Psychical Research (SPR) and permitting the mass audience of cheap periodicals to participate in the collection of extrasensory evidence.[60]

In fact, Stead considered that the *Review of Reviews*'s practice of abstracting and indexing articles from the world's press could actually make a significant contribution to the advancement of scientific knowledge by rendering the rapid growth of specialist information more manageable. 'Scientific workers', he reported, 'are complaining of the ever-increasing difficulty of keeping abreast of current scientific literature, even the literature of one particular science', and he bemoaned the fact that as yet 'no one has invented a *Scientific Review of Reviews*'. Even the Royal Society's momentous *Catalogue of Scientific Papers* (1867–) was judged a 'very incomplete and unsatisfactory' work that failed to fulfil adequately the function of an index of modern science.[61] The *Review* gave encouragement to a scheme for a bibliography of zoological literature employing methods similar to its own, but suggested that in the meantime its own abstracts and indexes could be of use even to the most prominent scientific writers.[62] In an abstract of the contents of the *Fortnightly* in September 1890 Stead remarked, 'I am glad to see that Mr. A. R. Wallace is a diligent reader of the *Review of Reviews*', noting that Wallace's paper on 'Human Selection' in the *Fortnightly* 'reviews the various summaries of articles on the subject of the improvement of the race which appeared in recent numbers of the *Review*'.[63] Wallace, however, took exception to the presumptive tone of the abstract, and forced Stead, just two months after his embarrassing blunder over Huxley's abstract, to apologize for doing him 'an injustice in the terms of my reference to your article', which, Stead conceded, could 'be read to imply . . . that you had only read the summaries' in the *Review of Reviews* rather than the original articles.[64] Despite the concern of prominent men of science like Huxley and Wallace with the reliability of his method of abstracting articles from other journals, Stead nevertheless continued to believe that the formal techniques of the new journalism could be of immense benefit to elite science in a period which witnessed an unprecedented growth in scientific information.

POPULAR READING

The *Review of Reviews* supplemented its abstracts of scientific articles from other periodicals with original essays commissioned from prominent popularizers like Grant Allen, author of, among many other things, the bestselling *The Evolutionist at Large* (1881), and John Munro, who penned works like *The Romance of Electricity* (1893) for the Religious Tract Society. This specially commissioned science writing appeared primarily in the short-lived 'Our Scientific Causerie' feature, as well as in character sketches of major scientific figures like Lord Kelvin and Robert Koch. In all of these formats, however, Stead insisted that science should be presented to the general reading public in as concise and succinct a form as possible. When it came to science, it seems that Stead always felt that the shorter the better, and he praised Edward Clodd's 'little book' *A Primer of Evolution* (1895) for its comprehensive 'presentment of the theory of evolution in so short a space'.[65] Even the most prolific of popularizers, however, did not share Stead's enthusiasm for pithy abridgement and hasty summary. Allen, who had contributed over eighty articles to the *Pall Mall Gazette* during the 1880s, was now commissioned to write the very first 'Our Scientific Causerie' for the *Review*'s June 1890 number. At the beginning of his two-page essay, which discussed August Weismann's recent experimental work on the continuity of the germ-plasm, he informed the reader that a 'small difference of opinion has occurred between my friend the Editor and myself' concerning the form that the article should take. The 'Editor', Allen observed, 'says science has made itself into a Brahmin caste, which holds aloof from the people' and wants the *Review of Reviews* to carry 'every month . . . a couple of pages of summary, showing what the scientific world is just then mainly engaged in thinking and debating'. Allen, on the other hand, was of the opinion that

You can't explain these things off-hand in so short a space to the general public . . . Outsiders who want to know, even cursorily, what these things are driving at, must make up their minds to devote to them a great deal more time and thought than is involved in glancing over a page or two of criticism in a general review.

Although he knew it 'will be heresy to the editor', Allen suggested that the unintelligibility of his own article ('the reader is as much at sea as at the outset', he concludes) has 'proved my point' that 'you really cannot compress' the latest findings on a recondite subject like heredity 'into two columns, so as to make it intelligible at a glance to the meanest understanding'.[66] Stead had earlier labelled Allen 'the most indefatigable of all mags-men', but his new journalistic ideal of popular science diverged widely even from that of such a highly prolific professional writer.[67]

This difference of opinion over the journalistic popularization of science was part of a more general disagreement over the ways that periodicals and newspapers were to be consumed by a mass audience. Allen's concern that readers should 'devote . . . a great deal' of 'time and thought' to reading rather than just 'glancing over a page or two' mirrored a wider concern with working-class reading practices, especially of periodicals, in the 1880s and 1890s.[68] The 'periodical literature' which is full of 'miscellanea, advertisements, and answers to correspondents', George R. Humphrey observed in the *Nineteenth Century* in 1893, 'begets loose, desultory habits of reading, and the idea that the study of a given subject is the height of monotony'. These desultory habits of reading, moreover, were particularly damaging to the popular understanding of science, because, Humphrey insisted, while 'novels are *read only* . . . Scientific books are studied'.[69] Even Allen's journalistic popularization of science in titles like the *Cornhill Magazine* and the *Popular Science Monthly* required that readers invest a considerable amount of time and effort in the process of reading and understanding.

The new journalism of Stead and others, however, was predicated on a very different conception of how a popular audience could and should read periodicals. Another practitioner of the new journalistic style, Thomas Power O'Connor, insisted in the *New Review*:

We live in an age of hurry and of multitudinous newspapers. The newspaper is not read in the secrecy and silence of the closet as is the book. It is picked up at a railway station, hurried over in a railway carriage dropped incontinently when read. To get your ideas through the hurried eyes into the whirling brains that are employed in the reading of a newspaper there must be no mistake about your meaning.[70]

The process of reading encouraged by the new journalism was not only different from the way that books were consumed, but also from the way that expensive monthly reviews were read. Articles that frequently ran to thirty or forty pages posed considerable difficulties for readers who could not afford the 2s 6d cover price of these reviews. As John Burns, leader of the 1889 dockers' strike, told Stead, 'Being unable to purchase the *Fortnightly*...I have looked at the first two pages on a bookstall at Charing Cross, the next few at Waterloo, and finished the article at Victoria some days later, compelled, of course, to buy a paper to justify my staying the time at each.'[71] The prohibitive cost, though, was not the only impediment to plebeian readers of titles like the *Fortnightly*. Rather, working-class readers generally could not afford to give the same amount of time to reading as the prosperous middle-class readers at whom the monthly reviews were principally aimed.

From the very outset, the *Review of Reviews* was intended to cater precisely to those readers with neither the money nor the leisure to read the monthly reviews. While organs of the so-called 'higher journalism' like the *Nineteenth Century* and *Fortnightly* were still aimed primarily at members of the intellectual elite who could read in the comfortable surroundings of metropolitan clubs, the *Review* was aimed defiantly at hardworking commuters who did much of their reading in crowded railway carriages. Advertisements declared proudly that it was 'UNIVERSALLY ACKNOWLEDGED TO BE THE BEST MAGAZINE FOR BUSY MEN' (adding that it was 'also the BEST FOR BUSY WOMEN'), and newspapers like the *Morning Post* agreed that the *Review* was 'of considerable value in an age when few have the time to read the leading articles in the magazines, and the majority have neither the time nor the opportunity' (fig. 7.1).[72] With characteristic hyperbole (and a lingering memory of the Dissenting traditions of reading in which he was brought up), Stead had initially proclaimed that his new journal should be 'read as men used to read their Bibles, not to waste an idle hour, but to discover the will of God'.[73] However, with its concise digests of current news

THE REVIEW OF REVIEWS

EDITED BY W. T. STEAD

(Monthly, Sixpence),

IS UNIVERSALLY ACKNOWLEDGED TO BE THE

Best Magazine for Busy Men

And it is also the BEST FOR BUSY WOMEN, for MISS FRANCES WILLARD, surely one of the best and busiest of women, says :—

"Your Magazine has the brightest outlook window in Christendom for busy people who want to see what is going on in the great world."

IT CONTAINS ALL THE BEST THOUGHTS OF THE BEST WRITERS IN CONTEMPORARY PERIODICAL LITERATURE.

THE NEW VOLUME   **STILL TO BE HAD.**

(Volume IV.)

Is NOW READY.   VOL. I. (Jan.-June, 1890), 4s. 6d.
                         VOL. II. (July-Dec., 1890), 5s.
Handsomely Bound in Cloth   VOL. III. (Jan.-June, 1891), 4s. 6d.
Gilt (656 pages),
Price 4s. 6d ; by Post, 5s.
                         Postage 6d. extra on each Volume.

Publishing Office—   Publishing Office—
125, FLEET STREET, E.C.   **125, FLEET STREET, E.C.**

"The Review of Reviews" will be sent Post Free for 12 Months to any part of the World for Eight Shillings and Sixpence.

Send Address, with Postal Order, to the Editorial Office, Mowbray House, NORFOLK STREET, LONDON, W.C.

Figure 7.1. Advertisement included in *Index to the Periodical Literature of the World (Covering the Year 1891)* (London: Office of the *Review of Reviews*, 1892). By permission of the British Library, PP.1483.c.

and opinion the *Review* in practice encouraged partial forms of browsing and skim-reading rather than the intensive reading traditionally granted to Scripture. While Stead acknowledged that the 'craze to have everything served up in snippets, the desire to be fed on seasoned and sweetened tit-bits' was 'deplored' by many middle-class commentators, he nevertheless defended his journalistic practice by insisting that 'although mincemeat may not be wholesome as a staple diet, it is better than nothing'.[74] The format of the *Review* self-consciously encouraged a form of what detractors termed 'desultory' reading that would allow readers without the time to cultivate more intensive modes of reading to have at least some understanding of – and sense of involvement in – the latest developments in subjects, like science, from which they had previously been excluded.[75]

In a similar vein, the *Review* also offered readers notices of 'the leading books that have been published' which would 'enable the reader far removed from libraries to grasp the nature of their contents'.[76] In exceptional cases, however, readers were advised to a adopt a more intensive style of reading for certain monographs. James Sully's *Studies of Childhood* (1895), for instance, was recommended as 'a book which it behoves every parent to read, and not to read lightly'.[77] Stead later elucidated the kind of careful reading practice he had in mind, suggesting that 'Whenever you read a book have a pencil in your hand, and mark lightly in the margin whatever passages you wish to remember', but he also acknowledged the problems that this intensive mode of reading posed for the audience of cheap periodicals by observing, 'If you have borrowed the book from a public library . . . be careful to erase every pencil mark before you return [it].'[78] Similarly, in a 'Character Sketch' of Herbert Spencer readers were told that, while they could use a recently published *Epitome* of Spencer's philosophy as 'a refresher or index', they 'must read [his work] through, not once or twice, but "tearfully and prayerfully" many times over' in order to 'assimilate its inner meaning'.[79] Such a devotional and intensive form of reading, especially of the secularist works of Spencer, was a serious matter with significant moral and physiological consequences. As one abstract of an article from the American magazine *Arena* recounted, a mother who '"became engrossed in Herbert Spencer's writings"' during pregnancy had given birth to a '"child [who] reflects the mother's mental condition in a most striking manner"' and is '"one of the finest reasoners . . . among children"'.[80] Indeed, the desultory and miscellaneous form of reading generally encouraged by the *Review* would at least prevent the fearful consequences of intensive reading revealed in another abstract, again from *Arena*, which claimed that the 'way in which Colonel [Robert] Ingersoll became an Atheist . . . was clearly traceable to his mother's reading during the time immediately preceding his birth'.[81] As well as allowing busy plebeian readers to become informed on a wide variety of subjects, the miscellaneous reading practice encouraged by the *Review* could also prevent the fanaticism and unbelief that might possibly result from intensive but narrow styles of reading.

Reading the *Review of Reviews* was enlivened by a distinctive and eye-catching use of typography (headlines and crossheads, for instance), as well as a style of writing 'with such vividness and graphic force as to make a distinct even although temporary impact upon the mind'. Each article, Stead enjoined, should be written 'in such a fashion as to strike the eye and compel the public at least to ask, "What is it all about?"'. Such 'Sensationalism in journalism', he insisted, was 'justifiable up to the point that it is necessary to arrest the eye of the public'.[82] The physical act of reading the *Review*, then, would stimulate, at least temporarily, the jaded senses of readers fatigued by the drudgery of daily life. Indeed, after perusing the *Review*'s first number, a contributor to the weekly *Methodist Recorder* reported that 'no sooner did our eyes light on a paragraph than we were compelled to read'.[83] It was precisely this capacity to attract the eye of overworked plebeian readers with sensational and exciting accounts of its findings that, according to Stead, had been relinquished by an increasingly specialized modern science. When the 1895 meeting of the British Association for the Advancement of Science at Liverpool 'passed without notable or sensational incident', Stead asserted:

the scientific picnic of the year has seldom yielded less amusement for the general public, and one feels more and more the lack of a lucid intelligible survey of the progress of scientific discovery in all fields. Science is so specialised and scientists tend to become such Brahmins that the ignorance of the average man seems likely to become denser the more minutely the field of knowledge is surveyed.[84]

What was needed to interest the general reader in scientific subjects were enticing works of synthesis like Max Nordau's *Degeneration* (1895), which, although 'generally wrong-headed', was at least 'as strenuous and fearless as the most sensation-loving reader could desire'.[85] Works of science, according to Stead, should excite and physically stimulate their readers, and this capacity for arousing heightened feelings was considerably more important than their actual accuracy. Similarly, Benjamin Kidd's *Social Evolution* (1894) was, as the *Review* noted, 'one of the few philosophic or sociological books of our time, which have had the run of a sensational novel'.[86] Stead had claimed earlier that Kidd's enticing and 'universally-talked-of' monograph was 'the scientific basis for the social gospel of the REVIEW OF REVIEWS', and the *Review* itself likewise offered abstracts and articles on scientific subjects that were 'served with piquante sauce' and were 'racy to read'.[87] Stead's new journalistic ideal of popular science was predicated upon a reading practice that was, paradoxically, both desultory and physically stimulating, but, most importantly, eschewed the kind of intensive and studious engagement with the printed page demanded by more traditional popularizers like Allen.

Allen's disagreement with Stead over the most appropriate way of reading popular science made it virtually impossible for him to continue to contribute to the *Review*. In a letter to Stead, Allen maintained that he would still be 'very glad to write you another scientific causerie', but his insistence on certain 'conditions', and especially that 'every word I write . . . be printed', suggests that he was no longer willing to supply the highly abbreviated and easily consumed form of popular science that Stead desired for the *Review*.[88] As Allen remarked in another letter to Stead, the two were 'so much alike in our aims, though so little in our means'.[89] The proposed 'Our Scientific Causerie' (along with a review of Darwin's *Autobiography* [1892] that Stead tried to commission from Allen) never appeared, and Allen's only other original contribution to the *Review* – a 'Character Sketch' of John Tyndall – appeared almost four years later in January 1894.[90] Stead nevertheless ensured Allen's continued presence in the *Review*'s pages by, among other things, casually mentioning in an abstract of an article on the pathological consequences of riding bicycles that he had recently been 'discussing the question . . . with Mr. Grant Allen'.[91] With Allen preferring to write for more conventional journals like the *Cornhill* and the *Fortnightly*, however, the *Review* largely abandoned the attempt to incorporate traditional, essay-based, forms of science popularization within its new journalistic format, and instead embarked on more elaborate methods of bringing science to the mass audience for cheap periodicals.

INTERVIEWING EXPERTS

Without Allen's high-profile contributions, the 'Our Scientific Causerie' feature lasted only another four months. The final article, written by Kidd, appeared in December 1890 and, like Allen's initial contribution, it once again considered Weismann's recent findings concerning the germ-plasm. Kidd, however, attempted to convey this abstruse theory of heredity to the mass audience of the *Review of Reviews* in a very different way to Allen. Whereas Allen had offered readers a dense and closely argued exposition of Weismann's embryological researches that was almost identical to a review on the same subject he had written for the highbrow *Academy*,[92] Kidd's much less imperious article was based on 'an interview which Professor Weismann was good enough to give me a few weeks ago at his home'. It began by giving a detailed and chatty description of the German scientist's 'detached English-looking house' and 'the view from [its] front windows' over 'vine-clad slopes', while photographs interspersed within the text showed the 'tall, handsome-looking man with much of the poet in his striking face'. The text of the actual interview was rendered as a dialogue which retained many traces of direct speech and attempted to recover the immediacy of the event and give a sense of how Weismann 'speaks English very fairly'. In recreating this convivial 'conversation' with the 'hero of the hour in biological science', Kidd even invited readers to enter the private space of Weismann's study, a 'charming little sanctum' where a 'bust of Darwin' sat 'in the place of honour ... over the Professor's desk'.[93] Unlike Allen's abstract theoretical essay, the profusion of personal and domestic details in Kidd's illustrated interview provided precisely the kind of piquant and easily comprehensible science writing that Stead demanded for the pages of the *Review*.

Interviews and other forms of personality-based journalism, however, were not merely passive and trivializing modes of popularization. The format of the interview, one of the most distinctive of the new journalism's borrowings from North America, deliberately created a sense of intimacy (as well as the frisson of illicit intrusion) between the mass audience of journals such as the *Review of Reviews* and intellectual luminaries like Weismann. In interviews conducted at the subject's home, moreover, details of the topography of the private domestic space and the objects contained therein were recorded by the interviewer in order to reveal traces of the 'authentic' personality and 'inner' beliefs of the celebrity subject.[94] In the case of science, such celebrity interviews provided important new ways of understanding the increasingly specialized researches of prominent practitioners.

The apparently incidental domestic detail of the positioning of Darwin's bust above Weismann's desk, for instance, was in fact integral to Kidd's contentious claim in the article about the degree of continuity that existed between the views of Darwin and Weismann. Allen, in his earlier 'Scientific Causerie', had emphasized Darwin's acceptance of the Neo-Lamarckian doctrine of the inheritance of acquired characteristics (which Weismann's germ-plasm theory now powerfully contradicted), and suggested that once 'Weismannism became the fashionable creed of the day ... even the ideas ... of Darwin himself ... began to be looked upon as antiquated and unphilosophical'.[95] Kidd, on the other hand, grudgingly acknowledged that 'Darwin in some measure lent his name, after going the rounds for a quarter of a century' to the inheritance of acquired characteristics, but insisted that, far from being convinced of the pivotal role of use and disuse, Darwin had 'left unsolved' the 'answer to this riddle' which 'Professor Weismann ha[d] since attempted to give'. The presence of Darwin's bust, positioned 'appropriately' at the centre of his study, proved beyond question that Weismann 'remain[ed] a Darwinian' and that 'the great English naturalist' was the 'presiding genius of the Professor's life work'.[96] The intimate personal details revealed in the interview format allowed Kidd to strengthen, at least implicitly, his controversial argument for the unbroken intellectual lineage between Darwin and Weismann.

As well as lionizing the celebrity subject as an exceptionally talented or interesting individual, the format of the interview also insisted, paradoxically, upon a quotidian intimacy which helped elide the boundaries between the subject and the reader. The revelation, for example, that the homes of even notable personalities contained everyday commodities similar to ones owned by the readers of cheap periodicals helped engender what has been termed the '"democratization" of . . . celebrity' in late nineteenth-century popular culture.[97] There was, of course, nobody more acutely aware of the levelling potential of the interview than Stead, who proclaimed that 'No one is too exalted to be interviewed and no one too humble.'[98] Interviews with men of science provided Stead with another means of overcoming their alleged aloofness and of reducing the hierarchical distance between professional scientists and the general public. After all, in the assumed intimacy of an interview even the most overpowering of scientific intellects could be humanized and shown to be not so very different from the more prosaic minds of readers. As an interview with Thomas Edison, which appeared in the *Review* in 1893, revealed, the inventor who 'sums up in his personality and achievements [the] genius of the American race' nevertheless struggled constantly with the 'forms and minutiae of business affairs' and other burdensome 'financial operations'.[99] The interview, more than any other format of the brashly demotic new journalism, insisted that, beneath the veneer of celebrity, everyone had similar material concerns, whether genius, journalist, or journeyman.

Some members of the scientific community were extremely wary of the consequences of giving such unrestricted access to their personal affairs. In the late 1870s both Darwin and Tyndall had been featured in the pioneering 'Celebrities at Home' series in the *World*. When, however, Stead's *Pall Mall Gazette* reprinted in 1887 an article from the *American Magazine* in which 'Mr. Grant Allen interviews himself after the fashion of the *World*'s "Celebrities at Home"', Allen protested vehemently about the infringement of his privacy. The unauthorized publication of this auto-interview describing his 'modest Surrey cottage', Allen alleged, had caused him 'acute discomfort' and 'profound regret', and he even claimed that he 'would rather have cut off my right hand than have had it printed here in England'.[100] The growth of intrusive personality-based journalism, as with other new journalistic innovations such as the encouragement of 'desultory' reading, perturbed more traditional popularizers of science like Allen, who wished to maintain a certain distance between themselves and their plebeian readers, at least on this side of the Atlantic (Allen claimed that his own use of the interview format was only meant to 'suit a peculiar American taste' and 'was not intended for English readers').[101] For populist editors like Stead, though, it afforded a further means of critiquing the increasingly hierarchical nature of professional science, and formed part of a wider campaign against the alleged arrogance of scientific experts.

Stead's profound antipathy towards anyone with specialist expertise was prompted, in part, by his distrust of their ability to communicate meaningfully with the general public. They might be the subjects of celebrity interviews and 'Character Sketches', but so-called 'experts' were not permitted to contribute original articles to any of the periodicals with which Stead was involved. In 'editing a newspaper', he admonished,

never employ an expert to write a popular article on his own subject . . . If the expert writes he will always forget that he is not writing for experts but for the public, and will assume that they need not be told things which, although familiar to him as ABC, are nevertheless totally unknown to the general reader.[102]

Certainly this strict prohibition on the writing of unintelligible 'experts' was adhered to throughout Stead's long editorship of the *Review of Reviews*. Even as late as 1910 he assured Wallace, 'I am not going to let any one-eyed specialist of a biologist loose upon your book [*The World of Life*]', insisting that 'Its importance is far greater than that, and I will allow no one but myself to summarise it.'[103] Stead proposed that editors such as himself were in the unique position of being able to communicate with the mass audience of cheap periodicals whilst also having almost unrestricted 'access to experts', and he claimed, in a disturbingly vampiric metaphor, that on any important question an 'editor can have sucked the brains of every living authority in England or in Europe, and printed their opinions in his columns'.[104] Like Dracula, who was to become one of the mythic figures of 1890s popular culture, Stead envisaged the editor sucking the intellectual lifeblood of the 'expert', and then transfusing it into the veins of an army of loyal plebeian readers.

Editors of popular journals, in Stead's estimate, were singularly well-placed to intercede between increasingly specialized professional experts and a rapidly expanding periodical readership who were eager to know about recent scientific discoveries. Such a mediating role, however, was not the limit of Stead's didactic ambitions. Even more urgently, he argued, the oligarchic authority of scientific experts needed to be reined in and redirected by energetic editors working in conjunction with the mass audiences of their periodicals. Editors, in Stead's immodest conception, were the new demagogues of the nascent era of popular democracy, and could readily enlist and mobilize the support of huge readerships. The 'secret power in all journalism', as Stead observed, was 'the establishment of close touch between the Editor and his readers'.[105] Like the hugely successful penny weekly *Answers to Correspondents* which Alfred Harmsworth began in 1888, the *Review of Reviews* granted a large amount of space to letters and contributions submitted by ordinary (and, of course, unpaid) readers, who were encouraged to consider themselves an integral part of the production of each monthly number of the *Review*. Stead prided himself, above all, on having a relationship with the audience of the *Review* that was 'so much closer than those which exist between the editors and readers of most periodicals', and he bolstered this sense of intimacy by appealing directly to readers' judgements on particular subjects above the heads even of acknowledged experts.[106]

The support of the *Review*'s readers was eagerly solicited in Stead's incessant campaigns to overcome the dogmatic hostility of the scientific establishment towards heterodox forms of knowledge. He requested readers to, amongst many other things, take 'the trouble to write out' the 'confirmatory evidence . . . of any apparition known to you' and 'send it in to "REVIEW OF REVIEWS, London", marked *Ghosts*'.[107] The active participation of the mass audience of cheap periodicals in the collection of evidence based on their own experience, as has already been seen in relation to psychical research, was, in Stead's view, the most effective way of proving beyond reasonable doubt the reality of myriad phenomena currently beyond the boundaries of orthodox scientific enquiry. The avowedly inclusive and populist agenda of the *Review of Reviews* could thereby become a means of repudiating the condescending and intolerant scepticism exhibited by professional scientific experts.

Such contributions of amateur evidence were of particular value when they came from the most ordinary of readers, and plebeian patrons of the *Review* were exhorted to 'guard against the mistaken assumption that it is only ladies and gentlemen of leisure and culture who can render valuable service' in such matters.[108] The 'ghostly census-taker', Stead counselled his working-class readers, must 'overcome a most unscientific reluctance on the part of the ordinary citizen to speak, or still more to write and append his name to a statement' regarding spectral apparitions.[109] Once such ordinary citizens conquered their instinctive reticence on scientific subjects, moreover, it would soon become evident just how much they had to contribute to the supposedly expert knowledge of specialist professionals. Even 'the tourist', as Stead noted in a review of books on Arctic exploration, 'is an invaluable ally of the scientific investigator', and if only 'summer travellers could be induced to visit' little-known regions such as Spitsbergen then 'it might be possible to get a portion of the Arctic land minutely studied and exactly surveyed'.[110] Inevitably, Stead's appeals for lowly readers to contribute to the discussion of important scientific issues, especially with regard to occult phenomena, were viewed with considerable distaste and suspicion at the more expensive end of the periodical market. The highbrow *Saturday Review*, for instance, greeted the opening number of *Borderland* by warning that 'a democratic congregation of inquirers is not likely to be cautious', and noted contemptuously that such a populist approach would 'bring vulgarity and twaddle, and perhaps even "interviewing", into our association with the world beyond the grave'.[111] Journalistic innovations such as celebrity interviews and the prominent involvement of ordinary readers, however, had the combined effect of making scientific experts appear more accessible, and even ordinary, while at the same time encouraging commonplace plebeian amateurs to consider themselves as active participants in the making of scientific knowledge. The boundaries between what might be considered 'élite' and 'popular' understandings of science were constantly and deliberately blurred in the self-consciously democratic pages of the *Review of Reviews*.

The so-called 'positivist diffusionist model' of science popularization, which disdainfully rejects the role of popularizers as well as the wider reading public in the production of scientific knowledge, has been increasingly called into question in recent years. Historians are now admonished to 'be suspicious of any model that, in granting to scientists the sole possession of genuine scientific knowledge, supports their epistemic authority', and enjoined to instead 'treat popularizations of science as sophisticated productions of knowledge in their own right' and to 'become more open to examining a variety of sites of scientific activity'.[112] One of most significant of these miscellaneous sites of scientific activity, as this chapter has argued, was the cheap periodical press in late-Victorian Britain, and particularly those titles that were identified as the purveyors of a novel and disturbingly different style of journalism. The *Review of Reviews*, the self-styled flagship of this new journalism, employed a range of innovative methods of science popularization, including the abstracting and recasting of élite scientific knowledge, the promotion of 'desultory' reading, personality-based formats like the celebrity interview, and reader participation, which make it clear that the growing division between 'élite' science and public discourse in the final decades of the nineteenth century was contested much more actively than has generally been recognized.

New journalistic methods of presenting science, as has been seen throughout this chapter, posed serious problems to ageing scientific naturalists such as Huxley and Wallace, as well as to traditional popularizers like Allen. The increasingly troubled encounters between such scientific practitioners and writers and the new type of campaigning editor exemplified by Stead signalled wider changes in the relationship between the spokesmen of élite groups, popularizers, and the reading public that would become ever more apparent in the twentieth century as the dynamics of the periodical marketplace were transformed by the exponential increase in titles aimed specifically at a mass audience.

Section B: Themes

CHAPTER 8

Tickling Babies: Gender, Authority, and 'Baby Science'

Sally Shuttleworth

From the 1860s to the 1890s the periodical press played a crucial role in the development of a new subject of scientific study: babies. Although early anthropological and evolutionary writings had stressed the close relationship between the physical characteristics and behaviour of infants and those of the 'lower' races, no systematic studies of the development of the European infant were published in England until the late 1870s, when articles by Hippolyte Taine and Charles Darwin opened up this field for scientific enquiry in the early issues of *Mind*.

The story of the emergence of baby science is one that raises significant issues about the interrelations between specialist and general periodicals, from high to low brow, and the construction and gendering of scientific authority. It also highlights the ways in which a new field of science was not merely reported but actively constructed in the pages of the periodical press.[1] Two key figures in this tale, G. H. Lewes and James Sully, were both relative outsiders to the scientific community, struggling initially to make names for themselves in scientific circles whilst financing their work through extensive popular journalism. In addition to their scientific writings, both contributed to a wide range of general periodicals, from the pages of the fiction-oriented *Cornhill*, through (in the case of Sully) to the pages of *Baby: An Illustrated Monthly Magazine for Mothers*, started in 1887 by the ardent campaigner for dress reform, Ada Ballin. For such writers, baby science possessed ambiguous attractions: it was clearly a topic which would appeal to female readers of the periodicals, but, in its very associations with the feminine domain of the nursery, it risked tainting the scientific credibility that Lewes and Sully were struggling so hard to establish.

This chapter explores the major periodical contributions to this debate, from Lewes, Sully, and other writers, focusing particularly on the various discursive strategies each writer adopted in his attempts to appeal equally to a male and female audience, and to bring that last bastion of female influence, the nursery, under the sway of male science. It will also consider the ways in which writers tailored their contributions to the specific genre of periodical for which they were writing, and the significant interrelations between the specialist scientific journal *Mind: A Quarterly Review of Psychology and Philosophy*, initiated by George Croom Robertson in 1876, and more populist writings in this field.

In 1857 the radical *Westminster Review* carried the highly influential essay, 'Progress: Its Law and Cause' by Herbert Spencer. 'If further elucidation be needed', he remarks, of his theory concerning the higher evolution of the European,

we may find it in every nursery. The infant European has sundry marked points of resemblance to the lower human races; as in the flatness of the alae of the nose, the depression of its bridge, the divergence and forward opening of the nostrils, the form of the lips, the absence of a frontal sinus, the width between the eyes, the smallness of the legs.[2]

Spencer has given bodily definition to earlier claims that the development of the child parallels that of the human race. He has invited us all into the nursery to see for ourselves, but has resolutely stopped short of any analysis of movement or behaviour. His babies are utterly passive and still, mere physiognomical forms. Spencer speaks with his usual dogmatic authority, but his assertions raise questions about the gathering of empirical evidence in this uncharted scientific domain. One cannot, somehow, imagine the great author of the Synthetic Philosophy entering the nursery at all, let alone having the patience to study its bawling, squirming inhabitants.[3]

No doubt nervousness of such a 'feminine' topic hindered the emergence of baby study. One of the first detailed English explorations of baby development appears not, as one might expect, in a medical or scientific periodical, but rather in an 1863 article by G. H. Lewes on 'The Mental Condition of Babies', published in that general fiction-oriented family periodical, the *Cornhill*, started under the editorship of Thackeray in 1860, and under Lewes's own guidance between 1862 and 1864. The subject was a review of a little-known tract by Dr Kussmaul of Erlangen who was the first, Lewes claims, to have examined this question in a scientific spirit.[4] The book was not reviewed in the *Lancet* or the *British Medical Journal*, and Lewes no doubt first encountered it in his extensive reading of German medical and scientific periodicals.[5] The subject itself was not one that would attract much attention from the British scientific world until the late 1870s. Lewes thus has to negotiate the dual difficulties of writing for a general audience, and also reporting on a new potential field for scientific inquiry. Whilst appearing to treat the research seriously, Lewes nonetheless adopts a comic and facetious tone: his instincts as a scientist are clearly being undermined by his own uneasy relations to his potential audiences. To understand the discursive strategies employed by Lewes in this piece we need to place the article in the context of his career as a whole.

For anyone interested in the intersection of science writing and periodicals Lewes offers a fascinating study as he moves from early arts reviewing, acting, and novel writing in the 1830s and 1840s, through to being one of the scientific stalwarts of *Mind* from its inception in 1876. He was co-founder and literary editor of the radical weekly the *Leader* from 1850 to 1854, chief adviser to the *Cornhill* from 1862 to 1864 after Thackeray's resignation, and editor of the new high-brow periodical, the *Fortnightly Review,* from 1865 to 1866.

His movement into the arena of science in the 1850s received a serious setback in 1854 when T. H. Huxley, flexing his own scientific muscles, attacked his *Comte's Philosophy of the Sciences* in the *Westminster Review* for its mere book-knowledge, and lack of the understanding which would arise from a *practical* engagement with science.[6] (Ironically, Huxley himself was unable to make science pay, and had accepted the *Westminster* reviewing, at twelve guineas per sheet, in order to further his own pursuit of a scientific career).[7] Lewes set to work to prove his scientific credentials, undertaking his own experimental research which led to the publication of *Sea-Side Studies* (1858) as an article series in *Blackwood's* in 1857 prior to book publication. His first major contribution to the emerging science of psychology, *The Physiology of Common Life* (1859–60), also appeared first in *Blackwood's* in 1859–60, whilst *Studies in Animal Life* (1862) graced the first *Cornhill* numbers in 1860. To garner more scientific status Lewes had also contributed no less than three papers to the 1859 British Association meeting at Aberdeen, and was delighted by praise from Huxley.[8] From hints dropped that year by 'various eminent scientific men' he felt he was 'no longer considered by them as a literary alien' but had 'won my "freedom of the city" in their community'.[9]

Nonetheless, a scientific career constructed almost entirely through popular publication in the quarterlies or shilling monthlies would always have its dangers, and indeed Lewes's problematic professional status has been replicated in subsequent scholarship which has tended either to ignore or underestimate the importance of his scientific work.[10] One of the difficulties Lewes faced in writing 'The Mental Condition of Babies' was how to introduce a field of science which undermined disciplinary boundaries by taking place not in the well-equipped, and hence fortified, laboratory, but in that feminizing and infantilizing arena, the nursery.

Lewes's choice of title signals his divided loyalties, with the high-flown scientism of 'mental condition' linked with almost comic bathos to 'babies'. For Kussmaul's term 'new-born', he has chosen to substitute the alliterative 'baby', which captures in its very sound the early babblings of an infant, and carries an almost defiant non-scientific tone. (Darwin, and virtually all subsequent medical and psychological authors, opt for the more emotionally neutral terms of 'infant' or 'child'.)[11] Lewes opens his article with comic depictions of men and women disputing over a baby's cradle, the mothers' claims for their adored ones' achievements being met by scepticism and 'combative opinionativeness' from the males. Science, however, will settle all, Lewes decrees, for Dr Kussmaul has sought to resolve these issues 'by making new-born infants subjects of *experiment*'.[12] Anticipating the 'voluble execrations of outraged womanhood' in response to such an idea, Lewes places Kussmaul's work in the context of his own:

Experiment on babies! We remember that, in a communication we submitted to the British Association for the Advancement of Science, the mention of experiments performed on sleeping children was not very well received by some mothers, although the experiments carried with them no operation more formidable than tickling the sleepers' cheeks. The sanctity of the infant was felt to have been violated! Perhaps, also, the experiments being mentioned in conjunction with others on decapitated frogs and salamanders, the timorous imagination at once conjured up visions of remorseless physiologists decapitating babies to detect the laws of nervous action.[13]

Unfortunately, no records survive of these outraged mothers, but the material which formed the basis of Lewes's communications to the BAAS is to be found in *The Physiology of Common Life* where Lewes does indeed pass directly from describing his experiments on lively decapitated frogs to those of tickling sleeping infants' cheeks. He concludes:

If any one will institute a series of such experiments, taking care to compare the actions of the animal before and after decapitation, he will perceive that there is no more difference between them than between those of the sleeping and the waking child.* [Lewes's footnote:]* It is better simply to remove the brain, than to remove the whole head, which causes a serious loss of blood.[14]

Whilst Lewes is undoubtedly correct in asserting that no harm is threatened to the infants, the linguistic associations are powerful, particularly those summoned up by that final unfortunate footnote. Lewes's own language and syntax erase distinctions between tickling and decapitation, or between babies and frogs. As readers, however, we are clearly expected to participate in the amused condescension he extends to these irrational mothers who set emotions before science. Although obliged to address, however obliquely, disturbing questions as to the precise relationship between babies and animals, and scientific entitlement with regard to experimentation on both humans and animals, Lewes tries his best to deflect such issues through the use of humour.

Dr Kussmaul's experiments, although presented as entirely innocuous, are more extensive and intrusive than Lewes's own. New-born babies, including those who were premature, were subjected to a series of tests on their senses, including bitter and sweet-tasting substances dropped on their tongues before they had sucked, and in the case of one unresponsive child, acid. With regard to hearing, Lewes agrees with Kussmaul's quite remarkable conclusion that this 'is the only one of the special senses in which the infant seems absolutely deficient'. Centuries of female experience is to be set aside on the authority of male science (and indeed subsequent studies in the 1880s happily take this scientific proclamation of infant deafness as their starting point).[15] Did 'voluble execrations' reach the offices of the *Cornhill* or were female readers suitably cowed by this scientific dismissal of the 'superfluous solicitude of mothers and nurses "not to wake baby"'?[16] Behind these assertions lie the politics of domestic space: the Englishman's home is to remain his to control, and considerations of the nursery are not to impinge on the drawing room. Using the twin techniques of lofty assertion and comic ridicule, Lewes seeks to press forward the claims of baby science. His strategies, however, help to highlight the uncertain authority of the male in this gendered domain. As a doctor supervising pregnancy and infant care, the scientist's word is law – but could he retain his dignity if he stooped to tickle babies' cheeks? And would women willingly relinquish their sway over the nursery in favour of masculine science? Lewes's scenario of cold-hearted male experimenters clashing with female vessels of sympathetic emotion anticipates the vivisection debates of the 1870s when women did seek to challenge the authority of masculine science, and Lewes, alongside Darwin, testified to the scientific need for vivisection.[17] Lewes attempts, facetiously, to disarm female opposition by claiming that science, which is represented throughout as female, will vindicate mothers' claims about their wondrous offspring. He calls on 'the mothers of Cornhill, and its "circumambient parishes"' to offer a ready ear to scientific research.[18] His conclusion, however, rather surprisingly takes a sudden swerve into mystical Idealism, with extensive quotation from Wordsworth and his Platonic vision of the child 'trailing clouds of glory' from his previous existence.[19] Lewes's uncertain relations to his subject matter and audiences are reflected in this dramatic narrative shift. The poetry functions, however, as a way

of decontaminating, or sanctifying, the whole question of baby experimentation, at the same time as subtly aligning psychological theories of
evolutionary descent with those of the most respected representatives of
high moral culture.

Although Lewes opened up an area for experimentation and debate,
no English scientists rushed into the breach; the light-hearted tone, and
the article's placement in the family-orientated *Cornhill*, militated against
any serious scientific response. Evolutionary discussions seemed content to
stop with the homological structures displayed in the embryo, or with large
generalizations about the shared characteristics of children and primitive
races. Even in Darwin's *Descent of Man* (1871) there is a surprising absence
of any sustained discussion of infant behaviour, whilst *The Expression of
Emotions in Man and Animals* (1872) draws only intermittently on the
observations he had made of his own infants – the development of smiling,
laughing, frowning, weeping, and, most importantly, screaming, for which
he commissioned a series of plates.[20] The disruption of domestic peace is
given an evolutionary explanation in his observation that, whilst the habits
of laughing and weeping are gradually acquired, 'The art of screaming, on
the other hand, from being of service to infants, has become finely developed
from the earliest days.'[21] Science can explain, if not contain, the infant.

Baby study in its own right seems to have received no real attention
until the foundation of the scientific journal, *Mind: A Quarterly Review
of Psychology and Philosophy* in 1876. Designed as the first British journal devoted to mental science, it was financed until 1891 by the eminent
physiological psychologist Alexander Bain, and edited by George Croom
Robertson, Professor of Mental Philosophy and Logic at University College,
London.[22] The contents list of the first issue read like a roll-call of authorities
in the field, including Herbert Spencer on 'The Comparative Psychology
of Man', and, significantly, articles by both Lewes and Sully, a testimony
to their having achieved scientific status.[23] In the second volume, Croom
Robertson published a translation of Hippolyte Taine's brief article 'On
the Acquisition of Language by Children', republished from the French
journal, *Revue Philosophique*, which had been instituted in the same year
as *Mind*. The article was based on a study of just one child, who was used
by Taine to confirm the identification of primitive cultures and child men-
tality. 'Speaking generally', he concluded, 'the child presents in a passing
state the mental characteristics that are found in a fixed state in primitive
civilisations.'[24]

The article, carrying with it the authoritative intellectual imprimatur of
Mind, spurred Darwin into action. He returned to the journal he and Emma

had kept of their first-born, William, thirty-seven years before, and rapidly produced an article which he sent, unsolicited, to Croom Robertson. It was published as 'A Biographical Sketch of an Infant' in the very next issue. The labour involved here for Darwin was not insubstantial – chronological jottings were transformed into a developed argument under subject headings, including 'Anger', 'Fear', 'Association of Ideas', 'Moral Sense', and 'Means of Communication' (and in the process most of Emma's contributions were excised).[25] There were a few vague references to heredity in the original version, and these were developed and placed in an evolutionary frame so that, in one case, anxious parents could actually take comfort from notions of hereditary transmission. On visiting the Zoological Gardens, William experienced real fear when seeing the 'beasts in houses'. Darwin noted, 'May we not suspect that the vague but very real fears of children, which are quite independent of experience, are the inherited effects of real dangers and abject superstitions during ancient savage times?'[26] His explanation bypasses completely the category confusion identified by William, and turns instead to the idea of inherited memories in order to offer parents a reassuring account of the seemingly irrational behaviour of their offspring.

Darwin was very diffident towards, and even embarrassed by, this article. He expressed surprise that *Mind* would actually want to publish it, and when besieged by requests from France and Germany for permission to translate it, he repeatedly stated that it was not worthy of such attention.[27] The combination of Darwin's name and the intellectual prestige of *Mind* proved irresistible, however: 'baby science' was now set firmly on the scientific agenda. The article also placed Darwin in correspondence with Wilhelm Preyer in Germany who had already started work on infants and whose *Die Seele des Kindes* (1882) was to become the definitive work in the field for some time. The pages of *Mind* now carried a flurry of articles on infant development,[28] so much so that Joseph Jacobs could claim in 1886 that 'Observation on children's minds, as attempted by Charles Darwin, has almost grown into a separate study, to which the apt name of Baby-lore has been given.'[29]

The dominant figure in this field in England was James Sully, who reviewed Preyer's *Die Seele des Kindes* for *Mind* in 1882.[30] Although his major work, *Studies of Childhood* (itself a compilation of general periodical articles), was not published until 1895, he had staked his claim by the early 1880s. A scholarly review of an earlier Preyer article in *Mind*, 1880, was followed by a popular article on 'Babies and Science' for the *Cornhill* in 1881, which in many ways looked back to Lewes's earlier piece.[31]

Like Lewes, who became his friend and semi-patron, Sully started writing initially for popular journals, and always felt a tension between his need to make money (which became acute around 1879–80 with his father's business failure) and his desire to develop his scientific interests. Both men were outsiders with regard to the intellectual establishment. Sully, unlike Lewes, had taken a degree, but in arts at a Baptist College at Regent's Park, London. Despite periods spent studying with Ewald and Lotze at Göttingen, and with Helmholtz in Berlin, he had difficulty gaining professional acceptance, and was repeatedly passed over for preferment until he was finally offered Croom Robertson's chair of the Philosophy of Mind and Logic at University College, London in 1892.

His career follows a pattern all too familiar today as he scrabbled to put together bits of teaching and examining whilst writing furiously for an enormous number of periodicals drawn from across the cultural spectrum, including the *Fortnightly, Saturday, Westminster*, and *Contemporary Review*s, the *Examiner, Academy, Cornhill, Longman's, Popular Science Monthly, English Illustrated Magazine*, and *Baby*, not to mention unpaid 'high-brow' work for *Mind*.[32] His first book, *Sensation and Intuition* (1874) on physiology and aesthetics, which brought together some of his earlier articles, received considerable praise from the scientific community, including Darwin, without seeming particularly to advance his career.

In his autobiography Sully characterized his writing for the *Cornhill* as midway 'between the more serious and the lighter kind of article'.[33] Following Lewes's pattern, he opens 'Babies and Science' with a light-hearted depiction of the battle between the sexes over the cradle – female 'baby-worship' is once more set against male indifference and even contempt. Science, Sully suggests, will now change all this for it has become 'a champion of the neglected rights of infancy' and hence will become for women the 'avenger of a whole sex'.[34]

Sully's interest in babyhood is primarily evolutionary. 'The attentive eye', he observes, 'may . . . find in seemingly meaningless little infantile ways hints of remote habits and customs of the human race.' Masculine science is to rescue infancy from 'meaninglessness' by transforming babies into palimpsestic records of past civilization. Such interest, Sully suggests, has led to the creation of a new breed of scientific father:

The tiny occupant of the cradle has had to bear the piercing glance of the scientific eye. The psychological papa has acquired a new proprietary right in his offspring; he has appropriated it as a biological specimen.[35]

Although the alliteration casts the proprietorial 'psychological papa' in a humorous light, the article works, finally and unevenly, to establish baby science as a serious male domain. Science herself is portrayed as female, luring the male to the cradle, but scientific practice is to remain resolutely male.

The domestic dynamics are those captured in the *Punch* cartoon of 1 April 1871, 'A Logical Refutation of Darwin's Theory' responding to the publication of the *Descent* (fig. 8.1). The man is placed ingratiatingly at the woman's feet, book in hand, as he attempts to convince his wife of the truth of Darwin's theories. The domestic cat, 'a hairy quadruped with pointed ears and a tail' looks on, envying the place occupied in the woman's warm lap by the child. The woman's superior response, with its lofty rejection of all things animal, demonstrates her inferiority, as hugging the child more tightly to her, she repulses this invasion into her domain of both man and science.[36]

Women, Sully notes in his article, at first pleased by the man's new interest in the infant, become alarmed 'when the rash enthusiast for science proposes to introduce the experimental method as superior to that of passive observation'. Mothers impede the progress of science if they too become 'infected with the scientific ardour of the father' since none of their observations, coloured as they must be by maternal instincts, can be trusted. The nurse too becomes an 'invincible obstacle' to scientific progress and 'may succeed in effectually barricading the cradle against [the father's] scientific approaches'.[37] Intellectually and physically women stand in the way of baby-science.[38]

Sully concludes the paper with a thinly veiled account of his observations of his baby son, who was born the previous year. Although modelled on Darwin's pattern established in *Mind*, even this part of the paper is comic in tone, poking fun at the abstruser musings of the father with regard to his son's connection to primitive human history.[39] The 'psychological papa' is viewed through the eyes of the sceptical wife, but without ever fully undercutting the value of his work. Sully's divided attitude to childhood studies, and his own role therein, which emerges so strongly in this article, is also expressed in his further periodical writings in the 1880s on the subject. These are strictly divided between serious scholarly reviews of childhood research in *Mind* and what Sully termed 'lighter' pieces in a range of journals including *Longman's*, the *English Illustrated Magazine,* and *Baby*.[40] Uncertainties about his own professional position, and the scientific dignity of the area itself, no doubt contributed to the long delay between his early interest in developmental studies and the final publication of *Studies of Childhood* in 1895 which brought together many of his periodical pieces.[41]

The gender-inflected concerns over questions of scientific authority in the emerging area of baby-science parallel in many ways the battles that

Figure 8.1. [George Du Maurier], 'A Logical Refutation of Mr Darwin's Theory', *Punch* 60 (1871), 130.

had recently been fought between midwives and doctors. A civilization, Tyler Smith declared in the *Lancet* of 1847, should be judged on how well it treats its women. Despite appearances, this was not a statement supporting the cause of midwives, but the very reverse. True respect for womanhood, according to Tyler Smith, could only be shown if the incompetent midwife was banished from the lying-in room, to be replaced by the omnicompetent male physician.[42] Similar struggles were being repeated in the domain of the nursery and the pages of the popular periodical press as male scientists sought to usurp a traditional area of female knowledge. Science would become the 'avenger' of women, but only if they agreed to relinquish their observational role in the nursery to men. Such arguments were particularly difficult to make, however, if scientists earned their keep by writing for periodicals aimed at both a male and female audience, and not just a closed male fraternity, and were also dependent on women for their data.

By the 1890s the scientific field of infant study opened up by *Mind* had become a major area of interest across the periodical spectrum.[43] One of the most prolific authors was Dr Louis Robinson, who published 'Darwinism in the Nursery' in the *Nineteenth Century* (1891) (other resonant titles include 'The Meaning of a Baby's Footprint' (1892) and 'Darwinism and Swimming' (1893)).[44] Despite some of the extraordinary claims made in these articles, the humorous, self-mocking tone adopted by Lewes and Sully had disappeared, and had been replaced by the pompous solemnity of self-satisfied science. 'It may be well', Robinson observes in 'The Meaning of a Baby's Footprint', 'to dwell upon the evolutionary interpretation of the strange inscriptions on this newly-discovered and most ancient historic document, the infantile sole'.[45] Theological probings of the soul are to be replaced by readings of the foot, as the denizen of the nursery is flourished before the readers' eyes in the guise of a newly unearthed pre-historic relic.

Robinson did not confine his research to vague speculation, but was one of the first to follow Kussmaul's example and actually experiment on babies. 'Darwinism in the Nursery' opens with the now customary declaration of female observational ineptitude: 'the average mother, in spite of many unquestioned merits, is about as competent to take an unprejudiced view of the facts bearing on the natural history of her infant as a West African negro would do to carry out an investigation of the anatomy and physiology of a fetish'.[46] The extraordinary condescension of this passage draws on the standard ethnological grouping of women, children, and savages to position them as figures outside the charmed circle of scientific reasoning.

Robinson set out to prove our arboreal ancestry by testing babies' power of grip. 'Finding myself,' he notes, without clarification, 'in a position in which material was abundant, and available for reasonable experiment' – he tested sixty babies under a month old, half within an hour of their birth, to see if they could hang from a bar. He had one 'performer', he claimed, of three weeks who held on for two minutes and thirty-five seconds.[47] He also claimed to have taken photographs, although as the *Review of Reviews* in reporting this article noted sardonically, 'Mr. Knowles has not yet developed sufficient enterprise to enable him to publish Dr. Robinson's photographs.'[48] Robinson observed that the posture of the hanging babies 'and the disproportionately large development of the arms compared with the legs, give the photographs a striking resemblance to a well-known picture of the celebrated chimpanzee "Sally" at the Zoological Gardens'.[49] In an interesting reversal, the affectionate evolutionary anthropomorphism lying behind the public's delight in 'Sally' is transferred to the babies themselves.

Other delights in this Darwinian line include S. S. Buckman's 'Babies and Monkeys', also in the *Nineteenth Century*, which made a plea for parental tolerance:

It is remarkable how much unnecessary suffering is inflicted on infants and children because parents fail to recognize the ancestry from 'animals', and consequently the instincts, different from those of adults, which children have inherited.[50]

Mothers are once more in trouble, not this time for treating their infants like fetishes, but for attempting to impose human rules of behaviour on their animalistic offspring. Every facet of child life is here explained for us – midnight feasts arise from the instinct of dragging food into the lair, the tearing of wallpaper re-enacts the process of searching for ants under bark, whilst 'Lullaby baby on the tree top' becomes a folk memory of our arboreal ancestry.[51]

Sully's contributions to this debate were more measured. In 1893 *Mind* published his appeal to parents and teachers to 'supply him with facts bearing on the characteristics of the childish mind. What he especially desires is first-hand observations carried out on children during the first five or six years of life.' Observations were to be classed under a range of thirteen headings including 'Memory', 'Language', 'Fear', and 'Self-Feeling'.[52] The appeal itself arises from Sully's awareness that authoritative research requires more data than can be gathered easily within the confines of the family circle, but he is clearly concerned about the quality of information that might be submitted. Informants are required to give exact age, timing, and facts of temperament, surroundings, and experience, so that he can properly assess the data.

In his first major piece arising from this research, 'The New Study of Children' in the *Fortnightly Review* (1895), Sully returned again to gendered issues of authority.[53] The article actively engaged with the recent contributions to the debate in the *Nineteenth Century*. Sully endorsed Robinson's experiments on hanging babies from bars, but found Buckman's article 'fantastic'. He also clearly had difficulty with the observations which flooded into him as a result of his appeal in *Mind*: 'Ask any mother untrained in observation to note the first appearance of that complex facial movement which we call a smile, and you know what kind of result you are likely to get.'[54] (Darwin, in reworking his notebook material for the 'Biographical Sketch', had similarly discounted Emma's observation that their third child, Henrietta, had smiled at three weeks.)[55] The discipline needed, he argued, 'qualified workers' who possess 'A divining faculty, the offspring of child-love, perfected by scientific training.'[56] Male and female traits are clearly to be combined, but only men, it would seem, were fitted to achieve such a harmonious union. Mothers would not be sufficiently skilled nor bold enough to attempt the experiments conducted by medical men like Dr Robinson. Such activities would be viewed as a form of sacrilege:

> To propose to test the little creature's sense of taste by applying drops of various solutions, as acids, bitters, &c., to the tongue ... would pretty certainly seem a profanation of the temple of infancy, if not fraught with danger to its tiny deity. And as to trying Dr Robinson's experiment of getting the newly-arrived treasure to suspend his whole precious weight by clasping a bar, it is pretty certain that, as women are at present constituted, only a medical man could have dreamt of so daring a feat.

Even if women did obtain scientific training, and *also* become mothers, they would not be disposed to undertake the 'rather dry and teasing work' of taking a scientific inventory of 'infantile sense-capacity'. Such experimental work should be left to the 'coarser-fibred man'.[57]

Yet in the very next paragraph Sully recognizes that women will have to play a larger role if men are to obtain consistent data. He is at pains to point out, however, that even the apparently simple task of recording children's early talk can be marred by lack of scientific understanding. His dissatisfaction with the quality of data he received in response to his appeal to parents is evident:

> The unskilled observer of children is apt to send scraps, fragments of facts, which have not their natural setting. The value of psychological training is that it makes

one as jealously mindful of wholeness in facts as a housewife of wholeness in her porcelain.[58]

In yet another attempt to master this complex field of gender politics, the male scientist is humorously depicted as a fussy housewife, but the implied distinction between male and female abilities remains. Sully concludes the article with an apparent compromise, offering the pious hope that one day 'some duly qualified mother, aided by a quick-eyed and sympathetic young teacher [earlier identified as male] may soon give us the history of a child's mind'.[59]

In Sully's next piece in the *Fortnightly*, 'The Child in Recent English Literature' (1897), he tears to shreds a production by a mother, Alice Meynell, who has presumed to offer her observations unaided by a masculine guide. He pours scorn on her 'pretty' treatment of a 'pretty theme' and notes sarcastically that 'she comes certificated by an authoritative hand as trained by maternal sympathy in the unlocking of children's secrets'. Her presumption in offering observations which contradict those of 'trained observers', Darwin and Preyer, is mercilessly attacked.[60]

As all these foregoing articles suggest, by the 1890s 'baby science' had become not only an acceptable area in science, but a 'hot topic' for periodical discussion. From its humorous beginnings in Lewes's *Cornhill* article in the 1860s, through Darwin's intervention in *Mind* in the late 1870s, to Sully's prolific range of journalism in the 1880s and 1890s, one can trace the growth of a new domain of science. The debate in these journals, however, was largely one-sided, as male writers sought to show their male and female readers how mothers, the traditional keepers of the keys to this kingdom, were naturally disqualified from participation in this new science. There were, however, some dissenting voices, one of which comes, most unusually, from a woman writing for that authoritative, and male-dominated journal, *Mind*. Granted the daunting job of reviewing Sully's *Studies of Childhood*, Alice Woods dares to take him to task for a naive and sentimentalized view of childhood (precisely his own complaint against Meynell). Children are not so immune, she suggests, as Sully would like to think from the stresses of our introspective and worldly nineteenth century. She makes her point humorously, not through the lumbering, uneasily comic voice so often adopted by her male peers, but with a quiet, gentle humour which completely deflates the evolutionary scientists' pretensions to knowledge. Far from tracing humanity back to its simplest sources, and observing impartially in ways only men can achieve, these baby scientists are actively creating the subjects they seek. The subjects learn, however, to answer back.

Alice Woods offers her own, subversive, observation of nineteenth-century childhood:

'Don't be so silly K' said a parent to his ten-year-old daughter. 'I can't help it Father', was the prompt reply, 'I've inherited it from Mother.'[61]

In the quick-witted response of this child, the evolutionists' theories of female inferiority become a weapon of offence.

Amidst the male writers who dominated coverage of the field in *Mind* and the high-brow range of periodicals at the time, Woods's is a rare voice. The establishment of baby science as a legitimate area of study, however, also led to the creation of a range of new child-care magazines, where women often took a leading role. One of the most prominent of these new periodicals was *Baby: An Illustrated Magazine for Mothers and Those Who Have the Care of Children, being A Guide to their Management in Health and Disease*, started in 1887 by Ada S. Ballin.[62] While magazines like the *Englishwoman's Domestic* had always drawn upon medical science in their childcare columns,[63] Ballin, who styled herself 'Lecturer to the National Health Society', adopted an explicit scientific orientation for *Baby*. The magazine aimed to offer 'the opinions of the highest authorities in medicine, hygiene, and education, as to the best means of physical, mental and moral training'.[64] Inevitably, such medical authorities were invariably male. The first volume, for example, carried, in addition to Sully's article on 'Children's Fears', a series by Dr Edmund Owen, Surgeon at the Great Ormond St Hospital, on 'The Science of the Nursery', and, prominently placed on the third page, 'How to Observe a Baby' by 'Francis Warner, M.D., F.R.C.P., F.R.C.S., Hunterian Professor of Comparative Anatomy and Physiology in the Royal College of Surgeons, England'.[65] In the pages of a female-edited and oriented magazine, women were to be taught, by a much-garlanded professor, a skill that had always resided traditionally, without contestation, in the female domain.

Ballin herself contributed some excellent articles on Froebel and the Kindergarten system of education, and employed a range of female authors to write on aspects of childcare and child development, but the aims of the magazine itself were firmly restricted to the education of *mothers*. Thus the opening editorial of the second volume expressed 'disgust' at an article published elsewhere by 'New Woman' writer, Mona Caird, on the upbringing of children:

A woman who would voluntarily delegate her maternal duties to a stranger, no matter how scientifically trained she may be, is no more worthy of the name of mother than an incubating machine.[66]

Respect for scientific training was tempered by an inflexible adherence to traditional gender roles: a scientifically trained woman poses a threat to maternal centrality.

Ballin's conflicted position on the question of science and babyhood offers, in some respects, a gendered mirror image of the difficulties faced by Lewes and Sully. Whilst they sought to wrest observational control of the nursery from women, without compromising the masculinity of their scientific practice, Ballin wished to promote understanding of masculine science, whilst keeping the nursery itself firmly under maternal control.

Although *Baby*, by its very title,[67] would appear to have targeted an exclusively female audience, Ballin was quick to announce, in her opening editorial for volume 3, that she had received so many interesting letters from gentlemen that she was changing the sectional title of 'Mother's Parliament', which published readers' handy hints and child observations, to 'Parents' Parliament'. Her claim raises interesting questions about reading patterns and audiences. Did men surreptitiously read their wives' copies, and then write in to Ballin? Or had the new respectability of 'baby science' altered family dynamics, so that husband and wife both read *Baby* and debated its contents? Alternatively, was this a ploy by Ballin to encourage a new masculine reading constituency?

Ballin's primary audience, however, was undoubtedly female, and armed with a firm sense of a devoted audience, and secure in her sense of the right of women to address the issues of child development, she looks out critically on the male domain of periodicals. She comments favourably on the fact that the *Nineteenth Century* had published an article by 'one of Professor Huxley's talented daughters', Jessie Waller, on the physical and mental training of children.[68] It was, she noted, a very good sign of the times when such material was placed before the *Nineteenth Century*'s readers 'who, I take it, are mostly serious-minded men, politicians, scientists, and clubmen'. The hint of mockery offered here is further developed in her following observations on the *British Medical Journal*:

It having recently become the fashion to discuss matters connected with children in the public press, we are not surprised to find the *British Medical Journal* gravely debating the question of thumb-sucking.[69]

The embarrassment which Lewes and Sully had displayed in attempting to turn baby study into a domain of science is here wickedly turned against the male scientist. Insult is added to injury by Ballin's dismissive claim that the author is probably a bachelor, and hence the article quite worthless. We are back once more to the domain of gender wars, with Lewes's image of the male and female struggling for control of the cradle.

The development of baby science in the second half of the nineteenth century enacted a series of territorial struggles over space: domestic, discursive, and professional. Periodicals played a crucial role in its rise, as male scientists sought to convince both male and female readers of science's right to enter the hallowed space of the nursery. On the domestic front, scientists faced the very real problem of how to obtain data in the face of female opposition; and also how to maintain dignity whilst penetrating into a traditional female domain. The story of the initial growth of baby science is not one primarily of laboratories and experiments, but rather of tentative debate in the periodical press. With the publication of Darwin's article in *Mind*, the field acquired a new legitimacy, and rapid growth ensued, leading to the publication of a spate of articles in *Mind* itself and in other scientific and popular journals, and the institution of female-targeted magazines such as *Baby*. Questions of scientific legitimacy and masculine entitlement, which Lewes had playfully addressed in his early article, survived well into the 1890s, however, kept alive by periodical debate.

In histories of psychology, James Sully is generally acknowledged as the founder of England's first major psychological laboratory, at University College, London. Given his interests, one would have expected it to focus on, or at least encompass, early child development. In an article in the *Journal of Education*, designed to publicize the proposal and appeal for funds, he is at pains, however, to point out that this will not be the case:

the proposed laboratory is not, as one London journal appeared to think, a place where confiding mothers may deposit their infants in order that a learned professor may ascertain by experiment whether, for example, they can discriminate what are to us offensive tastes, or, like their simian ancestors, hang with their whole weight on to a bar ... The laboratory modestly proposes merely to study the familiar mental processes as they can be observed in older children and adults.[70]

Despite the attempts by Lewes, Sully, and others to dignify and legitimize the experiments of Kussmaul and Robinson, they had clearly not convinced the British reading public.[71] Sully might not have been met by the 'voluble execrations of outraged womanhood' which Lewes claimed were his lot, but he is clearly not prepared to take on the might of public opinion expressed within the periodical press. His scientific agenda is thus curtailed, and only older children will be involved in experiments within his laboratory. British baby science, from its early comic emergence in the pages of the *Cornhill*, through to its stately coming of age within *Mind*, and institutionalization in the 1890s, was both framed and shaped by periodical debate.

CHAPTER 9

Scientific biography in the periodical press

Geoffrey Cantor

Following the fresh impetus imparted to biography by the writings of Johnson and Boswell, the 'lives' of eminent individuals streamed from the presses throughout the nineteenth century. This thirst for biography created the expectation that a famous person's 'life' would appear in the bookshops soon after the mourners had returned from the funeral. Not satisfied with a single volume commemorating a favourite statesman, poet, or scientist, biographers often indulged their readers with two – and sometimes more – bulky volumes filled with copious information about their subject's life. As Edmund Gosse noted, in England we 'bury our dead under the monstrous catafalque of two volumes (crown octavo)'.[1] Recognizing the popularity of the genre but the high cost of such octavo volumes, some publishers launched cheap editions in the hope of tapping a less affluent readership and increasing sales. For example, the Society for the Diffusion of Useful Knowledge published a number of low-priced biographies and in the 1840s commenced an over-ambitious project for an extensive biographical dictionary.[2] Publishers, authors, and editors also collaborated in producing collected biographies, often spanning a number of volumes. Thus Lardner's 'Cabinet Cyclopædia', which retailed at 6 shillings per volume, included the lives of 'the most eminent literary and scientific men of Great Britain' (three volumes), eminent lawyers (1 volume), British admirals (three volumes), military commanders (three volumes) and eminent British statesmen (seven volumes).

At the apogee of the Victorian cult of biography stands the *Dictionary of National Biography*, which provided a magnificent overview of Britain through the lives of its many eminent public figures. The initial series of sixty-three volumes was published between 1885 and 1900. Biographies also frequently prefaced other types of book; for example, an edition of a poet's writings or a scientist's collected papers. Encyclopaedias likewise often carried large numbers of biographical entries; although biography was omitted from the first (1771) edition of the *Encyclopædia Britannica*, potted biographies accounted for a substantial proportion of articles in the Victorian editions.[3] Numerous diaries, journals, and collected letters, containing undigested biographical material, were also published, thus adding to the market in other people's 'lives'.

The size of the market for biography can be gauged by analysing the *Nineteenth Century Short Title Catalogue* (*NSTC*),[4] which indicates that some 50,000 books of biography were published between 1801 and 1870.[5] While the absolute number of biographies is impressive, it is not very informative. Of greater significance is the market share achieved by biographies, which was approximately 6.7 per cent.[6] The *NSTC* data also indicate that the annual production of biographies rose fivefold over these seven decades, from about 250 at the century's beginning to 1,200 by the late 1860s. Thus by the latter date some twenty-five 'lives' (or collected 'lives') were published every week, and the rate of publication rose even higher by the century's end.

The *NSTC* data also suggest that the popularity of biography relative to all other subject areas was fairly constant, but increased slightly over the period 1801 to 1870. Most interestingly, literary biography, which is often taken as the thoroughbred in the stable of biographies, increased less dramatically over this period than did other types of biography. Among the larger categories, religious biography increased significantly, as did the rather unmanageable category comprising 'Biography – History, Travel, Other; Heraldry; Genealogy; Wills'. Yet the most impressive increase was in the lives of engineers, doctors, printers, and agriculturalists (again a rather amorphous grouping), while scientific biography and collective biography (which also includes biographies of bibliographers, librarians, and journalists) also grew relative to the overall book trade and expanded significantly faster than literary biography. Of particular interest are scientific biographies, which increased from seven titles a year at the beginning of the century to about forty in the late 1860s. Although these conclusions are tentative and the data require closer analysis, they indicate some interesting historical changes in the patterns of the production and reading of biography. To concentrate on books, however, is to overlook another major source for biographies.

PERIODICALS: 'CAPSULE LIVES'

While readers avidly consumed books of biography, the periodical press provided a further rich and diverse source of biographical information. As Richard Altick has commented, from the 1830s 'the condensed biographical narrative was a journalistic staple. The *Penny Magazine* and *Chambers's*

Journal and their many imitators abounded with earnestly written capsule lives.'[7] Most general periodicals – even those predating the 1830s – explicitly included biography within their compass. To provide two contrasting formulations: a flier dated 1824 for the *Literary Gazette* listed the inclusion of the 'Memoirs of Eminent and Literary Characters', while the editors of the *British Friend*, founded in 1843 to serve members of the Society of Friends, stated in their first number that they would include 'records of the lives, labours, and sufferings, for the sake of the Gospel, of those worthies who have gone before us, after having borne the burden and heat of the day'.[8] While the editor of the *Literary Gazette* used biography to extol worldly eminence, the *British Friend* employed biography to inculcate piety among its readers.

As the following example relating to Newton's life indicates, 'capsule lives' often reached a much larger readership than did weighty book-length biographies. The two main nineteenth-century 'lives' of Newton were *The Life of Sir Isaac Newton* and the *Memoirs of the Life, Writings and Discoveries of Sir Isaac Newton*, both written by the Scottish natural philosopher David Brewster who helped to maintain himself and his research career by writing and editing popular scientific works.[9] Brewster's *Life of Newton*, enhanced by a plate of Newton as its frontispiece and several woodcuts within the text, was published by John Murray in 1831, as part of his 'Family Library' series of duodecimo volumes. Yet Murray had been over-optimistic in printing 12,500 copies of Brewster's book, which sold at 5s. Sales were disappointing and Murray sustained a considerable loss, having to sell more than half his stock to Thomas Tegg, who subsequently reissued the volume under his own name in 1858.[10] Brewster's more expensive, substantial, and handsome two-volume *Memoirs of Newton* was first published by Constable in 1855 at 24s. The print run and sales figures are not known, but it is unlikely that the circulation exceeded 1,000 copies.[11] Although relatively few people and institutions purchased Brewster's *Memoirs of Newton*, the book's main themes would have been familiar to a much larger readership through the many reviews that appeared in the periodical press during the months following its publication. Review articles appeared in six of the titles covered by the *Wellesley Index* – *British Quarterly Review*, *Dublin Review*, *Dublin University Magazine*, *Edinburgh Review*, *North British Review* and the *Rambler* – with a combined circulation of 15,000 to 20,000.[12] To these six periodicals, most of which sold for about 5s, must be added the many non-*Wellesley* titles that also reviewed Brewster's *Memoirs of Newton*, among which was the widely circulated *Athenaeum*, which sold about 18,000 each week at 4d unstamped, or 5d stamped.[13] Even this very incomplete list of periodicals that reviewed Brewster's *Memoirs of Newton* indicates that the circulation of reviews vastly outstripped the distribution of the book itself. Moreover the reviews published *c.*1855 considerably outstripped the sales over the previous quarter century of his earlier *Life of Newton*. In these cases, and many others, the life of a scientist was more likely to be known from reviews in the general periodical press than from book-length biographies.

MODES OF BIOGRAPHICAL WRITING IN THE NINETEENTH CENTURY

Not only did biography become a highly popular genre but several contending forms of biographical writing were widely deployed in nineteenth-century Britain. Saints' lives provided a traditional model for biography (and one that continued in various forms throughout the nineteenth century, including the 'testimonies' published in religious magazines). In recounting such lives, little attention would be paid to the saint's personality or the facts of his life; instead the aim was to raise the reader's level of spiritual awareness through contemplating the saint's trials, tribulations, and extraordinary deeds. However, although one might aspire to live a spiritual life by imitating the saint, the saint's life is, by definition, unlike that of an ordinary mortal. By contrast, during the sixteenth century and increasingly during the seventeenth, writers recorded the lives of living or deceased individuals. Although authors often combined fact with anecdote and fantasy, veracity was increasingly acknowledged as both necessary and desirable. The emphasis on truth was further nurtured by the publication of diaries recording everyday events, Samuel Pepys's being the most famous.

During the eighteenth century Enlightenment values impinged on biography; biographical writing became less concerned with denoting the peculiarities of a particular individual than with using the individual's life to provide insights into the human mind and behaviour.[14] In reaction to this view of human nature, biographers influenced by Romanticism provided a crucially important change in outlook and helped biography emerge as a distinct literary genre. The focus was now on the subject's creative impulse; moreover, since a person's literary or artistic creation was a product of his or her personality, biography had to combine both creator and creation into a single narrative. Thus a poem was a highly personalized creation and an intimate part of the poet's unique qualities. Under the aegis of Romanticism, and particularly of Thomas Carlyle's *On Heroes, Hero-Worship and the Heroic in History* (1840),[15] many British biographers portrayed their subjects as heroes whose extraordinary qualities were intended to inspire the reader.

However, both Romantic and heroic biographies were open to the criticism that they created the cult of the extraordinary. In reaction, much nineteenth-century biography was factual and rather prosaic. One particularly interesting variety of anti-heroic biography that flourished from mid-century came to be associated with Samuel Smiles. In such works as *Self-Help, with Illustrations of Character and Conduct* (1859) and *Duty: With Illustrations of Courage, Patience, and Endurance* (1880) he urged his readers to pursue self-improvement, and social and economic advancement, by dint of their own efforts.[16] Smiles's writings contained copious examples of biographies illustrating this utilitarian theme. His paradigmatic examples of success were not blessed with genius or social advantage, but they possessed 'Courage, Patience, and Endurance' in large measure.

The critical reviewing function performed by the periodical press may have encouraged biographers to pay increasing attention to truth, in terms of both correct facts and valid judgements. In the nineteenth century, biographers were increasingly expected to recount with factual accuracy what their subjects actually said, did, or wrote. Yet, despite this emphasis on veracity, social convention decreed that, in contrast to its eighteenth-century predecessor, nineteenth-century biography should delicately skirt round such awkward issues as their subjects' sexual predilections, drunkenness, or debauchery. Although writers of 'advanced opinion' increasingly reflected on the topic of sexuality, they were reacting against a deadening sense of propriety and respectability that ensured that sexuality had no place in most biographies. With a few interesting exceptions, the proprietors of the book trade and the periodical press conspired in creating biographies that not only valued truth but also massaged it when it challenged conventional religious, social, and family values.

The main themes governing nineteenth-century biography were frequently employed in the sub-genre of scientific biography. The Romantic, the heroic, the utilitarian, and 'Smilesean' modes were all readily adapted in narrating the lives of scientists. The scientist could be portrayed as the Romantic genius, the heroic discoverer, or the exemplar of self-improvement. Likewise, the scientist's work could be depicted in any of a number of ways; for example, as a creative act or as a response to utilitarian market forces. In line with convention, any seamy aspects of a scientist's life could usually be overlooked.

Yet scientific biography also addresses three issues that are generally less relevant to the lives of novelists, statesmen, and admirals. First, with few exceptions, scientists were not readily recognized as celebrities by the general public. As the author of a biographical sketch of Lord Kelvin in the *Review of Reviews* lamented in 1893, scientists are rarely known out-side their professional circle and the public much prefers to read about the latest successful novelist or 'a boxing kangaroo'. Even among scientists Kelvin was relatively invisible since, unlike Darwin, he had not expounded a revolutionary theory nor challenged religious orthodoxy. That he was a Scot added further to his invisibility to Londoners. In demonstrating Kelvin's invisibility this particular biographer described a photographer's window in London in which photographs of well-known public figures were displayed. Although Kelvin's photo could be found in photographers' windows in Glasgow and Edinburgh, nevertheless it was absent from the London display.[17] As Richard Noakes points out in chapter 4, the number of scientific celebrities was small but it increased significantly during the closing decades of the century. Among this select band were Darwin and Faraday, whose portraits were widely distributed and who were depicted in *Punch* and in other magazines.[18] A surprisingly early portrait of Faraday was published in the Tory *Fraser's Magazine* for 1836, which was probably published to acknowledge Faraday's (unintended) support of the Tories (fig. 9.1).[19]

Scientific research was also becoming increasingly esoteric and, despite the impetus of scientists and some journalists, scientific innovations were generally less well known to the public than were the creations of artists, novelists, and engineers. Although some scientists were successful in dis-seminating their achievements to a wider audience, the public was excluded from the primary locus of scientific activity – the laboratory. Finally, while biographies of poets, for example, written in the Romantic mode sought to portray the poem arising from the poet's unique personal qualities, the con-nection between personality and product is far more difficult to sustain in the case of scientists. Although some biographers sought to make this con-nection, many scientific biographies – and not only nineteenth-century ones – demarcated the subject's life and work within separate chapters, thereby accentuating this disjuncture.

Scientific biography entered the periodical frame in a number of different contexts, which I shall group under four headings and discuss respectively in the ensuing sections of this chapter. The first is the obituary notice which by convention contained a biography of the deceased. Second, following the publication of a substantial biography of a scientist the periodical press generally published a flurry of reviews that raised public awareness of the subject's life and work. A third form of biography was the 'biographical sketch'. General periodicals often carried such sketches, which were frequently – but not always – published to coincide with a

AUTHOR OF 'CHEMICAL MANIPULATION'.

Figure 9.1. Faraday surrounded by apparatus, including an electrostatic generator, in the lecture theatre of the Royal Institution. This was one of the first published portraits of Faraday. *Fraser's Magazine* 13 (1836), facing 224. Reproduced with the kind permission of the Leeds Library.

centenary or other notable occasion. Finally, we encounter passing references to specific events in the lives of scientists. These references were either within articles on other subjects or acted as 'fillers' – an anecdote about Newton or Davy might be used to fill the small space remaining at the bottom of a column of print.

OBITUARIES

The death of a successful scientist usually generated a spate of obituary notices in both the general and the scientific press, the number of obituaries being a rough gauge of his or her perceived eminence. Although the proceedings of scientific societies rarely published other forms of biography, the death of a member was often noted, and in some cases an obituary published. For example, while the *Philosophical Transactions of the Royal Society of London* did not include obituaries, the *Proceedings of the Royal Society of London* (first published in 1830) contained obituary notices of deceased Fellows. A similar role was fulfilled by the *Monthly Notices of the Royal Astronomical Society*. Scientific periodicals that were not tied to societies, such as *Nature* and many of the specialist journals, also carried selected obituaries. These notices, usually written by a scientific colleague, briefly summarized the life of the deceased but generally paid far greater attention to his – rarely her – scientific achievements. However, in the general periodical press obituaries of scientists tended to concentrate on the subject's life and merely summarized the scientific achievements by employing terms that would be accessible to the non-specialist reader.

Special-interest and denominational periodicals also carried obituaries of scientists whose life or work fell within the journal's ambit. For example, the *Academy*, which sought to encourage British readers to become more aware of significant events on the Continent, included brief obituaries of Guglielmo Libri, the Italian mathematician, and the German physicist Heinrich Gustav Magnus.[20] Denominational periodicals celebrated those who shared their religious commitments; thus the *Youth's Magazine; or, Evangelical Miscellany* published in 1837 the funeral oration for the chemist Edward Turner, and the Quaker press carried obituaries of the eminent chemist John Dalton following his death in 1844.[21]

The obituaries that flowed from the presses following the death of Michael Faraday on 25 August 1867 illustrate both the wide and rapid dissemination of his 'life' and the construction of several parallel 'Faradays'. Over the next two or three days the dailies published anonymous notices, often with short biographies. While most were rather prosaic and factual, the obituary in the *Daily News* was considered particularly insightful and was reprinted in a number of other periodical publications. The scientific and medical weeklies, such as the *Mechanics Magazine*, *Chemical News*, and the *Lancet*, soon carried obituaries, as did such general weeklies as the *Illustrated London News* (including a portrait), the *Athenaeum*, *Punch* (in poetic form), and the *London Review*. Obituaries also appeared in several religious weeklies, especially periodicals associated with dissent (as Faraday was a Dissenter), such as the *English Independent*, the *Inquirer* (which drew on the notices in the *English Independent* and the *Daily News*), and the *Nonconformist* (which borrowed heavily from the *Examiner*). Most of these articles had clearly been composed at short notice by staff writers who were pleased to recycle material already in print, especially the well-written and informed obituary in the *Daily News*. While most of the dailies and weeklies, which were expected to respond rapidly to contemporary events, carried obituaries of Faraday, a far smaller proportion of monthlies and quarterlies published articles marking Faraday's passing. Among such publications were the *Pharmaceutical Journal*, the *Gentleman's Magazine*, the dissenting *British Quarterly Review*, *St. James Magazine*, and *Belgravia* – the last two being directed principally to affluent London women, some of whom would have heard Faraday lecture at the Royal Institution. Thus the obituary notice was most newsworthy soon after the subject's death but was no longer appropriate after a few weeks, except among specific interest groups.

Despite some examples of scissors-and-paste journalism, the obituary notices carried by the monthlies and quarterlies were mainly well-constructed, original articles that offered interestingly divergent accounts of Faraday, his science and its significance. While some obituaries concentrated on the basic facts of his life and on his acknowledged ability as a lecturer, others dilated on his personality. In many cases the Faraday they presented was based on personal experience and on widely circulating gossip. These articles – some of which were signed – praised his honesty, his simplicity, and his dedication to truth. The anonymous obituarist in the *London Review* was particularly fulsome, informing his readers that Faraday considered that 'the servants of science should be distinguished by a loftier aim and a purer life than the generality of men'. Since Faraday's life in science had exemplified these principles, the writer managed to draw a connection between his personality and the specific way he pursued science. His life also showed that '[t]he root of all true success lies in sincerity and love'.[22] These noble qualities were expressions of Faraday's sincere Christian beliefs.

Although a few obituaries avoided the subject of religion altogether – especially the over-formal notice in the *Gentleman's Magazine*[23] – most emphasized his deep religious feeling. Some writers even acknowledged his membership of a peculiar, dissenting sect – the Sandemanians – to which he had belonged for nearly half a century.[24] In particular, the *Nonconformist* stressed that he had been a member of 'this despised and dwindling community to the last'.[25] While ignoring his strong non-conformist principles, most periodicals recruited Faraday in support of general Christian values and virtues. Thus he was widely portrayed as a pious Christian who had combined an exemplary religious life with important, innovative scientific research. A few obituarists also explicitly drew connections between his Christianity and his scientific pursuits. For *Leisure Hour* – published by the evangelical Religious Tract Society – he was 'The Christian Philosopher' *par excellence*, while according to the *London Review*, 'he pursued his [scientific] investigations with the modesty, the candour, and the reverence of a Christian'.[26] Although subsequent writers expanded on this theme, these obituary notices formed part of the emerging hagiographical literature that created St Michael Faraday and raised his science to a pious vocation. In keeping with the genre's contemporary norms, his obituarists could find no serious flaw in his character.

In contrast to some writers later in the century who portrayed Faraday's achievements in starkly utilitarian terms, several obituaries depicted him as a disinterested philosopher seeking the truths of nature. 'In his own person', wrote one obituarist, 'he represented rather the philosophical than the utilitarian aspects of science, its love of knowledge rather than its search for practical utility.' This writer recognized that although posterity would judge Faraday by his discoveries, the man he was honouring exemplified the highest virtues of science.[27] As one of the main aims of an obituary is to sing the praise of the departed in the presence of family and friends, it provides a particularly appropriate locus for exhibiting religious and transcendental themes.

Contemporaries generally cited electromagnetic induction and the laws of electro-chemistry as Faraday's major scientific achievements, thus ignoring his more speculative ideas, such as field theory. Yet there was considerable divergence among obituarists over how to represent Faraday as a discoverer. For some he was the son of a poor ironsmith who had reached the pinnacle of British science by dint of hard labour. His accomplishments resulted from long hours spent in the laboratory and the rigorous application of the inductive method. His industry and perseverance allowed these writers to cite Faraday as a paradigmatic example of Smilesian self-help. Thus, according to the *Gentleman's Magazine* he was 'entirely a self-made man', while the *Engineer* branded him 'an example of what self-help can make a man'.[28] Others deployed a far less prosaic approach and instead adopted a Romantic perspective stressing his genius and transcendental qualities. One obituarist, who had known Faraday well, likened him to Goethe, while another described him as a 'chosen priest of nature' who at birth had received from a 'beneficent fairy... the mysterious baptism of genius'.[29] In these contrasting examples we see how conventional biographical tropes were deployed in narrating Faraday's life.

Many of the obituaries also contained personal information connecting the writer to Faraday. Thus the chemist John Scoffern, who contributed the obituary in *Belgravia*, gained some kudos and justified his 'life' of Faraday by claiming that he had been well acquainted with his eminent subject. Benjamin Abbott, writing in the *Friends' Quarterly Examiner*, reflected on their friendship stretching back over half a century to their youth – probably the longest association of any of Faraday's obituarists.[30] Such obituaries were often sprinkled with anecdotes, personal assessments of his character, and evidence of his success as a lecturer. The appearance of obituaries in the periodical press also sometimes prompted letters from readers containing reminiscences of their meetings with Faraday. While Faraday had taken great care in fashioning his public persona, its main features were posthumously confirmed in the periodical press and disseminated to a far larger audience than he could address in the theatre of the Royal Institution.[31] Moreover, in the days and weeks after his death the periodical press played a crucial role in fixing images of Faraday in the public mind.

REVIEWS OF BIOGRAPHIES

Writing in *Fraser's Magazine* for 1870, the lawyer William Frederick Pollock noted that with the passing of years '[p]ersonal recollections gradually fade away; the characteristic anecdote ceases to circulate... It is therefore a duty, no less of justice to the memory of the individual, than to the community for whose benefit the example of a great and good life is preserved, that provision should be made to keep the knowledge of it alive.'[32] In his opinion the circulation of biographies was a duty and it was therefore incumbent on the periodical press to carry extensive accounts of recently published biographies. According to this view, anecdotes and personal reminiscences fade with the passage of time and the published 'life' – together with the reviews it inspires – increasingly gains authoritative status. Biography becomes the principal source of collected memory.

The appearance of a new substantial biography would set the periodical press in motion with a flurry of reviews. Since reviews assisted sales of the original work, publishers were keen to distribute review copies to as many periodicals as possible. If the book's publisher also owned periodicals, then pressure could be exerted on editors not only to review the book but to review it extensively and glowingly. Public awareness of a new biography was also increased by advertisements, that were usually printed on the end-papers of periodicals. Through reviewing and advertising the periodical press became an arm of book publishing. As the earlier examples of Newton's biography showed, the periodical press enabled knowledge of the life of an eminent person to reach an audience far beyond the readership of the full biography.

Although reviews of scientific biographies often appeared in the scientific press – in such commercial journals as *Nature* and *Knowledge*, but rarely in the publications of scientific societies – the general periodical press frequently reviewed such biographies, sometimes at considerable length. By the closing decades of the century a biography of a reasonably well-known scientist would receive twenty or thirty reviews within a year or two of its publication. The quality and length of reviews varied considerably. In some cases the reviewer merely transcribed passages clipped from the biography with a minimum amount of linking material. This gave a wide readership access to the main contents of the biography (as mediated by the reviewer). However, as the century progressed, the scissors-and-paste review became less acceptable, especially in the more costly magazines, and reviewers were increasingly expected to produce original articles that engaged the subject under review. Thus the reviewer could elaborate on issues that particularly interested him or her, or were considered relevant to the target audience. Reviews did not simply reiterate the image of the subject contained in the biography under review, but instead introduced diversity that often reflected the ethos of the periodicals in which they were published.

We can appreciate some of the factors affecting reviewing if we look at the reviews of the two Faraday biographies that appeared within two and a half years of his death, on 25 August 1867. His younger colleague John Tyndall expanded the éloge, which he had delivered before members of the Royal Institution in January 1868, into a small compact volume entitled *Faraday as a Discoverer*, which was published in March 1868. Tyndall's was a very personal portrait of his friend and mentor. Moreover, under the influence of German Romanticism, Tyndall painted a transcendental Faraday whose soaring achievements were compared to the highest mountains in the Alps. Branding Faraday 'the greatest experimental philosopher the world has ever seen', Tyndall portrayed him as a genius, a prophet, and a seer.[33] This picture gained the approval of Faraday's widow, Sarah, and his unmarried niece,

Jane Barnard, who became the gatekeepers of Faraday's reputation after his death.[34]

Most reviewers were clearly attracted to Tyndall's story, which, according to one writer, 'has all the charms of a romance'.[35] However, a reviewer in the dissenting *Eclectic Review* was disappointed by the book, which was more of 'an oration, or eulogy' than a proper biography and he looked forward to the publication of a memoir that would do justice to its subject's life and work. Tyndall's slim volume, he complained, also added little to what was already widely known about Faraday's personality. This reviewer, who was clearly appalled by Tyndall's growing reputation as an atheist, also considered that his biography displayed a lack of humility, in marked contrast to the modesty that Faraday himself had evinced. More specifically, Tyndall was criticized for projecting himself in the role of Schiller, in relation to Faraday, who was cast as Goethe.[36]

In the autumn of the following year Henry Bence Jones, Faraday's physician and the Secretary of the Royal Institution (where Faraday had lived and worked), published his more substantial two-volume *Life and Letters of Faraday*.[37] Unlike Tyndall's personal portrait, Bence Jones's rather prosaic account was intended as the semi-official biography of the great man, sanctioned by his institution, family, and friends. Three parallel themes were maintained throughout: Faraday's personal life, his science, and his correspondence. In contrast to Tyndall's impressionistic sketch, Bence Jones's biography was firmly grounded in the primary sources, including letters, diaries, and lecture notes. Extensive quotations from these sources provided the reader with an entrée into the various facets of Faraday's life, many of which would not have been known outside his small circle of intimates. As one reviewer commented, Bence Jones's 'work reads like an autobiography'.[38] Another noted that Bence Jones had not so much provided a life of Faraday as 'an edition of diaries, letters, etc., of the great philosopher, from which we obtain interesting glimpses of his character, and of his peculiar methods of self-culture and study'.[39] Bence Jones had succeeded in enabling this reader to gain close access to Faraday.

Since both biographies were first published within thirty months of Faraday's death, notices in the periodical press often continued to be mixed with their authors' personal memories of, and tributes to, the deceased. Yet, the far fuller account of Faraday's personal life in Bence Jones's biography enabled some reviewers to focus on specific biographical themes that they considered important. A striking example appeared in Emily Faithfull's *Victoria Magazine*, a major voice of the women's movement which promoted the extension of women's education and prospects for employment. Under the title 'Plain Living and High Thinking. Michael Faraday', the reviewer noted that although Bence Jones's biography contained much scientific material that was unlikely to appeal to women, they would nevertheless find the book attractive because it demonstrated Faraday's qualities of nobility, morality, and generosity. Quoting passages from several of the letters published by Bence Jones, this anonymous reviewer engaged the intimate side of Faraday, stressing his moral strength and his determination in following his own noble path in science. But as the article drew to a close the writer directed attention to the issues of overriding concern to readers of the *Victoria Magazine*. Any woman who tried to follow Faraday in seeking a life in science, complained the writer, would be roundly condemned by society. Some of the familiar objections against women pursuing chemistry were mentioned but quickly dismissed as insubstantial by the reviewer.[40] Thus, perhaps to his surprise, Bence Jones's biography was used and championed by the women's movement. Yet this example shows how reviews of biographies could be deployed for purposes dictated by the editorial objectives of a particular periodical.

While there is no evidence that the writer in the *Victoria Magazine* had known Faraday, Juliet Pollock, who was married to William Frederick Pollock (cited above, p. 226), clearly did. Her review in the monthly *St. Paul's* wove together extracts supplied by Bence Jones with her own recollections. Although she had little to say about his science and the basic biographical sketch occupied less than a page, she portrayed Faraday as a genius, a perfect human being, and a Christian. His personality was faultless; he was 'a complete master' at lecturing; he was humorous, simple, sincere, and his 'presence was always stimulating'; he was pious; he was devoted to Sarah. Juliet Pollock's warm and intimate prose helped to paint this luminous portrait, as did the many personal details she added. For example, she informed her reader that when Sarah was suffering from lameness, 'There are some [of us] who will remember how tenderly he used to lead her to her seat at the Royal Institution.'[41] Pollock clearly identified herself as a member of the Institution and as an intimate of both Faradays. Some of his light was thereby reflected onto her. Moreover, in her review Pollock transcended Bence Jones's dry prose in order to create an even more angelic Faraday and one that was particularly congenial to her female readership. Together with several similar contributions to the periodical press, her review helped to create and maintain the saintly public images of Faraday that both Tyndall and Bence Jones had also sought to fashion.

BIOGRAPHICAL SKETCHES

Scattered throughout the general periodical literature were numerous sketches of the life and work of individual scientists. Although these sketches were often produced for specific occasions, such as centenaries, some periodicals had a more constant commitment to biography, publishing one or more biographical articles in each number, and even devoting a regular 'slot' to the topic. For example, separate biography sections were included in the *Mirror of Literature*, the *Wesleyan-Methodist Magazine*, and the *Boys' Own Paper* – in the last case under the heading 'Some Boys who Became Famous'. Each issue of the *Review of Reviews* likewise included a 'character sketch'. Most famously, beginning in 1868, the widely selling weekly *Vanity Fair* carried cartoons of eminent people, each cartoon being accompanied by a one-page biographical sketch. Scientists – both amateur and professional – were among those whose lives were recounted in the periodical press. For example, although scientists were far outnumbered by statesmen, lawyers, and novelists, the cartoons carried by *Vanity Fair* included many of the more prominent members of the late nineteenth-century scientific community, such as Thomas Henry Huxley, John Tyndall, George Biddell Airy (the Astronomer Royal), Lord Kelvin, and the physician and physiologist John Burdon-Sanderson and Richard Owen the naturalist.

The early volumes of the *Review of Reviews* contained biographical sketches of several scientists including Lord Kelvin, Thomas Alva Edison – who was unrivalled as a self-publicist – and John Tyndall. The article on Kelvin ran to ten quarto pages printed in double columns and was illustrated by several photographs (figs. 9.2 and 9.3). The author, a mechanical engineer named John Munro who had studied under Kelvin, opened with an apologia – mentioned above, p. 221 – for profiling a scientist. He then engaged several themes that deserve our attention. Although Kelvin's innovative scientific ideas and technological advances were discussed, Munro stressed his genius, personal strength, and heroic status. The scientist was thus portrayed as a Romantic figure before a largely non-scientific audience; for example, we are told that his students were treated to 'the rapid medley of bright ideas, invaluable precepts, and sublime speculations, often expressed in eloquent phrases that stuck in the memory as the true romance, the grander poetry of Science'. In sum, Kelvin was a 'really great man . . . the Napoleon of Natural Philosophy'.[42] While such transcendental qualities were emphasized, the author also stressed certain facets of Kelvin's work and character: he was a powerful thinker and an eminently practical man who had contributed immensely to the development of the telegraph;

Figure 9.2. An intimate portrait of Kelvin at work. J. Munro, 'Character Sketch: August. Lord Kelvin, P. R. S.', *Review of Reviews* 8 (1893), 138. Reproduced by kind permission of Leeds University Library.

Figure 9.3. 'Lord Kelvin's seat at Netherhall, Largs', from J. Munro, 'Character Sketch:
August. Lord Kelvin, P. R. S.', *Review of Reviews* 8 (1893), 137. Reproduced by kind permission
of Leeds University Library.

he was a sportsman who enjoyed sailing on his private yacht; he was active in
the public life of Scotland; he was honourable, honest, and sincere; he was
adored by his students (although they were sometimes rowdy in his class!);
and he was even celebrated for his kindness to animals. A highly human and
humane picture emerged; thus we see him sitting 'by his fireside, with a
cigar in his mouth, reading the ponderous tomes of some old philosopher
laid upon his knee, or thinking out some difficult problem, while now
and again a look of deep satisfaction would overspread his countenance'
(cf. fig. 9.2).[43]

Although substantial biographical sketches are frequently encountered
in the periodical literature, there were also many much shorter entries.
For example, in the late 1820s and early 1830s the *Youth's Magazine; or,
Evangelical Miscellany* ran an occasional series of short biographical sketches
of the ancients who had contributed to the sciences, including Thales,
Euclid, and Epicurus, in each case mentioning their achievements.[44] In this
instance, educating the reader was probably the main reason for introducing
such snippets of biographical information, since the ideas promulgated by
these ancients had long been dismissed as invalid. Yet educational aims
were not confined to those periodicals directed specifically at young readers

and many editors catering for a wide variety of adult readerships stressed the importance of periodicals in the dissemination of knowledge, including biographical knowledge.

Despite the emphasis on celebrities, the periodical press also sometimes focused on the place of science in the lives of people who would not be ranked as scientists. For example, the *Wesleyan-Methodist Magazine* for 1826 included a moralizing memoir of a fellow Methodist, George Newton of Thorncliffe near Sheffield, who as an apprentice had spent his leisure 'in the study of Mechanics, Geography, and Astronomy. With much ingenuity he constructed a terrestrial globe, and a sun-dial, which were both very correct.' Yet these apparently trivial biographical facts were turned to moral purpose. The author proceeded to contrast George Newton's serious and economical habits with the tendency of many children to waste their pocket money on 'depraved connexions' and 'expensive habits'. As an adult George likewise 'gratified his love of reading by procuring a choice collection of books on science and divinity'.[45] Thus even an amateur interest in science could be given significance within a specific biographical context. More generally, as Jonathan Topham notes in chapter 3, Methodists placed great emphasis on biography, which formed 'part of a wider confessional culture'. In charting the 'spiritual progress of their subjects' biographers often introduced scientific and medical issues.

PASSING REFERENCES

One of the most fascinating aspects of the general periodical press is the extensive deployment of passing references to scientific issues in non-scientific articles. Such intertextual material sometimes included biographical references, usually relating to well-known or startling aspects of a famous scientist's life. Writers and readers could thus draw on a common cultural resource. One of the best-known anecdotes about Newton was his observation of the fall of an apple, which (allegedly) resulted in his discovery of gravitation.[46] In 1842 *Punch* capitalized on this hackneyed anecdote in an article 'Punch's Letters to His Son', in which biography and fantasy were explosively mixed. According to Mr Punch, Newton was drunk when he made his great discovery. On watching the apple fall he was struck by a 'nascent idea'. However, only after imbibing a few more bottles was he convinced, 'that not only had the apple spun as it fell, but that the whole world turned round'. Scientific creativity merged with inebriation. In stark contrast to conventional biographical narratives, Newton was no soaring genius but an old soak.[47]

The celebrated events in Galileo's life likewise provided writers with a rich repertoire that could be used constructively in a variety of contexts. For example, a postscript was added to the *Mirror of Literature*'s astronomy column for January 1827 in which readers were reminded that Galileo had been forced to abjure the Copernican system before the Inquisition. 'After going through the humiliating ceremony, he stamped with his foot on the earth, saying, *e pur si muove*, "it moves notwithstanding".'[48] With the Catholic question frequently in the news and anti-Catholic feeling running high, writers could cite Galileo's trial as a widely known example of that Church's repressive attitude. *Punch*, which as Richard Noakes notes above (chapter 4) was stridently anti-Catholic, made frequent use of Galileo to mock any pronouncement by the Church of Rome. For example, when Cardinal Wiseman claimed that Catholicism and science were in harmony, *Punch* maliciously suggested that history should now be rewritten so as to show that the Church did not thwart Galileo's work.[49] The example of Galileo was likewise employed in the context of a discussion of the law of libel in the radical *Black Dwarf* in 1817. In arguing that the censorship of speculative ideas has been the characteristic 'of a barbarous age, or the resort of jealous tyrants', the author cited the example of Galileo's inquisitors who had imprisoned him for publicly espousing the Copernican system.[50] Galileo was an easily recognized symbol of persecution by the enemies of enlightenment. The Catholic Church – here taken to represent the political establishment in England – had sought to repress truth. Scientists' lives could therefore be recruited for many purposes including diatribes against political and religious authority.

ILLUSTRATIONS

Ludmilla Jordanova has observed that during the latter half of the eighteenth century the obituary notices of scientists and medical men carried by general periodicals began to be accompanied by engraved portraits.[51] Often these engravings contained funerary emblems and motifs illustrating the area of science or medicine pursued by the deceased. Likewise, throughout the nineteenth century many periodicals regularly carried 'likenesses' to accompany obituary notes and other types of biographical article. Such illustrations helped to sell periodicals like the mass-circulation *Mirror of Literature*, which is examined in chapter 2. The *Illustrated London News*, established in 1842, specialized in high-quality engravings and regularly contained portraits of the individuals discussed in its pages. With advances in photographic technology during the latter decades of the century, photographs began to replace engravings. This widespread diffusion of portraits by the periodical press enabled readers who would not otherwise have encountered the biographical subject or had the opportunity of seeing a painted portrait to 'see' eminent scientists.

Forms of illustration varied widely. For example, classical themes were frequently employed; thus a laurel crown would symbolize the scientist's victory over nature. The portraits of scientists also often included books and scientific instruments which related to the biographical subject's major area of research, such as the 1836 portrait of Faraday in *Fraser's Magazine* (fig. 9.1). Sometimes the subject was drawn or photographed in a laboratory or on a field trip, thus providing the reader with a visual context in which to appreciate the scientist's activities. As Gowan Dawson has noted in chapter 7, with particular reference to the *Review of Reviews*, scientific journalism towards the end of the century was becoming increasingly intrusive. Biographical articles, based on an interview, often contained a wealth of personal details about a scientific celebrity. Photographs or engravings were published showing readers the house in which the scientist lived and the library and study in which he worked (figs. 9.2 and 9.3). Thereby they could see the scientist 'at home' and relate to him via familiar domestic imagery.[52] Visual material played an increasingly important role in conveying 'scientific lives' within the periodical frame.

READING BRIEF SCIENTIFIC LIVES

So widespread was biography within the periodical literature that a reader who never consulted a work of collected biography or bought or borrowed a single memoir could glean a vast amount of biographical information from the proliferating periodical press. In contrast to the financial and temporal investment involved in purchasing and reading a full book-length biography, the reader of the general periodical press encountered numerous abbreviated 'scientific lives' as part of his or her general reading. Likewise, the historian of scientific biography will find the periodical press to be a wonderfully rich resource. One of its attractions is that biographical material was not presented in a uniform manner but that 'scientific lives' were subject to many different interpretations and were used to support a wide variety of social, political, and religious positions ranging from jingoism to internationalism and from atheism to evangelical Christianity. Moreover, I have suggested four contexts in which scientific biography entered the periodical frame – as obituary notices, reviews of biographies, biographical sketches, and passing references – each of which treated scientific 'lives' in a different way.

As emphasized in chapter 1, the nineteenth-century periodical press was highly differentiated. While some periodicals aimed at a wide audience, others concentrated on a specific readership, perhaps defined by religious commitment or geographical locality. Also, as far as the individual was concerned, price was a limiting factor on the availability of titles, unless accessed through a library or reading room. As Alvar Ellegård showed in his seminal monograph, the differentiation among periodicals enables the historian to ascertain how evolutionary ideas were disseminated to different audiences.[53] A similar exercise could be conducted to ascertain how scientific lives were presented to readerships possessing, say, different religious or political commitments. Thus, as indicated above, the presentation of Faraday's religion and its relationship to his science depended on the religious orientation of the periodical. Likewise, the *Victoria Magazine* presented Faraday from a woman's perspective, as did Juliet Pollock writing in *St. Paul's*. Different audiences received different 'Faradays'. While no necessary connection exists between a periodical's stance and its portrayal of individual scientists, the latter is likely to be influenced by the author, the editor, the proprietor, the readers, and other factors involved in periodical production.

Finally, biographies of scientists not only narrate the subject's life and work but also contain the author's views about the nature of science and the value of a life in science.[54] As in the case of Faraday, brief scientific biographies can identify the personal qualities necessary for a successful scientist. Likewise the portrayal of the scientist through biography was often intended to make science appear attractive and thus encourage readers to participate in science. As a contributor to the popular science journal *Knowledge* commented, 'the life of a man like Faraday is an inspiration' to the reader. His life 'should [therefore] be widely known and emulated'.[55] Repeatedly his biographers also emphasized the importance of experiment and his unwillingness to speculate beyond the legitimate inferences from his data. Here was an example of good scientific practice that the reader was urged to emulate. More generally, biographies frequently carried value judgments about certain scientific theories and scientific methods that their authors sought to propagate.

One of the outstanding questions for the historian is to determine the extent to which the general periodical press shaped public understandings of science. The short 'scientific lives' published within general periodicals

clearly played a crucial role in this respect. Not only do such 'lives' encapsulate notions of 'the scientist', but they also address many of the scientific
ideas and activities pursued by the biographical subject. Through these short
biographies, readers would therefore have encountered information about
scientific theories, experiments, and scientific method, and also discussions
of the controversies in which the scientist participated. The biographical
account became the locus for contemporary debate, whether, for example, on political issues, female emancipation, or the relationship between
science and religion. Far from simply offering the details of an individual
life, articles on scientific biography helped shape the nineteenth-century
cultural engagement with science.

CHAPTER 10

Profit and prophecy: electricity in the late-Victorian periodical

Graeme Gooday

What the revival of learning was to the Renaissance, what the discovery of the new world was to the Elizabethans, what the steam-engine was to the century of the Revolution, the application of electricity is to the New Generation. We are standing at the day-dawn of the Electric Age . . . There is an electric thrill in the air which is affecting the nerves of civilization, and galvanizing into new and serviceable activity the sluggish imaginations of our people. Hence I have selected for presentation in a condensed form in this REVIEW the work of an American author, republished in the last days of 1889 . . .

[W. T. Stead], 'Looking Forward: A Romance of the Electrical Age', *Review of Reviews* (1890).[1]

This chapter examines the adoption of a popular 'futurist' mode of writing on electricity in general periodicals of the 1890s. I show that this was inspired in part by the enormous popularity of *Looking Backward, 2000–1887* (1888), in which American author Edward Bellamy used a technological-egalitarian utopia set in the year 2000 to illustrate the injustices of late nineteenth-century life.[2] Periodical and monograph writing about the possible or probable future social effects of technology predated Bellamy's novel, of course. Antecedents can readily be found in optimistic forecasts about the impact of the steam railway in the 1830s and 40s, and the electric telegraph from the 1840s to the 1860s – as well as sharp satirical responses, notably from *Punch*, founded in 1841.[3] In 1883 the Scottish-American polymath John Macnie published an electrical utopia of the ninety-sixth century entitled *The Diothas: Or, A Far Look Ahead* under the pseudonym 'Ismar Thiusen' – but soon afterwards its main premise was undermined by the financial collapse of Edison and Swan electric lighting schemes. Six years later, with sales of *Looking Backward* booming and the prospects of electrical technology invigorated by new political and technical developments, Macnie republished his novel, now retitled *Looking Forward*, and with a preface claiming priority for the *Diothas* over a 'somewhat similar but much more widely known work'.[4] A new British sixpenny monthly, *Review of Reviews*, soon offered its readers this work in a form that, although shortened, took up a full quarter of the forty pages in the March 1890 issue. As we shall see, this presentation by editor-proprietor William Stead signalled the great significance of 'Looking Forward: A Romance of the Electrical Age' for the species of 'new journalism' that he promoted in sympathy with the socialist utopianism of Bellamy's *Looking Backward*.

Thanks to the work of Peter Broks we know that by 1896 (and up to 1907) electricity was presented as the principal generator of future societal progress in such diverse periodicals as *Pearson's Magazine*, *Pearson's Weekly*, *Cassell's Magazine*, *Cassell's Saturday Journal*, *The Clarion*, and the *Cottager and Artisan*.[5] Broks's suggestion that this univocal utopianism developed in response to H. G. Wells's popular scientific romances, specifically the *Time Machine* of 1895, is uncompelling, since Wells's futurist writings in this period neither refer to electricity nor promote optimistic views of human progress.[6] I argue instead that electrical futurist writing can be traced back to Stead's promotion of this genre from the very first issue of *Review of Reviews* in January 1890. In this and subsequent issues Stead and his staff presented readers with a transatlantic array of imaginative journalism on electricity as the destining force of life – a major component of the scientific responses to Bellamy's *Looking Backward*.

As Gowan Dawson points out in chapter 7, Stead's implementation of the 'new journalism' enabled readers of this sixpenny monthly to gain access to British, American, and European periodical literature on politics, religion, science, otherwise well beyond their means.[7] Such was the circulation and impact of Stead's radical new kind of periodical that, I suggest, fiction writers, journalists, scientists, and entrepreneurs appropriated this new genre of 'prophetical romance' to articulate the future cultural significance of electrical light, power, and communication to readers of a broad range of publications. Moreover, the ascendancy of electrical futurism in contemporary journalism can be registered in the way that the *Review of Reviews* commented upon instances of it – sometimes in a highly critical vein. One particular target for criticism was William Crookes's 'Some Possibilities of Electricity' in the *Fortnightly Review* of February 1892. Importantly, Crookes had recently been criticized for significantly different reasons by the Tory *Spectator* and the premier journal of professional engineering, *The Electrician*. Since their criticisms can be seen as appealing to a more traditional 'authoritative' mode of writing, the first part of this chapter will document the principal pre-futurist mode genre of electrical journalism: the technical-didactic exegesis.

While giving centre-stage to Stead it is important not to overstate his role in moulding the genre of electrical futurism. Stead could hardly have nurtured this literary genre unless industrial experts such as Park Benjamin, William Crookes, Thomas Edison, Alice Gordon, William Gordon, and Frank Sprague had agreed to adopt this new mode of writing for periodicals.[8] Even those few writers on electricity who did not rely on its application for their primary income, such as William Coutts Keppel (Viscount Bury, later Earl of Albermarle)[9] and Edith Faithfull,[10] evidently wrote on the subject with some personal stake in the future success of applications of electricity. Moreover, writers and editors alike recognized the importance of treating their readers as socio-economic agents whose actions were crucial in deciding which of the possible electrical futures presented in periodicals would come into existence and which would not.[11]

DIDACTIC WRITING IN THE *QUARTERLY REVIEW* AND *NINETEENTH CENTURY*

> Our old men remember when it took many months to get a letter to India; but the rising generation would think themselves ill-treated if they did not read in the 'Times' each morning the report of any important event which had occurred in India the day before. Electricity rings our bells, lights our shores, runs our errands, and, as we hope, will blow up our enemies if they approach our coasts. It has become indispensable in peace and doubly indispensable in war. Last, not least, it has [a] young and vigorous literature, and a special language of its own.
>
> 'The Science of Electricity as Applied in Peace and War',
> *Quarterly Review* (July 1877)[12]

In contrast to the excited coverage of futurism in the 1890s, writing on electricity featured only occasionally in established British general periodicals in the preceding decades, generally less frequently than for the cognate issues of physical science (meteorology and cosmology) or technology (railways and shipping). Upmarket monthlies, such as *Macmillan's Magazine* launched in 1859 and the *Fortnightly Review* in 1865, had recently come to dominate the scene, but quarterly periodicals were neither totally eclipsed nor forced to alter the journalistic practices they adopted during their heyday earlier in the century.[13] The *Quarterly Review* long maintained the Tory commitments with which it was founded in 1809, and the pricing of six shillings per quarterly issue (a year's subscription was still less expensive than monthlies typically costing two shillings and sixpence per issue). And whereas the new monthlies published named contributions from the ambitious secular community of middle-class academic scientists, for example T. H. Huxley, John Tyndall, and Norman Lockyer, the *Quarterly* continued its tradition of anonymity well into the twentieth century – albeit occasionally subverted by authors' subsequent self-identification.[14] Using the *Wellesley Index* to identify *Quarterly* authors between 1873 and 1889, we can see that while Herbert Spencer, Richard Owen, St George Mivart, and Alfred Wallace wrote very occasional contributions, most articles on natural science were penned by 'men of letters' or marginal scientific figures. For the period from January 1876 to July 1880, William Coutts Keppel (Viscount Bury), contributed six articles on the physical and navigational sciences and a seventh on international politics.[15] With the exception of a single piece on electric lighting published in October 1881, however, the *Quarterly*'s coverage of science in the 1880s focused predominantly on the life sciences and colonial exploration.

Science writers for the *Quarterly* wrote within the long-established repertoire of house styles astutely characterized by Walter Bagehot in the 1850s as 'review-like essays' and 'essay-like reviews'. While some reviews clearly set out to engage with the books whose titles graced their headings, many essays only had the semblance of being reviews, insofar as they used one or more books as rhetorical 'pegs' on which to hang independent accounts.[16] As Walter Houghton and Joanne Shattock have noted, the partisan character and broad scope of such pieces went far beyond an analysis of the books cited: their wider themes were indeed clearly signalled in ensuing page headers.[17] Some *Quarterly* essays encompassed a broad temporal scope, and discussions were by no means tied to new or even recent publications. The three-monthly cycle of publication importantly enabled more reflective writing for the *longue durée*, constituting publications more likely to be kept, bound, and consulted by posterity than ephemeral weeklies or shilling monthlies. Befitting a publication that spoke to its presumptive readership of landed, military, and political interests, *Quarterly* writing narrated the past and present accomplishments of the establishment more often than it addressed prospects for social improvement. While playing to the conservative mores of readers, *Quarterly* writers nevertheless used various devices – some distinctly didactic – to acclimatize readers to unfamiliar concepts in the sciences.

The July 1877 issue of the *Quarterly Review* carried a forty-page 'Article V' nominally devoted to reviewing six diverse publications on electricity dating from 1870 to 1876. Only four of these were explicitly addressed in this 'review-like essay' on 'The Science of Electricity as Applied in Peace and War'. Two theoretical treatises of five years' vintage, Sir William Thomson's *Papers on Electrostatics and Magnetism* (1872) and Sir William Snow Harris's

Magnetism (1872), were explored to illustrate decades of argument about the cause of variations in terrestrial magnetism that had so vexed navigators. Rather than 'further weary our readers' with unresolved arguments, the piece followed both Thomson and Snow Harris in conceding that the subject remained a mystery.[18] By contrast, the first five volumes of the *Journal of the Society of Telegraph Engineers* (1871–6) furnished definitive diagnoses on the hazards of lightning strikes and heralded the successes of thirty years of submarine and land telegraphy, especially in the colonies.[19] In this context the official *Report from the Select Committee of the House of Commons on the Post Office Telegraph Department* (1876) served to highlight how German military forces had made great tactical use of telegraph technology.

The didactic-historicist genre of writing instantiated in this *Quarterly* article is most clearly epitomized, however, in its excursions into sources not listed in its header. Note, for example, the concluding passage on the devastating use of the (static) electric torpedo in the American Civil War drawn from the 1865 *Report of the Secretary of the United States Navy*. Reinforcing the interpretation of the 1876 *Select Committee Report*, *Quarterly* readers were offered yet more evidence that electrical techniques had become decisive in modern warfare. Between such historical anecdotes, the narrative explicitly positioned readers as students more or less expert in the important but arcane wisdom of electricity. After the conventional admission that not even experts knew what electricity actually was, one quarter of the article was devoted to a standard textbook exegesis of how electricians had created instead a working *language* of electricity, including such terms as voltage, resistance, current, and induction.[20] Acknowledging the heterogeneous nature of the *Quarterly* audience, both the 'well-informed' and the 'very idle' reader were 'solemnly warned to skip' this lengthy discussion of technicalities. A third (majority) category of reader was thereby implied: the attentive learner who sought to attain the knowledge presupposed in texts addressed to a 'professional' audience. By gaining some such knowledge, readers would then find the *Journal of the Society of Telegraph Engineers* a 'mine of interesting information', and thereby come to comprehend the pronouncements of electrical experts contained within its pages.[21]

The significance of this didactic mode both for the writer and for the standing of the *Quarterly* as an anonymized reference volume is clear when we consider the opening sentences of William Coutts Keppel's article 'Electric Light and Force' published by the *Nineteenth Century* in July 1882:

In July 1877 the *Quarterly Review* had an article of mine on 'Electricity as applied in Peace and War', to which I refer here because it forms a convenient landmark.

Though it was written by me five years ago, and was intended to give in a popular form an account of electrical science as it then existed, it is quite curious to remark how completely recent inventions have left its statements in arrear... The very nomenclature of the science, which I took some pains to expound, is as archaic as Chaucer's English.[22]

Keppel conceded that electrical science had greatly altered since he had introduced *Quarterly* readers to the professional language of electricity in 1877; indeed in October 1881 *Quarterly* readers encountered a piece on electric lighting using a very different discourse (see below, p. 536). Keppel admitted that so 'rapid and violent' had been the change in language – at a speed indeed to 'rival that of the imponderable agent' itself – that such familiar household words as 'phonograph' and 'telephone' had only come into existence since his earlier article. And whereas Bury wrote in 1877 of 'voltaic electricity' measured in webers, the retitled 'direct current' was now customarily registered in amperes. Given the resilient status of the *Quarterly* as a repository of considered periodical wisdom, it is plausible to suggest that Keppel retrospectively revealed his authorship of the 1877 article because it was important to inform periodical readers that the earlier piece was no longer definitive. This was especially significant since the introduction of electric light a few years earlier had engendered a fast-growing demand for knowledge of electricity: 'The newspaper and the popular lecturer have taken it up, and instilled it into us, so to speak, with our tea and toast at breakfast.'[23]

Writing in the *Nineteenth Century* in 1882 was indeed an effective way of reaching an important audience interested in the implications of new developments in science and technology. Daniel Rutenberg has suggested that this 'serious' campaigning monthly, founded in 1877 by the former editor of the *Contemporary Review*, James Knowles, exercised a 'very striking influence' on both periodical literature and on 'liberal thought' in general. No more so than in 1882 when Knowles secured enormous support for his personally grounded opposition to plans for a Channel Tunnel.[24] Moreover, individual articles on science were a customary feature of its monthly schedule, as were the regular abstracts of recent research provided first by Thomas H. Huxley and later by Prince Kropotkin.

Bury's piece is discernibly attuned to the house-style, readers of his article being presumed to be well-informed about such features of modern life as the telephone.[25] Presuming 'everyone nowadays knows' how to maintain an electric current using a battery and electrical conductor, readers of 'Electric Light and Force' were invited to extend such knowledge to new forms of artificial lighting and power supply. Hopefully without 'wearying' readers,

244 Science in the Nineteenth-Century Periodical

Bury offered to guide them through the bewildering novelty of vocabulary needed to understand the Edison and Brush forms of 'dynamo', especially as textbooks treated such topics in exasperatingly different ways.[26] Tellingly, when the same author published again on the 'Electrical Transmission of Power' in the *Nineteenth Century* ten years later, he recycled much of the same material, but updated his vocabulary yet again to include 'energy' rather than the now antiquated terminology of 'electrical force'. He also now candidly revealed that his own financial interests in the electrical industry had been thwarted in the collapse following the brief boom of 1882. Evidently his didacticism was not that of a disinterested man of letters, but a mode of writing designed to give readers an understanding of contemporary entrepreneurial projects of 1892 that were now, he implied, on a much sounder footing. As the recently elevated Duke of Albemarle put it: 'the *bona fide* investor may fairly consider that in matters electrical his turn has come at last'.[27] Readers of the *Nineteenth Century*, like earlier readers of the *Quarterly*, were thus configured in two correlated modes: both as leisurely scholars of electricity and as prospective stakeholders in electrical ventures.

This pattern of didactic writing on electricity inflected with entrepreneurial undertones was not unique to Bury's journalism, but characteristic of most periodical writing on this subject up to about 1890. Consider, for example, 'Article IV' in the October 1881 issue of the *Quarterly Review*. This was an overtly partisan interpretation of the *Catalogue Général Officiel* of the Paris Exposition Internationale d'Electricité of August 1881 that attacked the conclusion of the Parliamentary Blue Book *Lighting by Electricity* of August 1879 that house-to-house electricity supply was economically unviable. Alluding to the scepticism with which contrary claims had been treated, the article claimed that the 'dream of the visionary and enthusiast has been realized': what had been deemed impossible two years earlier could be seen 'in daily action' at the exhibition in Paris.[28] Citing evidence on machines listed in the catalogue, and the writer's own visits and interviews at the Paris Exposition, technical arguments were offered to show that the ideal dynamo must be robustly designed to run at high speeds. By showing readers exactly *how* electrical machinery could be so efficiently constructed as to render the enterprise profitable, the wealthiest of *Quarterly* readers were thus offered inducements to be treated as potential shareholders in the electrical industry.[29] When the engineer James Gordon claimed authorship of this piece at the Society of Arts in 1883 (and subsequently in its journal), he effectively claimed priority for what was by then his characteristic technique of designing dynamos for his employer, the Telegraph Construction and Maintenance Company.[30]

Nevertheless, when Gordon published on 'The Latest Electrical Discovery' in the *Nineteenth Century* two months after Albemarle's piece for the same periodical in January 1892, his approach to writing about the subject had changed markedly. Gone were the detailed technical specifications and performance data that were meant to impress readers of the *Quarterly* with the combined rhetorical resources of the advanced science textbook and engineering company prospectus. Also vanished was the presumption that dreamers and visionaries stood, of necessity, at odds with conventional mainstream wisdom. Gordon presented Nikola Tesla's recent lecture on fluorescent lighting at the Royal Institution (on 3 February) as a dazzling extension of William Crookes's theatrical use of cathode ray tubes to produce 'radiant matter'. In exploring the use of very high frequency currents, this experimenter entered 'a region of mystery and hope': the generation of artificial light without the need for wire connections presented an astonishing new array of possibilities. If application of Tesla's results were ever to fulfil the 'bold dreams of scientific imagination', Gordon speculated that readers of the *Nineteenth Century* would see social and political change on a scale at least as significant as that already associated with the railway and telegraph systems:

Most manual labour will become unnecessary, as unlimited power will be available at every man's hand. Engineering works will be carried out on a far greater scale than has yet been even contemplated, and doubtless a corresponding era of material prosperity will set in.[31]

Why had Gordon adopted this rather different mode of writing on electricity as the fulfilment of progressivist 'dreams'? Explanations of this utopian strain of writing cannot be found in simple biographical accounts, but rather in understanding the widespread adoption of futurist writing during the preceding two years.

LOOKING BACKWARD AND ELECTRICAL FUTURISM IN THE *REVIEW OF REVIEWS*

A somewhat provoking paper by Mr Pack [*sic*] Benjamin, in the *Forum*, discusses the possibilities of electricity with more scientific imagination than literary skill.

William Stead, 'The Miracles of Electricity', *Review of Reviews* (January 1890).[32]

Following the broadly positive American response to the publication of Bellamy's *Looking Backward* in 1888, the first sustained production of futurist writing on electricity developed in the USA. These writers aimed at attracting a readership for their work by extrapolating a plausible Bellamyian utopian future from contemporary novelties in electrical science and technology. As William Stead was founding an American version of the *Review of Reviews* at the same time as the British edition in late 1889, he had unique access to transatlantic journalism. Stead in turn reproduced in summary form some of these writings in early issues of the *Review of Reviews*, thus bringing into one periodical otherwise disparate and dispersed electricity-centred responses to *Looking Backward*. To understand why he did this we should note both Stead's political sympathy for Bellamy's representation of the year 2000 as a Christian world of social justice facilitated by nationalized technologies of communication and transport, and his shrewd recognition of the great popularity of *Looking Backward* in the United Kingdom. Stead's anthologizing of futurist writing thus showed the tens of thousands who were to read the *Review of Reviews* how present-day developments in electrical technology could plausibly realize Bellamy's egalitarian vision of life a little more than a century in the future. At the same time, Stead was by no means an uncritical cut-and-paste purveyor of futurist writings. His editorial interventions not infrequently passed harsh judgement on self-indulgent or ill-composed journalism, especially gadget-based fantasies that failed to conform to his sober Congregationalist ethic.

In its very first issue of January 1890 the British *Review of Reviews* abstracted Park Benjamin's 'The Miracles of Electricity' from the American engineering journal *Forum*. Stead's criticism of its implausibility and literary demerits is evident from the epigraph above. Benjamin blithely forecast the arrival of electric light without heat; instant photography across continents; electric trains travelling at three hundred miles an hour; the telegraphing of tastes and smells for remote medical diagnosis; telegraphic and telephonic transmissions without wires; and the use of electrical heating for welding, cookery, and institutional warmth. Noting the sybaritic possibility of 'music on tap' in every dwelling, the sceptical *Review of Reviews* noted with astonishment Benjamin's intimation that wallpaper might soon be electrically illuminated. As if to counter these excesses, this article on electrical miracles was immediately followed by an abstract of 'Electricity in the Household' published by A. E. Kennelly, Thomas Edison's senior electrician, in *Scribner's Magazine*. This 'interesting' and generally demure paper offered the more immediate utilitarian prospect of using electricity in a burglar-alarm service; to regulate domestic temperature; keep clocks on time; power carpet-sweepers; operate a table train to serve meals; and heat large quantities of coffee.[33]

Although neither Benjamin nor Kennelly explicitly mentioned Bellamy, we can understand Stead's abstracting and republication of their writings in the context of his quasi-Bellamyan agenda as owner-proprietor. A few pages later in the same issue we find an abstract of an 'admirable' piece from the *Contemporary Review* on 'Two New Utopias'. This offered readers a history of philosophical utopianism from Plato to Bellamy, comments on Peruvian state socialism, and a review of 'Mon Utopie' by an eminent French professor of philosophy. Significantly, Stead placed immediately after this article some highlights from an interview with the author of *Looking Backward* drawn from the American *Our Day*. Stead's editing reveals a striking commonality between his wholesome interests and Edward Bellamy's. Much is made of how Bellamy's novel promoted marital equity, state ownership of principal technologies, especially those of transportation and telegraphic communication, and the religious praxis of working collectively towards a peacefully built utopia. Of the widespread organization of activist clubs formed to enact his goals Bellamy is reported as saying: 'Christians form the best class in society, but they have lacked a practical working plan, and our movement supplies that lack.'[34] By his detailed and sympathetic reporting of Bellamy's plan, Stead effectively endorsed an active form of devout technological egalitarianism that enabled readers of the *Review of Reviews* to see how an utopia could be created in their lifetime.

Wherever possible, Stead's editing of electrical futurist writing highlighted the distinctly theological concomitants of electrical innovation. An adulatory piece from *Harper's Magazine*, 'The Genius of this Electric Age', in the February 1890 issue of *Review of Reviews* closed with Thomas Edison's reply to questions about an Intelligent Creator: 'The existence of such a God, can to my mind, almost be proved from chemistry.'[35] Nevertheless, Stead's ecumenical editorial policy could also accommodate less reverent visions of an electrical world to come. That same issue re-published from the *North American Review* an article on 'The Future and What Hides in It – A Scientific Prophecy by Professor Thurston'. This broad-ranging narrative examined the wider possibilities of human development and technologically induced harmony, focusing on the probable impact of electrical agency in global transmission of power, voices, and pictures:

Nothing is more probable than that in the next few years the triumphs of electricity will be extended from the earth to the air, and a flying machine will be as common in the twentieth century as an electric tramcar is to-day. It is only a question of the number of years that must pass before we are able to emulate the angels, if not in their virtues, at least in the manner of their locomotion.[36]

Indeed with an eye to maintaining the circulation figures needed for profitability, Stead was tactical in choosing to republish the racier and more imaginative sources – especially given the prosaically unliterary qualities of *Looking Backward*. As Stead noted in an editorial piece from March 1890:

> The great success which has attended Mr. Edward Bellamy's 'Looking Backward,' a prophetico-realist romance of an American idealist is a welcome sign of the times. 'Looking Backward' as a story is as dull as ditchwater. It is only because it is a kind of apocalyptic vision, if not of the new heaven, then of the new earth, for which the hearts of men and women are longing all over the world, that 200,000 copies have been sold in the America, and the sale in this country in the last few months has mounted up to 100,000. The success of 'Looking Backward' has naturally stimulated the tendency of a certain class of theorists to resort to the historico-prophetic form of romance as a popular vehicle for infusing these ideas into the public mind.

Not only did Stead seek out livelier writing than Bellamy's to capture popular literary taste, he also pinpointed narratives that placed at centre-stage the most plausible means for bringing his utopia into existence. Electricity, he contended, was the 'most puissant of all the servants of man', no less than the 'destined agent' that would banish war from the world by making next-door neighbours of nations in all continents.[37] Such was the editorial flourish with which he introduced his condensed version of *Looking Forward* as a 'romance of the electrical age'.[38] Stead explained that this was among the best of such contemporary romances, since it offered an ingenious speculation upon the probable political and social results to be expected from harnessing the 'universal force' of electricity. Stead noted approvingly the author's claim that this forecast was drawn from present conditions and tendencies framed within the bounds of 'sober reason' – in contrast to the wild fancifulness of some futurist writing surveyed in previous months.[39] Tellingly though, Stead took no notice of the anti-socialist preface that 'Ismar Thiusen' included in the 1889 edition of his work.[40]

Politics aside, the commonality of themes between 'Looking Forward' and *Looking Backward* explains why Stead found the former a useful vehicle for re-articulating Bellamy's programme. A mesmerically induced sleep takes the narrator to an egalitarian and co-operative 96th-century world characterized by a three-hour working day for all men and women. The ubiquitous electric light and the phonograph sustain a high quality of domestic life and an automated food service obviates the need for servants – but not the obligation for a prayer of thanks before each meal. The modernity of global life is further characterized by the abolition of the papacy and the free availability of intercontinental electric transportation and telecommunication. Stead spares his readers the central love-story (advising readers to purchase the complete novel), but not the tragedy in which the narrator's nineteenth-century unfamiliarity in handling a battery-powered boat leads to the death of his 96th-century fiancée – while he miraculously returns to his year of origin.[41]

This genre of cautious technological extrapolation, framed in an egalitarian utopia and narrated as populist romance, was calculated, as Stead noted, to reinvigorate the imaginations of readers in order to see how electricity could 're-energize' the world to egalitarian reform. Accordingly he and his staff of writers on the *Review of Reviews* were critical of any subsequent popular writing on electrical futurism that failed to meet these demanding moral standards. In the final section I consider their critical response to electrical writing in a liberal highbrow monthly, entire issues of which were regularly abstracted in a section entitled 'The Reviews Reviewed'.

FUTURISM IN THE *FORTNIGHTLY REVIEW* – AND ITS CRITICS

> The scientific authorities of today have fallen into a rather provoking and tantalising habit of taking the public into their confidence, making known to it discoveries that are as yet only half known to themselves, and building upon them the basis of those discoveries a bewildering fabric of conjectural possibilities.
>
> 'Science and Conjecture', *The Spectator* (21 November 1891)[42]

Symptomatic of the literary response to Bellamy's millennial bestseller epitomized in the *Review of Reviews*, a range of periodicals soon discussed the future possibilities and possible futures engendered by science, often aided and abetted by scientific experts, who generally welcomed such congenial debates. Between spring 1890 and 1892 the 'future' featured as a central motif in the titles of eight *Fortnightly Review* pieces on warfare, religion, marriage, American literature, geography, cosmology and art.[43] Two of the three articles on electricity published by the *Fortnightly* in this period borrowed from the futurist genre popularized by Stead in the widely read *Review of Reviews*. A third, 'Human Electricity' by Professor John McKendrick of Glasgow University, showed, however, the resilience of the didactic mode of writing among the academic fraternity[44] – elements of which were also apparent in William Crookes's 'Some Possibilities of Electricity', published in February 1892. Nevertheless, substantial portions of the latter epitomize the tendency of expert electrical writers to borrow from the imaginative literature of the future that we saw illustrated earlier in J. E. H. Gordon's

'The Latest Electrical Discovery', published in the *Nineteenth Century* one month before Crookes's article.

'The Development of Decorative Electricity' by Alice (Mrs J. E. H.) Gordon appeared in the February 1891 issue of the *Fortnightly*. As I have discussed elsewhere, this was written concurrently with her book on the same subject.[45] Both presented the prospect of men and women in the wealthier middle classes enjoying the results of electric light tastefully installed to modernize their home comforts. In commenting on this article in the *Fortnightly*, the *Review of Reviews* presented Mrs Gordon as contributing to the discourse of electrical prophecy, summarizing her principal claim: 'In the drawing-room the light of the future will be a reflected light.' Nevertheless, like other periodical critics, scepticism was expressed about her wanton use of the 'scientific imagination' to propose the placing of electrical cigar-lighters near everyone's front door and the indulgent installation of electric lamps in the obscurity of cupboards, cellars and housemaid's closets. At best her suggestions were 'interesting' but were judged by the moralistic narrator of the *Review of Reviews* to constitute a project of gratuitous luxury.[46]

William Crookes's 'Some Possibilities of Electricity' was a departure in style from his previous quasi-didactic expositions, although we can readily trace the introduction of the 'future' as a topic for public discussion. In his Presidential address to the Institution of Electrical Engineers (IEE) a year earlier, in January 1891, Crookes spoke cautiously to that expert audience, suggesting that cultivating 'pure research' on electricity offered the best hope for the future, hinting that the 'discrepancies' apparent in residual phenomena 'promise a rich harvest of future discoveries to the experimental philosopher'. Otherwise his IEE presentation was a highly technical report of experiments involving cathode ray tubes.[47] However, at an after-dinner speech at the Picadilly Hotel in London in November that year, Crookes was less guarded in his speculation. There were, he suggested, 10,000 foot-tons of energy locked up in each cubic foot of universal ether, and the tasks of unlocking this 'vast storehouse of power' fell to the 'electrician of the future'.[48] The Tory weekly *Spectator*, characteristically sceptical of claims from ambitious scientists, dwelt at length on the apparent similarities between Crookes's outlandish claim and the dubious pronouncements of contemporary charlatans who inspired similarly regrettable credulity among the 'unscientific host'.[49] Undeterred by this criticism, however, Crookes continued with further futurist speculation on electricity in a more overtly popular format for the *Fortnightly* in February 1892.

Expanding upon several of the themes in his recent after-dinner speech at the Piccadilly, for the *Fortnightly* Crookes cast expert electrical researchers as heroes of the coming generation. Undeterred by the resiliently mysterious nature of electricity, their task was to imagine and instantiate practical possibilities for the future utilitarian application of electricity. Alluding perhaps to one of the 'miracles' of electricity forecast by Park Benjamin two years earlier, Crookes articulated in considerable detail the possible operation of a system of telegraphy that dispensed with the expensive encumbrance of wires. Establishing his authority for *Fortnightly* readers by using the didactic mode of exegesis for several paragraphs, he then distanced this account from the more fantastical electrical journalism of the non-expert by emphasizing the informed modesty of his extrapolation:

This is no dream of a visionary philosopher. All the requisites needed to bring it within the grasp of daily life are well within the possibilities of discovery, and are so reasonable and so clearly in the path of researches which are now being actively prosecuted in every capital of Europe that we may any day expect to hear that they have emerged from the realms of speculation into those of sober fact.

Such communication, he emphasized, was indeed already possible within a distance of a few hundred yards, and he himself could claim credibility for having participated in similar experiments several years earlier.[50] And it was not just long-distance communication that could take place through the ether in an electrified future. Like Gordon writing for the *Nineteenth Century*, Crookes quoted intensively from Tesla's recent dazzling theatrical display illustrating how vacuum tubes could be made incandescent without recourse to ungainly connecting wires. This, Crookes noted, would be the 'ideal way' of lighting a room; such was the intrinsic beauty of the coloured light that even Mrs Gordon's elaborate aesthetic of lampshades might prove otiose.

Drawing inspiration from the imminent prospects of success in these two familiar technological enterprises, Crookes then undertook a considerable departure from his own areas of expertise. In the latter part of the article he adopted the imaginative rather than didactic mode, speculating on the future application of electricity to public services. The enhancement of agricultural productivity, the treatment of sewage, the destruction of disease, the elimination of London fogs and the control of rainfall might yet be attempted, he suggested, by exploiting the electrical mechanism responsible for their particular operations. Recognizing that such optimistic speculations might arouse derision, Crookes reflected that he would 'perhaps, be styled a dreamer, or something worse, if I remotely hint at still further amending the ways of Nature'. To curtail such thoughts, he re-minded readers of their non-expert status by suggesting that such matters could safely be left to the devices and 'inspirations' of electrical engineers. 'Sufficient for this generation are the wonders thereof!' exclaimed Crookes in closing.[51]

In the 'Reviews Reviewed' section of the *Review of Reviews* in February 1892 Stead disparaged Crookes's piece, which he somewhat archly charac-terized as the 'most interesting' in that month's issue of the *Fortnightly*. It was 'sufficient to take away one's breath' for its indulgence in futurism beyond what might have been warranted by contemporary accomplishments:

The writer maintains that there is no reason to doubt that, in a short time, we shall be able to telegraph without wires in any direction. As we have the telegraph without wires, so we shall have electric light without connecting the lamp to any current. Professor Crookes gives a clear run to his fancy, and thinks that we may, by electrical action, rout the parasitical insects and fungi which in some seasons rob us of no less than the tenth of our crops. At present there is 796,800 horse-power of the sun's rays wasted on our land. If it could be yoked by electricity, what could not be done? Electricians, he thinks, should aim at nothing less than the control of the weather, and always make it wet at nighttime and sunshiny all the day; and when it was to rain, rain a downpour never a drizzle. Incidentally he would abolish London fogs and sterilise all germs in the water supply.[52]

This response to Crookes shows us clearly that, despite being a conve-nient part of the rhetorical weaponry employed by the youthful electrical industry to win the confidence of future consumers and investors, the le-gitimacy of electrical futurism could be contested in a variety of ways.[53] For Stead, Crookes's undisciplined conjectures were symptomatic of the unenlightened worldly hubris of electricians. Stead's critique in such a high-circulation monthly as the *Review of Reviews* served to undermine Crookes's broad status as an electrical expert of the highest rank. The prob-lematic position of futurist writing by experts was recognized elsewhere in the periodical world by an electrical journal that had eulogized Crookes as President of the Institution of Electrical Engineers in the previous year. In commenting on Crookes's piece, the *Electrician* of 5 February 1892 referred its readers back to its discussion of the *Spectator*'s comments in the previous November on the humbug of scientific conjecture.

If the science, so far as it goes, is correct, and the conjectures which go beyond are fairly logical, such dissertations have a JULES VERNE-like romance, and harmlessly amuse the public with ideas of these "half-baked" notions with which some thinkers are busying themselves.

The *Electrician* judged Crookes's 'Some Possibilities of Electricity' to be a contribution to this kind of literature, noting knowingly that the 'initiated' would observe a number of 'slips' that it then documented in some detail. Even while sharing Crooke's interest in promoting an electricity-dominated future, the *Electrician* criticized his account so as to pre-empt further scepticism concerning the trustworthiness of expert writers engaging in futurist speculation.[54]

RE-ASSESSING THE ORIGINS OF FUTURIST WRITING ON SCIENCE

William Stead's journalism for the *Review of Reviews* was crucial in forging electrical futurism as an identifiable genre of writing out of the responses of electrical scientists and engineers to Bellamy's *Looking Backward*. Having seen the flourishing of electrical futurism due to Stead's efforts from 1890, we can appreciate – *pace* Broks – that H. G. Wells's *Time Machine* of 1895 was arguably more a reaction *against* utopian futurism about electricity than a stimulus to it. Although Wells deployed a *technology* of time-travel rather than conventional mesmeric devices to transport his protagonist into the future, its mechanism was not electrical. More tellingly still, the two futurist narratives in the *Time Machine* present discomfiting extrapolations from other areas of contemporary science: a Darwinian dystopia of human degeneration and an entropic eschatology of universal heat death.[55] Although Stead remained silent about the uncongenially anti-progressivist ramifications of the former, the *Review of Reviews* did publish writings on the theological implications of the latter. After all, from Stead's perspective there was no incongruity in juxtaposing the journalism of electrical liberation with that of thermodynamic catastrophe eons later: an imminent future of socialist electrical utopias was quite compatible with the eventual passing of the material world to herald the resurrection of Christian souls.[56]

Importantly, however, neither readers of the *Review of Reviews* nor those whose writings it published need have subscribed to Stead's religious-political assumptions in order to appreciate the narratives of electrical futures that he edited and commented upon during the 1890s. For less affluent consumers, the *Review of Reviews* provided an affordable panoply of imaginative views of what the wonder-working agent of electricity might soon do for them – sparing them both the expense of reading several periodicals and the tedium of dry didactic treatments that hitherto abounded. For industrial propagandists of electricity, the *Review of Reviews* furnished useful examples of how to treat the subject so as to capture the interest of the reading public – and some salient warnings about the reasonable limits of journalistic hyperbole.

Imaginative technological futurism never became the sole mode of writing on electrical topics; it supplemented and eclipsed traditional didacticism as the most popular mode of writing about technical subjects, if not necessarily the most credible. But ever since Stead's endeavours in the 1890s, experts in science and technology have enjoyed the benefits of the precedents he created, enabling them to speculate about the future implications of their work without fear that they would necessarily be seen as breaching the boundaries of professional decorum.

Notes

I. INTRODUCTION

1. 'Are there Real Analogies in Nature? [1856]', in Lewis Campbell and William Garnett, *The Life of James Clerk Maxwell, with a Selection From his Correspondence and Occasional Writings and a Sketch of his Contributions to Science* (London: Macmillan and Co., 1882), pp. 235–44 (243).
2. Margaret Beetham, 'Towards a Theory of the Periodical as a Publishing Genre', in *Investigating Victorian Journalism*, ed. by Laurel Brake, Aled Jones, and Lionel Madden (Basingstoke: Macmillan, 1990), pp. 19–32 (21).
3. James A. Secord, *Victorian Sensation: The Extraordinary Publication, Reception, and Secret Authorship of 'Vestiges of the Natural History of Creation'* (Chicago: University of Chicago Press, 2000), pp. 126–38.
4. Alvar Ellegård, *Darwin and the General Reader: The Reception of Darwin's Theory of Evolution in the British Periodical Press, 1859–1872*, 2nd edn (Chicago: University of Chicago Press, 1990), p. 21.
5. Secord, *Victorian Sensation*, p. 351.
6. Ellegård, *General Reader*, p. 341.
7. Robert M. Young, 'Natural Theology, Victorian Periodicals, and the Fragmentation of a Common Context', in *Darwin's Metaphor: Nature's Place in Victorian Culture* (Cambridge: Cambridge University Press, 1985), pp. 126–63, 265–71.
8. Richard Yeo, *Defining Science: William Whewell, Natural Knowledge, and Public Debate in Early Victorian Britain* (Cambridge: Cambridge University Press, 1993), pp. 38–48 (47). See also Jürgen Habermas, *The Structural Transformation of the Public Sphere: An Inquiry into a Category of Bourgeois Society*, trans. by Thomas Burger (Cambridge, Mass.: MIT Press, 1991); Thomas Broman, 'The Habermasian Public Sphere and "Science in the Enlightenment"', *History of Science* 36 (1998), 123–49; Thomas Broman, 'Periodical Literature', in *Books and the Sciences in History*, ed. by Marina Frasca-Spada and Nick Jardine (Cambridge: Cambridge University Press, 2000), pp. 225–38; and Terry Eagleton, *The Function of Criticism: From The Spectator to Post-Structuralism* (London and New York: Verso, 1984).
9. Jon P. Klancher, *The Making of English Reading Audiences, 1790–1832* (Madison: University of Wisconsin Press, 1987), p. 12.

10. See, particularly, Adrian Desmond, 'Artisan Resistance and Evolution in Britain, 1819–1848', *Osiris* 2nd ser. 3 (1987), 77–110; and Adrian Desmond, *The Politics of Evolution: Morphology, Medicine, and Reform in Radical London* (Chicago and London: University of Chicago Press, 1989).

11. Charles H. Timperley, *Encyclopaedia of Literary and Typographical Anecdote*, 2 vols. (London: H. G. Bohn, 1842), p. 952.

12. Roger Cooter and Stephen Pumfrey, 'Separate Spheres and Public Places: Reflections on the History of Science Popularization and Science in Popular Culture', *History of Science* 32 (1994), 237–67 (255).

13. Bernard Lightman, '"The Voices of Nature": Popularizing Victorian Science', in *Victorian Science and Culture*, ed. by Bernard Lightman, (Chicago and London: University of Chicago Press, 1997), pp. 187–211 (191).

14. Gillian Beer, *Darwin's Plots: Evolutionary Narrative in Darwin, George Eliot and Nineteenth-Century Fiction* (London: Routledge & Kegan Paul, 1983); Sally Shuttleworth, *George Eliot and Nineteenth-Century Science: The Make-Believe of a Beginning* (Cambridge: Cambridge University Press, 1984); George Levine, *Darwin and the Novelists: Patterns of Science in Victorian Fiction* (Cambridge, Mass.: Harvard University Press, 1988).

15. John S. North (ed.), *The Waterloo Directory of English Newspapers and Periodicals, 1800–1900*, 50 vols. (Waterloo, Ontario: North Waterloo Academic Press, 1994–), vol. 1, p. 9. See also J. S. North (ed.), *The Waterloo Directory of Scottish Newspapers and Periodicals, 1800–1900*, 2 vols. (Waterloo, Ontario: North Waterloo Academic Press, 1989); and J. S. North (ed.), *The Waterloo Directory of Irish Newspapers and Periodicals, 1800–1900* (Waterloo, Ontario: North Waterloo Academic Press, 1986).

16. See, for instance, Beetham, 'Towards a Theory'; Lyn Pykett, 'Reading the Periodical Press: Text and Context', in *Investigating Victorian Journalism*, ed. by Laurel Brake, Aled Jones, and Lionel Madden (Basingstoke: Macmillan, 1990), pp. 3–18; and Laurel Brake, 'Writing, Cultural Production and the Periodical Press in the Nineteenth Century', in *Writing and Victorianism*, ed. by J. B. Bullen (London: Longman, 1997), pp. 54–72.

17. Geoffrey Cantor, Gowan Dawson, Richard Noakes, Sally Shuttleworth, and Jonathan R. Topham, *Science in the Nineteenth-Century Periodical: An Electronic Index* (forthcoming, Hri Online, University of Sheffield, 2004). For details see <http://www.sciper.leeds.ac.uk>.

18. The phrase comes from Michael Wolff's classic article 'Charting the Golden Stream: Thoughts on a Directory of Victorian Periodicals', in *Editing Nineteenth-Century Texts*, ed. by John M. Robson (Toronto: University of Toronto Press, 1967), pp. 37–59.

19. George Saintsbury, *A History of Nineteenth Century Literature, 1780–1895* (New York and London: Macmillan and Co., 1896), p. 166.

20. Michael Harris, 'Periodicals and the Book Trade', in *Development of the English Book Trade, 1700–1899*, ed. by Robin Myers and Michael Harris (Oxford: Oxford Polytechnic Press, 1981), pp. 66–94; and John Feather,

A History of British Publishing (London and New York: Routledge, 1988), pp. 106–15.

21. [William Hazlitt], 'The Periodical Press', *Edinburgh Review* 38 (1823), 349–78 (350).
22. Lee Erickson, *The Economy of Literary Form: English Literature and the Industrialization of Publishing, 1800–1850* (Baltimore and London: Johns Hopkins University Press, 1996), p. 7; Mark Parker, *Literary Magazines and British Romanticism* (Cambridge: Cambridge University Press, 2000), p. 1.
23. Marilyn Butler, 'Culture's Medium: The Role of the Review', in *The Cambridge Companion to Romanticism*, ed. by Stuart Curran (Cambridge: Cambridge University Press, 1993), pp. 120–47 (131).
24. 'Preface', *Gentleman's Magazine* 90, pt 1 (1820), iii–iv.
25. G. N. Cantor, 'The Academy of Physics at Edinburgh, 1797–1800', *Social Studies of Science* 5 (1975), 109–34; Thomas H. Cook, 'Science, Philosophy, and Culture in the Early *Edinburgh Review*, 1802–1829', unpublished PhD thesis, University of Pittsburgh, 1976; John Clive, *Scotch Reviewers: The 'Edinburgh Review', 1802–1815* (London: Faber, 1957).
26. Roy Porter, 'Lay Medical Knowledge in the Eighteenth Century: The Evidence of the *Gentleman's Magazine*', *Medical History* 29 (1985), 138–68 (142).
27. Butler, 'Culture's Medium', p. 143; Yeo, *Defining Science*, pp. 43, 44, 80, 82, 84; Joanne Shattock, *Politics and Reviewers: The 'Edinburgh' and the 'Quarterly' in the Early Victorian Age* (Leicester: Leicester University Press, 1989), p. 90.
28. Secord, *Victorian Sensation*, pp. 410–16.
29. Eagleton, *Function of Criticism*, p. 55.
30. Porter, 'Lay Medical Knowledge'; Roy Porter, 'Laymen, Doctors and Medical Knowledge in the Eighteenth Century: The Evidence of the *Gentleman's Magazine*', in *Patients and Practitioners: Lay Perceptions of Medicine in Pre-Industrial Society*, ed. by Roy Porter (Cambridge: Cambridge University Press, 1985), pp. 283–314.
31. 'Preface', *Gentleman's Magazine* 52 (1782), ii.
32. James Grant, *The Great Metropolis*, 3rd edn, 2 vols. (London: Saunders and Otley, 1838), vol. II, p. 271.
33. Porter, 'Lay Medical Knowledge', 164.
34. 'Preface', *Gentleman's Magazine* 90, pt 1 (1820), iii–iv (iii).
35. The figures here are based on Robert Mortimer Gascoigne, *A Historical Catalogue of Scientific Periodicals, 1665–1900: With a Survey of their Development* (New York and London: Garland Publishing, 1985); Henry Carrington Bolton, *A Catalogue of Scientific and Technical Periodicals, 1665–1895, Together with Chronological Tables and a Library Check-List*, 2nd edn (Washington: Smithsonian Institution, 1897); Samuel H. Scudder, *Catalogue of Scientific Serials of all Countries Including the Transactions of Learned Societies in the Natural, Physical and Mathematical Sciences, 1633–1876*, reprint (New York: Kraus Reprint Corp., 1965 [1879]); and William R. Lefanu, *British Periodicals of Medicine: A Chronological List 1640–1899*, revised edn, ed. by Jean Loudon (Oxford: Wellcome Unit for the History of Medicine, 1984).

36. William Jerdan, *The Autobiography of William Jerdan*, 4 vols. (London: Arthur Hall, Virtue, & Co., 1852–4), vol. II, p. 187. We are grateful to Janice Cavell for this reference.
37. Jerdan, *Autobiography*, vol. IV, pp. 291–2. The high rate of taxation on newspapers of course restricted their circulation at this period; however, it is a significant omission that no serious attention has been given to date to the extent of scientific reportage in daily and weekly newspapers. See, however, James A. Secord, 'Extraordinary Experiment: Electricity and the Creation of Life in Victorian England', in *The Uses of Experiment: Studies in the Natural Sciences*, ed. by David Gooding, Trevor Pinch, and Simon Schaffer (Cambridge: Cambridge University Press, 1985), pp. 337–83; and Jonathan R. Topham, 'Beyond the "Common Context": The Production and Reading of the *Bridgewater Treatises*', *Isis* 89 (1998), 233–62 (257–9).
38. Jonathan R. Topham, '"An Infinite Variety of Arguments": The *Bridgewater Treatises* and British Natural Theology in the 1830s', PhD thesis, University of Lancaster (1993), chapter 7. See also Joel Wiener, *Radicalism and Freethought in Nineteenth-Century Britain: The Life of Richard Carlile* (Westport, Conn. and London: Greenwood Press, 1983); and Roger Cooter, *The Cultural Meaning of Popular Science: Phrenology and the Organization of Consent in Nineteenth-Century Britain* (Cambridge: Cambridge University Press, 1984). On later radical periodicals and science see Desmond, 'Artisan Resistance'.
39. See, for instance, Sujit Sivasundaram, 'The Periodical as Barometer: Spiritual Measurement and the *Evangelical Magazine*', in *Culture and Science in the Nineteenth-Century Media*, ed. by Louise Henson *et al.* (Aldershot: Ashgate, 2004), pp. 43–55; and Jonathan R. Topham, 'Science, Natural Theology, and the Practice of Christian Piety in Early Nineteenth-Century Religious Magazines', in *Science Serialized: Representations of Science in Nineteenth-Century Periodicals*, ed. by Geoffrey Cantor and Sally Shuttleworth (Cambridge, Mass.: MIT Press, 2004).
40. Cynthia White, *Women's Magazines 1693–1968* (London: Michael Joseph, 1970); and Margaret Beetham, *A Magazine of Her Own? Domesticity and Desire in the Woman's Magazine, 1800–1914* (London: Routledge, 1996), p. 18.
41. Ann B. Shteir, 'Green-Stocking or Blue? Science in Three Women's Magazines, 1800–50', in Henson *et al.*, *Culture and Science*, pp. 1–13. See also A. B. Shteir, '"Let us Examine the Flower": Botany in Women's Magazines, 1800–1830', in Cantor and Shuttleworth, *Science Serialized*.
42. Jonathan R. Topham, 'Periodicals and the Making of Reading Audiences for Science in Early Nineteenth-Century Britain: The *Youth's Magazine*, 1828–37', in Henson *et al.*, *Culture and Science*, pp. 57–69.
43. This discussion draws on R. D. Altick, *The English Common Reader: A Social History of the Mass Reading Public, 1800–1900*, 2nd edn (Columbus: Ohio State University Press, 1998), pp. 318–64; W. H. Brock, 'The Development of Commercial Science Journals in Victorian Britain', in *Development of Science Publishing in Europe*, ed. by A. J. Meadows (Amsterdam:

Elsevier Science Publications, 1980), pp. 95–122; and Feather, *British Publishing*, pp. 129–79.

44. Patricia Anderson, *The Printed Image and the Transformation of Popular Culture 1790–1860* (Oxford: Clarendon Press, 1991), p. 3.
45. T. K. Derry and Trevor I. Williams, *A Short History of Technology From the Earliest Times to A.D. 1900* (Oxford: Oxford University Press, 1960), p. 647.
46. The fall in prices is succinctly illustrated in Alvar Ellegård, 'The Readership of the Periodical Press in Mid-Victorian Britain', *Göteborgs Universitets Årsskrift* 63 (1957), 1–41 (17–22).
47. Brock, 'Commercial Science Journals'; Susan Sheets-Pyenson, 'Popular Science Periodicals in Paris and London: The Emergence of a Low Scientific Culture, 1820–1875', *Annals of Science* 42 (1985), 549–72; Ruth Barton, 'Just Before *Nature*: The Purposes of Science and the Purposes of Popularisation in some English Popular Science Journals of the 1860s', *Annals of Science* 55 (1998), 1–33.
48. Barton, 'Just Before *Nature*'.
49. Richard Yeo, 'Science and Intellectual Authority in Mid-Nineteenth Century Britain: Robert Chambers and the "Vestiges of the Natural History of Creation"', in *Energy and Entropy: Science and Culture in Victorian Britain*, ed. by P. Brantlinger (Bloomington: Indiana University Press, 1989), pp. 1–27.
50. Secord, *Victorian Sensation*, esp. pp. 126–38.
51. For the development of illustrated periodicals see Celina Fox, *Graphic Journalism in England During the 1830s and 1840s* (New York and London: Garland Publishing, 1988); and Anderson, *Printed Image*.
52. See also Secord, *Victorian Sensation*, pp. 437–70.
53. Altick, *Common Reader*, p. 394.
54. Louise Henson, '"In the Natural Course of Physical Things": Ghosts and Science in Charles Dickens's *All the Year Round*', in Henson *et al.*, *Culture and Science*, pp. 113–23.
55. Beetham, *Magazine of Her Own*; White, *Women's Magazines*, pp. 39–50.
56. Sally Shuttleworth, Gowan Dawson, and Richard Noakes, 'Women, Science and Culture: Science in the Nineteenth-Century Periodical', *Women: A Cultural Review* 12 (2001), 57–70.
57. Kirsten Drotner, *English Children and their Magazines, 1751–1945* (New Haven and London: Yale University Press, 1988), p. 67.
58. Diana Dixon, 'Children's Magazines and Science in the Nineteenth Century', *Victorian Periodicals Review* 34 (2001), 228–38.
59. Editor [George Henry Lewes], 'Farewell Causerie', *Fortnightly Review* 6 (1866), 890–6 (890).
60. Editor [John Morley], 'Valedictory', *Fortnightly Review* n.s. 32 (1882), 511–21 (514).
61. José Harris, *Private Lives, Public Spirit: Britain 1870–1914*, (Harmondsworth: Penguin, 1994), p. 21.
62. Quoted in Raymond Williams, *The Long Revolution* (London: Chatto & Windus, 1961), p. 217.

63. Mark Pattison, 'Books and Critics', *Fortnightly Review* n.s. 22 (1877), 659–79 (663). On the Royal Commission on Copyright, see Altick, *Common Reader*, pp. 310–12.

64. Pattison, 'Books and Critics', 663.

65. Young, 'Natural Theology', pp. 128 and 156.

66. Peter Broks, *Media Science Before the Great War* (London: Macmillan, 1996), pp. 131 and 40.

67. Louis Dudek, for instance, contends that the *Review of Reviews*, one of the leading organs of the new journalism, was 'an excellent intellectual periodical'. Louis Dudek, *Literature and the Press: A History of Printing, Printed Media, and Their Relation to Literature* (Toronto: Ryerson, 1960), p. 117.

68. Klancher, *English Reading Audiences*, p. 4.

69. Steven Shapin and Arnold Thackray, 'Prosopography as a Research Tool in History of Science: The British Scientific Community, 1700–1900', *History of Science* 12 (1974), 1–28 (14).

70. William Baker (ed.), *The Letters of George Henry Lewes*, 3 vols. (Victoria, B.C.: University of Victoria, 1995–99), vol. 1, p. 292.

71. [Walter Bagehot], 'The First Edinburgh Reviewers', *National Review* 1 (1855), 253–84 (276).

72. W. T. Stead, 'Government by Journalism', *Contemporary Review* 49 (1886), 653–74 (655).

73. H. M. Collins and T. J. Pinch, 'The Construction of the Paranormal: Nothing Unscientific is Happening', in *On the Margins of Science: The Social Construction of Rejected Knowledge*, ed. Roy Wallis (Keele: Keele University Press, 1979), pp. 237–70 (241).

74. See, for example, Ellegård, *General Reader*; Desmond, *Politics*; Pietro Corsi, *Science and Religion: Baden Powell and the Anglican Debate, 1800–1860* (Cambridge: Cambridge University Press, 1988); and Yeo, *Defining Science*.

75. Secord, 'Extraordinary Experiment'; Secord, *Victorian Sensation*.

76. Gowan Dawson, 'Intrinsic Earthliness: Science, Materialism and the Fleshly School of Poetry', *Victorian Poetry* 41 (2003), 113–29 (115).

77. [George H. Lewes], 'Studies in Animal Life', *Cornhill Magazine* 1 (1860), 198–207 (202).

78. [George H. Lewes], 'Studies in Animal Life', *Cornhill Magazine* 1 (1860), 61–74 (68), and [George H. Lewes and Robert H. Patterson], 'Our Survey of Literature, Science, and Art', *Cornhill Magazine* 6 (1862), 271–81 (278).

79. Shuttleworth, Dawson, and Noakes, 'Women, Science and Culture', 67–8.

80. Louise Henson, '"Matters Arising from the Scenes of our Too-Long Neglect": Charles Dickens, Victorian Chemistry, and the Folklore of the Ghost', *Victorian Review* 26 (2000), 6–23.

81. 'The Quarterly Review (Just Published)', *Mirror of Literature* 16 (1830), (306).

82. 'Some Autograph Introductions', *Review of Reviews* 1 (1890), 3–13.

83. *Mirror of Literature*, 16 (1830), 303.

2. THE *MIRROR OF LITERATURE, AMUSEMENT AND INSTRUCTION* AND CHEAP MISCELLANIES IN EARLY NINETEENTH-CENTURY BRITAIN

1. [Anon.], 'Contemporary Journals', *Monthly Repository* 15 (1820), 540–3, 601–2, 672–4.
2. On the circulation of the *Mirror of Literature* see Jonathan R. Topham, 'John Limbird, Thomas Byerley, and the Production of Cheap Periodicals in the 1820s' (forthcoming).
3. The use of the term 'masses' in the sense of an undivided populace dates from around this period, although the use of 'mass' to describe audiences or publications is later. See Raymond Williams, *Keywords: A Vocabulary of Culture and Society* (London: Fontana Press, 1988).
4. See, for instance, Barry Barnes and Stephen Shapin, 'Science, Nature and Control: Interpreting Mechanics' Institutes', *Social Studies of Science* 7 (1977), 31–74.
5. Jon P. Klancher, *The Making of English Reading Audiences, 1790–1832* (Madison: University of Wisconsin Press, 1987), pp. 3, 16, 96, 80, 77.
6. Quoted in Barnes and Shapin, 'Science', 56.
7. Susan Sheets-Pyenson, 'Popular Science Periodicals in Paris and London: The Emergence of a Low Scientific Culture, 1820–1875', *Annals of Science* 42 (1988), 549–72.
8. Letter from Susan to Charles Darwin, 12–18 November 1832, in *The Correspondence of Charles Darwin*, ed. by Frederick Burkhardt *et al.*, 12 vols. (Cambridge: Cambridge University Press, 1988–), vol. 1, pp. 283–5 (284).
9. W. Roberts, 'Our Early Contemporaries: Pioneers of the Periodical Press', *Chambers's Journal* 5th ser. 8 (1936), 20–4 (20).
10. Adrian Johns, 'Miscellaneous Methods: Authors, Societies and Journals in Early Modern England', *British Journal for the History of Science* 33 (2000), 159–86 (160).
11. *Athenaeum*, 28 April 1832, p. 274. See also *Athenaeum*, 14 July 1832, p. 455, and 15 September 1832, pp. 60–4; and *Literary Gazette*, 22 Feburary 1834, p. 136.
12. On the popularity of the illustrations see 'The Pioneer of Cheap Literature', *Bookseller*, 30 November 1859, pp. 1326–7 (1326). For a more detailed account of the origin and production of the *Mirror* see Topham, 'John Limbird'.
13. *Mirror* 5 (1825), iii.
14. The vast majority lasted only for a very short period; note that the rapid increase in the early 1820s is followed by a plateauing, and even a decline in 1826. The *Gentleman's Magazine* noted that the financial crash of 1825–6 had affected the 'Scissars and Paste-Man' as well as the 'Man of Genius' (*Gentleman's Magazine* 96 pt 1 (1826), iii). See also *True Half-Penny Magazine* 1 (1832), 1–2.
15. Richard D. Altick, *The English Common Reader: A Social History of the Mass Reading Public, 1800–1900*, 2nd edn (Columbus: Ohio State University Press, 1998), pp. 324–6.

16. Charles Knight, *Passages of a Working Life During Half a Century: with a Prelude of Early Reminiscences*, 3 vols. (London: Bradbury & Evans, 1864), vol. 1, pp. 234–57; William Chambers, *Memoir of Robert Chambers, with Autobiographic Reminiscences of William Chambers*, 3rd edn (London and Edinburgh: W. & R. Chambers, 1872), pp. 162–71, 226.

17. [Charles Knight], 'Preface', *Penny Magazine* 1 (1832), iii–iv; [Charles Knight], 'The Commercial History of a Penny Magazine', *Penny Magazine* 2 (1833), 377–84, 417–24, 465–72, and 505–11.

18. D. C. Coleman, *The British Paper Industry, 1495–1860: A Study in Industrial Growth* (Oxford: Clarendon Press, 1958), pp. 195–6, 203, 205.

19. *Mirror* 7 (1826): 240.

20. *Literary Gazette*, 3 January 1818, p. 1; Topham, 'John Limbird'.

21. Charles Knight, *The Old Printer and the Modern Press* (London: John Murray, 1854), p. 267.

22. *Mirror* 1 (1823), 32.

23. 'Pioneer of Cheap Literature', 1326; *Mirror* 7 (1826), [iii].

24. Mirror 5 (1825), iv; *Mirror* 8 (1826), 440.

25. Henry Peter Brougham, *Practical Observations upon the Education of the People, Addressed to the Working Classes and their Employers* (London: Longman, Hurst, Rees, Orme, Brown, and Green, 1825), p. 3.

26. *Mirror* 5 (1825), iii.

27. On the distinction between 'the people' and 'the populace' see W. D. Washington, 'The *Penny Magazine*: A Study of the Genesis and Utilitarian Application of the Popular Miscellany', unpublished PhD thesis, Ohio State University (1967), p. 123.

28. *Literary Journal* 1 (1818), 1.

29. *Mirror* 3 (1824), iii.

30. *Mirror* 5 (1825), iii–iv.

31. *Literary Gazette*, 13 May 1826, p. 294.

32. 'Pioneer of Cheap Literature', 1326; 'Obituary', *Bookseller*, 5 January 1884, p. 6.

33. *Mirror* 4 (1824), 208; 'Pioneer of Cheap Literature', 1326; 'Obituary', 6.

34. Klancher, *English Reading Audiences*, p. 78.

35. Ibid., p. 96.

36. *Mirror* 1 (1823), iii.

37. *Monthly Literary Advertiser*, 10 December 1822, p. 94.

38. The older monthlies generally began with original contributions, proceeding to other named sections typically including book reviews, original poetry, and some form of historical register, containing home and foreign news, commercial, agricultural, and meteorological reports, and births, deaths, and marriages.

39. On Byerley see Topham, 'John Limbird'.

40. John Timbs, 'My Autobiography: Incidental Notes and Personal Recollections', *Leisure Hour* (1871), 20–3, 85–8, 181–4, 212–15, 266–9, 293–5, 347–51, 394–8, 420–4, 469–72, 500–3, 596–600, 612–15, 644–8, 685–8, 692–6, 730–3, and 794–9 (614). I am grateful to Jim Secord for showing me this publication.

41. See, for instance, *Mirror* 7 (1826), 192.

42. *Mirror* 7 (1826), 82–5, 98–100, 132–7, 242–6; 8 (1826), 131–3; 9 (1827), 362–3.
43. Richard Yeo, *Encyclopaedic Visions: Scientific Dictionaries and Enlightenment Culture* (Cambridge: Cambridge University Press, 2001), pp. 35–98.
44. *Mirror* 7 (1826), 82.
45. *Mirror* 3 (1824), 325–6; *Mirror* 4 (1824), 19–21, 115–16, 217–18.
46. As Peter Murphy has shown, exclusively working-class periodicals were generally free from such classical quotations, allusions, or translations. Paul Thomas Murphy, *Towards a Working-Class Canon: Literary Criticism in British Working-Class Periodicals, 1816–1858* (Columbus: Ohio State University Press, 1994), p. 38.
47. *Mirror* 4 (1824), 5–6; cf. *Mirror* 3 (1824), 388.
48. *Mirror* 4 (1824), 168–9.
49. Ibid., 162–4.
50. Ibid., 90.
51. Ibid., 459–60.
52. Ibid., 428–30.
53. *Mirror* 7 (1826), 376.
54. See James Mussell, '"This is Ours and for Us": The *Mechanic's* Magazine and Low Scientific Culture in Regency London,' in *Sidelined Science*, ed. by Martin Willis, David Clifford, and Elizabeth Wadge (London: Anthem Press, forthcoming).
55. *Mirror* 3 (1824), iv.
56. *Literary Chronicle* 1 (1819), 1.
57. *Mirror* 4 (1824), 462.
58. Ibid., 397–8.
59. *Mirror* 1 (1822–3), 90. The original appeared in *Blackwood's Edinburgh Magazine* 12 (1822), 635–8; the attribution to Maginn is given in Alan Strout, *A Bibliography of Articles in Blackwood's Magazine, Volumes 1 through 17, 1817–1825* (Lubbock, Tex.: Texas Technological College Library, 1959).
60. *Mirror* 4 (1824), 4–5.
61. *Mirror* 2 (1823), 488, 489. The original, signed 'Titus', appeared in *Blackwood's Edinburgh Magazine* 14 (1823), 507–11; it was by Henry Thomson (Strout, *Bibliography*).
62. Marilyn Butler, 'Culture's Medium: The Role of the Review', in *The Cambridge Companion to British Romanticism*, ed. by Stuart Curran (Cambridge: Cambridge University Press, 1993), pp. 120–47 (145).
63. *Mirror* 7 (1826), 416. See also ibid., 192.
64. Thomas Frognall Dibdin, *The Library Companion; or, The Young Man's Guide, and the Old Man's Comfort, in the Choice of a Library,* 2 vols. (London: Harding, Triphook, and Lepard, and J. Major, 1824), vol. 1, p. xv.
65. See Leslie A. Marchand, *The Athenaeum: A Mirror of Victorian Culture* (Chapel Hill, N.C.: University of North Carolina Press, 1941), esp. pp. 52–4; and Susan Holland and Steven Miller, 'Science in the Early *Athenaeum*: A Mirror of Crystallization', *Public Understanding of Science* 6 (1997), 111–30.

66. See Michael Twyman, *Printing 1770–1970: An Illustrated History of its Development and Uses in England*, new edn (London: British Library, 1998), pp. 94f.

67. On the *Observer* see Mason Jackson, *The Pictorial Press: Its Origin and Progress* (London: Hurst and Blackett, 1885), pp. 219f.

68. Patricia Anderson, *The Printed Image and the Transformation of Popular Culture* (Oxford: Clarendon Press, 1991), pp. 16–49.

69. *Mirror* 1 (1822–23), iii.

70. Timbs, 'Autobiography', 614.

71. Topham, 'John Limbird'; Brian Maidment, *Into the 1830s: Some Origins of Victorian Illustrated Journalism. Cheap Octavo Magazines of the 1820s and their Influence* (Manchester: Manchester Polytechnic Library, 1992), p. 9; Peter W. Sinnema, *Dynamics of the Pictured Page: Representing the Nation in the 'Illustrated London News'* (Aldershot: Ashgate, 1998), p. 18.

72. *Mirror* 1 (1822–3), 1.

73. Ibid., 17. See Richard D. Altick, *The Shows of London* (Cambridge, Mass. and London: Belknap Press, 1978), pp. 302–3.

74. *Mirror* 1 (1822–3), 49, 65.

75. Iwan Morus, Simon Schaffer, and Jim Secord, 'Scientific London', in *London – World City 1800–1840*, ed. by Celina Fox (New Haven and London: Yale University Press in association with the Museum of London, 1992), pp. 129–42.

76. Fox, *London*, pp. 415, 418–21; William Jerdan, *Men I Have Known* (London: George Routledge and Sons, 1866), pp. 72–4; Altick, *Shows*, pp. 235–52.

77. *Mirror* 1 (1822–23), 113–14 (113); 129–30 (130); 146–8.

78. *Mirror* 7 (1826), 145; Altick, *Shows*, pp. 308–16; Fox, *London*, pp. 423–4.

79. *Mirror* 7 (1826), 146, 147. On prints see David Bindman, 'Prints', in *An Oxford Companion to the Romantic Age: British Culture, 1776–1832*, ed. by Ian McCalman (Oxford: Oxford University Press, 1999), pp. 207–13.

80. *Mirror* 7 (1826), 146, 147.

81. Ibid., 148–52.

82. Ibid., 166–8, 178–9, 207, 217–18, 221–4, 238–9, 249.

83. On the remodelling of London see Andrew Saint, 'The Building Art of the First Industrial Metropolis', in Fox, *London*, pp. 51–76; and J. Mordaunt Crook, 'Metropolitan Improvements: John Nash and the Picturesque', in Fox, *London*, pp. 77–96.

84. *Mirror* 2 (1823), 259–61.

85. *Mirror* 6 (1825), 143–4.

86. See, for instance, *Mirror* 4 (1824), 314–15; this article, extracted from the *New Monthly Magazine*, was prefaced by a quotation from *Gulliver's Travels* describing the schemes of the Academy of Lagado.

87. *Mirror* 5 (1825), 54–5 (55).

88. *Mirror* 4 (1824), 350.

89. *Mirror* 5 (1825), 60–1.

90. Maidment, *Into the 1830s*, p. 9.

91. See, e.g., Roy Porter, 'Lay Medical Knowledge in the Eighteenth Century: The Evidence of the *Gentleman's Magazine*', *Medical History* 29 (1985), 138–68.

92. Little has been written on this transformation, but see John O. Hayden, 'Introduction', in *British Literary Magazines: The Romantic Age, 1789–1836*, ed. by Alvin Sullivan (Westport, Conn. and London: Greenwood Press, 1983), pp. xv–xxv (xx); Butler, 'Culture's Medium', 143; Porter, 'Lay Medical Knowledge', 167–8; Richard Yeo, *Defining Science: William Whewell, Natural Knowledge, and Public Debate in Early Victorian Britain* (Cambridge: Cambridge University Press, 1993), pp. 44–8; and Joanne Shattock, *Politics and Reviewers: The 'Edinburgh' and the 'Quarterly' in the Early Victorian Age* (London: Leicester University Press, 1989), p. 90.

93. 'Pioneer of Cheap Literature', 1326.

94. 'John Timbs, F.S.A.', *Illustrated London News*, 10 February 1855, pp. 125–6.

95. On Phillips see also Timbs, 'Autobiography', 394–6, 470–2; John Timbs, 'Thirty Years of the Reign of Victoria: Personal Recollections', *Leisure Hour* (1872), 58–60, 100–4, 157–60, 189–91, 221–3, 252–4, 293–5, 396–400, 471–2, 549–52, 621–3, 650–3, 707–11, 773–6, and 821–3 (221–2); and John Timbs, *Walks and Talks about London* (London: Lockwood & Co., 1865), pp. 94–123.

96. Timbs, 'Autobiography', 396 and 614. Timbs's editorial duties began with number 275 of the journal, dated 29 September 1827. On Timbs's editorship see also Timbs, 'Thirty Years', 102, 158, and 622–3.

97. *DNB* and H. R. Fox Bourne, *English Newspapers: Chapters in the History of Journalism*, 2 vols. (London: Chatto & Windus, 1887), vol. II, p. 120.

98. *Mirror* 9 (1827), 184.

99. *Mirror* 11 (1828), 340–1, 419–20.

100. On the move towards self-consciously 'popular science' in the weekly literary journals of this period see Holland and Miller, 'Science'.

101. *Literary Gazette*, 18 February 1832, p. 104.

102. *Mirror* 12 (1827), iv.

103. 'Pioneer of Cheap Literature', 1326; Madeleine House and Graham Storey, *The Letters of Charles Dickens: The Pilgrim Edition*, vol. I, *1820–1839* (Oxford: Clarendon Press, 1965), p. 412.

3. THE *WESLEYAN-METHODIST MAGAZINE* AND RELIGIOUS MONTHLIES IN EARLY NINETEENTH-CENTURY BRITAIN

1. John Tyndall, 'Miracles and Special Providences', *Fortnightly Review* n.s. 1 (1867), 645–60 (647). I am grateful to Richard Noakes for this reference. 'The Providence of God Asserted' was a section during the second series (1804–21) of the magazine, which ended before Tyndall's second birthday. On Tyndall's somewhat ambivalent attitude towards Methodism see John Brooke and Geoffrey Cantor, *Reconstructing Nature: The Engagement of Science and Religion* (Edinburgh: T. & T. Clark, 1998), p. 254.

2. Benjamin Gregory, *Autobiographical Recollections* (London: Hodder and Stoughton, 1903), pp. 13–14. Richard Altick discusses Gregory's reading, drawing on this extraordinarily rich autobiography, in R. D. Altick, *The English Common Reader: A Social History of the Mass Reading Public, 1800–1900*, 2nd edn (Columbus: Ohio State University Press, 1998), pp. 117–21.

3. On the early nineteenth-century religious press see Josef L. Altholz, *The Religious Press in Britain, 1760–1900* (New York: Greenwood Press, 1989); Louis Billington, 'The Religious Periodical and Newspaper Press, 1770–1870', in *The Press in English Society from the Seventeenth to the Nineteenth Century*, ed. by Michael Harris and Alan Lee (London: Associated Universities Press, 1986), pp. 113–32 and 231–9; and Francis Mineka, *The Dissidence of Dissent: The 'Monthly Repository', 1806–1838, Under the Editorship of Robert Aspland, W. J. Fox, R. H. Horne, and Leigh Hunt. With a Chapter on Religious Periodicals, 1700–1825* (Chapel Hill, N.C.: North Carolina University Press, 1944), pp. 27–97.

4. [Anon.], 'Magazines and Reviews', *Literary Panorama* 2 (1807), cols. 65–6. A similar proportion of religious to secular publications prevailed more generally. See Simon Eliot, '*Patterns and Trends* and the *NSTC*: Some Initial Observations', *Publishing History* 42 (1997), 79–104, and 43 (1998), 71–112 (72).

5. Similar average prices (10d versus 1s 11½d) prevailed in 1820. [Anon.], 'Contemporary Journals', *Monthly Repository* 15 (1820), 540–3, 601–2, 672–4.

6. [Sydney Smith], '[Review of *Causes of the Increase of Methodism and Dissension*, by R. A. Ingram]', *Edinburgh Review* 11 (1807–8), 341–62 (342).

7. Quoted in Marsh Wilkinson Jones, 'Pulpit, Periodical, and Pen: Joseph Benson and Methodist Influence in the Victorian Prelude', unpublished PhD thesis, University of Illinois at Urbana-Champaign (1995), p. 243.

8. [Thomas Carlyle], 'Signs of the Times', *Edinburgh Review* 49 (1829), 439–59 (443).

9. Altholz, *Religious Press*, p. 10.

10. Mark Clement, 'Sifting Science: Methodism and Natural Knowledge in Britain, 1815–1870', unpublished DPhil thesis, University of Oxford (1996), pp. 24–7 and 284.

11. See, for instance, Sujit Sivasundaram, 'The Periodical as Barometer: Spiritual Measurement and the *Evangelical Magazine*', in *Culture and Science in the Nineteenth-Century Media*, ed. by Louise Henson *et al.* (Aldershot: Ashgate, 2004), pp. 43–55; and Topham, 'Periodicals'.

12. Thomas Jackson, *Recollections of My Own Life and Times*, ed. by B. Frankland (London: Wesleyan Conference Office, 1878), p. 26. On the treasuring of back issues see also *Wesleyan-Methodist Magazine* (hereinafter *WMM*) 1 (1822), 2.

13. Quoted in Frank Cumbers, *The Book Room: The Story of the Methodist Publishing House and Epworth Press* (London: Epworth Press, 1956), p. 5.

14. See Cumbers, *Book Room*; Thomas W. Herbert, *John Wesley as Editor and Author* (Princeton: Princeton University Press, 1940); Henry D. Rack, *Reasonable Enthusiast: John Wesley and the Rise of Methodism* (London: Epworth Press, 1989), pp. 343–60; Isabel Rivers, 'Dissenting and Methodist Books of Practical Divinity', in *Books and their Readers in Eighteenth-Century England*, ed. by Isabel Rivers (Leicester: Leicester University Press, 1982), pp. 127–64; H. F. Matthews, *Methodism and the Education of the People, 1791–1851* (London:

Epworth Press, 1949); Samuel J. Rogal, 'John Wesley's *Arminian Magazine*', *Andrews University Seminary Studies* 22 (1984), 231–47; and Jones, 'Pulpit', pp. 195–200.

15. Jones, 'Pulpit', pp. 197–98, 239–45; Smith, 'Review of *Causes*', p. 342.

16. On Wesley and the Enlightenment see, for instance, Rack, *Reasonable Enthusiast*, pp. 32–3, 383–8; and David Bebbington, *Evangelicalism in Modern Britain: A History from the 1730s to the 1980s* (London: Unwin Hyman, 1989), pp. 20–74 *passim*. On Wesley and science see, for instance, R. E. Schofield, 'John Wesley and Science in Eighteenth-Century England', *Isis* 44 (1953), 331–40; J. W. Haas, 'John Wesley's Views on Science and Christianity: An Examination of the Charge of Antiscience', *Church History* 63 (1994), 378–92; and Haas, 'Eighteenth-Century Evangelical Responses to Science: John Wesley's Enduring Legacy', *Science and Christian Belief* 6 (1994), 83–102.

17. John Wesley, *A Survey of the Wisdom of God in the Creation: or, A Compendium of Natural Philosophy*, 3rd edn, 5 vols. (London: sold at the Foundry, 1777), vol. i, p. iv.

18. Jones, 'Pulpit', pp. 200–9; and Jackson, *Recollections*, p. 211.

19. Jones, 'Pulpit', pp. 199, 208, and 232–4; Benjamin Gregory, *Side Lights on the Conflicts of Methodism During the Second Quarter of the Nineteenth Century, 1827–1852*, popular edn (London: Cassell, 1899), pp. 116–24; and Jackson, *Recollections*, pp. 211–12, 247–52.

20. Jones, 'Pulpit', pp. 200–1, 237, and 245–6; Cumbers, *Book Room*, pp. 15, 48, and 77; and 'Book Room Committee Minutes, 1797–1817', Methodist Archives, MAW MS640.

21. 'Book Room Committee Minutes, 1822–1827', Methodist Archives, MAW MS641. There are wrappers for most of the numbers of the 6d edition for 1829 in the Rare Book, Manuscript, and Special Collections Library at Duke University. For a contemporary reading of similar adverts from the *Evangelical Magazine*, see Smith, 'Review of *Causes*', pp. 106–7.

22. Haas, 'Evangelical Responses', 93; and Matthews, *Methodism*, p. 172.

23. Jones, 'Pulpit', p. 375.

24. 'Announcement', Methodist Archives, PLP.7.12.31.

25. *Methodist Magazine* 27 (1804), 33.

26. *Christian Observer* 1 (1802), i.

27. Ibid., 15.

28. Joseph Benson, *The Inspector of Methodism Inspected, and the 'Christian Observer' Observed. Being an Answer to a Pamphlet, Entitled, 'Methodism Inspected', Published by William Hales, D. D. Rector of Killesandra in Ireland: And to the Review Thereof in the 'Christian Observer'* (London: Conference-Office, 1803), p. 3.

29. John Kent, 'The Wesleyan Methodists to 1849', in *A History of the Methodist Church in Great Britain*, ed. by Rupert Davies, A Raymond George, and Gordon Rupp, 4 vols. (London: Epworth Press, 1965–88), vol. ii, pp. 213–75 *passim*.

30. Jackson, *Recollections*, pp. 210–16.
31. *WMM* 1 (1822), 2.
32. Ibid., 4, 5.
33. Ibid., 5, 370.
34. Ibid., 3.
35. Jonathan R. Topham, 'Science, Natural Theology, and the Practice of Christian Piety in Early Nineteenth-Century Religious Magazines', in *Science Serialized: Representations of the Sciences in the Nineteenth-Century Periodical*, ed. by Geoffrey Cantor and Sally Shuttleworth (Cambridge, Mass.: MIT Press, 2004) pp. 37–66. See also Clement, 'Sifting', pp. 29–56.
36. Wesley, *Survey*, vol. v, pp. 191, 211n. Wesley's natural theology requires further study, but see John C. English, 'John Wesley and Isaac Newton's "System of the World"', *Proceedings of the Wesley Historical Society*, 48 (1991), 69–86 (74); and M. Elton Hendricks, 'John Wesley and Natural Theology', *Wesleyan Theological Journal* 18 (1983), 7–17.
37. E.g. Jackson, *Recollections*, pp. 322, 325–36, 402; *WMM* 2 (1823), 7–19; 3 (1824), 21; 5 (1826), 370–7.
38. *WMM* 1 (1822), 19–27, 83–90.
39. *WMM* 5 (1826), 675.
40. *WMM* 8 (1829), 842.
41. *WMM* 6 (1828), 174–6.
42. *WMM* 1 (1822), 571–3.
43. Ibid., 233.
44. Ibid., 169–71.
45. *WMM* 3 (1824), 738.
46. *WMM* 1 (1822), 574. See also *WMM* 1 (1822), 649–50; 2 (1823), 28–9.
47. *WMM* 2 (1823), 240. Rogerson was probably the astronomer and Methodist local preacher, born in Pocklington in 1797. See Clement, 'Sifting', p. 36.
48. See L. G. Stevenson, 'Religious Elements in the Background of the British Anti-Vivisection Movement', *Yale Journal of Biology and Medicine* 29 (1956), 125–57; and Adrian Desmond, *The Politics of Evolution: Morphology, Medicine, and Reform in Radical London* (Chicago and London: Chicago University Press, 1989), pp. 183–92.
49. *WMM* 5 (1826), 312, 313, and 333.
50. *WMM* 1 (1822), 260, 323; 2 (1823), 47, 183–4; 8 (1829), 260–1.
51. *WMM* 3 (1824), 193.
52. *WMM* 1 (1822), 318. On the Methodist response to Lawrence see Clement, 'Sifting', pp. 85–91.
53. *WMM* 1 (1822), 20; 3 (1824), 21.
54. *WMM* 1 (1822), 158–63; 3 (1824), 804.
55. *WMM* 2 (1823), 287–93, 431–41, 723; 3 (1824), 367.
56. *WMM* 2 (1823), 378; (1824), 319.
57. The scientific education of mechanics was welcomed for its possible 'moral effect' in 'substituting intellectual for low and sensual enjoyments' (*WMM* 1 (1822), 52), but the need for its combination with religious education was also

felt (*WMM* 2 (1823), 185). See also Jonathan R. Topham, 'Science and Popular Education in the 1830s: The Role of the *Bridgewater Treatises*', *British Journal for the History of Science* 25 (1992), 397–430; and Clement, 'Sifting', pp. 46–56.

58. *WMM* 8 (1829), 112–13, 177–8.

59. See, for instance, Geoffrey Cantor, *Michael Faraday: Sandemanian and Scientist* (London: Macmillan, 1991); John Hedley Brooke, 'Religious Belief and the Content of the Sciences', *Osiris* 16 (2001), 3–28; and Jonathan R. Topham, '*Not* Thinking about Science and Religion', *Minerva* 40 (2002), 203–9. See also Topham, 'The Practice of Christian Piety'.

60. Smith, 'Review of *Causes*', 342.

61. Gregory, *Recollections*, p. 35.

62. Bebbington, *Evangelicalism*, pp. 10–12.

63. *WMM* 5 (1826), 522.

64. *WMM* 1 (1822), 178.

65. *WMM* 3 (1824), 688.

66. *WMM* 5 (1826): 451. The same point was made with regard to William Edward Parry's endurance of 'ten thousand nameless ills' in his search for a North-West passage for the 'paltry lure' of 'science, honour, [and] fame'. *WMM* 2 (1823), 347.

67. *WMM* 1 (1822), 476–7.

68. *WMM* 8 (1829), 823.

69. *WMM* 5 (1826), 522.

70. Ibid., 380–5, 455–60, 523–9, 556, 596–605, and 698.

71. Ibid., 236–41.

72. Ibid., 628; 8 (1829), 773–4.

73. *WMM* 5 (1826), 558.

74. *WMM* 8 (1829), 488.

75. *WMM* 2 (1823), 199.

76. Herbert, *John Wesley*, p. 34.

77. *WMM* 1 (1823), 1–2.

78. See the breakdown of production costs given in 1804 in the 'Minutes of the Book Room Committee, 1797–1817', Methodist Archives, MAW MS640.

79. Isabel Rivers, '"Strangers and Pilgrims": Sources and Patterns of Methodist Narrative', in *Augustan Worlds: Essays in Honour of A. R. Humphreys*, ed. by J. C. Hilson, M. M. B. Jones and J. R. Watson (Leicester: Leicester University Press, 1978), pp. 189–203.

80. Ibid., 194–5; Matthews, *Methodism*, pp. 168–9.

81. Matthews, *Methodism*, p. 78.

82. Clement, 'Sifting', pp. 167–8. Cf. Roberta Topham, 'Making Ministers, Making Methodism: An Anthropological Study of an English Religious Denomination', unpublished PhD thesis, University of Cambridge (2000), pp. 78–89.

83. *WMM* 5 (1826), 727.

84. *WMM* 2 (1823), 709, 711–12.

85. Ibid., 501–2.

86. See, for instance, *WMM* 2 (1823), 634.
87. Ibid., 555.
88. *WMM* 3 (1824), 63.
89. *WMM* 2 (1823), 412. See also *WMM* 5 (1826), 732.
90. *WMM* 8 (1829), 6. See also *WMM* 3 (1824), 645, which relates that Henry Taft 'relinquished an extensive and lucrative practice of medicine, for which he had been regularly educated' to become a Methodist minister.
91. *WMM* 8 (1829), 435.
92. Ibid., 433
93. Ibid., 434.
94. Ibid., 435. See also 510–11.
95. Ibid., 440, 506.
96. *WMM* 2 (1823), 65.
97. Ibid., 785–90.
98. Clement, 'Sifting', 167–80.
99. *WMM* 1 (1822), 699.
100. *WMM* 5 (1826), 6.
101. See Altholz, *Religious Press*; and Billington, 'Religious Press'. On the *Leisure Hour* see Aileen Fyfe, 'Periodicals and Book Series: Complementary Aspects of a Publisher's Mission', in Henson *et al.*, *Culture and Science*, pp. 71–82.
102. Alvar Ellegård, 'The Readership of the Periodical Press in Mid-Victorian Britain', *Göteborgs Universitets Årsskrift* 63 (1957), 1–41.
103. Henry D. Rack, 'Wesleyan Methodism, 1849–1902', in Davies *et al.*, *History*, vol. III, pp. 119–66 (164–5 n. 121); Thomas H. Yorty, 'The English Methodist Response to Darwin Reconsidered', *Methodist History* 32 (1994), 116–25 (118); and Stuart Andrews, 'The *Wesley Naturalist*', *History Today* 21 (1971), 810–17 (810).

4. PUNCH AND COMIC JOURNALISM IN MID-VICTORIAN BRITAIN

1. 'E.', 'The Philosophy of Punch', *Westminster Review* 38 (1842), 265–318 (316–17).
   I thank Patrick Leary, Jim Paradis, and Jim Secord for their help in preparation of this chapter. I am indebted to Patrick Leary who allowed me to draw on his unpublished researches on *Punch*. See Patrick Leary, 'Table Talk and Print Culture in Mid-Victorian Britain: The *Punch* Circle, 1858–1874' (unpublished PhD dissertation, University of Indiana, 2002). I would also like to thank Helen Walasek and Brigitte Istim for their help in locating *Punch* material. For permission to reproduce material in their collections I thank *Punch* Library, London. The source of attribution of *Punch* articles is from the contributor's ledger books held in *Punch* library. Throughout these notes *Punch* is abbreviated as '*P*'.
2. Richard D. Altick, *Punch: The Lively Youth of a British Institution, 1841–1851* (Columbus: Ohio State University Press, 1997), pp. 1–40.

3. The most informative studies of Victorian *Punch* are: M. H. Spielmann, *The History of 'Punch'* (London: Cassell, 1895); Charles L. Graves, *Mr. Punch's History of Modern England*, 4 vols. (London: Cassell, 1921–2); R. G. G. Price, *A History of Punch* (London: Collins, 1957); Susan Briggs and Asa Briggs (eds.), *Cap and Bell: Punch's Chronicle of English History in the Making, 1841–61* (London: Macdonald, 1972); Celina Fox, *Graphic Journalism During the 1830s and 1840s* (New York: Greenwood Press, 1988); Altick, *Punch*.

4. Altick, *Punch*, pp. 552–6, 646–52; James G. Paradis, 'Satire and Science in Victorian Culture' in Bernard Lightman (ed.), *Victorian Science in Context* (Chicago: Chicago University Press, 1997), pp. 143–75; James A. Secord, *Victorian Sensation: The Extraordinary Publication, Reception, and Secret Authorship of the Vestiges of the Natural History of Creation* (Chicago: Chicago University Press, 2000), pp. 455–60; Roy Porter, *Bodies Politic: Disease, Death, and Doctors in Britain, 1650–1900* (London: Reaktion Books, 2001), 262–71 (268); Richard Noakes, 'Representing "A Century of Inventions": Nineteenth-Century Technology and Victorian *Punch*', in Louise Henson, *et al.* (eds.), *Culture and Science in Nineteenth-Century Media* (Aldershot: Ashgate Press, 2004), pp. 151–62. Other discussions of *Punch*, science, technology, and medicine can be found in Graves, *Mr. Punch's History*, vol. I, pp. 61–80, vol. II, pp. 136–47, vol. III, pp. 198–212, vol. IV, pp. 181–93; Briggs and Briggs, *Cap and Bell*, pp. 106–7, 201–5; Asa Briggs, *Victorian Things* (London: Batsford, 1988), p. 382; and Suzanne Le-May Sheffield, 'The 'Empty-Headed Beauty' and the 'Sweet Girl Graduate': Women's Science Education in *Punch*, 1860–1890', in Henson *et al.* pp. 15–28.

5. See, for example, Anthony Wohl, *Endangered Lives: Public Health in Victorian Britain* (London: Dent, 1983); Briggs, *Victorian Things*.

6. Peter M. Sinnema, *The Dynamics of the Pictured Page: Representing the Nation in the 'Illustrated London News'* (Aldershot: Ashgate, 1998), pp. 1–2.

7. Roy Porter, 'Review Article: Seeing the Past', *Past and Present* (February 1988), 186–205; B. E. Maidment, *Reading Popular Prints 1790–1870* (Manchester: Manchester University Press, 1996), *Second, Victorian Sensation*. Citation from Maidment, *Reading Popular Prints*, p. 11. I am not suggesting that we should stop using *Punch* or any other comic periodical to gauge popular engagements with scientific culture: on the contrary, studies by Martin Rudwick and Janet Browne persuasively argue how much satirical material can reveal about otherwise undocumented attitudes towards scientific enterprises: Martin J. S. Rudwick, 'Caricature as a Source for the History of Science: De la Beche's Anti-Lyellian Sketches of 1831', *Isis* 66 (1975), 534–60; Janet Browne, 'Squibs and Snobs: Science in Humorous British Undergraduate Magazines Around 1830', *History of Science* 30 (1992), 165–97.

8. Janet Browne, 'Darwin in Caricature: A Study in the Popularisation and Dissemination of Evolution', *Proceedings of the American Philosophical Society* 145 (2001), 496–509 (509).

9. Altick, *Punch*, p. xix.

10. Brooks cited in Briggs and Briggs, *Cap and Bell* p. xviii.

11. Fox, *Graphic Journalism*.
12. In this chapter I do not consider *Punch's Almanacks* or the wrappers of individual issues of the periodical. From 1846 the *Almanacks* were issued separately from the periodical and so I treat them as an independent publication. For analysis of *Punch's Almanack* see Maureen Perkins, *Visions of the Future: Almanacs, Time and Cultural Change 1775–1870* (Oxford: Clarendon Press, 1996), pp. 145–9. *Punch's* wrappers are not considered owing to the difficulty of accessing such rare material. However, a complete run of *Punch* with wrappers is held in the *Punch* Library and deserves detailed analysis.
13. Leslie Stephen, 'Humour', *Cornhill Magazine* 33 (1876), 318–26 (324).
14. See, for example, [Gilbert Abbott à Beckett], 'The Disadvantages of Science', *P* 11 (1846), 179, which discusses the electric telegraph and the railways while [Douglas Jerrold], 'Hero Surgeons', *P* 18 (1850), 118, deems military surgeons to be 'people of science'.
15. Price, *History of Punch*, p. 370.
16. Altick, *Punch*, p. xvii.
17. Fox, *Graphic Journalism*; David Kunzle, 'Between Broadsheet Caricature and 'Punch': Cheap Newspaper Cuts for the Lower Classes in the 1830s', *Art Journal* 43 (1983), 339–46; Amanda-Jane Doran, 'The Development of the Full-Page Wood Engraving in *Punch*', *Journal of Newspaper and Periodical History* 7 (1991), 48–63; Marcus Wood, *Radical Satire and Print Culture 1790–1822* (Oxford: Clarendon Press, 1994); Maidment, *Reading Popular Prints*.
18. Patricia Anderson, *The Printed Image and the Transformation of Popular Culture 1790–1860* (Oxford: Clarendon Press, 1991), pp. 16–83; Maidment, *Reading Popular Prints*, pp. 145–8.
19. Nigel Cross, *The Common Writer: Life in Nineteenth Century Grub Street* (Cambridge: Cambridge University Press, 1985).
20. Paradis, 'Science and Satire'; Porter, *Bodies Politic*; Richard M. Koppel, 'English Satire and Science, 1660–1750', unpublished PhD thesis, University of Rochester, New York, (1978).
21. Richard D. Altick, 'Punch's First Ten Years: The Ingredients of Success', *Journal of Newspaper and Periodical History* 7 (1991), 5–16.
22. Altick, *Punch*, p. 4.
23. Wood, *Radical Satire*, pp. 270–1.
24. Cited in Arthur A. Adrian, *Mark Lemon: First Editor of Punch* (Oxford: Oxford University Press, 1966), p. 58.
25. See, for example, [Anon.], 'British Association for the Advancement of Everything in General, and Nothing in Particular', *P* 3 (1842), 6–7; [Douglas Jerrold], 'British and Foreign Destitute', *P* 6 (1844), 231. For *Punch* and Buckingham see Altick, *Punch*, pp. 637–42.
26. [Tom Taylor], 'The Truth after Thomson', *P* 61 (1871), 62–3.
27. Fox, *Graphic Journalism*, pp. 218–19.
28. For *Punch* and Ireland see R. F. Foster, *Paddy and Mr. Punch: Connections in Irish and English History* (Harmondsworth: Penguin Books, 1995), pp. 171–94. For Jews and the Victorian comic press see Anthony S. Wohl,

'"Dizzi-Ben-Dizzi": Disraeli as Alien', *Journal of British Studies* 34 (1995), 365–411. For *Punch* on America and Roman Catholicism see Altick, *Punch*, pp. 367–79, 466–92.

29. See Altick, *Punch*, pp. 343–50, 683–6, 698–707.
30. Darwin to Huxley, 22 May 1861, in Frederick H. Burkhardt, Duncan Porter, Joy Harvey, and Marsha Richmond (eds.), *The Correspondence of Charles Darwin*, volume IX, 1861 (Cambridge: Cambridge University Press, 1994), pp. 134–5 (134).
31. Briggs and Briggs, Cap and Bell (eds.), p. xxvi.
32. Based on his analysis of the 'paper and print' ledger books in the *Punch* archive, Patrick Leary has claimed that in the late 1850s and early 1860s, *Punch* achieved weekly sales of between 56,000 and 61,000: personal communication from Patrick Leary. Circulation figures for *Fun* and *Tomahawk* in Alvar Ellegård, *Darwin and the General Reader: the Reception of Darwin's Theory of Evolution in the British Periodical Press, 1859–72* (Chicago: Chicago University Press, 1990), pp. 374, 383.
33. See comments of Mark Lemon recorded by Henry Silver in his Diary: Henry Silver's Diary, *Punch* Library, London (hereafter 'Silver Diary'), entry for 27 June 1866. For recent explanations of *Punch*'s success see Briggs and Briggs, *Cap and Bell*, pp. xiv–xv; Altick, *Punch*, pp. 41–66; Cross, *Common Writer*, p. 107.
34. [Andrew Halliday], 'Comic Literature', *Temple Bar* 9 (1863), 590–3 (590). For attribution see Silver Diary, entry for 4 November 1863.
35. See note 1. The ledger books list names of authors, titles of articles, and amount of column space for each article. They begin with the issue of 4 March 1843 and continue, with several short breaks, to the twentieth century. Approximately 75 per cent of the articles in any given issue are listed, but many of the smaller ones are omitted.
36. Paradis, 'Science and Satire', pp. 149–50.
37. For Leigh, Smith, and Du Maurier see *DNB*. For Mayhew see Price, *History of Punch*, 27. Although Albert Smith left *Punch* in 1843 he was responsible for one of its most famous portrayals of medical students, the 1841 series 'The Physiology of the London Medical Student'.
38. George Somes Layard, *A Great "Punch" Editor: Being the Life, Letters, and Diaries of Shirley Brooks* (London: Sir Isaac Pitman & Sons, 1907), pp. 323, 339, 495, 516, 518, 579. Brooks's poem was published as 'The Dodo Demolished', *P* 66 (1874), 19.
39. Silver Diary. For analysis see Leary, 'Table Talk and Print Culture'.
40. Silver Diary, entries for 1 September 1858 (Stephenson), 23 February 1859 (phrenology), 3 May 1865 (Fitzroy).
41. Silver Diary, entry for 9 April 1862. The last sentence is from [Henry Silver], 'Iron-Clad Jack. A Sea-Song of the Future', *P* 42 (1862), 146. For the interaction between *Punch* artists and 'suggestors' of illustrations see John Bush Jones and Priscilla Shaw, 'Artists and "Suggestors": The *Punch* Cartoons 1843–1848', *Victorian Periodicals Review* 2 (1978), 2–14.

42. [John Leech], 'The "British Tar" of the Future', *P* 42 (1862), [147].
43. Cross, *Common Writer*, p. 102. [Mark Lemon?], 'The Moral of Punch', *P* 1 (1841), 1.
44. Stephen, 'Humour', 320.
45. [Percival Leigh], 'A Philosopher Afloat', *P* 29 (1855), 26; [John Leech], 'Faraday Giving His Card to Father Thames', *P* 29 (1855), [27].
46. [Anon.], 'The Locomotive Table Company', *P* 24 (1853), 209.
47. [John Leech], 'How to Insure Against Railway Accidents', *P* 24 (1853), 125.
48. See Silver Diary, entries for 8 and 15 August 1860, 26 February, 5 March 1862, and 19 March 1862 which reveal *Punch* contributors' scepticism towards spirit-rapping.
49. For the symbiosis between *Punch* and other Victorian periodicals see Altick, *Punch*, pp. 67–90.
50. 'Gorilla' [Anon.], 'Monkeyana', *P* 40 (1861), 206; Thomas H. Huxley, 'Man and Apes', *Athenaeum*, 13 April 1861, 498
51. [Shirley Brooks], 'Punch's Essence of Parliament', *P* 34 (1858), 233–4 (233).
52. [Anon.], 'A Philosopher Afloat'.
53. [Percival Leigh], 'Will it Wash?', *P* 33 (1857), 183.
54. [Horace Mayhew], 'Light and Hair', *P* 49 (1865), 114.
55. [Anon.], '"Science Gossip"', *P* 54 (1868), 202.
56. [Percival Leigh], 'The Irish Yahoos', *P* 41 (1861), 245.
57. Foster, *Paddy and Mr. Punch*, pp. 171–94; Perry Curtis, *Apes and Angels: The Irishman in Victorian Caricature* (Washington and London: Smithsonian Institution, 2nd edn, 1996).
58. [Henry Silver], 'St. Januarius at it Again', *P* 37 (1859), 149.
59. [Percival Leigh], 'Representative Rascals', *P* 41 (1861), 25.
60. J[ohn] L[eech], 'Quite a Novelty', *P* 27 (1854), 40.
61. [Gilbert Abbott à Beckett], 'A Railway Map of England', *P* 9 (1845), 163.
62. [George] D[u] M[aurier], 'The Keeper Nightmare', *P* 60 (1871), [6–7]; C[harles] H. B[ennett], 'The British Association', *P* 49 (1865), 113–14.
63. R[ichard] D[oyle], 'Manners and Customs of ye Englyshe (New Series) No. 10: A Scientific Institution – During ye Lecture of an Eminent 'Savan'', *P* 19 (1850), 136; [Leech], 'Faraday'.
64. J[ohn] L[eech], 'Animal Magnetism; Sir Rhubarb Pill Mesmerising the British Lion', *P* 1 (1841), [67]; J[ohn] Leech, 'Lord Brougham's Railway Nightmare', *P* 8 (1845), [207]; J[ohn] L[eech], 'Effect of the Submarine Telegraph; or, Peace and Good-Will Between England and France', *P* 19 (1850), [117]; John Leech, 'The Use of Adulteration', *P* 29 (1855), [47]; [John Leech], 'Father Thames Introducing His Offspring to the Fair City of London', *P* 35 (1858), [5]; J[ohn] T[enniel], 'Another Eclipse for India', *P* 35 (1858), [101]; [John Leech?], 'The New Russell Six-Pounder', *P* 38 (1860), [121]. [John Leech?], 'The Lion of the Season', *P* 40 (1861), [213]; [John Leech?], 'The Parliamentary Python', *P* 42 (1862), [85]; T[enniel], 'The Political Cow-Doctors', *P* 50 (1866), [69].
65. T[enniel], 'Another Eclipse'.

66. [Tom Taylor], 'Eclipse in India', *P* 55 (1868), 104–5.
67. [Mark Lemon], 'Fourth Meeting of the Brightish Association for the Advancement of Everything: Section A – Mathematical and Physical Science', *P* 5 (1843), 167.
68. [Lemon], 'Fourth Meeting'. For *Punch*'s tussles with Bunn see Altick, *Punch*, pp. 698–707.
69. [Percival Leigh], 'Political Zoology: The Red-Tapeworm', *P* 28 (1855), 71.
70. For analysis of Scriblerians see Koppel, 'English Satire', pp. 196–234.
71. [Anon.], 'Buns', *P* 4 (1843), 72.
72. [Anon.], 'Grand Railway from England to China', *P* 3 (1842), 205.
73. 'Simon Hodgskins' [Percival Leigh], 'Fudge for Farmers', *P* 11 (1846), 40 Leigh's italics.
74. See [Shirley Brooks], 'Punch's Essence of Parliament', *P* 50 (1866), 208–9; [Percival Leigh], 'Fresh Air! Or, Victoria Park Preserved', *P* 50 (1866), 214; C[harles] H. B[ennett], 'Punch on the People's Parks', *P* 50 (1866), 138.
75. 'Audi Alteram Patrem' [Percival Leigh], 'A Gas Plant at Victoria Park', *P* 50 (1866), 258.
76. Amy Cruse, *The Victorians and their Reading* (Boston: Houghton Mifflin Co., 1935), p. 394.
77. Henry James, 'Du Maurier and London Society', *Century Magazine* 26 (1883), 49–65 (51). Cited in Altick, *Punch*, p. xx.
78. Browne, 'Darwin in Caricature'. See also Bert Hansen, 'America's First Medical Breakthrough: How Popular Excitement about a French Rabies Cure in 1885 Raised New Expectations for Medical Progress', *American Historical Review* 103 (1998), 373–418. I owe this reference to Jim Secord.
79. This is based on the principle that the actual number of readers of a periodical is roughly five times the number of copies sold. Thus copies of *Punch* in the 1860s would have been read by approximately 5 × 60,000 = 300,000 people. For this principle see Altick, *Punch*, p. 38.
80. [Henry Silver], 'Effects of the Recent Eclipse', *P* 39 (1860), 39.
81. For sociological analysis of scientists' jokes see G. Nigel Gilbert and Michael Mulkay, *Opening Pandora's Box: A Sociological Analysis of Scientists' Discourse* (Cambridge: Cambridge University Press, 1984), pp. 172–87. For science and rhetoric see Alan G. Gross, *The Rhetoric of Science* (Cambridge, Mass.: Harvard University Press, 1990).
82. Lord Rayleigh, 'Presidential Address', *Proceedings of the Society for Psychical Research* 30 (1918–19), 275–90 (276). Rayleigh was referring to [Anon.], 'Very Odd!', *P* 24 (1853), 120.

5. THE *CORNHILL MAGAZINE* AND SHILLING MONTHLIES IN MID-VICTORIAN BRITAIN

1. Quoted in *Saturday Review*, 7 January 1860, p. 32.
2. [Richard Allen?], 'Paper', *Cornhill Magazine* [hereafter *CM*] 4 (1861), 609–23 (616 and 622).

3. Mrs Richmond Ritchie, 'The First Number of the *Cornhill*', *CM* 1 n.s. (1896), 1–16 (1).
4. [William Makepeace Thackeray], 'The Adventures of Philip', *CM* 5 (1862), 129–52 (136).
5. [William Makepeace Thackeray], 'Roundabout Papers. – No. VIII. De Juventute', *CM* 2 (1860), 501–12 (504).
6. The endemic artificiality of pastoral as a genre is, of course, discussed at length in Raymond Williams, *The Country and the City* (London: Chatto and Windus, 1973).
7. *Bookseller*, 26 April 1860, p. 213.
8. Ritchie, 'First Number', 2.
9. Gordon N. Ray (ed.), *The Letters and Private Papers of William Makepeace Thackeray*, 4 vols. (London: Oxford University Press, 1946), vol. IV, p. 161.
10. Edgar F. Harden (ed.), *The Letters and Private Papers of William Makepeace Thackeray: A Supplement to Ray* (London: Garland, 1994), pp. 937–8.
11. R. J. Morris, *Class, Sect and Party: The Making of the British Middle Class, Leeds 1820–1850* (Manchester: Manchester University Press, 1990), pp. 264–79.
12. John Sutherland, '*Cornhill*'s Sales and Payments: The First Decade', *Victorian Periodicals Review* 19 (1986), 106–8 (106); Richard D. Altick, *The English Common Reader: A Social History of the Mass Reading Public*, 2nd edn (Columbus: Ohio State University Press, 1998), p. 395.
13. Quoted in Altick, *Common Reader*, p. 359.
14. Ray, *Letters*, vol. IV, p. 158; quoted in Barbara Quinn Schmidt, 'The Patron as Businessman: George Murray Smith (1824–1901)', *Victorian Periodicals Review* 16 (1983), 2–14 (8).
15. *Economist*, 9 March 1861, p. 261; William Baker (ed.), *The Letters of George Henry Lewes*, 3 vols. (Victoria, B.C.: University of Victoria, 1995–9), vol. III, p. 71.
16. Ray, *Letters*, vol. IV, p. 160.
17. Harden, *Supplement*, p. 1004.
18. Ray, *Letters*, vol. IV, p. 158.
19. Ibid., vol. IV, p. 161.
20. [Thomas Henry Huxley], 'Darwin on the *Origin of Species*', *Westminster Review* 17 n.s. (1860), 541–70 (541); T. H. Huxley, 'Time and Life: Mr. Darwin's *Origin of Species*', *Macmillan's Magazine* 1 (1859), 142–8 (146–8).
21. Alvar Ellegård, *Darwin and the General Reader: The Reception of Darwin's Theory of Evolution in the British Periodical Press, 1859–1872*, 2nd edn (Chicago: Chicago University Press, 1990), p. 26.
22. Certainly the footnotes to the sections on the *Cornhill* in Ellegård's book make reference only to these instalments of 'Studies in Animal Life'. See ibid., pp. 26, 41, 205, and 292.
23. Jennifer Glynn, *Prince of Publishers: A Biography of George Smith*, (London: Allison and Busby, 1986), p. 128.
24. *Economist*, 9 March 1861, p. 260.
25. Quoted in Altick, *Common Reader*, p. 338.
26. Baker, *Letters*, vol. I, p. 292.

27. Ibid., vol. I, p. 291.
28. [George Henry Lewes], 'Studies in Animal Life', *CM* I (1860), 61–74 (63 and 61n.).
29. Ibid., 438–7 (442).
30. Ibid., 598–607 (603).
31. Gordon S. Haight (ed.), *The George Eliot Letters*, 9 vols. (New Haven: Yale University Press, 1954–78), vol. III, p. 227.
32. [Lewes], 'Studies', 605.
33. Ibid., 445–7.
34. Baker, *Letters*, vol. II, p. 23.
35. Ibid., vol. II, p. 12.
36. Alfred McKinley Terhune and Annabelle Burdick Terhune (eds.), *The Letters of Edward Fitzgerald*, 2 vols. (Princeton: Princeton University Press, 1980), vol. II, p. 353.
37. Quoted in Rosemary Ashton, *G. H. Lewes: A Life* (Oxford: Clarendon Press, 1991), p. 215.
38. Ibid., p. 215.
39. [Eneas Sweetland Dallas], 'The Poor Man's Kitchen', *CM* I (1860), 745–54 (754).
40. Ibid., 747.
41. [James Hinton], 'Food – How to Take It', *CM* 4 (1861), 281–94 (281); [James Hinton], 'Food – What It Is', *CM* 3 (1861), 460–72 (460).
42. [Andrew Wynter], 'First Beginnings', *CM* 5 (1862), 481–94 (483).
43. [George Henry Lewes], 'Aids to Beauty, Real and Artificial', *CM* 7 (1863), 391–400 (391).
44. Baker, *Letters*, vol. II, p. 23.
45. N. John Hall (ed.), *The Letters of Anthony Trollope*, 2 vols. (Stanford: Stanford University Press, 1983), vol. I, p. 58.
46. Ibid., vol. I, p. 447.
47. [Anthony Trollope], 'The Struggles of Brown, Jones, and Robinson', *CM* 4 (1861), 675–91 (690).
48. Charles Darwin, *On the Origin of Species* (London: John Murray, 1859), p. 445.
49. [Edmund Saul Dixon], 'A Vision of Animal Existences', *CM* 5 (1862), 311–18 (311–12).
50. Ibid., 313.
51. Ibid., 315–17.
52. The only other allusion to threatening aspects of Darwinism came in Richard Ashe King's 'A Tête-à-tête Social Science Discussion' (*CM* 10 [1864], 569–82), which I discuss in 'Women, Science and Culture: Science in the Nineteenth-Century Periodical', *Women: A Cultural Review* 12 (2001), 57–70 (66–67).
53. Dixon's use of the dream as a way of exploring Darwinism perhaps draws on the 'Dreamland' chapter of Charles Kingsley's *Alton Locke* (1850) which charts the progressive development of man from 'the lowest point of created life' in a series of feverish hallucinations. My thanks to Rebecca Stott for this suggestion.

54. [Dixon], 'Animal Existences', 318.
55. [Thackeray], 'Adventures of Philip', *CM* 3 (1861), 385–408 (389).
56. 'Monkeyana', *Punch* 40 (1861), 206; [Thackeray], 'Philip', 389 and 392; 'Adventures of Philip', *CM* 6 (1862), 217–40 (236).
57. [William Makepeace Thackeray], 'Roundabout Papers. – No. XVI. On Two Roundabout Papers which I Intended to Write', *CM* 4 (1861), 377–84 (381–2).
58. Ibid., 382–4.
59. Ibid., 384.
60. Harden, *Supplement*, p. 1047.
61. James A. Secord, *Victorian Sensation: The Extraordinary Publication, Reception, and Secret Authorship of 'Vestiges of the Natural History of Creation'* (Chicago: University of Chicago Press, 2000), p. 37.
62. Parts of this section have appeared in a different form in my 'Stranger than Fiction: Spiritualism, Intertextuality, and William Makepeace Thackeray's Editorship of the *Cornhill Magazine*, 1860–62', *Journal of Victorian Culture* 7 (2002), 220–38.
63. Darwin, *Origin*, p. 184.
64. [James Fitzjames Stephen], 'Spiritualism', *CM* 7 (1863), 706–19 (706).
65. [Robert Bell], 'Stranger than Fiction', *CM* 2 (1860), 211–24 (213 and 219).
66. Ibid., 215, 223, and 224.
67. Ibid., 215.
68. Harden, *Supplement*, pp. 914–16.
69. [Bell], 'Stranger than Fiction', 211n.
70. Harden, *Supplement*, p. 982.
71. Haight, *Letters*, vol. III, p. 335.
72. Charles Richard Weld, *Last Winter in Rome* (London: Longmans, 1865), p. 181.
73. Quoted in 'Elegant Extracts', *Spiritual Magazine* 1 (1860), 433–43 (437–8).
74. 'Notices of New Books', *Spiritual Magazine* 1 (1860), 416–25 (425).
75. [George Henry Lewes], 'Seeing is Believing', *Blackwood's Edinburgh Magazine* 88 (1860), 381–95 (384).
76. Harden, *Supplement*, p. 980.
77. [William Makepeace Thackeray], 'A Roundabout Journey. Notes of a Week's Holiday', *CM* 2 (1860), 623–40 (625).
78. [James Hinton], 'The Brain and its Uses', *CM* 5 (1862), 409–25 (420).
79. [James Fitzjames Stephen], 'Superstition', *CM* 5 (1862), 537–49 (537–9).
80. [Anthony Trollope], 'Framley Parsonage', *CM* 1 (1860), 296–321 (310).
81. Elizabeth Barrett Browning, 'Little Mattie', *CM* 3 (1861), 736–7 (737).
82. [William Makepeace Thackeray], 'Roundabout Papers. – No. XX. The Notch on the Axe. – A Story à la Mode' (I), *CM* 5 (1862), 508–12 (512 and 511).
83. Ibid. (II), 634–40 (637).
84. Ibid. (III), 754–60 (760).
85. Haight, *Letters*, vol. IV, p. 29.
86. [James Hinton], 'Seeing with the Eyes Shut', *CM* 6 (1862), 64–70 (66 and 64).
87. G. Smith to J. Herschel, 6 May 1862, Herschel Papers 16.185, Royal Society.
88. [George Henry Lewes], 'Our Survey of Literature, Science, and Art', *CM* 6 (1862), 103–20 (103).

89. [John Herschel], 'Our Survey of Literature and Science', *CM* 7 (1863), 132–44 (142–3).
90. G. Smith to J. Herschel, 5 August 1862, Herschel Papers 16.188; J. Herschel to G. Smith, 6 August 1862, Herschel Papers 25.15.19.
91. Frederick H. Burkhardt *et al.* (ed.), *The Correspondence of Charles Darwin*, 13 vols. (Cambridge: Cambridge University Press, 1985–), vol. x, p. 550.
92. Ibid., vol. x, p. 589. The notice of Cohn's book appeared in [John Herschel], 'Our Survey of Literature and Science', *CM* 6 (1862), 842–56 (853–4).
93. Baker, *Letters*, vol. ii, p. 49.
94. Ibid., vol. ii, pp. 70–1.
95. Ibid.
96. Ibid., vol. ii, p. 75.

6. THE *BOY'S OWN PAPER*, SCIENCE, AND LATE-VICTORIAN JUVENILE MAGAZINES

I would like to thank Aileen Fyfe for her help in preparation of this chapter. For permission to quote from unpublished material in their collections I would like to thank the United Society for Christian Literature.

1. Edward Salmon, *Juvenile Literature as It Is* (London: Henry J. Drane, 1888), pp. 13, 203.
2. [G. A. Hutchison?], 'Correspondence', *BOP* 2 (1879–80), 319. For circulation figures see Richard D. Altick, *The English Common Reader: A Social History of the Mass Reading Public* (Chicago: Chicago University Press, 1957), p. 395. See also Patrick A. Dunae, 'The *Boy's Own Paper*: Origins and Editorial Developments', *Private Library* 9 (1976), 123–58, 133–4.
3. For the *Daily Telegraph* see Altick, *English Common Reader*, p. 395. In 1879 the *Boys of England* was selling 250,000 copies a week: Kirsten Drotner, *English Children and their Magazines, 1751–1945* (New Haven and London: Yale University Press, 1988), p. 75.
4. Jack Cox, *Take a Cold Tub Sir! The Story of the Boy's Own Paper* (Guildford: The Lutterworth Press, 1982), pp. 78, 88.
5. Patricia Mary Barnett, 'English Boys' Weeklies, 1866–1899', unpublished PhD thesis, University of Minnesota (1974), chapters 4 and 5; John M. Mackenzie, *Propaganda and Empire: The Manipulation of British Public Opinion, 1880–1960* (Manchester: Manchester University Press, 1984), pp. 199–226 (204).
6. Barnett, 'English Boys' Weeklies', pp. 151–3; Aileen Kennedy Fyfe, 'Industrialised Conversion: The Religious Tract Society and Popular Science Publishing in Victorian Britain', unpublished PhD thesis, University of Cambridge (2000); Diana Dixon, 'Children's Magazines and Science in the Nineteenth Century', *Victorian Periodicals Review* 34 (2001), 228–38; Jonathan R. Topham, 'Periodicals and the Making of Reading Audiences for Science in Early Nineteenth-Century Britain: The *Youth's Magazine*, 1828–37' in Louise Henson *et al.* (eds.), *Culture and Science in Nineteenth Century Media*, (Aldershot: Ashgate, 2004), pp. 57–69.

7. Greg Myers, 'Science for Women and Children: The Dialogue of Popular Science in the Nineteenth Century', in John Christie and Sally Shuttleworth (eds.), *Nature Transfigured: Science and Literature, 1700–1900* (Manchester: Manchester University Press, 1989), pp. 171–200; Bernard Lightman, '"The Voices of Nature": Popularising Victorian Science', in Bernard Lightman (ed.), *Victorian Science in Context* (Chicago: Chicago University Press, 1997), pp. 187–211; Aileen Fyfe, 'Young Readers and the Sciences', in N. Jardine and others (eds.), *Cultures of Natural History* (Cambridge: Cambridge University Press, 1995), pp. 276–90; Fyfe, 'Industrialised Conversion', chapter 1; Topham, 'Periodicals'.

8. David Reed, *The Popular Press in Britain and the United States 1880–1960* (London: The British Library, 1997), p. 253.

9. Lightman, '"The Voices of Nature"', p. 191.

10. *Publisher's Circular* 42 (1879), 61.

11. Reed, *Popular Press*, pp. 92–3; J. S. Bratton, *The Impact of Victorian Children's Fiction* (London: Croom Helm, 1981), pp. 191–2.

12. For the religious press and children's literature see Fyfe, 'Industrialised Conversion'.

13. John Springhall, '"Disseminating Impure Literature": The 'Penny Dreadful' Publishing Business since 1860', *Economic History Review* 3 (1994), 567–84 (568). See also John Springhall, '"Pernicious Reading"? The 'Penny Dreadful' as Scapegoat for Late-Victorian Juvenile Crime', *Victorian Periodicals Review* 27 (1994), 326–49. The *OED* cites the earliest use of 'penny dreadful' in *The Slang Dictionary: Etymological, Historical, and Anecdotal* (London: Chatto and Windus, 1873).

14. The *Wild Boys of London* boasted weekly sales of 1 million: see the *Waterloo Directory of English Newspapers and Periodicals, 1800–1900*, ed. by John North (Waterloo, Ontario: North Waterloo Academic Press, 2001), accessed 23 January 2003 <http://www. victorianperiodicals.com>.

15. For the *GOP* see Wendy Forrester, *Great-Grandmama's Weekly. A Celebration of the Girl's Own Paper 1880–1901* (Guildford: The Lutterworth Press, 1980). For a comparison of the contents of the *BOP* and *GOP* in 1890 see Reed, *Popular Press*, p. 253.

16. Bennett cited in Dunae, '*Boy's Own Paper*', 136.

17. Hutchison cited in Dunae '*Boy's Own Paper*', 132. Hutchison was here paraphrasing the eminent nineteenth-century educationist and clergyman, Thomas Arnold: Fyfe, 'Industrialised Conversion', p. 86.

18. Drotner, *English Children*, pp. 63–111; Bratton, *Impact*, p. 102.

19. Diana Dixon, 'Children and the Press, 1866–1914', in Michael Harris and Alan Lee (eds.), *The Press in English Society from the Seventeenth to Nineteenth Centuries* (Rutherford: Fairleigh Dickinson Press, 1986), pp. 133–48 (133).

20. Dixon, 'Children's Magazines', 229–31.

21. Fyfe, 'Young Readers', p. 288; Myers, 'Science for Women and Children'; Lightman, '"The Voices of Nature"'.

22. The following discussion draws on Fyfe, 'Periodicals and book series: complementary aspects of a publisher's mission', in Henson *et al.*, *Culture and Science*, pp. 71–82. The circulation of the *Leisure Hour* reached 100,000 in its first decade: Alvar Ellegård, *Darwin and the General Reader: The Reception of Darwin's Theory of Evolution in the British Periodical Press, 1859–72* (Chicago: Chicago University Press, 1990), p. 376. For the history of the RTS see Fyfe, 'Industrialised Conversion', chapter 1; Bratton, *Impact*, pp. 32–46.

23. Drotner, *English Children*, 75.

24. For Macaulay, see Dunae, '*Boy's Own Paper*', 130. For the *Leisure Hour* see Fyfe, 'Periodicals'.

25. For Hutchison see Cox, *Take a Cold Tub*, pp. 76–81; Dunae, '*Boy's Own Paper*', 129–32.

26. Many of the biographies appearing in the *BOP* were expanded versions of articles appearing in the *Leisure Hour*. See, for example, [anon.], 'Some Boys who Became Famous. George and Robert Stephenson', *BOP* 3 (1880–81), 579–80, 595–6, which was based on [anon.], 'Robert Stephenson', *Leisure Hour* (1860), 711–14, 722–7.

27. Dixon, 'Children's Fiction', 233.

28. One of the few statements on atonement is in [anon.], 'Why I am Not a Christian', *BOP* 5 (1883–84), 795.

29. Dunae, '*Boy's Own Paper*', 145.

30. [G. A. Hutchinson?], 'Correspondence', *BOP* 4 (1882–3), 824.

31. John Macbeath, 'Where the "Boy's Own Paper" Began', *BOP* 51 (1929–31), 224.

32. John Scoffern, for example, believed it was within the capacity of 'any boy' to follow his recipes for illustrating abstract scientific theories: Dr Scoffern, 'Optical Toy Sports', *BOP* 4 (1882–3), 228–9.

33. Cox, *Take a Cold Tub*, p. 12.

34. For science in late-Victorian secondary schools see Michael Argles, *From South Kensington to Robbins: An Account of English Technical and Scientific Education Since 1851* (London: Longman, 1964), pp. 21–56; Gordon W. Roderick and Michael D. Stephens, *Scientific and Technical Education in Nineteenth-Century England* (Newton Abbott: David and Charles, 1972), pp. 25–41.

35. For J. G. Wood, see Theodore Wood, *The Rev. J. G. Wood* (London: Cassell, 1890); Lightman, '"Voices of Nature"', pp. 200–3; Lightman, 'The Visual Theology of Victorian Popularizers of Science: From Reverent Eye to Chemical Retina', *Isis* 91 (2000), 651–80.

36. For Stables see Walter N. Menzies, 'Facing Fearful Odds: William Gordon Stables, MD, LM, RN, 1837–1910', *Aberdeen University Review* 47 (1977–78), 133–48, 249–55; Cox, *Take a Cold Tub*; Patrick A. Dunae, 'New Grub Street for Boys', in Jeffrey Richards (ed.), *Imperialism and Juvenile Literature* (Manchester: Manchester University Press, 1989), pp. 12–33, 30–1.

37. For Verne and the *BOP* reprints of his works see Brian Taves and Stephen Michaluk Jr (eds.), *The Jules Verne Encyclopaedia* (Lanham, Md: Scarecrow Press, 1996), *passim*.

38. For Scoffern see Cox, *Take a Cold Tub!*, p. 55; J[ohn] Scoffern, *A Manual of Chemical Analysis for the Young* (London: Office of the National Illustrated Library; W. S. Orr, [1854]).

39. Gordon Stables, 'Ferrets as Pets, and How to Keep Them', *BOP* 2 (1879–80), 746–7 (746).

40. Dixon, 'Children's Magazines', 232.

41. Dr Scoffern, 'Indoor Amusements. Chemical Odds and Ends. How to Make a Shower of Fire', *BOP* 2 (1879–80), 757–8 (757).

42. Dr Scoffern, 'Seasonable Indoor Amusements: Chemistry and Conjuring', *BOP* 2 (1879–80), 165–6 (166).

43. Jules Verne, 'The Giant Raft; or, Eight Hundred Leagues on the Amazon', *BOP* 3 (1880–1), 659–60 (660).

44. [Anon.], 'Insect Life in the Amazon Country', *BOP* 2 (1879–80), 822.

45. Revd. J. G. Wood, 'Shore-Hunting', *BOP* 2 (1879–80), 3–4 (3). Wood's italics.

46. John Mackenzie, 'Hunting and the Natural World', in Richards, *Imperialism*, pp. 144–72 (155).

47. Mary Ann Elston, 'Women and Anti-Vivisection in Victorian England', in Nicolaas A. Rupke (ed.), *Vivisection in Historical Perspective* (London: Croom Helm, 1987), pp. 259–94.

48. [G. A. Hutchison], 'Correspondence', *BOP* 5 (1882–3), 48.

49. Revd. J. G. Wood, 'On Killing, Setting, and Preserving Insects. I – Killing', *BOP* 1 (1879), 431–2 (431).

50. [George Hutchison], [Editorial Note], *BOP* 1 (1879), 431.

51. United Society of Christian Literature (Archives), School of Oriental and African Studies, University of London: R.T.S./U.S.C.L. Executive Committee (H-8501), Box 9, Fiche #425, 18 November 1884, Minute 857.

52. [Anon.], 'Some Boys who Became Famous. The Father of English Potters', *BOP* 2 (1879–80), 163–5 (165); [Anon.], 'Some Boys who Became Famous. Robert Dick, the Baker-Geologist', *BOP* 2 (1879–80), 684–6 (686).

53. [Anon.], 'Men who are Talked About', *BOP* 4 (1881–2), 764–6 (766).

54. Jules Verne, 'The Boy Captain: A Tale of Adventure by Land and Sea', *BOP* 2 (1879–80), 12–14 (14).

55. [Anon.], 'Boys We Have Known – The Duffer', *BOP* 2 (1879–80), 502–3, 503.

56. Bratton, *Impact*, 103.

57. Verne, 'Boy Captain', *BOP* 2 (1879–80), 604–6 (606); T. S. Millington, 'Our Holiday Tramp', *BOP* 2 (1879–80), 598–601 (599).

58. Richards, *Imperialism*; Mackenzie, *Propaganda*, pp. 210–13; Barnett, 'English Boys' Weeklies', pp. 219–54.

59. For a detailed analysis of this material see Stuart Hannabus, 'Information Clinic: The Correspondence Columns of the *Boy's Own Paper* in 1894–95', *Library Review* 26 (1977), 279–85.

60. [Anon.], 'Correspondence', *BOP* 5 (1882–3), 752.

61. [Anon.], 'Correspondence', *BOP* 3 (1880–1), 775. The works referred to are Henry E. Roscoe, *Chemistry* (London: Macmillan, 1872) and Roscoe, *A Treatise on Chemistry*, 2 vols. (London: Macmillan, 1877–9).

62. On Harmsworth see Drotner, *English Children*, pp. 115–30.

7. THE *REVIEW OF REVIEWS* AND THE NEW JOURNALISM IN LATE-VICTORIAN BRITAIN

1. 'The Topic of the Month', *Review of Reviews* [hereafter *RR*] 16 (1897), 457–65 (457–8).
2. See Joel H. Wiener, 'How New was the New Journalism?' in *Papers for the Millions: The New Journalism in Britain, 1850s to 1914*, ed. by Joel H. Wiener (New York: Greenwood, 1988), pp. 47–71.
3. W. T. Stead, 'The Future of Journalism', *Contemporary Review* 50 (1886), 663–79 (663); W. T. Stead, 'Government by Journalism', *Contemporary Review* 49 (1886), 653–74 (664).
4. Alan J. Lee, *The Origins of the Popular Press in England, 1855–1914* (London: Croom Helm, 1976), p. 120; J. O. Baylen, 'The "New Journalism" in Late Victorian Britain', *Australian Journal of Politics and History* 18 (1972), 367–85 (369 and 371).
5. See Peter D. McDonald, *British Literary Culture and Publishing Practice 1880–1914* (Cambridge: Cambridge University Press, 1997), pp. 48 and 149.
6. See Frederic Whyte, *The Life of W. T. Stead*, 2 vols. (London: Jonathan Cape, 1925), vol. II, p. 55.
7. See J. O. Baylen, 'W. T. Stead as Publisher and Editor of the *Review of Reviews*', *Victorian Periodicals Review* 12 (1979), 70–84 (71).
8. Stead, 'Future of Journalism', 663; 'To All English-Speaking Folk', *RR* 1 (1890), 15–20 (15).
9. 'To All English-Speaking Folk', 15 and 18.
10. Baylen, 'W. T. Stead', 74.
11. 'Programme', *RR* 1 (1890), 14.
12. 'To all English-Speaking Folk', 19; Matthew Arnold, 'Up to Easter', *Nineteenth Century* 21 (1887), 629–43 (638).
13. 'To My Readers', *RR* 1 (1890), 363.
14. On Stead's nervous breakdown, see Whyte, *Life*, vol. II, p. 67.
15. See Grant Richards, *Memories of a Misspent Youth 1872–1896*, (London: William Heinemann, 1932), pp. 125–7; *Index to the Periodical Literature of the World (Covering the Year 1891)* (London: Office of the *Review of Reviews*, 1892), 28.
16. Baylen, 'W. T. Stead', 74–6.
17. Hulda Friederichs, *The Life of Sir George Newnes* (London: Hodder and Stoughton, 1911), p. 116. Stead claims a 'circulation of well on to 200,000 copies in all parts of the English speaking world' in 'After Two Years', *RR* 4 (1891), 551–5 (551).
18. 'To All English-speaking Folk', 15.
19. 'Programme', 14.
20. J. Knowles to T. H. Huxley, 20 January 1890, Huxley Papers 20.123, Imperial College of Science, Technology, and Medicine Archives, London.
21. 'The Judgement of the Journalists', *RR* 1 (1890), 166–8 (166).

22. 'To My Readers', 363.
23. 'Judgement of the Journalists', 166.
24. On nineteenth-century copyright law, see John Feather, *Publishing, Piracy and Politics: An Historical Study of Copyright in Britain* (London: Mansell, 1994); and Catherine Seville, *Literary Copyright Reform in Early Victorian England* (Cambridge: Cambridge University Press, 1999).
25. 'The Book of the Month', *RR* 11 (1895), 569–78 (569).
26. 'Some Autograph Introductions', *RR* 1 (1890), 3–13 (9).
27. On Huxley's concern with copyright law, see Paul White, *Thomas Huxley: Making the 'Man of Science'* (Cambridge: Cambridge University Press, 2002), pp. 141–2.
28. Adrian Johns, *The Nature of the Book: Print and Knowledge in the Making* (Chicago: University of Chicago Press, 1998), pp. 32–3.
29. See James A. Secord, *Victorian Sensation: The Extraordinary Publication, Reception, and Secret Authorship of 'Vestiges of the Natural History of Creation'*, (Chicago: University of Chicago Press, 2000), p. 126.
30. Joseph Hatton, *Journalistic London: A Series of Sketches of Famous Pens and Papers of the Day* (London: Sampson Low, 1882), p. 248.
31. Leonard Huxley, *Life and Letters of Thomas Henry Huxley*, 2 vols., (London: Macmillan, 1900), vol. 1, p. 424.
32. See ibid., vol. 11, pp. 116–17, which prints a letter from January 1886 in which Huxley tells Knowles, 'I shall send you the MS. of the *Evolution of Theology* to-day or to-morrow. It will not do to divide it, as I want the reader to have an *aperçu* of the whole process from Samuel of Israel to Sammy of Oxford. I am afraid it will make thirty or thirty-five pages . . . Please have it set up in slip, though, as it is written after the manner of a judge's charge.'
33. W. T. Stead to T. H. Huxley, 31 December 1889, Huxley Papers 27.3.
34. 'Is "Progress and Poverty" all Fudge?', *RR* 1 (1890), 128.
35. 'Culture and Current Orthodoxy', *RR* 2 (1890), 43.
36. W. T. Stead to T. H. Huxley, 29 October 1890, Huxley Papers 27.12.
37. *Index to the Periodical Literature of the World*, p. 28.
38. Richards, *Memories*, p. 147.
39. 'Culture and Current Orthodoxy', 43.
40. Adrian Desmond, *Huxley: Evolution's High Priest* (London: Michael Joseph, 1997), p. 202.
41. 'Professor Huxley as Controversialist', *RR* 2 (1890), 143.
42. T. H. Huxley, 'The Lights of the Church and the Light of Science', *Nineteenth Century* 28 (1890), 5–22 (21).
43. 'The Nineteenth Century', *RR* 2 (1890), 466–7 (467).
44. T. H. Huxley to W. T. Stead, 8 July 1890, Huxley Papers 27.5; T. H. Huxley to W. T. Stead, 9 July 1890, Huxley Papers 27.6.
45. See Desmond, *Huxley*, p. 145; and Bernard Lightman, 'Ideology, Evolution and Late Victorian Agnostic Popularizers', in *History, Humanity and Evolution*, ed. by James R. Moore (Cambridge: Cambridge University Press, 1989), 285–309 (303).

46. *The Times*, 24 January 1891, p. 13; W. T. Stead to T. H. Huxley, 24 January 1891, Huxley Papers 27.23.
47. W. T. Stead to T. H. Huxley, 27 January 1891, Huxley Papers 27.25.
48. J. Knowles to T. H. Huxley, 20 January 1890, Huxley Papers 20.123.
49. '"Borderland"', *RR* 7 (1893), 675–8 (675).
50. 'How We Intend to Study Borderland', *Borderland* 1 (1893–4), 1–6 (1).
51. 'The Response to the Appeal', *Borderland* 1 (1893–4), 10–23 (18).
52. T. H. Huxley to W. T. Stead, 18 July 1893, Huxley Papers 27.26.
53. This was not, though, the first time that such a suggestion had been made in one of Stead's journals. In January 1889, Huxley wrote to Stead complaining that 'The *Pall Mall Gazette* of the 20th December contains a quotation from a Chicago newspaper, in which not only is it stated that I have taken part in "a series of experiments, chiefly with the medium Home", but it is pretty plainly suggested that I am disposed to judge what is called "Spiritualism" more or less favourably. The statement and the suggestion are alike erroneous.' *Pall Mall Gazette*, 1 January 1889, p. 1.
54. See T. H. Huxley to W. T. Stead, 21 June 1894, Huxley Papers 27.32.
55. Roger Cooter and Stephen Pumfrey, 'Separate Spheres and Public Places: Reflections on the History of Science Popularisation and Science in Popular Culture', *History of Science* 32 (1994), 237–67 (248).
56. 'Prussian Annals', *RR* 7 (1893), 53.
57. 'Do Dead Men Dream?', *RR* 1 (1890), 111.
58. '"Borderland"', 675.
59. Quoted in Joseph O. Baylen, 'W. T. Stead's *Borderland: A Quarterly Review and Index of Psychic Phenomena*, 1893–97', *Victorian Periodicals Newsletter* 1 (1969), 30–5 (30).
60. On Stead's relations with the SPR, see Roger Luckhurst, *The Invention of Telepathy 1870–1901* (Oxford: Oxford University Press, 2002), pp. 121 and 127.
61. 'Catalogues and Indexes of Scientific and Technical Literature', *RR* 10 (1894), 194.
62. See 'Zoological Bibliography', *RR* 11 (1895), 430.
63. 'The Fortnightly Review', *RR* 2 (1890), 255.
64. W. T. Stead to A. R. Wallace, 17 September 1890, Wallace Papers, British Library, Add. 46436 f. 229.
65. 'Our Monthly Parcel of Books', *RR* 11 (1895), 387–9 (389).
66. Grant Allen, 'Our Scientific Causerie', *RR* 1 (1890), 537–8 (537–8).
67. 'Mr. Grant Allen', *RR* 1 (1890), 198.
68. See Kelly J. Mays, 'The Disease of Reading and Victorian Periodicals', in *Literature in the Marketplace: Nineteenth-Century British Publishing and Reading Practices*, ed. by John O. Jordan and Robert L. Patten (Cambridge: Cambridge University Press, 1995), pp. 165–94.
69. George R. Humphrey, 'The Reading of the Working Classes', *Nineteenth Century* 33 (1893), 690–701 (693–4).
70. T. P. O'Connor, 'The New Journalism', *New Review* 1 (1889), 423–34 (434).
71. 'Our Welcome', *RR* 1 (1890), 96–9 (99).

72. Advertisement included in *Index to the Periodical Literature of the World*; quoted in 'Judgement of the Journalists', 166.
73. 'To All English-Speaking Folk', 20.
74. 'Government by Journalism', 673.
75. A Welsh miner, Percy Wall, recalled how in his youth he read periodicals in the local Miners' Institute Library where 'Above all I could study the *Review of Reviews* and learn the complexities of foreign affairs.' Quoted in Jonathan Rose, *The Intellectual Life of the British Working Classes* (New Haven: Yale University Press, 2001), p. 244.
76. 'Ten Years of Modern History', *RR* 20 (1899), advertising supplement.
77. 'Our Monthly Parcel of Books', *RR* 13 (1896), 277–80 (279).
78. W. T. Stead, 'My System', *Cassell's Magazine* (1906), 292–7 (296).
79. 'Character Sketch. Mr. Herbert Spencer', *RR* 12 (1895), 399–407 (407).
80. 'The Rights of the Unborn', *RR* 12 (1895), 264.
81. 'Against Compulsory Motherhood', *RR* 11 (1895), 328–9 (328).
82. 'Government by Journalism', 671.
83. Quoted in 'Judgement of the Journalists', 167.
84. 'The Progress of the World', *RR* 14 (1896), 289–96 (296).
85. 'Our Monthly Parcel of Books', *RR* 12 (1895), 183–5 (183).
86. 'One of the Notable Books of the Age-End', *RR* 11 (1895), 472–3 (472).
87. 'Our Monthly Parcel of Books', *RR* 9 (1894), 522–6 (523); 'Ten Years of Modern History'.
88. G. Allen to W. T. Stead, ?1890, Stead Papers, Churchill Archives Centre, Churchill College, Cambridge, fl. 1 ALS.
89. G. Allen to W. T. Stead, n.d., Stead Papers, fl. 5 TLS.
90. Grant Allen, 'Character Sketch. Professor Tyndall', *RR* 9 (1894), 21–6. On the proposed review of Darwin's *Autobiography*, see G. Allen to W. T. Stead, 6 October [1892], Stead Papers, fl. 4 ALS.
91. 'Cyclomania Morbus', *RR* 15 (1897), 157.
92. See Allen, '[Review of] *Essays upon Heredity and Kindred Biological Problems* by August Weismann', *Academy* 37 (1890), 83–4.
93. Benjamin Kidd, 'Our Scientific Causerie', *RR* 2 (1890), 647–50 (647–9).
94. See Richard Salmon, 'Signs of Intimacy: The Literary Celebrity in the "Age of Interviewing"', *Victorian Literature and Culture* 25 (1997), 159–77.
95. Allen, 'Our Scientific Causerie', 538.
96. Kidd, 'Our Scientific Causerie', 647–8 and 650.
97. Salmon, 'Signs of Intimacy', 169.
98. Quoted in Harry Schalk, 'Fleet Street in the 1880s: The New Journalism', in *Papers for the Millions*, ed. by Wiener, pp. 73–87 (80).
99. Charles D. Lanier, 'Character Sketch. Thomas Alva Edison', *RR* 8 (1893), 598–607 (604).
100. *Pall Mall Gazette*, 4 October 1887, p. 13; *Pall Mall Gazette*, 6 October 1887, p. 7.
101. *Pall Mall Gazette*, 6 October 1887, p. 7.
102. Stead, 'My System', 297.

103. W. T. Stead to A. R. Wallace, 15 December 1910, Wallace Papers, Add. 46438 f.161.
104. Stead, 'Government by Journalism', 666.
105. 'A Word to Those Who are Willing to Help', *RR* 1 (1890), 53.
106. 'Some Pages of a Busy Life', *RR* 19 (1899), 537–43 (537).
107. 'Wanted, a Census of Ghosts!', *RR* 4 (1891), 257–8 (258).
108. '"England at the End of the Century"', *RR* 4 (1891), 370–71 (371).
109. 'The Census of Ghosts', *RR* 4 (1891), 347.
110. 'Some Notable Books of the Month', *RR* 15 (1897), 593–600 (600).
111. Quoted in 'Some Press Comments on "Borderland"', *Borderland* 1 (1893–4), 203–6 (203).
112. Bernard Lightman, 'Marketing Knowledge for the General Reader: Victorian Popularizers of Science', *Endeavour* 24 (2000), 100–6 (100).

8. TICKLING BABIES: GENDER, AUTHORITY, AND 'BABY SCIENCE'

1. Standard histories of developmental psychology tend to take Darwin's essay as an originary moment, and then move forward to Freud, and twentieth-century psychology. For a brief corrective view, see Ben S. Bradley, *Visions of Infancy: A Critical Introduction to Child Psychology* (London: Polity Press, 1989). By placing the debate in the context of periodical discussion, this chapter outlines a very different story of the emergence of a scientific field. The best introduction to the development of child study is to be found in Lyubov Gurjeva, 'Everyday Bourgeois Science: The Scientific Management of Children in Britain, 1880–1914', unpublished PhD thesis, University of Cambridge (1998). I am indebted to Dr Gurjeva for sharing her work with me.
2. Herbert Spencer, *Essays: Scientific, Political, and Speculative* (London: Longman, Brown, Green, Longmans, and Roberts, 1858), p. 10.
3. Spencer has become legendary for his romantic rejection of Marian Evans (the future George Eliot) and his lifelong bachelor status.
4. Adolf Kussmaul, *Untersuchungen über das Seelenleben des Neugeborenen Menschen* (Leipzig and Heidelberg, 1859). Lewes's heavily annotated copy of Kussmaul's tract is amongst his books at Dr Williams's Library, London.
5. The Kussmaul tract was reviewed in the *Zeitschrift für Rationelle Medicin* (Leipzig and Heidelberg, 1861), pp. 516–17 which is also in G. H Lewes's books at Dr Williams's Library.
6. T. H. Huxley, *Westminster Review* n.s. 5 (1854), 254–6.
7. See Adrian Desmond, *Huxley: The Devil's Disciple* (London: Michael Joseph, 1994), and James A. Secord, *Victorian Sensation: The Extraordinary Publication, Reception, and Secret Authorship of 'Vestiges of the Natural History of Creation'* (Chicago: University of Chicago Press, 2000), pp. 498–500.
8. GHL Journal, 27 October 1859, in Gordon S. Haight (ed.), *The George Eliot Letters*, 9 vols. (New Haven: Yale University Press, 1954–78), vol. III, p. 189.

9. Lewes to John Blackwood, 30 January 1859, in William Baker (ed.), *The Letters of G. H. Lewes*, 2 vols. (Victoria, B.C.: University of Victoria, 1995), vol. I, p. 281.

10. Lewes is also in the unusual position of having been eclipsed in cultural reception and memory by his partner, George Eliot. His science is often seen as a mere adjunct to her literary life, whilst his major work, the three-part *Problems of Life and Mind* (1874–9), is portrayed as the deluded labour of a scientific Casaubon. Historians of science have also replicated this neglect, giving precedence to Spencer in the field of psychology, and ignoring the scientific impact of *The Physiology of Common Life*, 2 vols. (Edinburgh and London: William Blackwood and Sons, 1859–60), which became a set university text across Europe, and Lewes's innovative work on the multiple levels of consciousness, and the role of the cultural environment in fashioning self-hood.

11. The *Lancet*, for example, usually classified any work on babies under the heading infant, apart from the emotive issue of 'baby-farming' where it used the more popular term in its long-running campaign against such abuses in order to play upon popular sentiment.

12. [G. H. Lewes], 'The Mental Condition of Babies', *Cornhill Magazine* 7 (1863), 649–56 (651).

13. Ibid., 651.

14. Lewes, *Physiology*, vol. II, pp. 239–43. For summaries of Lewes's papers see *Report of the Twenty-Ninth Meeting of the British Association for the Advancement of Science* (London: John Murray, 1860), pp. 166–70. There were replies in the *Athenaeum*, on 24 September and 8 October 1859, 407 and 471.

15. The major study of child development in the 1880s, W. Preyer's *Die Seele des Kindes* (1882), reiterates this point that the new-born infant has no sense of hearing. The idea of new-born deafness did not, however, originate with Kussmaul. In his notes on the Kussmaul text, Lewes marks out a quotation from Bichat's *Recherches Physiologiques sur la Vie et la Mort* where he notes deficiencies in all the new-born's senses, including the fact that 'leur oreille n'entend presque rien' (p. 10).

16. Lewes, 'Mental Condition', p. 651.

17. Frances Power Cobbe and George Eliot's friend, Cara Bray, were leading lights of the anti-vivisection movement which led to the passing of the Cruelty to Animals Act in 1876. For Lewes's involvement on the opposing side see Rosemary Ashton, *G. H. Lewes: A Life* (Oxford: Clarendon Press, 1991), p. 268.

18. Lewes, 'Mental Condition', p. 651.

19. Lewes quotes extensively, with manifest approval, from Wordsworth's 'Ode: Intimations of Immortality from Recollections of Early Childhood' (1802–4, 1807).

20. For an interesting history of Darwin's difficulties in acquiring these plates, and their less than scientific nature, see Phillip Prodger, 'Rejlander, Darwin, and the Evolution of "Ginx's Baby", in *History of Photography* 23 (1999), 260–8. I am indebted to Greg Radick for this reference.

21. Charles Darwin, *The Expression of Emotions in Man and Animals* (London: John Murray, 1872), p. 212.

22. Although Bain initially tried to pay his contributors, payments were soon cut back to reviews only. This shift did not seem to deter his primary writers, however, who were eager to support the endeavour, and to be associated with its intellectual agenda.

23. G. H. Lewes contributed 'What is Sensation' (157–61) and Sully a long article on Wundt, 'Physiological Psychology in Germany' (20–43), and a shorter one on 'Art and Psychology' (467–78) to *Mind* 1 (1876).

24. H. Taine, 'On the Acquisition of Language by Children', *Mind* 2 (1877), 252–9, translation of an article that appeared in *Revue Philosophique* 1 (January 1876).

25. The original journal is reproduced as an appendix to F. Burkhardt and S. Smith (eds.), *The Correspondence of Charles Darwin*, 12 vols. (Cambridge: Cambridge University Press, 1988-), vol. IV, pp. 411–33.

26. Charles Darwin, 'A Biographical Sketch of an Infant', *Mind* 2 (1877), 283–94 (288).

27. See Frederick Burkhardt and Sydney Smith (eds.), *Darwin Calendar of Correspondence* (Cambridge: Cambridge University Press, 1994), letters 10968, 11011, 11047, 11088.

28. For example, volume 3 (1878) carried F. Pollock's, 'An Infant's Progress in Language', notes made, he observes, 'in humble following of Mr. Darwin's and M. Taine's example', 392–401 (392), and Pollock's review of Bernard Perez, *Les Trois Premières Années de L'Enfant* (Paris, 1878), a work subsequently published in English in 1885 with a preface by Sully. Volume 5 (1880) contained a review by Sully of an article by Preyer in *Deutsche Rundschau* which returned to the earlier experiments of Kussmaul, reviewed by Lewes in the *Cornhill,* and repeated his assertions that 'New-born children are all deaf', 385–6. Volume 6 (1881), contained 'Notes on an Infant' by F. H. Champneys, 104–7, again explicitly modelling itself on Darwin's 'Sketch'. Volume 7 (1882), carried Sully's review of Preyer's *Die Seele des Kindes,* 416–23.

29. Joseph Jacobs, 'The Need of a Society for Experimental Psychology', *Mind* 11 (1886), 51. Interestingly, Jacobs suggests that Galton's practical researches into the contents of individuals' minds should be complemented by reading the works of George Eliot and Meredith. This suggestion follows an earlier article by Sully in 1881 on 'George Eliot's Art', 378–94, which commends her work to psychologists in quest of 'scientific precision'. Although *Mind* was resolutely scientific in its orientation, it was sufficiently open-minded to grant the possibility of fiction contributing to the development of the science of psychology.

30. James Sully, critical notice of Preyer, *Die Seele des Kindes*, in *Mind* 7 (1882), 416–23. Sully greets the volume as 'the first systematic record of the mental development of a young child' (416). He accepts without question Preyer's reiteration of Kussmaul's finding that babies are born deaf, but interestingly raises queries regarding Preyer's endorsement of Darwin's theory that fears are

all inherited, preferring himself a combined explanation of shock and inherited association. In assessing Preyer's theories of language acquisition, he draws on his own scientific observations.

31. These articles preceded the more scholarly *Outlines of Psychology with special reference to the Theory of Education* (London: Longmans, Green, and Co., 1884). Although this was not a detailed study of child development, it did have an explicit focus, as its secondary title implies, on 'what may be called the embryology of mind' (p. vii). For a discussion of Sully's contributions to the *Cornhill* just prior to 'Babies and Science' see Ed. Block, Jr., 'Evolutionist Psychology and Aesthetics: *The Cornhill Magazine, 1875–1880*', *Journal of the History of Ideas* 45 (1984), 465–75.

32. As Secord has noted, 'the number of hungry writers on science is striking' (*Victorian Sensation*, p. 438). Detailed attention has been paid to the economic difficulties of novelists and literary journalists, but not to the equivalent problems experienced by fledgling scientists attempting to support themselves through journalism.

33. James Sully, *My Life and Friends: A Psychologist's Memories* (London: T. Fisher Unwin, 1918), p. 163.

34. J. S. [James Sully], 'Babies and Science', *Cornhill Magazine* 43 (1881), 539–54 (540).

35. Ibid., 545.

36. For another reading of this cartoon see Gillian Beer, *Open Fields: Science in Cultural Encounter* (Oxford: Clarendon Press, 1996), pp. 132–3.

37. Sully, 'Babies and Science', 546.

38. As Lyubov Gurjeva notes, Sully's views on women elsewhere were decidedly liberal ('Everyday Bourgeois Science', ch. 5).

39. Sully, 'Babies and Science', 551.

40. *Baby: An Illustrated Monthly Magazine for Mothers* was started by the proponent of rational dress, Ada S. Ballin, in December 1887. Its primary focus was on the healthcare of children. Sully contributed a short article on 'Children's Fears' to the first volume (July 1888), 195–7.

41. *Studies of Childhood* (1895) drew on material from 'Babies and Science' as well as articles published in *Popular Science Monthly*, *English Illustrated Magazine*, *Longman's Magazine* and the *Fortnightly Review*. Its publication occurs once Sully's professional position has been assured by his appointment in 1892 to the Chair at University College, London.

42. W. Tyler Smith, 'Introductory Lecture to a Course of Lectures on Obstetrics, Delivered at the Hunterian School of Medicine, 1847–48', *The Lancet* 2 (1847), 371.

43. For example, a detailed study of the *Lancet* reveals very little attention paid to child development until 1884 when it takes up the cause of 'over-pressure schools' in response to James Crichton Browne's report (see editorials on 11 October, 15 and 22 November, and the responding letter 'Overpressure in Schools' on 29 November 1884). Thereafter there are numerous articles on this topic which turn, in the 1890s, into the wider preoccupation with the

development of child study. On 25 January 1896 ('A Study of Childhood', 249), it offers its own addition to 'baby-lore', printing what it terms a 'delicious production' of a seven-year old child, which it commends to the notice of Professor Sully. With the exception of baby-farming and questions of infant mortality, children figure remarkably little in the pages of the *Lancet* until the 1880s when the number of headings under which they feature rapidly diversifies. Even surgical reporting of infant cases partakes of this new level of interest.

44. Louis Robinson, 'Darwinism in the Nursery', *Nineteenth Century* 30 (1891), 831–42; 'The Meaning of a Baby's Footprint', *Nineteenth Century* 31 (1892), 795–806; 'Darwinism and Swimming: A Theory', *Nineteenth Century* 34 (1893), 721–32.
45. Robinson, 'Baby's Footprint', 804.
46. Ibid., 832.
47. Ibid., 837–8. Robinson's work was highly influential, and provoked extended debate in the periodical press. In 1897, for example, the *Lancet* published a letter entitled 'The Prehensile Powers of the Hands of the Human Infant' by Walter Kidd (16 October), attempting to refute the theory, which in turn provoked supportive letters (23 October and 20 November).
48. '"Darwinism in the Nursery": Curious Experiments with Babies', *The Review of Reviews* 4 (1891), 500.
49. Robinson, 'Baby's Footprint', 838.
50. S. S. Buckman, 'Babies and Monkeys', *Nineteenth Century* 36 (1894), 727–43 (733).
51. Ibid., 733–4 and 736.
52. James Sully, *Mind* n.s. 2 (1893), 420–1. The thirteen categories are:
    1. Attention and Observation
    2. Memory
    3. Imagination and Fancy
    4. Reasoning
    5. Language
    6. Pleasure and Pain
    7. Fear
    8. Self-feeling
    9. Sympathy and Affection
    10. Artistic Taste
    11. Moral and Religious Feeling
    12. Volition
    13. Artistic Production.
53. James Sully, 'The New Study of Children', *Fortnightly Review* 58 (1895), 723–37. This article formed the basis of his introductory chapter for *Studies of Childhood*.
54. Ibid., 725 and 729.
55. See Burkhardt and Smith (eds.), *Correspondence of Charles Darwin*, vol. IV, p. 417.

56. Sully, 'New Study', 731. In reworking this material for *Studies of Childhood*, Sully retained this passage, but excised a subsequent one where he notes that 'the child-lover, like other lovers, seeks the object of his love' (p. 731). Although the sensitivities which today surround the term 'child-love' were clearly not operative in the Victorian era, it is probable that this textual change was motivated by the sense that the analogy with romantic love undermined the vaunted objectivity of the male scientific observer.

57. Sully, 'New Study', 733.

58. Ibid., 735–6.

59. Ibid., 737. Sully's difficulties in negotiating this gendered terrain are reflected in his rewriting of this passage for the book version, where women are simultaneously given a higher profile, but also more directly excluded from professional observation. See James Sully, *Studies of Childhood* (New edn: London: Longmans, Green, and Co., 1896), pp. 22–4.

60. James Sully, 'The Child in Recent English Literature', *Fortnightly Review* 61 (1897), 218–28 (218–20).

61. Alice Woods, Review of James Sully, *Studies of Childhood*, *Mind*, n.s. 5 (1896), 256–61 (260).

62. For a list of British child-care and child-study periodicals from this period see Gurjeva, 'Everyday Bourgeois Science', p. 243.

63. See Sally Shuttleworth, Gowan Dawson, and Richard Noakes, 'Women, Science and Culture: Science in the Nineteenth-Century Periodical', in *Women: A Cultural Review* 12 (2001), 57–70 (62–4).

64. 'Editorial Address', *Baby* 1 (1887), 13.

65. Francis Warner, 'How to Observe a Baby', *Baby* 1 (1887), 3–4. Warner went on to write a range of texts on child development, including *The Study of Children and their School Training* (1897), and *The Nervous System of the Child* (1900).

66. Editorial, *Baby* 2 (1888–9), 1. The offending article was probably Mona Caird, 'Marriage', *Westminster Review* 130 (1888), 186–201.

67. The emergence of scientific child study brought with it a whole new range of Latinate vocabulary to create an aura of greater dignity: Paediatric (1893–4); Paedology (the study of the nature of children 1894); Paedotrophy (the rearing of children). The OED cites Sully in *Harper's Magazine* (June 1889).

68. Jessica Waller, 'Mental and Physical Training of Children', *Nineteenth Century* 26 (1889), 659–67. Editorial Note, *Baby* 2 (1888–9), 266.

69. Editorial note, *Baby* 2 (1888–9), 267.

70. Sully, *Journal of Education*, (1897), 355, quoted in Elizabeth R. Valentine, 'The Founding of the Psychological Laboratory, University College London: 'Dear Galton . . . Yours truly, J. Sully', *History of Psychology* 2 (1999), 204–218 (210). For further details of Sully's role see Gurjeva, 'Everyday Bourgeois Science', ch. 5.

71. Similar anxieties regarding child research were recorded in the *Lancet* on 20 February 1897 in a report on the founding of a Manchester branch of the British Association of Child Study: 'To those who had read the delightful essays of Professor Sully it was not necessary to explain the object of the society. During

the last few months some of their candid friends had asked if they were going to experiment on newly-born babies – if they were going to put pepper on their tongues to try to find out at what exact period they appreciated these useful condiments. They were asked if they were going to repeat the experiments on the prehensile faculty of infants in order to demonstrate their affinities with our lower relations, and if it was intended to make the nursery a temple and the baby an idol' (533). This arch mode of reporting nonetheless conveys very well how deeply ingrained these iconic images of baby experimentation had become.

9. SCIENTIFIC BIOGRAPHY IN THE PERIODICAL PRESS

1. Cited in Laurel Brake, *Subjugated Knowledges. Journalism, Gender and Literature in the Nineteenth Century* (Basingstoke: Macmillan, 1994), p. 192.
2. *The Biographical Dictionary of the Society for the Diffusion of Useful Knowledge*, ed. by G. Long, 4 vols. (London: SDUK, 1842–4). These volumes covered only the range Aa to Az!
3. Richard Yeo, *Encyclopaedic Visions. Scientific Dictionaries and Enlightenment Culture* (Cambridge: Cambridge University Press, 2001).
4. Electronic version of the *Nineteenth Century Short Title Catalogue, series I and II*, produced by Avero Publications Ltd., Newcastle-upon-Tyne, 1996.
5. The raw calculation was 60,000, but this figure is inflated because a proportion of entries are listed twice in the 'biography' subject indexes – under both the author's and the subject's name. For example, John Whishaw, *Some Account of the Late Smithson Tennant* (London: Baldwin, 1815) is included twice – against the names of both Whishaw and Tennant. Also, many entries carry more than one *NSTC* subject classifier; hence, a specific book may be both a biography and a contribution to natural history. In order to correct for the latter overestimate I suggest that the lower figure of 50,000 biographies provides us with a better estimate of the genre's popularity. Among the many other issues raised by this statistical analysis is the inclusion of works that are not normally counted among biographies – for example, testimonials for scientists applying for university posts.
6. As indicated in the previous note many books are attributed with more than one subject classifier. Thus if we were to add all the percentage market shares for all subjects the total would be well in excess of 100 per cent.
7. Richard D. Altick, *Lives and Letters. A History of Literary Biography in England and America* (Westport, Conn.: Greenwood Press, 1965), p. 77.
8. Flier for *Literary Gazette* in the author's possession; *British Friend* 1 (1843), 1.
9. D. Brewster, *The Life of Sir Isaac Newton* (London: John Murray, 1831); D. Brewster, *Memoirs of the Life, Writings and Discoveries of Sir Isaac Newton*, 2 vols. (London: Constable, 1855). For Brewster's career see *Martyr of Science: Sir David Brewster 1781–1868*, ed. by A. D. Morrison-Low and J. R. R. Christie (Edinburgh: Royal Scottish Museum, 1984), esp. W. H. Brock, 'Brewster as a Scientific Journalist', pp. 37–42.

10. James Secord, *Victorian Sensation: The Extraordinary Publication, Reception, and Secret Authorship of 'Vestiges of the Natural History of Creation'* (Chicago: University of Chicago Press, 2000), pp. 49–51; Scott Bennett, 'John Murray's Family Library and the Cheapening of Books in Early Nineteenth Century Britain', *Studies in Bibliography* 29 (1978), 139–66.

11. Only one other edition appeared during the nineteenth century, an 1860 re-publication by Edmonton and Douglas of Edinburgh.

12. Anon., *British Quarterly Review* 22 (1855), 317–46; G. W. Abraham, *Dublin Review* 39 (1855), 273–90; Anon., *Dublin University Magazine* 46 (1855), 308–20; Baden Powell, *Edinburgh Review* 103 (1856), 499–534; Augustus de Morgan, *North British Review* 23 (1855), 261–4; Richard Simpson, *Rambler* 16 (1855), 199–207. Circulation figures obtained from the on-line version of John S. North, *Waterloo Directory of English Periodicals and Newspapers, 1800–1900.*

13. Reviewed by C. R. Weld in *Athenaeum*, 16 June 1855, 697–9.

14. Much of the discussion in this section is based on Altick, *Lives and Letters.*

15. Thomas Carlyle, *On Heroes, Hero-Worship, and the Heroic in History: Six Lectures Reported, with Emendations and Additions* (London: Chapman and Hall, 1840).

16. Samuel Smiles, *Self-Help: with Illustrations of Character and Conduct* (London: John Murray, 1859); *Duty: with Illustrations of Courage, Patience, and Endurance* (London: John Murray, 1880).

17. J. Munro, 'Character Sketch: August. Lord Kelvin, P. R. S.', *Review of Reviews* 8 (1893), 135–44; David N. Livingstone, 'Science, Region, and Religion: The Reception of Darwinism in Princeton, Belfast, and Edinburgh', in *Disseminating Darwinism: The Role of Place, Race, Religion and Gender*, ed. by Ronald L. Numbers and John Stenhouse (Cambridge: Cambridge University Press, 1999), pp. 387–408.

18. Gertrude M. Prescott, 'Faraday: Image of the Man and the Collector', in *Faraday Rediscovered. Essays on the Life and Work of Michael Faraday 1791–1867*, ed. by David C. Gooding and Frank A. J. L. James (London: Macmillan, 1985), pp. 15–32; Janet Browne, 'Darwin in Caricature: A Study in the Popularisation and Dissemination of Evolution', *Proceedings of the American Philosophical Society* 145 (2001), 496–509.

19. *Fraser's Magazine* 1 (1836), 224 and facing. A few months earlier Faraday had unintentionally fuelled *Fraser's* campaign against the Whigs by (allegedly) refusing a pension from the Prime Minister, Lord Melbourne.

20. *Academy: A Monthly Record of Literature, Learning, Science, and Art* 1 (1869–70), 45 and 207.

21. *Youth's Magazine; or, Evangelical Miscellany* 10 (1837), 207–12; *Friend* 2 (1844), 197–8.

22. *London Review of Politics, Society, Literature, Art, and Science* 15 (1867), 236–7.

23. *Gentleman's Magazine*, n.s. 4 (1867), 534–6.

24. Geoffrey Cantor, *Michael Faraday, Sandemanian and Scientist* (Basingstoke: Macmillan, 1991).

25. *Nonconformist* 27 (1867), 731.

26. *Leisure Hour* 17 (1868), 176; *London Review of Politics, Society, Literature, Art, and Science* 15 (1867), 236–7.

27. *English Independent* 1 (1867), 1151–2, quoting *Daily News*. For later utilitarian accounts see Geoffrey Cantor, 'The Scientist as Hero: Public Images of Michael Faraday', in *Telling Lives in Science: Essays on Scientific Biography*, ed. by Michael Shortland and Richard Yeo (Cambridge: Cambridge University Press, 1996), pp. 171–93.

28. *Gentleman's Magazine*, n.s. 4 (1867), 534–6; *Engineer* 24 (1867), 182. Faraday had been cited by Smiles as a paradigm example of self-help: Smiles, *Self-Help*, p. 12.

29. J. Scoffern, 'Michael Faraday', *Belgravia* 3 (1867), 421–8; *British Quarterly Review* 47 (1868), 434–74. Simon Schaffer, 'Genius in Romantic Natural Philosophy', in *Romanticism and the Sciences*, ed. by Andrew Cunningham and Nicholas Jardine (Cambridge: Cambridge University Press, 1990), pp. 82–98.

30. On Faraday's role in creating his own public image see several of the papers in Gooding and James, *Faraday Rediscovered*.

31. Scoffern, 'Michael Faraday'; Benjamin Abbott, 'The late Professor Faraday', *Friends' Quarterly Examiner* 2 (1868), 122–8.

32. [William Frederick Pollock], 'Faraday', *Fraser's Magazine* 1 (1870), 326–42 on 326.

33. John Tyndall, *Faraday as a Discoverer* (London: Longmans, Green, 1868). On Tyndall's commitments to Romanticism see Ruth Barton, 'John Tyndall, Pantheist. A Rereading of the Belfast Address', *Osiris* 3 (1987), 111–34.

34. Cantor, *Michael Faraday*, pp. 83–5.

35. *London Review of Politics, Society, Literature, Art, and Science* 16 (1868), 289–90.

36. 'Tyndall on Faraday', *Eclectic and Congregational Review* 14 (1868), 389–410. See also 'Faraday as a Discoverer', *Saturday Review* 25 (1868), 619–21.

37. Henry Bence Jones, *The Life and Letters of Faraday*, 2 vols. (London: Longmans, Green, 1869). A second edition appeared in 1870.

38. 'Faraday, his Life, his Letters', *Journal of Science* 7 (1870), 232–7.

39. *Student and Intellectual Observer* 4 (1870), 436–45.

40. 'T.', 'Plain Living and High Thinking. Michael Faraday', *Victoria Magazine* 14 (1869), 331–8.

41. Juliet Pollock, 'Michael Faraday', *St. Paul's; a Monthly Magazine* 6 (1870), 293–303.

42. The copy in Leeds University Library contains a manuscript note by Charles Thomas Whitmell who suggests an alternative epithet: 'The Newton of the Nineteenth Century'.

43. Munro, 'Character Sketch', *passim*.

44. *Youth's Magazine; or, Evangelical Miscellany* 3rd ser. 1 (1828), 29–30; 3 (1830), 245–6; 4 (1831), 239–40. For a broader discussion see chapter 2, above.

45. 'Memoir of Mr. George Newton, of Thorncliffe, near Sheffield', *Wesleyan-Methodist Magazine*, 3rd ser. 5 (1826), 725–34.

46. *Let Newton Be!*, ed. by John Fauvel, Raymond Flood, Michael Shortland, and Robin Wilson (Oxford: Oxford University Press, 1988); Patricia Fara, *Newton: The Making of Genius* (London: Macmillan, 2002).
47. *Punch* 3 (1842), 229.
48. 'Astronomical Observations for January', *Mirror of Literature* 9 (1827), 3–4.
49. 'Science and the Pope', *Punch* 24 (1853), 80. See also 'The Ultramontane Crab', 27 (1854), 132; 'Guy Fawkes' Day in Vienna', 29 (1855), 218–19; 'The Pope's Syllabus', 57 (1869), 161; 'Rome's Ups and Downs (as Sung before a Select Committee of the Œcumenical Council)', 58 (1870), 20.
50. 'Law of Libel. – Letter V', *Black Dwarf* 1 (1817), 427–30. Galileo was only placed under house arrest.
51. Ludmilla Jordanova, *Defining Features. Scientific and Medical Portraits 1660–2000* (London: National Portrait Gallery and Reaktion Books, 1988), pp. 26–9.
52. See, for example, the character sketch of Lord Kelvin cited in Munro, 'Character Sketch'.
53. Alvar Ellegård, *Darwin and the General Reader. The Reception of Darwin's Theory of Evolution in the British Periodical Press, 1859–1872* (Gothenburg: University of Gothenburg, 1958; revised edn Chicago: Chicago University Press, 1990).
54. See several of the essays in *Telling Lives in Science*.
55. Review of S. P. Thompson, *Michael Faraday: His Life and Work* in *Knowledge* 24 (1901), 110.

10. PROFIT AND PROPHECY: ELECTRICITY IN THE LATE-VICTORIAN PERIODICAL

1. [W. T. Stead], 'Looking Forward: A Romance of the Electrical Age', *Review of Reviews* [hereafter *RR*] 1 (1890), 230–41, (230).
2. Edward Bellamy, *Looking Backward, 2000–1887 Or, Life in the Year 2000 A.D.* (Boston: Ticknor, 1888; London: Ward, Lock, & Co., 1888).
3. For literary responses to the steam engine see Wolfgang Schivelbusch *The Railway Journey: The Industrialization of Time and Space in the 19th Century* (Leamington Spa: Berg, 1986). For *Punch*'s satirical comment on railways and telegraphs see Richard Noakes, 'The Rage for "Portable" This, That, and Everything': Representing Technology in *Punch* 1841–61', in Louise Henson *et al.* (eds.), *Culture and Science in the Nineteenth Century Media* (Aldershot: Ashgate, 2004), pp. 151–63.
4. Ismar Thiusen [Pseud. John Macnie], *The Diothas, Or, A Far Look Ahead* (New York: Putnam, 1883). The second edition was published as Ismar Thiusen [pseud. John Macnie], *Looking Forward or The Diothas* (New York/London: Putnam, 1890), the quote is from p. iii. Without mentioning *Looking Backward* or its author by name, Macnie's preface to the second edition hints at possible plagiarism by Bellamy, while emphasizing the absence of 'socialistic doctrines' or 'new social gospel' in *Looking Forward*. 'Ismar Thiusen' is the name given to the novel's narrator by his 96-century interlocutors, his nineteenth-century name being left unspecified. For more

general discussion of science and technology in the history of US utopianism see Howard Segal, *Technological Utopianism in American Culture* (Chicago: Chicago University Press, 1985), and John Carey and John J. Quirk, 'The Mythos of the Electronic Revolution', *American Scholar*, 39 (1970), 219–41 and 395–424.

5. Peter Broks, *Media Science Before the Great War* (London: Macmillan, 1996), pp. 98–110, 155–8.

6. Wells's student piece 'The Chronic Argonauts' was published in the *Science School Journal* (of which he was editor) in spring 1887. Some themes from this were presented to the *Fortnightly Review* in 1891 as 'The Universe Rigid' but forcefully rejected by editor Frank Harris – see Herbert George Wells, *Experiment in Autobiography: Discoveries and Conclusions of a Very Ordinary Brain (since 1866)*, 2 vols. (London: Victor Gollancz/The Cresset Press, 1934), vol. 1, pp. 214–15, 356–9). Parts of the 'Argonauts' appeared in Wells's miscellaneous writings for the *Pall Mall Gazette*. With considerable editorial assistance from W. E. Henley the piece was recast and was published serially by *The New Review* in 1895, the monograph version being published as Herbert G. Wells, *The Time Machine: An Invention* (London: Heinemann, 1895). For biographical information see David Smith, *H. G. Wells: A Biography* (Yale: Yale University Press, 1986), pp. 46–86, 501. 'The Lord of the Dynamos', a bloody and anti-imperialist fable, is Wells's only electricity-related short story. See H. G. Wells, 'Lord of the Dynamos', *Pall Mall Budget*, September 6, 1894, reproduced in H. G. Wells, *Complete Short Stories* (London: Ernest Benn, 1927), pp. 284–93. For Wells's destructive student encounter with experimental physics see *Experiment in Autobiography*, vol. 1, pp. 206–18.

7. For details of the *Review of Reviews* and other contemporary periodicals discussed in this chapter, see Joanne Shattock, *Politics and Reviewers: The 'Edinburgh' and the 'Quarterly' in the Early Victorian Age* (Leicester: Leicester University Press, 1989), pp. 12 and 99; Alvin Sullivan, ed., *British Literary Magazines*, 4 vols. (Westport, Conn.: Greenwood Press, 1983–6).

8. For the continuing interest in biography see Geoffrey Cantor's discussion in ch. 9.

9. As a wealthy landed aristocrat, the Eton-educated William Coutts Keppel, Viscount Bury (1832–94), was able to make substantial investments in electrical industry in the 1880s and early 1890s. His previous career had been in military service, colonial duties in India and Canada, and parliamentary work as a Liberal (1856) then Conservative (1876). With a record of writing upon army and imperial duties in monographs and for *Fraser's Magazine*, Keppel's reputation in military matters was such that Disraeli appointed him Under-Secretary for War in 1878. For biographical details on Bury see 'Keppel, William Coutts' in *DNB*, and obituary in *The Times*, 29 August 1894, 8f, which reported that he 'took a great interest in the problems of electricity'.

10. At a time when controversial homeopathic remedies were widely discussed in the periodical press (especially the *Review of Reviews*), Edith Faithfull told readers of the *Contemporary Review* that electrical therapy had reliably cured

her of cancer. Edith Faithfull, 'The Electrical Cure of Cancer', *Contemporary Review* 61 (1892), 408–21.

11. For the alternative view that periodical readerships respond passively to the authoritative writing of electrical experts see Carolyn Marvin, *When Old Technologies Were New: Thinking about Communications in the Late Nineteenth Century* (Oxford: Oxford University Press, 1988).

12. 'The Science of Electricity as Applied in Peace and War', *Quarterly Review* 144 (1877), 138–79 (144).

13. Dawson, this book, ch. 5. Notwithstanding its name, the *Fortnightly* became a monthly publication from 1866.

14. For identification of some key professional scientists writing for monthlies, see introduction to this book. For the development of signed publications in the monthlies see Shattock, *Politics and Reviewers*, 15–18, and Catherine Judd, 'Male Pseudonyms and Female authority in Victorian England' in John Jordan and Robert Patten (eds.), *Literature in the Marketplace: Nineteenth Century Publishing and Reading Practices* (Cambridge: Cambridge University Press, 1995), pp. 250–68. While the threepenny weekly *Punch* long continued its playful editorial ventriloquism of 'Mr Punch', William Stead adopted a new form of 'mononymous' editorial ubiquity in the sixpenny monthly *Review of Reviews*. See Dawson, this book, ch. 7.

15. William Coutts Keppel's *Quarterly Review* (hereafter *QR*) articles are 'Modern Methods in Navigation and Nautical Astronomy', *QR* 141 (1876), 137–70; 'Sir William and Caroline Herschel', *QR* 141 (1876), 323–52; 'Modern Philosophers on the Probable Age of the World', *QR* 142 (1876), 202–32; 'Geographical and Scientific Results of the Arctic Expedition', *QR* 143 (1877), 146–86; 'The Science of Electricity as Applied in Peace and War', *QR* 144 (1877), 138–79; 'The Aggression of Russia and the Duty, of Great Britain', *QR* 145 (1878), 534–70; 'Recent and Future Arctic voyages', *QR* 150 (1880), 111–40.

16. Shattock, *Politics and Reviewers*, pp. 104–24.

17. Ibid., p. 110.

18. 'The Science of Electricity', 143–4.

19. The title refers to Richard Culley, *Handbook of Practical Telegraphy* (London: Longmans, Green, Reader, & Dyer, no year or edition specified. 1st edn 1863, most recent edition the 6th of 1874), and H[einrich] Schellen, *Der Elektromagnetische Telegraph* (Braunschweig: n.p., 5th edn, 1870), but no explicit evidence is given of their use in preparing the *Quarterly* text.

20. 'The Science of Electricity', 145–55.

21. Ibid, 145. Readers were frequently reminded of what they should and should not be able to judge, e.g. 'the reader will now, we hope, follow us when we speak of the resistance of a wire, a battery, or an electric circuit of any kind' (152); 'Our readers are probably acquainted with the principle on which the signalling apparatus on land (telegraph) lines is constructed' (163); 'Those who have done us the favour of reading the earlier part of the paper will understand what is meant by the resistance of a given circuit' (167).

22. Viscount Bury, 'Electric Light and Force', *Nineteenth Century* 12 (1882), 98–119.

23. 'The Science of Electricity', 138.
24. Daniel Rutenberg, 'Nineteenth Century', in Sullivan (ed.), *British Literary Magazines*, vol. III, pp. 268 and 270.
25. Viscount Bury, 'Electric Light and Force', *Nineteenth Century* 12 (1882), 98–119 (98–9).
26. Ibid., 103 and 105–6.
27. Albemarle, 'Electrical Transmission of Power', *Nineteenth Century* 31(1892), 73–89 (85). He referred to 1882 as 'the unlucky year' in which costly failure and 'bitter disappointment' had been the norm. Keppel had not only been elevated to become Seventh Duke of Albemarle (February 1891), but he was also Chairman of the General Electric Power and Traction Company that for two years had produced and operated electric launches on the Thames (see *The Times* obituary cited above).
28. 'Parliamentary Blue Book – "Lighting by Electricity", Aug. 13, 1879. Exposition Internationale d'Electricité, Paris. Catalogue Général Officiel, Aug. 11, 1881', *QR* 153 (1881), 441–61 (459). The title 'The Development of Electric Lighting' is used in page headings from 442.
29. Ibid., 444.
30. Gordon later wrote: 'less than two years ago, I wrote an article in the *Quarterly Review* in which, if I recollect rightly, I said that if dynamos of the future "will, we believe, rotate much more rapidly than at present; their speed will only be limited by their tendency to fly to pieces". Then my friends and I set to work to build a dynamo on the principle I had laid down in the *Quarterly Review* article . . .' Quoted in J. E. H. Gordon 'The Development of Electric Lighting', *Journal of the Society of Arts* 31 (1882–3), 778–87 (780). The actual text from the *Quarterly* somewhat misquoted here was: 'We believe [the speed of revolution] should only be limited by the strength of the wheel to resist the centrifugal force tending to make it fly to pieces. It is probable that the machines of the immediate future will be made much stronger and will revolve many times faster than any at present time.' 'The Development of Electric Lighting', 444.
31. James Gordon, 'The Latest Electrical Discovery', *Nineteenth Century* 31 (1892), 399–402 (402).
32. William Stead, 'The Miracles of Electricity', *RR* 1 (1890), 33–4 (33). The quotation should refer to Park Benjamin (1849–1922), a New York patent lawyer, editor, and historian of electricity who wrote numerous essays in the *Forum*, *Independent*, and other periodicals. See *Who was Who in America* (Chicago: Marquis, 1943), vol. 1, p. 83.
33. [William Stead] 'Electricity in the Household', *RR* 1 (1890), 34.
34. 'Yet Another Utopia, by M Charles Secrétan', *RR* 1 (1890), 46. 'The Author of "Looking Backward": An Interview with Edward Bellamy', *RR* 1 (1890), 47.
35. 'The Genius of this Electric Age: Mr Edison and his Ideas', *RR* 1 (1890), 120.
36. 'The Future and What Hides in It – A Scientific Prophecy by Professor Thurston', *RR* 1 (1890), 115–16.
37. Ibid.

38. [W. T. Stead], 'Looking Forward: A Romance of the Electrical Age', *RR* 1 (1890), 230–41 (230).

39. Ibid.

40. 'It will be seen that the author is not deeply imbued with the communistic ideas so attractive to many. To become the well-fed slaves of an irresistible despotism with its hierarchy of walking delegates, seems hardly the loftiest conceivable destiny for the human race.' *Looking Forward*, p. iv.

41. Ibid.

42. 'Science and Conjecture', *Spectator* 67 (1891), 723–4. (723) See below, pp. 552–3, for further discussion.

43. Colonel W. W. Knollys, 'War in the Future', *Fortnightly Review* (hereafter *FR*) n.s. 48 (1890), 274–81; Theodore Watts, 'The Future of American Literature', *FR* 49 (1891), 910–26; Oswald Crawfurd, 'The Future of Portugal', *FR* 50 (1891), 149–62; Wordsworth Donisthorpe, 'The Future of Marriage' *FR* 51 (1892), 258–70; Susan Malmesbury, 'A Reply to "The Future of Marriage"', ibid., 272–81; Sir Robert Ball, 'How Long can the Earth Sustain Life?', *FR* 51 (1892), 478–90; The Duke of Marlborough, 'A Future School of Art', *FR* 52 (1892), 595–606; Revd Dr Momerie, 'Religion: Its Future', *FR* 52 (1892), 834–50.

44. John G. McKendrick, 'Human Electricity', *FR* 51 (1892), 634–51, followed up by John G. McKendrick, 'Electric Fishes', *FR* 54 (1893), 539–50. Compare with the similarly didactic mode of fellow Glaswegian professor Lord Kelvin, 'On the Dissipation of Energy', *FR* 51 (1892), 313–21.

45. Alice M. Gordon, 'The Development of Decorative Electricity', *FR* 49 (1891), 278–84; Graeme Gooday, '"I never will have the electric light in my house": Alice Gordon and the gendered Periodical Representation of a Contentious New Technology', in Henson *et al.*, *Culture and Science*, 173–85.

46. Stead, 'The Reviews Reviewed: The Fortnightly Review', *RR* 3 (1891), 165. For similar criticisms see 'Domestic Electric Light', *Saturday Review* 71 (1891), 453, discussed in Gooday, '"I never will have the electric light in my house"'.

47. William Crookes, 'Electricity in Transit: From Plenum to Vacuum', *Electrician* 26 (1891) 323–7, 354–60, 389–2 (323 and 356). Towards the end of his lecture Crookes deliberately distanced himself from his controversial research relating to spiritualism two decades earlier: 'Science has emerged from its childish days. It has shed many delusions and impostures. It has discarded magic, alchemy and astrology. And certain pseudo-applications of electricity, with which this institution is little concerned, in their turn will pass into oblivion' (392).

48. Speech reported in 'Dinner of the Institution of Electrical Engineers', *Electrician* 28 (1891), 70–2 (70). In replying to comments by Sir George Gabriel Stokes, Crookes briefly explored some unsolved questions about the possible use of electricity in agriculture, curing disease, sterilizing water, and treating sewage. He concluded 'These are problems that may safely be left to the devices and inspiration of our electrical engineers . . . What is really in store in the way of future wonders is folded in "shady leaves of Destiny"' (71–2). Compare with the conclusion of Crookes's 'Some Possibilities of Electricity' discussed

below. The quotation is a reference to a poem by Richard Crashaw (1612?–49), 'Wishes to his Supposed Mistress'. William B. Turnbull (ed.), *The Complete Works of Richard Crashaw* (London: John Russell Smith, 1858), pp. 133–8 (133).

49. 'Science and Conjecture', 723–4.

50. William Crookes, 'Some Possibilities of Electricity', *FR* 51 (1892), 173–81 (175–6). For the relation of this piece to Marconi's wireless telegraphy of 1896 see Sungook Hong, *Wireless: From Marconi's Black Box to the Audion* (Cambridge, Mass. and London: MIT Press, 2001), 22.

51. Crookes, 'Some Possibilities of Electricity', 178–81.

52. Stead, 'The Reviews Reviewed', 182.

53. Carolyn Marvin suggests that 'Some Possibilities' instantiates a wider trend of expert literary endeavour of using the 'raw material' of scientific discovery to mix fantasy and reality in 'equal proportions of the familiar and novel' see *When Old Technologies Were New*, p. 156.

54. 'Notes', *Electrician* 28 (1892), 341–2.

55. The best scholarly study of Wells's futurist writing is Patrick Parrinder, *Shadows of the Future: H. G. Wells, Science Fiction and Prophecy* (Liverpool: Liverpool University Press, 1995).

56. In the August 1890 Stead commented on Revd S. J. Vaughan's account for the *Dublin Review* showing how to calculate the date of the final apocalypse, 'The Final Destiny of the Earth: A Curious Speculation', *RR* 2 (1890), 160. The following April, Stead abstracted from the *Contemporary Review* an account that showed how electrical technologies would bring but temporary respite from the Earth's predicted heat death in 2,200,000 AD: 'The Last Days of the Earth by M. Camille Flammarion', *RR* 3 (1891), 370. The constraints of space do not permit a more detailed discussion of this topic here.

Select bibliography

PRIMARY BIBLIOGRAPHIES AND FINDING GUIDES

Bolton, Henry Carrington, *A Catalogue of Scientific and Technical Periodicals, 1665–1895, Together with Chronological Tables and a Library Check-List*, 2nd edn (Washington: Smithsonian Institution, 1897).

Doughan, David and Denise Sanchez, *Feminist Periodicals, 1855–1984: An Annotated Critical Bibliography of British, Irish, Commonwealth and International Titles* (Brighton: Harvester, 1987).

Harrison, Royden, Gillian B. Woolven, and Robert Duncan, *Warwick Guide to British Labour Periodicals, 1790–1970: A Check List* (Hassocks: Harvester Press, 1977).

Lefanu, William R., *British Periodicals of Medicine: A Chronological List 1640–1899*, revised edn, ed. by Jean Loudon (Oxford: Wellcome Unit for the History of Medicine, 1984).

North, John S., ed., *The Waterloo Directory of Irish Newspapers and Periodicals, 1800–1900* (Waterloo, Ontario: North Waterloo Academic Press, 1986).

The Waterloo Directory of Scottish Newspapers and Periodicals, 1800–1900, 2 vols. (Waterloo, Ontario: North Waterloo Academic Press, 1989).

The Waterloo Directory of English Newspapers and Periodicals, 1800–1900, 50 vols. (Waterloo, Ontario: North Waterloo Academic Press, 1994–).

Scudder, Samuel H., *Catalogue of Scientific Serials of all Countries Including the Transactions of Learned Societies in the Natural, Physical and Mathematical Sciences, 1633–1876*, reprint (New York: Kraus Reprint Corp., 1965 [1879]).

Shattock, Joanne, ed., *The Cambridge Bibliography of English Literature*, Vol. IV, *1800–1900*, 3rd edn (Cambridge and New York: Cambridge University Press, 1999).

Stewart, James D., ed., *British Union Catalogue of Periodicals: A Record of the Periodicals of the World from the Seventeenth Century to the Present Day, in British Libraries*, 4 vols. (London: Butterworths Scientific Publications, 1955).

The Times Tercentenary Handlist of English and Welsh Newspapers, Magazines and Reviews (London: The Times, 1920).

Ward, William S., *Index and Finding List of Serials Published in the British Isles, 1789–1832* (Lexington: University of Kentucky Press, 1953).

Wolff, Michael, John S. North, and Dorothy Deering, *The Waterloo Directory of Victorian Periodicals 1824–1900*, Phase I (Waterloo, Ontario: University of Waterloo, [1970]).

Wiener, Joel H., *A Descriptive Finding List of Unstamped British Periodicals, 1830–1836* (London: The Bibliographical Society, 1970).

SECONDARY BIBLIOGRAPHIES AND GENERAL WORKS

Griffiths, Dennis, ed., *The Encyclopedia of the British Press, 1422–1992* (New York: St Martin's Press, 1992).

Madden, Lionel, *The Nineteenth-Century Periodical Press in Britain: A Bibliography of Modern Studies 1901–1971* (New York and London: Garland, 1976).

Sullivan, Alvin, ed., *British Literary Magazines*, 4 vols. (Westport, Conn.: Greenwood Press, 1983–6).

Uffelman, Larry K., *The Nineteenth-Century Periodical Press in Britain: A Bibliography of Modern Studies, 1972–1987* (Edwardsville: Southern Illinois University at Edwardsville for the Research Society for Victorian Periodicals, 1992).

Vann, J. Don and Rosemary T. VanArsdel, eds., *Victorian Periodicals: A Guide to Research*, 2 vols. (New York: Modern Language Association of America, 1978–89).

eds., *Victorian Periodicals and Victorian Society* (Aldershot: Scolar, 1994).

Ward, William S., *British Periodicals and Newspapers, 1789–1932: A Bibliography of Secondary Sources* (Lexington: University Press of Kentucky, [1973]).

INDEXES TO PERIODICALS AND BOOK REVIEWS

Cantor, Geoffrey, Gowan Dawson, Richard Noakes, Sally Shuttleworth, and Jonathan R. Topham, 'Science in the Nineteenth-Century Periodical: An Electronic Index' (Forthcoming, Hri Online, University of Sheffield, 2004), see <http://www.sciper.leeds.ac.uk>

Cushing, Henry Grant and Adah V. Morris, eds., *Nineteenth Century Readers' Guide to Periodical Literature, 1800–1899, with Supplementary Listing 1900–1922*, 2 vols. (New York: H. W. Wilson Company, 1944).

Dameron, J. Lasley and Pamela Palmer, *An Index to the Critical Vocabulary of 'Blackwood's Edinburgh Magazine', 1830–1840* (West Cornwall, Conn.: Locust Hill Press, 1990).

Garside, Peter and Rainer Schöwerling, *The English Novel, 1770–1829: A Bibliographical Survey of Prose Fiction Published in the British Isles*, vol. II, *1800–1829* (Oxford: Oxford University Press, 2000).

Houghton, Walter E., *et al.*, eds., *The Wellesley Index to Victorian Periodicals, 1825–1900*, 5 vols. (Toronto: University of Toronto Press, 1966–89).

Lohrli, Anne, *'Household Words': A Weekly Journal 1850–1859, Conducted by Charles Dickens: Table of Contents, List of Contributors and their Contributions based on the Household Words Office Book in the Morris L. Parrish Collection of Victorian*

Novelists, Princeton University Library (Toronto: University of Toronto Press, 1973).

Oppenlander, Ella Ann, *Dickens' 'All the Year Round': Descriptive Index and Contributor List* (Troy, N.Y.: Whitston Pub. Co., 1984).

Palmegiano, Eugenia, *Women and British Periodicals, 1832–1876* (New York: Garland, 1976).

   The British Empire in the Victorian Press, 1832–1867: A Bibliography (New York: Garland, 1987).

   Crime in Victorian Britain: An Annotated Bibliography from Nineteenth-Century British Magazines (Westport, Conn. and London: Greenwood Press, 1993).

   Health and British Magazines in the Nineteenth Century (Lanham, Md. and London: Scarecrow Press, 1998).

Poole, William Frederick, *Poole's Index to Periodical Literature, 1802–1906*, rev. edn, 6 vols. (Gloucester, Mass.: Smith, 1963).

Richardson, Ruth, *The Builder: Illustrations Index, 1843–1883* (Gomshall: Builder Group and Hutton & Rostron, 1994).

Royal Society of London, *Catalogue of Scientific Papers*, 19 vols. (London: Clay, 1867–1925).

Ward, William S., *Literary Reviews in British Periodicals, 1798–1820: A Bibliography with a Supplementary List of General (Non-Review) Articles on Literary Subjects* (New York: Garland, 1972).

   Literary Reviews in British Periodicals, 1821–1826: A Bibliography, with a Supplementary List of General (Non-Review) Articles on Literary Subjects (New York and London: Garland, 1977).

PERIODICALS IN NINETEENTH-CENTURY BRITAIN

Adburgham, Alison, *Women in Print: Writing Women and Women's Magazines from the Restoration to the Accession of Victoria* (London: Allen & Unwin, 1972).

Altholz, Josef L., *The Religious Press in Britain, 1760–1900* (New York: Greenwood Press).

Altick, Richard D., *The English Common Reader: A Social History of the Mass Reading Public, 1800–1900* (Chicago: University of Chicago Press, 1957; 2nd edn Columbus: Ohio State University Press, 1998).

   The Presence of the Present: Topics of the Day in the Victorian Novel (Columbus: Ohio State University Press, 1991).

   Punch: The Lively Youth of a British Institution, 1841–1851 (Columbus: Ohio State University Press, 1997).

Anderson, Patricia J., *The Printed Image and the Transformation of Popular Culture 1790–1860* (Oxford: Clarendon Press, 1991).

Anderson, Patricia J. and Jonathan Rose, eds., *British Literary Publishing Houses, 1820–1880*, Dictionary of Literary Biography, 106 (Detroit: Gale Research, 1991).

Baylen, J. O., 'The "New Journalism" in Late Victorian Britain', *Australian Journal of Politics and History* 18 (1972), 367–85.

'W. T. Stead as Publisher and Editor of the *Review of Reviews*', *Victorian Periodicals Review* 12 (1979), 70–84.

Beetham, Margaret, 'Towards a Theory of the Periodical as a Publishing Genre', in *Investigating Victorian Journalism*, ed. by Laurel Brake, Aled Jones, and Lionel Madden (Basingstoke: Macmillan, 1990), pp. 19–32.

A Magazine of Her Own? Domesticity and Desire in the Woman's Magazine, 1800–1914 (London: Routledge, 1996).

Billington, Louis, 'The Religious Periodical and Newspaper Press, 1770–1870', in *The Press in English Society from the Seventeenth to the Nineteenth Century*, ed. by Michael Harris and Alan Lee (London: Associated Universities Press, 1986), pp. 113–32 and 231–9.

Boyce, George, James Curran, and Pauline Wingate, eds., *Newspaper History from the Seventeenth Century to the Present Day* (London: Constable, for the Press Group of the Acton Society, 1978).

Brake, Laurel, *Subjugated Knowledges: Journalism, Gender and Literature in the Nineteenth Century* (Basingstoke: Macmillan, 1994).

'Writing, Cultural Production and the Periodical Press in the Nineteenth Century', in *Writing and Victorianism*, ed. by J. B. Bullen (London: Longman, 1997), pp. 54–72.

Print in Transition, 1850–1910: Studies in Media and Book History (Basingstoke: Palgrave, 2001).

Brake, Laurel, Aled Jones, and Lionel Madden, eds., *Investigating Victorian Journalism* (Basingstoke: Macmillan, 1990).

Brake, Laurel, Bill Bell, and David Finkelstein, eds., *Nineteenth-Century Media and the Construction of Identity* (Basingstoke: Palgrave, 2000).

Brown, Allan Willard, *The Metaphysical Society: Victorian Minds in Crisis, 1869–1880* (New York: Columbia University Press, 1947).

Brown, Lucy, *Victorian News and Newspapers* (Oxford: Clarendon Press, 1985).

Butler, Marilyn, 'Culture's Medium: The Role of the Review', in *The Cambridge Companion to British Romanticism*, ed. by Stuart Curran (Cambridge: Cambridge University Press, 1993), pp. 120–47.

Campbell, Kate, ed., *Journalism, Literature and Modernity: From Hazlitt to Modernism* (Edinburgh: Edinburgh University Press, 2000).

Clive, John, *Scotch Reviewers: The 'Edinburgh Review', 1802–1815* (London: Faber, 1957).

Collins, A. S., *The Profession of Letters: A Study of the Relation of Author to Patron, Publisher and Public, 1780–1832* (London: George Routledge & Sons, 1928).

Cox, Jack, *Take a Cold Tub Sir! The Story of the 'Boy's Own Paper'* (Guildford: The Lutterworth Press, 1982).

Cross, Nigel, *The Common Writer: Life in Nineteenth Century Grub Street* (Cambridge: Cambridge University Press, 1985).

Demoor, Marysa, *Their Fair Share: Women, Power, and Criticism in the 'Athenaeum', from Millicent Garratt Fawcett to Katharine Mansfield, 1870–1920* (Aldershot: Ashgate, 2000).

Dixon, Diana, 'Children and the Press, 1866–1914', in *The Press in English Society from the Seventeenth to Nineteenth Centuries*, ed. by Michael Harris and Alan Lee (Rutherford: Fairleigh Dickinson Press, 1986), pp. 133–48.

Drotner, Kirsten, *English Children and their Magazines, 1751–1945* (New Haven and London: Yale University Press, 1988).

Dudek, Louis, *Literature and the Press: A History of Printing, Printed Media, and Their Relation to Literature* (Toronto: Ryerson, 1960).

Eagleton, Terry, *The Function of Criticism: From 'The Spectator' to Post-Structuralism*, Rpt. (London and New York: Verso, 1996).

Eliot, Simon, *Some Patterns and Trends in British Publishing, 1800–1919* (London: Bibliographical Society, 1994).

'Patterns and Trends and the *NSTC*: Some Initial Observations', *Publishing History* 42 (1997), 79–104; 43 (1998), 71–112.

Ellegård, Alvar, 'The Readership of the Periodical Press in Mid-Victorian Britain', *Göteborgs Universitets Årsskrift* 63 (1957), 1–41.

Erickson, Lee, *The Economy of Literary Form: English Literature and the Industrialization of Publishing, 1800–1850* (Baltimore and London: Johns Hopkins University Press, 1996).

Everett, Edwin Mallard, *The Party of Humanity: The 'Fortnightly Review' and Its Contributors 1865–1874* (Chapel Hill: University of North Carolina Press, 1939).

Feather, John, *A History of British Publishing* (London and New York: Routledge, 1988).

Finkelstein, David, *The House of Blackwood: Author–Publisher Relations in the Victorian Era* (University Park, Pa.: Penn State University Press, 2002).

Flint, Kate, *The Woman Reader, 1837–1914* (Oxford: Clarendon Press, 1993).

Fontana, Biancamaria, *Rethinking the Politics of Commercial Society: The 'Edinburgh Review' 1802–1832* (Cambridge: Cambridge University Press, 1985).

Forrester, Wendy, *Great-Grandmama's Weekly: A Celebration of the 'Girl's Own Paper' 1880–1901* (Guildford: The Lutterworth Press, 1980).

Fox, Celina, *Graphic Journalism in England During the 1830s and 1840s* (New York and London: Garland, 1988).

Gilmartin, Kevin, *Print Politics: The Press and Radical Opposition in Early Nineteenth-Century England* (Cambridge: Cambridge University Press, 1996).

Graham, Walter, *Tory Criticism in the 'Quarterly Review', 1809–53* (New York: Colombia University Press, 1921).

English Literary Periodicals (New York: Thomas Nelson & Sons, 1930).

Gross, John, *The Rise and Fall of the Man of Letters: Aspects of Literary Life Since 1800* (London: Weidenfeld and Nicolson, 1969).

Harris, Michael, 'Periodicals and the Book Trade', in *Development of the English Book Trade, 1700–1899*, ed. by Robin Myers and Michael Harris (Oxford: Oxford Polytechnic Press, 1981), pp. 66–94.

Hayden, John O., *The Romantic Reviewers, 1802–1824* (London: Routledge and Kegan Paul, 1969).

Hollis, Patricia, *The Pauper Press: A Study in Working-Class Radicalism of the 1830s* (London: Oxford University Press, 1970).

Houghton, Walter E., 'Periodical Literature and the Articulate Classes', in *The Victorian Periodical Press: Samplings and Soundings*, ed. by Joanne Shattock and Michael Wolff (Leicester: Leicester University Press, 1982), pp. 3–27.

Hughes, Linda K. and Michael Lund, *The Victorian Serial* (Charlottesville: University Press of Virginia, 1991).

Jackson, Kate, *George Newnes and the New Journalism in Britain, 1880–1910* (Aldershot: Ashgate, 2001).

Jackson, Mason, *The Pictorial Press: Its Origin and Progress* (London: Hurst and Blackett, 1885).

Jordan, John O. and Robert L. Patten, eds., *Literature in the Marketplace: Nineteenth-Century British Publishing and Reading Practices* (Cambridge: Cambridge University Press, 1995).

Klancher, Jon P., *The Making of English Reading Audiences, 1790–1832* (Madison: University of Wisconsin Press, 1987).

Lee, Alan J., *The Origins of the Popular Press in England 1855–1914* (London: Croom Helm, 1976).

Maidment, Brian, *Into the 1830s: Some Origins of Victorian Illustrated Journalism. Cheap Octavo Magazines of the 1820s and their Influence* (Manchester: Manchester Polytechnic Library, 1992).

Marchand, Leslie A., *The 'Athenaeum': A Mirror of Victorian Culture* (Chapel Hill, N.C.: University of North Carolina Press, 1941).

Metcalf, Priscilla, *James Knowles: Victorian Editor and Architect* (Oxford: Clarendon Press, 1980).

Mineka, Francis E., *The Dissidence of Dissent: The 'Monthly Repository' 1806–1838* (Chapel Hill, N.C.: University of North Carolina Press, 1944).

Murphy, Paul Thomas, *Towards a Working-Class Canon: Literary Criticism in British Working-Class Periodicals, 1816–1858* (Columbus: Ohio State University Press, 1994).

Nesbitt, G. L., *Benthamite Reviewing: The First Twelve Years of the 'Westminster Review', 1824–1836* (New York: Columbia University Press, 1934).

Onslow, Barbara, *Women of the Press in Nineteenth-Century Britain* (Basingstoke: Macmillan, 2000).

Parker, Mark, *Literary Magazines and British Romanticism* (Cambridge: Cambridge University Press, 2000).

Parry, Ann, 'The Grove Years 1868–1883: A "New Look" for *Macmillan's Magazine*?', *Victorian Periodicals Review* 19 (1986), 149–57.

'The Intellectuals and the Middle Class Periodical Press: Theory, Method and Case Study', *Journal of Newspaper and Periodical History* 4 (1988), 18–32.

Pearson, Jacqueline, *Women's Reading in Britain 1750–1835: A Dangerous Recreation* (Cambridge: Cambridge University Press, 1999).

Pearson, Richard, *W. M. Thackeray and the Mediated Text: Writing for Periodicals in the Mid-Nineteenth Century* (Aldershot: Ashgate, 2000).

Perkins, Maureen, *Visions of the Future: Almanacs, Time, and Cultural Change, 1775–1820* (Oxford: Clarendon, 1996).

Pykett, Lyn, 'Reading the Periodical Press: Text and Context', in *Investigating Victorian Journalism*, ed. by Laurel Brake, Aled Jones, and Lionel Madden (Basingstoke: Macmillan, 1990), pp. 3–18.

Raven, James, Helen Small, and Naomi Tadmor, eds., *The Practice and Representation of Reading in England* (Cambridge: Cambridge University Press, 1996).

Roper, Derek, *Reviewing Before the 'Edinburgh', 1788–1802* (London: Methuen, 1978).

Salmon, Richard, 'Signs of Intimacy: The Literary Celebrity in the "Age of Interviewing"', *Victorian Literature and Culture* 25 (1997), 159–77.

Saunders, J. W., *The Profession of English Letters* (London: Routledge and Kegan Paul, 1964).

Schmidt, Barbara Quinn, 'Novelists, Publishers, and Fiction in Middle-Class Magazines: 1860–1880', *Victorian Periodicals Review* 17 (1984), 142–53.

Scott, J. W. Robertson, *The Story of the 'Pall Mall Gazette', of its First Editor Frederick Greenwood and of its Founder George Murray Smith* (London: Oxford University Press, 1950).

Shattock, Joanne, *Politics and Reviewers: The 'Edinburgh' and the 'Quarterly' in the Early Victorian Age* (Leicester: Leicester University Press, 1989).

Shattock, Joanne and Michael Wolff, eds., *The Victorian Periodical Press: Samplings and Soundings* (Leicester: Leicester University Press, 1982).

Shine, Hill and Helen Chadwick Shine, *The 'Quarterly Review' under Gifford* (Chapel Hill, N.C.: University of North Carolina Press, 1949).

Sinnema, Peter M., *The Dynamics of the Pictured Page: Representing the Nation in the 'Illustrated London News'* (Aldershot: Ashgate, 1998).

Srebrnik, Patricia Thomas, *Alexander Strahan, Victorian Publisher* (Ann Arbor: University of Michigan Press, 1986).

Sutherland, Kathryn, '"Events . . . Have Made us a World of Readers": Reader Relations, 1780–1830', in *The Penguin History of Literature*, Vol. V, *The Romantic Period*, ed. by David B. Pirie (Harmondsworth: Penguin, 1994), pp. 1–48.

Thrall, Miriam M. H., *Rebellious Fraser's: Nol Yorke's Magazine in the Days of Maginn, Thackeray, and Carlyle* (New York: Columbia University Press, 1934).

Turner, Mark W., 'Toward a Cultural Critique of Victorian Periodicals', *Studies in Newspaper and Periodical History Annual* 3 (1995), 111–25.

   Trollope and the Magazines: Gendered Issues in Mid-Victorian Britain (London: Macmillan, 2000).

Webb, R. K., *The British Working-Class Reader, 1790–1848: Literacy and Social Tension* (London: George Allen and Unwin, 1955).

White, Cynthia L., *Women's Magazines, 1693–1968* (London: Joseph, 1970).

Wiener, Joel H., *The War of the Unstamped: The Movement to Repeal the British Newspaper Tax, 1830–1836* (Ithaca and London: Cornell University Press, 1969).

Wiener, Joel H., ed., *Innovators and Preachers: The Role of the Editor in Victorian England* (Westport, Conn.: Greenwood Press, 1985).

Papers for the Millions: The New Journalism in Britain, 1850s to 1914 (New York: Greenwood, 1988).

Wood, Marcus, *Radical Satire and Print Culture 1790–1822* (Oxford: Clarendon Press, 1994).

Worth, George J., '*Macmillan's Magazine*', 1859–1907: 'No Flippancy or Abuse Allowed' (Aldershot: Ashgate, 2003).

PERIODICALS AND THE HISTORY OF SCIENCE

Allen, David E., 'The Struggle for Specialist Journals: Natural History in the British Periodicals Market in the First Half of the Nineteenth Century', *Archives of Natural History* 23 (1996), 107–23.

Barnes, Barry and Steven Shapin, 'Science, Nature, and Control: Interpreting Mechanics' Institutes', *Social Studies of Science* 7 (1977), 31–74.

Barr, E. Scott, *An Index to the Biographical Fragments in Unspecialized Scientific Journals* (University, Ala.: University of Alabama Press, [1973]).

Barton, Ruth, 'Just Before *Nature*: The Purposes of Science and the Purposes of Popularisation in some English Popular Science Journals of the 1860s', *Annals of Science* 55 (1998), 1–33.

Baylen, J. O., 'The Mattei Cancer Cure: A Victorian Nostrum', *Proceedings of the American Philosophical Society* 113 (1969), 149–76.

'W. T. Stead's *Borderland*: A Quarterly Review and Index of Psychic Phenomena, 1893–97', *Victorian Periodicals Newsletter* 1 (1969), 30–5.

Bennett, Scott, 'Revolutions in Thought: Serial Publication and the Mass Market for Reading', in *The Victorian Periodical Press: Samplings and Soundings*, ed. by Joanne Shattock and Michael Wolff (Leicester: Leicester University Press, 1976), pp. 221–57.

'The Editorial Character and Readership of the *Penny Magazine*', *Victorian Periodicals Review* 17 (1984), 127–41.

Block, E., 'Evolutionist Psychology and Aesthetics: "The Cornhill Magazine" 1875–1880', *Journal of the History of Ideas* 45 (1984), 465–73.

Brock, W. H., 'The Development of Commercial Science Journals in Victorian Britain', in *Development of Science Publishing in Europe*, ed. by A. J. Meadows (Amsterdam: Elsevier Science Publications, 1980), pp. 95–122.

'Brewster as a Scientific Journalist', in *Martyr of Science: Sir David Brewster 1781–1868*, ed. by A. D. Morrison-Low and J. R. R. Christie (Edinburgh: Royal Scottish Museum, 1984), pp. 37–42.

'British Science Periodicals and Culture, 1820–1850', *Victorian Periodicals Review* 21 (1988), 47–55.

'Patronage and Publishing: Journals of Microscopy, 1839–1989', *Journal of Microscopy* 155 (1989), 249–66.

Brock, W. H. and A. J. Meadows, *The Lamp of Learning: Taylor & Francis and the Development of Science Publishing*, 2nd edn (London: Taylor and Francis, 1998).

Broks, Peter, 'Science, the Press and Empire: Pearson's Publications, 1890–1914', in *Imperialism and the Natural World*, ed. by John M. Mackenzie (Manchester: Manchester University Press, 1990), pp. 141–63.

Media Science Before the Great War (London: Macmillan, 1996).

Broman, Thomas, 'The Habermasian Public Sphere and "Science in the Enlightenment"', *History of Science* 36 (1998), 123–49.

'Periodical Literature', in *Books and the Sciences in History*, ed. by Marina Frasca-Spada and Nick Jardine (Cambridge: Cambridge University Press, 2000), pp. 225–38.

Browne, Janet, 'Squibs and Snobs: Science in Humorous British Undergraduate Magazines around 1830', *History of Science* 30 (1992), 165–97.

'Darwin in Caricature: A Study in the Popularization and Dissemination of Evolution', *Proceedings of the American Philosophical Society* 145 (2001), 496–509.

Bynum, W. F., S. Lock, and R. Porter, eds., *Medical Journals and Medical Knowledge: Historical Essays* (London and New York: Routledge, 1992).

Cantor, Geoffrey and Sally Shuttleworth, eds., *Science Serialized: Representations of the Sciences in the Nineteenth-Century Periodical Press* (Cambridge, Mass.: MIT Press, 2004).

Chew, Kenneth and Anthony Wilson, *Victorian Science and Engineering Portrayed in the 'Illustrated London News'* (Stroud: Science Museum, 1993).

Cooter, Roger and Stephen Pumfrey, 'Separate Spheres and Public Places: Reflections on the History of Science Popularization and Science in Popular Culture', *History of Science* 32 (1994), 237–67.

Corsi, Pietro, *Science and Religion: Baden Powell and the Anglican Debate, 1800–1860* (Cambridge: Cambridge University Press, 1988).

Crawford, Catherine, 'A Scientific Profession: Medical Reform and Forensic Medicine in British Periodicals of the Early Nineteenth Century', in *British Medicine in an Age of Reform*, ed. by Roger French and Andrew Wear (London: Wellcome Institute Series in the History of Medicine, 1991), pp. 203–30.

Currie, R. A., '"All the Year Round" and the State of Victorian Psychiatry', *Dickens Quarterly* 12 (1995): 18–24.

Dawson, Gowan, 'Stranger than Fiction: Spiritualism, Intertextuality, and William Makepeace Thackeray's Editorship of the *Cornhill Magazine*, 1860–62', *Journal of Victorian Culture* 7 (2002), 220–38.

'Intrinsic Earthliness: Science, Materialism and the Fleshly School of Poetry', *Victorian Poetry* 41 (2003), 113–29.

Desmond, Adrian, 'Artisan Resistance and Evolution in Britain, 1819–1848', *Osiris* 2nd ser. 3 (1987), 77–110.

The Politics of Evolution: Morphology, Medicine, and Reform in Radical London (Chicago and London: University of Chicago Press, 1989).

Huxley, 2 vols. (London: Michael Joseph, 1994–7).

Dixon, Diana, 'Children's Magazines and Science in the Nineteenth Century', *Victorian Periodicals Review* 34 (2001), 228–38.

Dunae, Patrick A., 'The *Boy's Own Paper*: Origins and Editorial Developments', *Private Library* 9 (1976), 123–58.

'New Grub Street for Boys' in *Imperialism and Juvenile Literature*, ed. by Jeffrey Richards (Manchester: Manchester University Press, 1989), pp. 12–33.

Ellegård, Alvar, *Darwin and the General Reader: The Reception of Darwin's Theory of Evolution in the British Periodical Press, 1859–72*, 2nd edn (Chicago: Chicago University Press, 1990).

Gascoigne, Robert Mortimer, *A Historical Catalogue of Scientific Periodicals, 1665–1900: With a Survey of their Development* (New York: Garland, 1985).

Gokyigit, E. A., 'The Reception of Francis Galton's "Hereditary Genius" in the Victorian Periodical Press', *Journal for the History of Biology* 27 (1994), 215–40.

Henson, Louise, '"Matters Arising from the Scenes of our Too-Long Neglect": Charles Dickens, Victorian Chemistry, and the Folklore of the Ghost', *Victorian Review* 26 (2000), 6–23.

et al., eds., *Culture and Science in the Nineteenth-Century Media* (Aldershot: Ashgate, 2004).

Holland, Susan, and Steven Miller, 'Science in the Early "Athenaeum": A Mirror of Crystallization', *Public Understanding of Science* 6 (1997), 111–30.

Hull, David L., *Darwin and His Critics: The Reception of Evolution in the Scientific Community* (Cambridge, Mass.: Harvard University Press, 1973).

Knight, David, 'Science and Culture in Mid-Victorian Britain: The Reviews and William Crookes' "Quarterly Journal of Science"', *Nuncius* 11 (1996), 43–54.

Kronick, David A., *A History of Scientific and Technical Periodicals: The Origin and Development of the Scientific and Technological Press, 1665–1790*, 2nd edn (New York: The Scarecrow Press Inc., 1976).

Lightman, Bernard, '"The Voices of Nature": Popularizing Victorian Science', in *Victorian Science in Context*, ed. by Bernard Lightman (Chicago: Chicago University Press, 1997), pp. 187–211.

MacLeod, Roy, *et al.* 'Centenary Supplement', *Nature* 224 (1969), 417–76.

Meadows, A. J., *Science and Controversy: A Biography of Sir Norman Lockyer, Founder of 'Nature'* (London and Basingstoke: Macmillan, 1972).

Meadows, A. J., ed., *Development of Science Publishing in Europe* (Amsterdam and New York: Elsevier Science Publishers, 1980).

Metz, N. A., 'Science in *Household Words*: The Poetic . . . Passed into our Common Life', *Victorian Periodicals Newsletter* 11 (1978), 121–33.

Ostry, Elaine, '"Social Wonders": Fancy, Science, and Technology in Dickens's Periodicals', *Victorian Periodicals Review* 34 (2001), 54–78.

Paradis, James G., 'Satire and Science in Victorian Culture', in *Victorian Science in Context*, ed. by Bernard Lightman (Chicago: Chicago University Press, 1997), pp. 143–75.

Peterson, M. Jeanne, 'Specialist Journals and Professional Rivalries in Victorian Medicine', *Victorian Periodicals Review* 12 (1979), 25–32.

'Medicine', in *Victorian Periodicals and Victorian Society*, ed. by J. Don Vann and Rosemary T. VanArsdel (Aldershot: Scolar Press, 1994), pp. 22–44.

Porter, Roy, 'Lay Medical Knowledge in the Eighteenth Century: The Evidence of the *Gentleman's Magazine*', *Medical History* 29 (1985), 138–68.

'Laymen, Doctors and Medical Knowledge in the Eighteenth Century: The Evidence of the *Gentleman's Magazine*', in *Patients and Practitioners: Lay Perceptions of Medicine in Pre-Industrial Society*, ed. by Roy Porter (Cambridge: Cambridge University Press, 1985), pp. 283–314.

Roos, David A., 'The Aims and Intentions of "Nature"', in *Victorian Science and Victorian Values*, ed. by James Paradis and Thomas Postlewait (New York: New York Academy of Sciences, 1981), pp. 159–80.

Secord, James A., 'Behind the Veil: Robert Chambers and *Vestiges*', in *History, Humanity and Evolution: Essays for John C. Greene*, ed. by James R. Moore (Cambridge: Cambridge University Press, 1987), pp. 165–94.

'Extraordinary Experiment: Electricity and the Creation of Life in Victorian England', in *The Uses of Experiment: Studies in the Natural Sciences*, ed. by David Gooding, Trevor Pinch, and Simon Schaffer (Cambridge: Cambridge University Press, 1989), pp. 337–83.

Victorian Sensation: The Extraordinary Publication, Reception, and Secret Authorship of 'Vestiges of the Natural History of Creation' (Chicago: Chicago University Press, 2000).

Sheets-Pyenson, Susan, 'Darwin's Data: His Reading of Natural History Journals, 1837–1842', *Journal of the History of Biology* 14 (1981), 231–48.

'A Measure of Success: The Publication of Natural History Journals in Early Victorian Britain', *Publishing History* 9 (1981), 21–36.

'From the North to Red Lion Court: The Creation and Early Years of the *Annals of Natural History*', *Archives of Natural History* 10 (1981), 221–49.

'Popular Science Periodicals in Paris and London: The Emergence of a Low Scientific Culture, 1820–1875', *Annals of Science* 42 (1985), 549–72.

Sholnick, Robert J., '"The Fiery Cross of Knowledge": *Chambers's Edinburgh Journal*, 1832–1844', *Victorian Periodicals Review* 32 (1999), 324–58.

Shuttleworth, Sally, Gowan Dawson, and Richard Noakes, 'Women, Science and Culture: Science in the Nineteenth-Century Periodical', *Women: A Cultural Review* 12 (2001), 57–70.

Topham, Jonathan R., 'Science and Popular Education in the 1830s: The Role of the *Bridgewater Treatises*', *British Journal for the History of Science* 25 (1992), 397–430.

'Science, Natural Theology, and Evangelicalism in Early Nineteenth-Century Scotland: Thomas Chalmers and the *Evidence* Controversy', in *Evangelicals and Science in Historical Perspective*, ed. by David N. Livingstone, D. G. Hart, and Mark A. Noll (New York: Oxford University Press, 1999), pp. 142–74.

'Scientific Publishing and the Reading of Science in Nineteenth-Century Britain: A Historiographical Survey and Guide to Sources', *Studies in History and Philosophy of Science*, 31A (2000), 559–612.

Young, Robert M., 'Natural Theology, Victorian Periodicals, and the Fragmentation of a Common Context', in *Darwin's Metaphor: Nature's Place in Victorian Culture* (Cambridge: Cambridge University Press, 1985), pp. 126–63, 265–71.

Yeo, Richard, 'Science and Intellectual Authority in Mid-Nineteenth-Century Britain: Robert Chambers and the "Vestiges of the Natural History of Creation"', *Victorian Studies* 28 (1984), 5–32.

Defining Science: William Whewell, Natural Knowledge, and Public Debate in Early Victorian Britain (Cambridge: Cambridge University Press, 1993).

Index

Abbott, Benjamin, 226
à Beckett, Gilbert Abbott, 102
Academy, 189, 206, 223
Academy of Physics, 11
Ackermann, Rudolph, 58
Addison, Joseph, 138
advertisements
  biographies, 227
  Boy's Own Paper (BOP), 154
  Cornhill Magazine, 126
  Punch, 31, 105
  Wesleyan-Methodist Magazine, 27, 73
Age, 91, 96
Agnostic Annual, 180
Airy, George Biddell, 230
Aldini, Giovanni, 79
All the Year Round, 18
Allen, Grant, 28, 183–184, 188–189, 191–192, 195
Allingham, John, 156
Altick, Richard, 93, 94, 97, 217
American Magazine, 191
Analytical Review, 10
Anderson, Patricia, 16
animal cruelty, 79, 167–168, 203
Answers to Correspondents, 193
Arcana of Science, 64–65
Arena, 187
Arminian Magazine, 70, 71–72, 85
Arnold, Matthew, 172
Athenaeum, 40, 96, 109, 218, 224
audiences *see* readership
Aunt Judy's Magazine, 155

Babbage, Charles, 79, 108
Baby: An Illustrated Monthly Magazine for Mothers, 199, 206, 207, 213, 215
baby science
  child-care magazines, 213
  comic/humour, 202, 203, 207, 209, 212
  Cornhill Magazine, 200–204, 205
  Darwin (Charles), 199, 204–205, 207, 211, 215

data collection, 209, 210–212
domestic peace, 204
evolution, 199, 200, 206, 209–210, 212, 213
experiments, 202, 209, 210, 211, 215
gender politics, 207–209, 211, 212
Lewes (George Henry), 200–204, 205–206
male science, 203, 206, 212, 214, 215
Mind, 7, 199, 204
natural knowledge, 29
primitive human history, 205, 206, 207
'psychological papa', 206, 207
racial superiority, 199, 200
scientific debates, 29, 199–215
Sully (James), 205–207
terminology, 202
women, 202, 203, 207–209, 211–212
Bagehot, Walter, 241
Bain, Alexander, 204
Baines, Edward, 51
Bakhtin, Mikhail, 26
Ballantyne, Robert Michael, 158, 160, 169
Ballin, Ada S., 199, 213–214
Bampton Lectures, 67
Barnard, Jane, 228
Barton, Ruth, 16, 17
Bates, Henry Walter, 148
Baylen, Joseph O., 173
Bebbington, David, 82
Beetham, Margaret, 2
Beeton, Samuel, 18–19, 155, 157
Belgravia, 126, 224, 226
Bell, Robert, 141–143, 144, 146
Bellamy, Edward, 238, 239, 246, 247, 248, 249, 253
Belloc, Marie, 175
Bence Jones, Henry, 32, 228–229
Benjamin, Park, 240, 245, 246, 247, 251
Bennett, Charles, 114
Bennett, James, 155
Benson, Joseph, 73–76, 77, 80

CAMBRIDGE STUDIES IN NINETEENTH-CENTURY
LITERATURE AND CULTURE

General editor
Gillian Beer, *University of Cambridge*

Titles published